Praise for Stephen Todd Walker's *Understanding Alternative Investments*

"Few finance books today capture the true essence of tactical allocation and why it is crucial to make adjustments to a portfolio like *Understanding Alternative Investments* does. By understanding that risk premiums change with market conditions, it can be possible to employ tactical asset allocation strategies to improve investment returns."

—Neil Peplinski, CFA, Managing Partner, Good Harbor Financial, LLC

"One of the best finance books ever written on venture capital. Venture capital moves in waves and riding the next wave is not always easy, which is why every investor, venture capital partner, and entrepreneur should study this book."

—Gary Rubinoff, Managing Partner, SummerHill Venture Partners

"His latest book is an excellent read for financial services professionals who want to deepen their knowledge of alternative investments. Todd has remarkable insights on how alternative investments can be integrated into variable annuities and 401(k) plans."

—David Nanigian, PhD, Assistant Professor of Investments, The Richard D. Irwin Graduate School

"Anyone who starts a business is a venture capitalist, an exercise highly valued by our society. This book will acquaint the reader with the amazing depth and span of venture capital markets and the opportunities they present to the investor."

—Dr. William C. Dunkelberg, Chief Economist, National Federation of Independent Business and former Dean of the Fox School of Business and Management, Temple University

"This book is a refreshing view of finance. Wave theory can also be applied to private equity, which has no boundaries."

—Rupert Harrington, Managing Director, Advent Private Capital

"Wave theory is timeless and should be learned by every business student. One can learn a lot from *Understanding Alternative Investments*. It should be mandatory reading."

—Brad Leve, Assistant Director, Farrell Corporate Innovation and Entrepreneurship Center, Smeal College of Business, The Pennsylvania State University

"Walker's new book, *Understanding Alternative Investments*, thoughtfully extends the application of his wave theory to real estate (as well as additional alternative investments) and provides valuable insights to investors and managers alike."

—Robert L. Cooney Jr., Cofounder and Managing Principal, Steel Castle Capital, LLC

"The nature of risk—and the appetite for it—have changed greatly since the onset of the Great Recession, and so has the landscape for alternative investments. In *Understanding Alternative Investments*, Walker has taken a thoughtful, building-blocks approach. It is a useful navigation tool for anyone interested in hedge funds or other alternative investments."

—Gregory J. Nowak, Esq., Partner, Pepper Hamilton LLP, and author and lecturer on alternative investments and structures

"Weathering today's investment market is more challenging than ever. Walker's book provides investors with the critical tools needed when allocating real estate as part of a diversified portfolio. *Understanding Alternative Investments* illustrates how alternative investments, such as real estate, can provide attractive risk-adjusted returns in an economic cycle."

—Jake E. Hannah, Commercial Real Estate Professional

"Crowdfunding is the next wave. Extremely helpful book for anyone raising capital or investing in early stage companies."

—Bill Marvin, CEO and Cofounder of InstaMed

"One needs to watch the waves when investing in or raising venture capital especially with technology."

—Bami Bastani, President and Chief Executive Officer, Meru Networks

"Pension plan sponsors, endowments and foundations as well as pension consultants have all warmed up to managed futures in a significant way over the past decade. This book clearly shows the merits of managed futures and how they can be used to further diversify a portfolio. The attractive long-term, risk-adjusted (and noncorrelated) returns are one important way institutions can generate much-needed alpha in an era where much more horsepower is required beyond the traditional paradigm of stocks and bonds."

—David Lerman, Senior Director, Asset Managers, Products and Services, CME Group

"*Understanding Alternative Investments* is an essential tool to prepare for finance interviews. It offers comprehensive yet accessible insight into portfolio diversification with alternative investments that I used to impress my interviewers and receive job offers from bulge bracket, private equity, and real estate firms."

—Tony Murphy, Student at the Wharton School of the University of Pennsylvania

"Perceptive work. Anyone truly interested in helping improve the cardiovascular problems of today should read this book whether they are passionate about seeing a deadly disease get eradicated or as an investor in this space. Todd has sparked a new movement with Cardio Companies as he calls them. Investors have the potential to make money as well as help those inflicted with the number one killer of women and men worldwide, cardiovascular disease."

—Roger Schwab, Sports/Medicine Director, Main Line Health and Fitness

"Venture capital has changed with the emergence of crowdfunding and P2P financing. This evolution makes a working understanding of alternative investments critical for entrepreneurs and those hoping to reshape the world of finance."

—Justin W. Askins, Esq., Attorney, Investor, Venture Capitalist

"This book provides any entrepreneur as well as investors valuable insight regarding crowdfunding."

—Steve Graham, CEO of Scitt Kits, LLC and Serial Entrepreneur

UNDERSTANDING ALTERNATIVE INVESTMENTS

CREATING DIVERSIFIED PORTFOLIOS THAT RIDE THE WAVE OF INVESTMENT SUCCESS

STEPHEN TODD WALKER

palgrave
macmillan

UNDERSTANDING ALTERNATIVE INVESTMENTS

First published in 2014 by
PALGRAVE MACMILLAN®
in the United States—a division of St. Martin's Press LLC,
175 Fifth Avenue, New York, NY 10010.

Where this book is distributed in the UK, Europe and the rest of the world, this is by Palgrave Macmillan, a division of Macmillan Publishers Limited, registered in England, company number 785998, of Houndmills, Basingstoke, Hampshire RG21 6XS.

Palgrave Macmillan is the global academic imprint of the above companies and has companies and representatives throughout the world.

ISBN: 978–1–137–37018–1

Library of Congress Cataloging-in-Publication Data

Walker, Stephen (Stephen Todd)
Understanding alternative investments : creating diversified portfolios that ride the wave of investment success / Stephen Todd Walker.
pages cm
ISBN 978–1–137–37018–1 (hardback)
1. Portfolio management. 2. Investment analysis. I. Title.

HG4529.5.W355 2014
332.6—dc23 2013047212

A catalogue record of the book is available from the British Library.

Design by Newgen Knowledge Works (P) Ltd., Chennai, India.

First edition: July 2014

10 9 8 7 6 5 4 3 2 1

DISCLAIMERS AND DISCLOSURES

This book is designed to provide accurate and authoritative information in regard to the subject matter covered, and the information, analysis, and data contained herein are based on sources believed to be reliable. The author and Stratosphere, LLC do not, however, guarantee the timeliness, accuracy, or completeness of the information provided. The author has been associated with a number of leading investment banking firms in his career but the opinions in this book are his alone. All information and opinions herein are subject to change without notice and are not intended to be the primary basis for any investment decision. The strategies described do not address individual financial objectives and may not be suitable in every situation. The appropriateness of a particular investment or strategy depends on an investor's particular circumstances and objectives. The author and Stratosphere, LLC do not intend to render individual financial, investment, tax, legal, accounting, or other professional advice or services in this book. If personal advice or services are required, the reader should engage a competent professional. Nothing in this book should be construed as a recommendation about the advisability of purchasing or selling any particular security. The charts and graphs are for illustrative purposes only, and past performance of any security described in this book is not necessarily indicative of and does not guarantee comparable future results. All investments are made at the reader's own risk, and the publisher, the author, or Stratosphere, LLC shall not be liable or cannot be held responsible for any losses or damages, including without limitation special, incidental, consequential, or other damages, incurred as a result of actions taken or not taken on the basis of the information, opinions, or strategies set forth or described herein. The author, the author's clients, and/or Stratosphere, LLC may invest in securities mentioned in this book.

Alternative investments are speculative and include a high degree of risk. They are typically highly illiquid, because, among other things, they often involve (i) securities that are not registered under the Securities Act of 1933 and/or (ii) securities that are subject to legal or contractual restrictions or requirements relating to their purchase, holding, or sale, or the exercise of rights and performance of obligations with respect to them. Most alternative investments are also very volatile. Investors could lose all of, or in some cases more than the original amount of, their investment. For these reasons, they are suitable only for experienced and sophisticated investors who are capable of understanding and assuming the risks involved and who are willing to forego liquidity and put capital at risk for an indefinite period of time. Some of the other risks involved in and factors affecting the price of the types of alternative investments discussed in this book are set forth below:*Gold*: Risks of investments in actual gold or securities backed by actual gold include but are not limited to forgery, fraud, theft, and loss. Prices of all types of investments in gold can be affected by, among other things, (i) speculation; (ii) hedging; (iii) expectations regarding inflation; (iv) supply and demand; (v) currency exchange rates; (vi) interest rates; (vii) global or regional instability; or (viii) political, financial, economic, and regulatory conditions or events.*Commodities*: Risks include but are not limited to geopolitical risk, leverage, speculation, and fraud. Prices can be affected by, among other things, (i) changes in supply and demand relationships; (ii) governmental programs and policies; (iii) national and international political and economic events, armed conflict, and terrorist activity; (iv) changes in interest and exchange rates; (v) trading activities in commodities and related contracts; (vi) technological change, climate change, and weather conditions; and (vii) the price volatility of a specific commodity.*Hedge funds*: Risks include but are not limited to (i) little or no regulation; (ii) leveraging, short selling, and other speculative investment practices; (iii) lack of transparency regarding underlying investments; (iv) unavailability of pricing or valuation information; (v) reduction of profits by high fees, some of which are not based on profitability; (vi) complex tax structures and delays in distributing important tax information; and (vii) the potential for regulatory changes.*Venture capital funds*: Risks include but are not limited to (i) business risks involved in investing in smaller, less established companies; (ii) availability of future capital or other financing; (iii) lack of liquidity of underlying investments; and (iv) dilution of underlying investments.*Leveraged buyout (LBO) funds*: Risks include but are not limited to the following: (i) Investments in LBO funds are speculative and carry a high degree of risk. (ii) LBO funds frequently have limited transparency and utilize different valuation methods. (iii) Private equity does not have the same regulatory requirements such as mutual funds. (iv) Investors in LBO funds might experience delays in receiving tax information. Similarly, investing in LBO funds might not be tax efficient. (v) Long lockups for funds are a risk. (vi) Economic and political developments can adversely affect LBO investments. (vii) Market risk exists. (viii) Managers can utilize leverage, which might increase their exposure to certain variables such as rising interest rates. (ix.) There is no guarantee of future results based on past leveraged buyout activities. Typically, there is no market for Limited Partnership Investments. (x) Investors in LBO funds rely on the General Partner as well as the investment advisor. (xi) There is no assurance that the funds' objectives will be achieved. (xii) Failure to make payments in a private equity fund might lead to a forced sale of its investments in the fund or preclusion from further investment. (xiii) LBO funds can have high fees for management, placement, and performance.*Managed futures*: Risks include but are not limited to (i) illiquidity; (ii) leveraging and other speculative investment practices; (iii) they are not required to provide periodic pricing or valuation information to investors; (iv) high fees; (v) may involve complex tax structures; (vi) delays in distributing important tax information; (vii) manager risk; (viii) market risk; (ix) reliance on certain strategies such as trend following, which might not work in certain environments; and (x) government and political risk.*Real estate*: Risks include but are not limited to (i) falling property values due to increasing vacancies or declining rents resulting from economic, legal, or technological developments; (ii) non-diversification (certain real estate funds can be classified as "non-diversified" under the 1940 Act and can invest a greater portion of its assets in obligations of a single issuer than a "diversified" fund); (iii) reliance on an investment adviser and subadviser; (iv) tax risks; (v) investment and market risk; (vi) competition can reduce the number of attractive portfolio investment opportunities available to a real estate fund); (vii) interest rate risk is the risk that debt securities in a fund's portfolio might decline in value because of increases in market interest rates; (viii) if a real estate fund holds mortgage backed or other such securities, there is credit risk where securities in the fund's portfolio might decline in price or the issuer thereof will fail to pay interest or principal when due; (ix) leverage risk (real estate funds can use leverage, which will magnify investment, market, and certain other risks); and (x) past performance is no guarantee of future results.

* * *

"All truly great thoughts are conceived by walking."

—Friedrich Nietzsche

CONTENTS

ILLUSTRATIONS

FIGURES

TABLES

RIDING THE WAVE

INTRODUCTION: THAT WAS THEN, THIS IS NOW

Alternative investments can be defined as any asset class or investment other than equities, bonds, or cash. Diversification can lead to alternative investments as obscure as coins, diamonds, comic books, rare earth, art, or even wine. One of my goals in writing my first book, *Wave Theory for Alternative Investments: Riding the Wave with Hedge Funds, Commodities, and Venture Capital*, was to help educate anyone interested in alternative investments, whether they are institutional investors, high net worth clients, wealth managers, financial advisors, financial planners, consultants, professors, trainees, or students. I would like investors to simply know more about the exciting world of alternative investments. Besides this professional or institutional audience, many others have expressed an avid interest in learning more about alternative investments. The world of financial products for alternative investments is rapidly expanding and the number of choices is substantial. In the past, the vast majority of research concerning investments has been focused primarily on equities and fixed income. However, times have changed and so has the investment process, which has evolved to include alternative investments. It is my firm belief that virtually any asset allocation model should include alternative investments. As authors Bodie, Kane, and Marcus explain in *The Investment Process in Investments*, "Investment assets can be categorized into broad asset classes, such as stocks, bonds, real estate, commodities, and so on."[1] *Understanding Alternative Investments* covers how alternatives work and why it might be wise for an investor to consider adding them to their portfolio. Essentially, alternative investments can be utilized to build better investment portfolios with less risk and higher returns if done in a prudent fashion.

Institutional money, otherwise known as "smart money," as well as ultra high net worth individuals, have utilized alternative investments for years and invested even more in alternative investments after the Great Recession. The *Dow Jones Newswire* reports that "A McKinsey & Co. study from this year on the mainstreaming of alternative investments found that year-round assets in global alternatives reached a record \$6.5 trillion in 2011, growing at a five-year rate of more than seven times that of traditional asset classes. By 2015, retail alternatives are expected to account for one-quarter of retail revenues, according to McKinsey & Co."[2] Institutions are currently adding more alternative investments than in the past. According to KPMG, "The majority of institutional investors intend to increase their allocations to alternative investments in the next 3 years."[3] Institutional investors can drive the market. Billions of dollars are flowing into alternative investments. In 2012 the New Jersey Division of Investment, Trenton, committed up to \$1.745 billion to new and existing alternatives investments.[4] Retail investors are adding alternative investments and mutual funds are creating vehicles for easier access. The rate at which investors are putting money into alternative mutual funds is making them mainstream. "According to data released by Cerulli Associates and Strategic Insight/SIMFUND, alternative mutual funds account for 2.8 percent of overall mutual fund assets today. But Cerulli projects they will account for 9.7 percent of all mutual fund assets in five years, and 15.8 percent of assets a decade from now."[5] Poor returns with equities during the tech bubble and the Great Recession, as well as numerous complications with bonds, have created curiosity amongst investors regarding alternative investments.

The market has grown and developed vehicles to enable many types of investors to further diversify. In 2012, the mutual fund behemoth Fidelity Investments offered investors access to hedge funds. "Fidelity Investments is offering retail clients access to hedge-fund firms through a mutual fund launched in partnership with Arden Asset Management."[6] Private-equity firms also set up new vehicles. Blackstone Group LP and Carlyle launched their first mutual funds in 2013. On the one hand, it is good news that alternative investments can be accessed for far less money than in the past. On the other hand, it has created a new set of problems. Not all vehicles being introduced today for alternative investments are worthwhile. "The

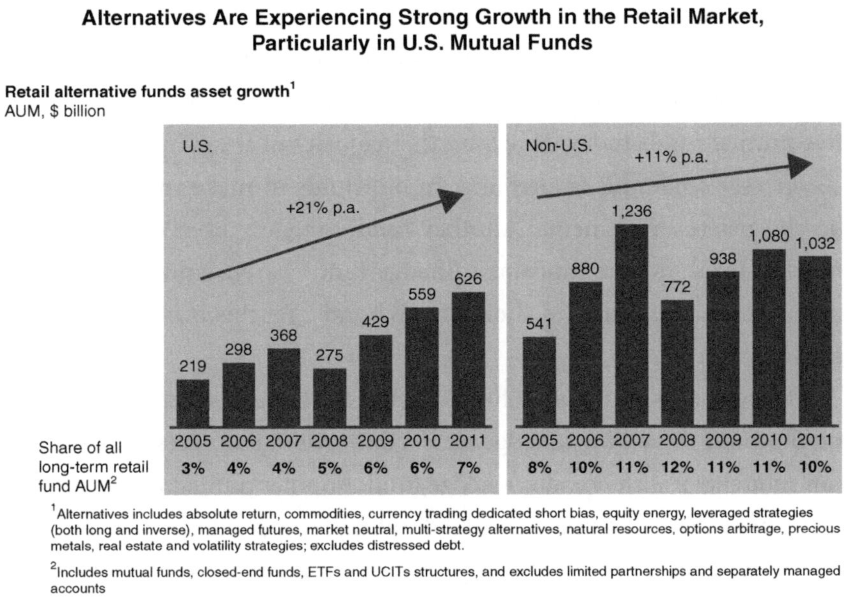

Figure 0.1 The Growing Interest in Alternative Investment Mutual Funds.

Source: The Mainstreaming of Alternatives: The Next Wave of Growth in Asset Management, McKinsey & Company, June 2012.

vast majority of the other 254 hedged mutual funds in the US—which pursue market-neutral, long-short, managed-futures and multi-alternative strategies—have proven to be even more lackluster."[7] Alternative investments continue to gain momentum with retail investors (Figure 0.1).

Risk has increased into areas that are both transparent and hidden. Hidden risk with alternative investments can be very troublesome, as seen by the real estate problems that caused the Great Recession. "In the years running up to the financial crisis, there was a much-discussed breakdown between what investors actually bought and what they understood they were buying…At its heart, the subprime debacle was a fundamental misunderstanding of real estate risk, and the perils of applying historical models (about potential default rates, for example) to the current environment. But it also represented a form of concentration risk, to the extent that so many investors relied on a handful of ratings agencies and their models."[8] Many new financial products have shown up on the market since the Great Recession, claiming to be "alternatives" or "alternative investments." These so called alternative products are entering the market at a rapid rate and causing much confusion. I met with a well-known mutual fund company that has historically specialized in fixed income and equities. The fund company (like many others) are now self-proclaimed experts with alternative investments. Essentially, all fund companies offer alternative mutual funds today. However, the majority of these fund companies are merely renaming or dressing up old funds to make them appear to be alternative investments. Another fund company even described one of their fixed income funds as a "hedge fund" because the mutual fund manager has the ability to short or sell bonds. Yet this is nothing new or earth-shattering.

Hedge funds and mutual funds are not the same. Just because a mutual fund can do something a hedge fund can do, does not necessarily mean it can suddenly transform into a hedge fund. Another mutual fund company that I know had a natural resources fund that morphed into a "commodities" fund. That is, representatives from the company are telling advisors or investors they are commodities experts. However, investing in a gold miner or exchange-traded fund (ETF) does not qualify them to be commodity experts. Essentially, mutual fund companies are new to the world of alternative investments. Investors should be careful about such products and perform proper due diligence. Historically, the biggest blowups often result from investors not asking enough intelligent questions. For example, many investors were duped by Bernie Madoff. They thought they were investing in a reputable hedge fund with good performance. Bernie Madoff deliberately made it awkward to ask detailed questions about his strategy and would make investors feel intimidated as though they were being disrespectful. Amaranth Advisors LLC was another blowup that could have been avoided by investors asking astute questions. Amaranth was an American hedge fund that collapsed in 2006 after losing billions in natural gas futures. The collapse was not about unpredictable market events but rather an oversight issue. Neither of these investments provided a clear or concise explanation as to what they were investing in and investors lost billions of dollars as a result. They were two of the worst investments anyone could ever make.

Investors should learn about how alternative investments function as well as all their hazards and whether or not it makes sense to add them to a diversified portfolio. Do they help or hinder the goals and objectives of an investment portfolio? Depending on the alternative investment, they can play a role in a prudent investor's portfolio because of their intrinsic

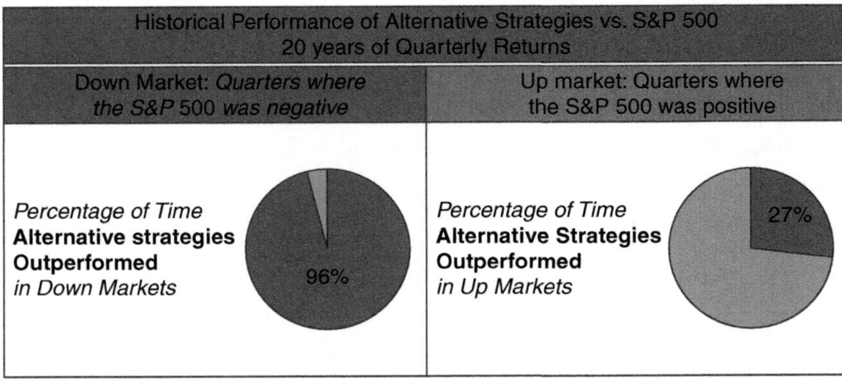

Source Zephyr StyleADVISOR (April 1, 1993–June 30, 2012). Alternative Strategies are represented by the Hedge Fund Research, Inc. (HFRI) Fund-of-Funds Composite, an equal-weighted index consisting of over 800 consultant hedge funds, including both domestic and offshore funds; U.S. Stocks are represented by the S&P 500, a market capitalization-weighted index of 500 widely held stocks often listed as proxy for the stock market. **Past performance does not guarantee future results. Illustration does not reflect performance of Principal Fund and does not take into account cost associated with investment. The Principal Global Multi-Strategy Fund is new and therefore does not have investment performance. Index performance information reflects no deduction for fees, expensed, or taxes. Indices are managed and individuals cannot invest directly in an index. Asset allocation/diversification does not guarantee a profit or protect against a loss.**

Figure 0.2 Historical Performance of Alternative Investments in Both Down and Up Markets.

Source: Dave Reichart, Senior Vice President, Principal Funds.

risk/reward characteristics. However, alternative investments are not a get-rich-quick or riskless investment. No investment is risk free. Investing in alternatives without clear and precise knowledge, just like the purchase of any other investment or product, seldom has beneficial results. Invariable the results are poor.

Wall Street typically offers guidance but created long-term skepticism among investors due to the subprime crisis and has since provided little solace. Over the past two decades, alternative investments have performed reasonably well in both down as well as up markets (Figure 0.2).

Understanding the magnitude of the problems and what led to them as well as the global domino effect that followed are crucial to seeing the role that alternative investments might play in a well-diversified portfolio. "The robustness check for the financial crisis reveals that the importance of alternative investments for risk diversification in defensive portfolios was underestimated. In spite of the financial crisis the results for alternative investments are even stronger."[9] The world witnessed a rogue (sometimes referred to as freak) financial wave that helped form the Great Recession, not too different from a rogue wave at sea. "An unusually high single wave event observed offshore is commonly called a freak wave. This definition is somewhat obscure since neither the cause of the occurrence nor criteria to define freak waves have been clarified. Freak waves have been observed only rarely and these observations occurred under unexpected condition[s]: hence, only few measured data are available."[10] It is also important to review this time period, otherwise known as the Great Recession, because it highlights risks found with alternative investments that can be either transparent or hidden.

The losses suffered by Wall Street were evidenced by the significant write-downs by banks and investment firms. They were heavily involved with subprime real estate. Years after, the Great Recession led to many financial institutions being downgraded, especially large banks in the United States: "S&P downgraded 15 big banks to reflect new rating methods the firm has been putting in place over the past year. The new guidelines sharpen the focus on how banks would hold up under market and economic stress, and on the likelihood of governments providing extraordinary support to troubled institutions."[11] When purchasing alternative investments, the firm used to make the purchase was not so much a concern as it is today. Historically, it was unheard of for a firm to go bankrupt. However, Lehman Brothers sold alternative investments and went bankrupt, which caused numerous problems for those who bought them. Moreover, alternative investments can be illiquid or not easily moved from one firm to another. Once the firm shut its doors, the former Lehman employees that sold the alternative investments were all gone and investors had no one to turn to for information. Certain proprietary products were completely wiped out. In other words, the "seller" risk became an issue. New risks emerged that had never been seen before. The Great Recession showed Wall Street and investors unforeseen risk that no one had considered let alone incorporated in any risk model, whether they were an institution or a retail investor.

Risk used to be somewhat simple to comprehend. "Each investment—each stock, bond, or physical asset—is associated with two types of risk: diversifiable risk and nondiversifiable risk. The sum of these two components is the investment's total risk."[12] But risk can change and new risk can emerge such as evidenced by the Great Recession. Throughout this book, transparent as well as hidden risks with alternative investments are covered. Figure 0.3 is a risk chart I devised to show both kinds of risk that one might consider along with other variables before acquiring an alternative investment.

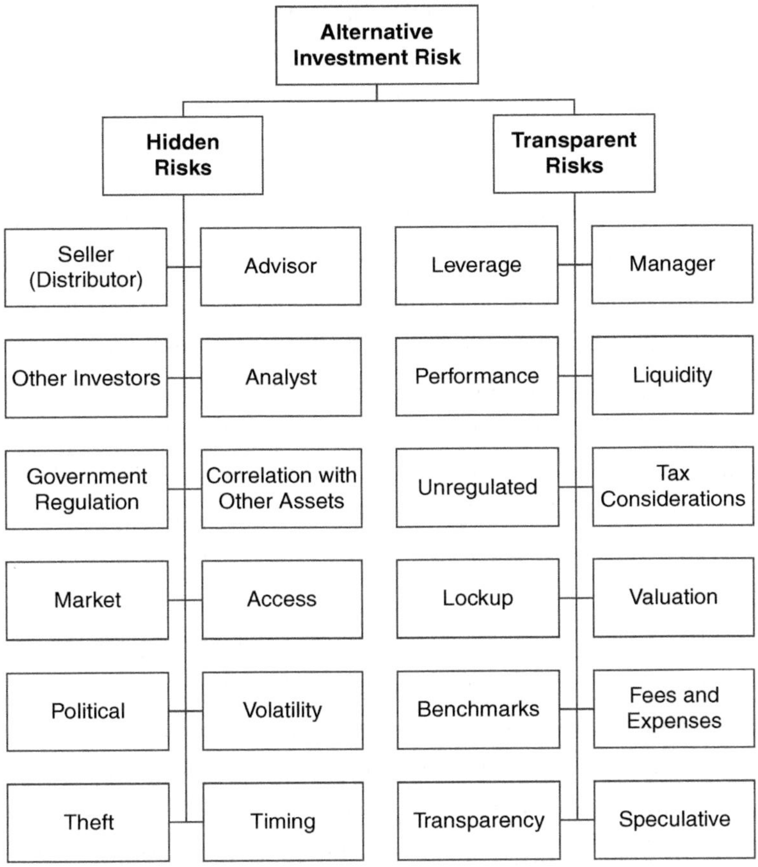

Figure 0.3 Transparent and Hidden Risks with Alternative Investments.
Source: Author.

How did banks become a risk to investors interested in alternative investments? One way was through real estate. Real estate is an alternative investment. Real estate is both commercial and residential:

> Real Estate for the vast majority of the public means a home or a condominium. And, that residential market is completely different, with a different set of dynamics, from the commercial market. The purchase of a home or condo is probably the last bastion of individual decision making, where the wrong decision has an immediate adverse impact on the purchaser. The commercial real estate market is no longer dominated by individual purchasers. Rather it

> is dominated by REITs, institutional investors, investment bankers and pension funds. The individual investor participates indirectly as a shareholder, pensioner, or investor in a pool.[13]

Like other alternative investments, real estate moves in waves. That is, commercial real estate tends to be correlated with the business cycle. As an investment, real estate can be quite compelling and provide a steady income stream. There are a lot of ways to invest in real estate. One can buy real estate outright, such as a house or apartment building. Investors can lend money privately to those wanting to buy houses. Real estate investment trusts (REITs) can be private or publicly traded. Yet real estate is not without risk. Wall Street took a segment of the real estate market and created a security that ultimately led to the Great Recession. The riskiest part of real estate, subprime real estate, involves loans being made to borrowers with bad credit ratings.

In *Wave Theory for Alternative Investments*, three primary alternative investments were covered—hedge funds, commodities, and venture capital. These are just a few of the many types of alternative investments. However, there are many other alternative investments such as real estate, managed futures, and LBO funds (private equity). Alternative investments, just like any other security, can be found to move in waves that I call "Wave Theory."

> Wave Theory is simply the belief that all securities move in waves (patterns, cycles, or trends). History sometimes repeats itself, but with alternatives an investor can typically see similar waves repeating themselves. Equities move in waves. Fixed income moves in waves. Cash moves in waves. There is now enough data to support the notion that alternatives move in waves.[14]

Many years ago, I devised the hypothesis that alternative investments move in waves. Waves never stop as we know. "The seas off the eastern and western coasts of Australia provide constant waves, rolling in as they do from half way across the world, in the Pacific Ocean on Australia's western coast, and really as far in the Indian Ocean that washes Western Australia's shores. A storm almost anywhere across two thirds of the world builds waves that eventually crash onto Australia's two main coastlines."[15] However, there was no reliable data that I could utilize to test this hypothesis so I had to collect it myself. Over the years, I gathered large amounts of data to prove my theory. I examined many alternative investments and found that they move in waves. For example, there are LBO waves. "The leveraged buyout (LBO) wave of the 1980s was an important phenomenon well studied by academics and practitioners. The recession of the early 1990s, however, brought most of that activity to an end, as many deals from later in that period defaulted. Nearly 15 years later, however, the pace of LBO activity reached new record levels, renewing questions about whether and how these deals create value."[16]

While data with alternative investments can sometimes be conflicting, LBO funds have been shown to outperform the S&P 500. Robert Harris of the University of Virginia's Darden School, Tim Jenkinson of Oxford University's Saïd Business School, and Steven Kaplan of the University of Chicago's Booth School of Business examined private-equity performance and found that it is "very likely" that private equity outperforms the S&P 500.[17] Similarly, Dr. Rüdiger Stucke, a research fellow in Finance and Economics at the Saïd Business School and the Oxford-Man Institute of Quantitative Finance, University of Oxford, states, "In particular, the claim that private equity has not outperformed public equity is unlikely to hold with true numbers."[18] LBOs are part of the alternative investments area known as private equity. Private equity also moves in waves. As David T. Robinson and Berk A. Sensoy explain in an abstract "Cyclicality, Performance Measurement, and Cash Flow Liquidity in Private Equity," "Public and private equity waves move together."[19] Another area that I researched was real estate. Like private equity, real estate moves in waves. "Real estate is not a highly liquid asset and the key to successful investing is one of timing…One thing is certain; whatever has happened in the past will be repeated in the future, although probably in a different form."[20] Figure 0.4 is a chart of real estate equity assets showing the market recovering and forming a new wave for real estate despite the fact that the Great Recession was caused by the real estate market collapse.

Real estate has moved in waves for centuries and there have been many housing booms long forgotten. "A truly healthy housing market boom

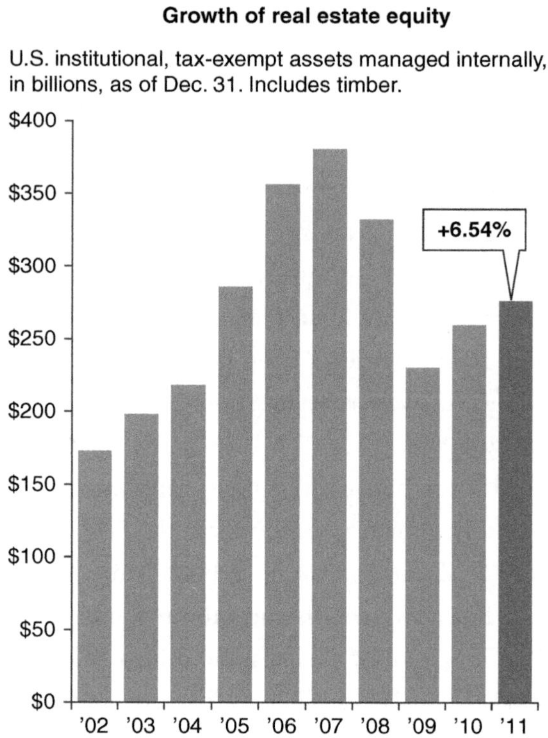

Figure 0.4 Real Estate Waves.

Source: "Graphic: Growth of real estate equity assets," *Pensions and Investments*, http://www.pionline.com, May 28, 2012.

occurred between 1940 and 1960. Supported by Fannie Mae as a quiet, behind-the scenes government corporation, the home ownership rate grew from 40 percent to 60 percent. The company provided liquidity for FHA mortgages and for U.S. Veterans Affairs' zero-down payment mortgages for returning World War II soldiers, which helped fuel the growth of the American middle class."[21] A plethora of information was put together in *Wave Theory for Alternative Investments*, in order to show waves that each alternative investment (hedge funds, commodities, and venture capital) exhibits over time. Real estate, which caused the Great Recession, is recovering. "Sales of previously owned homes were stronger than expected in October 2012, putting them on track to hit their highest annual level since 2007."[22] The residential real estate market is showing signs of recovery. (Figure 0.5).

New constructions is a way to gauge the real estate market. ETFs such as the Dow Jones U.S. Home Construction ETF are now available. "Over the past 20 years, home-related stocks have roughly tracked new construction,

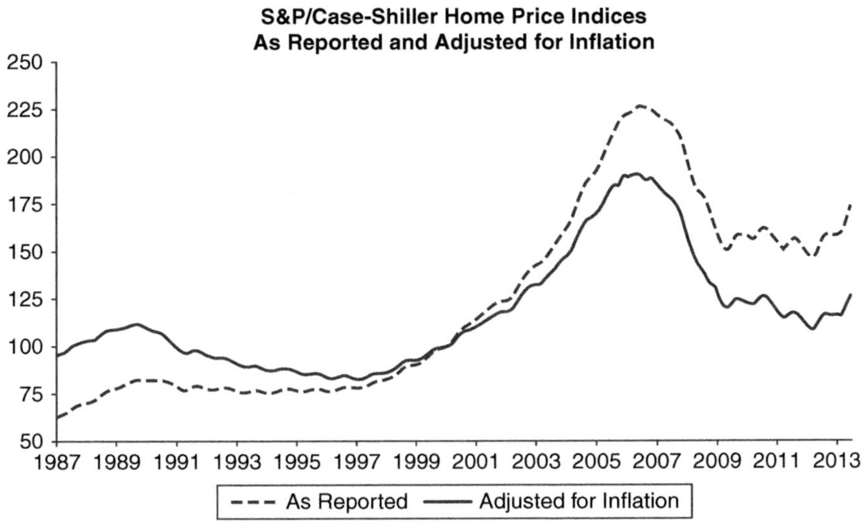

Figure 0.5 United States Residential Real Estate Recovering and Forming a New Wave.
Source: Rent vs. buy and inflation adjustments – S&P Dow Jones Indices – housing views.

itself perhaps the best indicator of the housing market's health. Plus, growth over a cycle can justify the high price/earnings ratios that housing stocks might have initially; future earnings and price appreciation can make those formerly costly-looking stocks seem cheap in hindsight."[23] The lumber industry, home-improvement stores, and homebuilders were some of the best performing industries in 2012.

Reminiscent of ocean waves, securities move in waves. Equities, for instance, move in waves. "Bull and bear markets are a common way of describing cycles in equity prices."[24] Patterns, trends, and cycles can be seen over time, again and again with alternative investments. Behavioral finance helps explain this phenomenon. "The forecasted change in price level is higher following a series of previous price increases than following price decreases, suggesting that investors indeed chase trends once they think they see them."[25] Fixed income moves in waves, as evidenced by the European debt crisis where there was a wave of selling. Many have accepted the fact that alternative investments move in waves and presently more research is being done. Waves exist and they exist with alternative investments.

Prudent investors can use this knowledge regarding Wave Theory to possibly help them make intelligent investment decisions as well as to build better portfolios. "Several recent studies have attributed this forecast ability to what has come to be known as the 'stock market overreaction' hypothesis, the notion that investors are subject to waves of optimism and pessimism and therefore create a kind of momentum which causes prices to temporarily swing away from their fundamental values."[26] Successfully investing money for institutions and high net worth individuals for more than two decades, I found this information to be quite useful. Based on the trends, patterns, or cycles that one observes, alternative investments can be used to further diversify a portfolio. Waves with different asset classes can also be found at the web site, http://www.InvestingWave.com. For instance, managed futures might be used to take advantage of these trends. "An initial under-reaction to a shift in fundamental value can potentially allow a managed futures strategy to invest before the information is fully reflected in prices. The trend then over extends due to herding effects."[27] "Managed Futures" refers to the Barclays CTA Index, an index that seeks to replicate the overall composition of the managed futures industry. Managed futures did well starting in 1990 when the equity market was bad, as well as in 2000, 2001, 2002, and 2008 (Figure 0.6).

A number of savvy investment pros have seen the value of investing when times are bad. "The secret is having the capital and courage when things look pretty gloomy to say, 'This will work,'" says George Siguler, whose New York-based Siguler Guff & Co. manages about $10 billion in private equity and distressed debt, including investments in Oaktree.[28] Many of these successful pros are experts in alternative investments. Carlyle Group frequently enters new areas before others, such as raising a sub-Saharan Africa private-equity fund, giving the firm a first-mover advantage. The largest hedge fund in the world, Bridgewater Associates, follows a strategy somewhat similar in nature to Wave Theory. The founder of Bridgewater Associates is Ray Dalio. Dalio, 62, built Bridgewater into the world's largest macro hedge-fund firm, with $110 billion in total assets, by tacking against consensus. He's created a distinct workplace culture and a research-driven investing process that spreads risk across scores of markets. "Making money is a zero-sum game, so to be successful you have to be willing to stand apart from the crowd," Dalio says, "And you have to be right."[29] These investments pros know when to buy or sell, unlike the typical investor that sells precisely at the wrong time (the bottom of the market) and buys at the wrong time (at the top).

Comparative Performance of Asset Classes Ranked by Annual Return (January 1990–June 2013)

1990	1991	1992	1993	1994	1995	1996	1997	1998	1999	2000	2001
Managed Futures 15.3%	NASDAQ 56.9%	Hedge Funds 21.2%	Hedge Funds 30.9%	MSCI World 5.6%	NASDAQ 39.9%	Real Estate 35.8%	S&P 500 33.4%	NASDAQ 39.6%	NASDAQ 85.6%	Real Estate 25.9%	Real Estate 15.5%
Global Bonds 12.0%	Real Estate 35.7%	NASDAQ 15.5%	MSCI World 23.1%	T-Bills 4.4%	S&P 500 37.6%	S&P 500 23.0%	NASDAQ 21.6%	S&P 500 28.6%	Hedge Funds 31.3%	Managed Futures 6.6%	Hedge Funds 4.6%
T-Bills 6.4%	Hedge Funds 32.2%	Real Estate 12.2%	Real Estate 18.5%	Hedge Funds 4.1%	Hedge Funds 21.5%	NASDAQ 22.7%	Real Estate 18.9%	MSCI World 24.8%	MSCI World 25.3%	T-Bills 6.0%	Managed Futures 3.8%
Hedge Funds 5.8%	S&P 500 30.5%	S&P 500 7.6%	NASDAQ 14.7%	Global Bonds 2.3%	MSCI World 21.3%	Hedge Funds 21.1%	Hedge Funds 16.8%	Global Bonds 15.3%	S&P 500 21.0%	Hedge Funds 5.0%	T-Bills 3.3%
S&P 500 -3.1%	MSCI World 19.0%	Global Bonds 5.5%	Managed Futures 13.4%	S&P 500 1.3%	Global Bonds 19.0%	MSCI World 14.0%	MSCI World 16.2%	Managed Futures 12.4%	T-Bills 4.8%	Global Bonds 1.6%	Global Bonds -1.0%
MSCI World -16.5%	Global Bonds 15.8%	T-Bills 3.4%	Global Bonds 13.3%	Real Estate 0.8%	Real Estate 18.3%	Managed Futures 12.8%	Managed Futures 12.0%	T-Bills 4.9%	Managed Futures 1.6%	S&P 500 -9.1%	S&P 500 -11.9%
Real Estate -17.3%	Managed Futures 14.7%	Managed Futures 2.5%	S&P 500 10.1%	Managed Futures -0.2%	Managed Futures 14.0%	T-Bills 5.1%	T-Bills 5.2%	Hedge Funds 2.6%	Global Bonds -4.3%	MSCI World -12.9%	MSCI World -16.5%
NASDAQ -17.8%	T-Bills 4.6%	MSCI World -4.7%	T-Bills 3.0%	NASDAQ -3.2%	T-Bills 5.6%	Global Bonds 3.6%	Global Bonds 0.2%	Real Estate -18.8%	Real Estate -6.5%	NASDAQ -39.3%	NASDAQ -21.1%

2002	2003	2004	2005	2006	2007	2008	2009	2010	2011	2012	2013
Global Bonds 19.5%	NASDAQ 50.0%	Real Estate 30.4%	MSCI World 10.0%	Real Estate 34.4%	Global Bonds 11.0%	Managed Futures 13.5%	NASDAQ 43.9%	Real Estate 27.6%	Real Estate 7.3%	Real Estate 20.2%	S&P 500 13.8%
Managed Futures 13.7%	Real Estate 38.5%	MSCI World 15.2%	Hedge Funds 9.3%	MSCI World 20.7%	Hedge Funds 10.0%	Global Bonds 10.9%	MSCI World 30.8%	NASDAQ 16.9%	Global Bonds 6.4%	MSCI World 16.5%	NASDAQ 12.7%
Real Estate 5.2%	MSCI World 33.8%	S&P 500 10.9%	Real Estate 8.3%	S&P 500 15.8%	NASDAQ 9.8%	T-Bills 1.3%	Real Estate 27.4%	S&P 500 15.1%	S&P 500 2.1%	S&P 500 16.0%	MSCI World 8.8%
T-Bills 1.6%	S&P 500 28.7%	Global Bonds 10.4%	S&P 500 4.9%	Hedge Funds 12.9%	MSCI World 9.6%	Hedge Funds -19.0%	S&P 500 26.5%	MSCI World 12.3%	T-Bills 0.1%	NASDAQ 15.9%	Real Estate 5.4%
Hedge Funds -1.5%	Hedge Funds 19.5%	Hedge Funds 9.0%	T-Bills 3.3%	NASDAQ 9.5%	Managed Futures 7.5%	S&P 500 -37.0%	Hedge Funds 20.0%	Hedge Funds 10.3%	NASDAQ -1.8%	Hedge Funds 6.4%	Hedge Funds 3.6%
MSCI World -19.5%	Managed Futures 15.5%	NASDAQ 8.6%	Managed Futures 2.4%	Global Bonds 6.1%	S&P 500 5.5%	Real Estate -37.3%	Global Bonds 2.6%	Managed Futures 6.4%	Managed Futures -4.3%	Global Bonds 1.7%	Managed Futures 0.5%
S&P 500 -22.1%	Global Bonds 14.9%	T-Bills 1.4%	NASDAQ 1.4%	Managed Futures 6.0%	T-Bills 4.5%	MSCI World -40.3%	T-Bills 0.2%	Global Bonds 5.2%	Hedge Funds -5.3%	T-Bills 0.1%	T-Bills 0.0%
NASDAQ -31.5%	T-Bills 1.0%	Managed Futures 0.9%	Global Bonds -6.9%	T-Bills 5.0%	Real Estate -17.8%	NASDAQ -40.5%	Managed Futures -4.8%	T-Bills 0.1%	MSCI World -5.0%	Managed Futures -1.8%	Global Bonds -5.7%

	S&P 500	NASDAQ	MSCI World	Global Bonds	T-Bills	Real Estate	Hedge Funds	Managed Futures
Compound Annual Return Jan 1990 - Jun 2013	9.0%	8.9%	6.4%	6.5%	3.2%	10.3%	10.9%	6.7%
Correlation of Monthly Returns to Managed Futures	(0.12)	(0.19)	(0.08)	0.29	0.08	(0.05)	(0.01)	1.00

Figure 0.6 Managed Futures Performance Compared to Other Asset Classes.

Source: Millburn Ridgefield Corporation; S&P 500 Index; NASDAQ Composite Index; MSCI World Index; World Government Bond Index; 90-day U.S. Treasury Bills; FTSE NAREIT US Real Estate Index Series; HFRI Fund Weighted Composite Index; Managed Futures Index refers to the Barclay BTOP50 Index; Managed Futures is a Managed Futures Index. Past Performance is not necessarily indicative of future performance. Unless noted otherwise, index returns do not reflect fees or transaction costs and reflect reinvestment of net dividends.

Diversification with companies is not too dissimilar from an investor making investment decisions. After all, both would like to increase rates of return while ideally lowering risk to build a better, more solid investment portfolio. "In today's business world, institutional investors are looking to outperform the foreseeable long period of low returns of the public and fixed income security markets caused by the economic turmoil of the last few years. They are looking to invest in alternative vehicles such as venture capital and private equity firms that benefit from demonstrable competitive advantages in territories where they invest, which, in turn, provide real advantages to their portfolio companies vis-à-vis their competitors from around the globe."[30] In other words, there appears to be many types of financial waves. Opportunities to invest exist in any environment but one needs to develop fundamental valuation principles, whether it is in a corporate setting or an individual building a sound investment portfolio. Finding intrinsic value is difficult with publicly traded securities but can be even more cumbersome with alternative investments. Alternative investments can be difficult to value since there might be no market for them nor a lot of information to make a rational decision. Liquidity is also not a benefit of most alternative investments.

Wall Street has been and still remains mainly devoted to stocks, bonds, and cash. For instance, many recommendations revolve around these three asset classes and in some cases do not mention or include real estate, private equity, managed futures, venture capital, commodities, or hedge funds as additional options. Bloomberg reporter Inyoung Hwang has made several tables for strategists recommending allocations for stocks, bonds, and cash.[30]

The American Association of Individual Investors (AAII) presents three different asset allocation models for investors called AAII Asset Allocation Models, which do not include alternative investments. That is, the aggressive, moderate, and conservative models have no alternative investments (Table 0.1).

By focusing on just stocks and bonds without alternative investments, investors are not considering an important part of the overall picture, which might possibly increase returns while at the same time lower risk, provided careful selection and appropriate timing are used.

Table 0.1 AAII Asset Allocation Models

Aggressive	**Moderate**	**Conservative**
20% large-cap stocks	20% large-cap stocks	25% large-cap stocks
20% mid-cap stocks	20% mid-cap stocks	10% mid-cap stocks
20% small-cap stocks	10% small-cap stocks	10% small-cap stocks
20% international stocks	15% international stocks	5% international stocks
10% emerging markets stocks	5% emerging markets stocks	0% emerging markets stocks
10% intermediate bonds	30% intermediate bonds	40% intermediate bonds
0% short-term bonds	0% short-term bonds	10% short-term bonds

Source: "Suggested Allocation Breakdowns," The American Association of Individual Investors, www.aaii.com/asset-allocation, April 2, 2013.

Historically, asset allocation was considered the Holy Grail for investing by Wall Street. In the infamous study "In Determinants of Portfolio Performance," authors Brinson, Hood, and Beebower examined 91 large pension plans over 1974–1983 and expressed the view that asset allocation is far more important than security selection or market timing. They found that asset allocation is responsible for around 93.6 percent of the variation in total plan return. While this study might have had some validity almost four decades ago, times have changed, especially with alternative investments. In *Trends in State Pension Asset Allocation and Performance* for 2012, Cliffwater states: "In fact, over the last 10 years, just the opposite has transpired. We find that asset allocation explained a mere 8% of the variation among state fund returns while manager/fund selection accounted for 92% of the variation among state fund returns."[32] Oddly, decades after this study, there are still investors who believe security selection and market timing do not play a significant role. An interesting but little-known fact is that Brinson, Hood, and Beebower did not incorporate alternative investments at the time partially since these investments were not nearly as developed as they are today. Brinson, Hood, and Beebower appeared to have been undecided as to how to incorporate alternative investments. Recognizing alternative investments was one thing, but including them in their study was another. Data was unavailable for them to use. Essentially, alternative investments were not well known back then as they are almost 40 years later.

Investing during the 1960s and 1970s was very different from today. The 1960s led investors to believe one should buy and hold but this did not last for long. Investors liked buying the 50 most popular stocks and then holding them for the long haul: "The Nifty Fifty were often called one-decision stocks: buy and never sell. Because their prospects were so bright, many analysts claimed that the only direction they could go was up."[33] The stock market declined in 1973–1974 and these stocks plummeted. By 1976, they were considered undervalued.

Most of the 1990s revolved around large cap growth names that investors bought and held like Cisco or Microsoft. A decade later, the financial landscape has changed once again. That is, investors have found a buy and hold strategy to be a troublesome strategy and bad for a portfolio. "The buy-and-hold strategy finds a theoretical basis in the Efficient Market Hypothesis (EMH), according to which stock prices always include all available information and are priced correctly. As a result, short term stock price movements are completely random and it is not possible to predict them."[34] While it is debatable whether or not the stock market is truly efficient or not, alternative investments are often private and not traded on an exchange, and it is difficult to obtain information about them.

Regarding when and how an investor deploys funds to buy or sell any security, timing is much more relevant today. Timing is not completely irrelevant and might not be summarily dismissed. Investors frequently have bad timing such as the tendency to sell winners too early or hold losing investments too long. "Prospect theory predicts a disposition to sell winners and ride losers when the proceeds realized are held, as opposed to being rolled over into another gamble."[35] Buying and simply holding without considering the market can lead to large losses:

> The main problem with the buy-and-hold strategy is the total lack of risk control that can result in huge losses. Market volatility is higher during drawdowns. Prices usually decrease quicker than they increase, and thus the absence of risk management techniques exposes a passive unmanaged portfolio, to large fluctuations that in a few days can completely wipe out positive returns that took years to achieve. A buy-and-hold strategy may be extremely risky in declining markets.[36]

Looking at the market is a prudent decision. Are we in an uptrend or a downtrend? What is the condition of the market?

Even though alternative investments have been found and shown to be useful for asset allocation purposes, Wall Street has been too timid to stray from their traditional investments mainly around stocks, bonds, and cash. That is, current asset allocation models frequently fail to include alternative investments despite the known benefits and merits of adding them to a portfolio. Countless investment professionals and many big banks to this day brandish pie charts showing asset allocation to be the biggest determinant for how returns are generated. Selecting which security to buy is important, as evidenced with the U.S. State Pension System. "Overall 10 year state fund returns were more influenced by manager/fund selection than by asset allocation; putting in question the conventional wisdom that 90% of performance is asset allocation. Private equity and real estate allocations were the primary driver behind the better performing state funds."[37] As investors, we typically frame securities; cognitive abilities of investors are somewhat narrow and confined. As a result, investors tend to box securities. In "Behavioral Portfolio Theory," Hersch Shefrin and Meir Statman explain:

> Labels, such as "stock" or "bond" provide help in processing information as they frame complex information into simple boxes. Behavioral investors begin the process of security screening by eliminating from consideration securities whose labels indicate that they are not likely to be suitable for a given layer. For example, investors might eliminate securities that carry the "stock" label from consideration for the downside protection layer because they know that, in general, stocks lack the desired properties for downside protection securities. Labels always simplify information. Unfortunately, labels also distort information.[38]

Like the research done by Brinson, Hood, and Beebower decades ago, Modern Portfolio Theory (MPT) is outdated and no longer modern. A new method for investing, which I call Modern Portfolio Allocation (MPA), might be more relevant in today's world of finance. MPA includes adding alternative investments to a stock and bond portfolio in order to create a well-diversified portfolio, with the goal of lowering risk and increasing returns. Alternative investments typically have a low correlation with stocks and bonds. As we saw with managed futures, they have a negative correlation with equities and a low correlation with global bonds. As part of our human nature, we tend to get caught up in the moment and our vision becomes myopic. Investors frequently fail to look ahead or even at what has happened in the past. While one could argue there is no guarantee of past performance continuing into the future, panicking and selling based on pure emotions tends to end in dire results. Once an investor loses money, they walk away and invariably miss the recovery. "Investors seem to attach disproportionate importance to short-run economic developments."[39]

Today, there is finally enough data to show alternative investments move in waves. Equities, on the other hand, have a longer and more measurable track record, as Professor Richard Sylla found (Figure 0.7).

An astute investor can devise strategies around the ebb and flow of the stock market. "A wide variety of trading strategies call for buying stocks

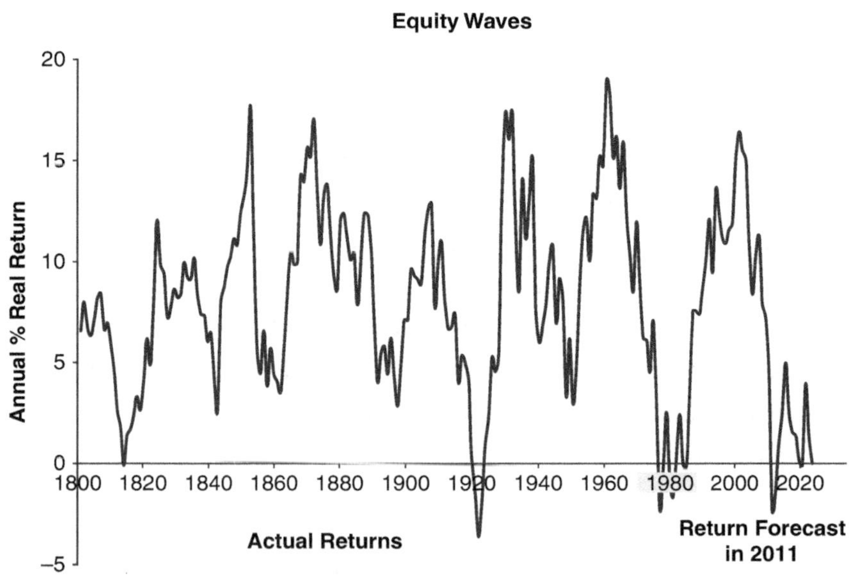

Figure 0.7 Equity Waves.

Source: Richard Sylla—Henry Kaufman Professor of the History of Financial Institutions and Markets; Professor of Economics, Stern School of Business—New York University.

when their prices rise and selling stocks when their prices fall."[40] Waves with equities are nothing new; waves have been observed quite some time ago. "Early in the history of stock market indexes developed by Charles Dow, editor of the Wall Street Journal from 1900–1902 and part-owner, commentators viewed their evolution as a series of nested irregular '*waves*.'"[41]

Equity and bond information can be traced for centuries but data regarding alternative investments has been difficult to obtain because of its private nature. It is difficult to track. For example, Gjergji Cici, the former associate director of research for Wharton Research Data Service (WRDS) at the Wharton School of Business (presently an assistant professor of economics and finance at William & Mary's Mason School of Business), developed the "WRDS Guide to IPO Databases and Research" and warns that "the most widely used database in IPO research" must be used with "caution" because "it has missing information and documented errors."[42] While data can differ from one organization to the next, it is becoming more accurate. In the past, this was not the case. It is very difficult to obtain information from a private transaction. More information is available with publicly traded companies. An increasing number of organizations are gathering data on LBO funds as well as on venture capital. Each organization might record data differently, which one needs to be cognizant about before making an investment decision. For instance, are we looking at apples to apples? Is the number of dollars raised or number of private-equity deals the same between the organizations collecting the data? One might record domestic data while the other records global data, which might be drastically different, leading the investor to a false conclusion about which way the private-equity market is moving. Private equity moves in waves and appears to be different from country to country. The venture capital/LBO market in Canada is different from that in the United States. For one, venture capital is much more mature in the United States as opposed to the venture capital market in Canada, which is more in its infancy; the U.S. venture capital market has been around for decades while the Canadian market has not been around as long. Therefore, waves associated with both might differ.

While the criteria are not the same, I believe that Thomson Reuters and DeaLogic are two helpful services to use for analyzing initial public

Table 0.2 Initial Public Offerings (2011–2012)

Year	# of IPOs	Aggregate proceeds
2001	79	$34.24 billion
2002	66	$22.03 billion
2003	62	$9.53 billion
2004	174	$31.31 billion
2005	160	$28.27 billion
2006	157	$30.48 billion
2007	160	$35.69 billion
2008	21	$22.76 billion
2009	41	$13.17 billion
2010	92	$29.85 billion
2011	81	$26.97 billion
2012	94	$31.12 billion

Source: Jay R. Ritter, Cordell Professor of Finance, University of Florida, "Initial Public Offerings: Updated Statistics," March 29, 2013

offerings (IPOs). Likewise, Jay Ritter and Professor Alexander Ljungqvist provide excellent research with IPO data (Table 0.2).

Data can be viewed differently, depending on the source, as well as the search criteria used. Some databases are also hard to access or are extremely expensive to use especially if one is not anticipating investing on a regular basis in venture capital or IPOs. Finally, there are other databases that are new and do not track data back to any meaningful length of time.

As anyone who understands anything about alternative investments knows, they are not easy to monitor or track. Hedge funds, for example, do not have the reporting requirements that mutual funds have and are also unregulated. Hedge fund data historically is conflicting. Even indexes that were created in recent years do not match up with one another despite the fact that they were attempting to create the same reliable index. One index might include hedge funds that went out of business while the other one did not. I have found HFRI (Hedge Fund Research Inc.) to be quite helpful. Like hedge funds, information for investors regarding commodities still differs mid 2011. For example, consider commodity indexes. Commodity indexes greatly vary in composition. Major commodity indexes dropped sharply in the first week of May 2011, but some fell more steeply than others, creating a significant performance gap among indexes and investment products linked to them.[43] Considering over 2,000 hedge funds vanished in 2009, the impact was large and the numbers are very different depending on whether or not one included the 2,000 hedge funds.

Whether one is running a $20 billion dollar pension or investing $10,000 in an individual retirement account (IRA), there is a lot to learn about alternative investments. To an extent, institutions and high net worth investors have similar needs. "Institutional investors also face complex decisions. Some institutions invest on behalf of their clients, but others, such as foundations and university endowments, are more similar to individuals in that they seek to finance a long-term stream of discretionary spending. The investment options for these institutions have also expanded enormously since the days when a portfolio of government bonds was the norm."[44]

1

DOES THE UNIVERSE MOVE IN WAVES?

Besides the exploration of alternative investments and how they move in waves, *Understanding Alternative Investments* reviews how occurrences in nature, such as waves, can be used in finance. That is, the study of waves can be used for additional knowledge about investing in alternative investments. Ocean waves are generated by wind energy: "Wind energy is imparted to the sea surface through friction and pressure, causing waves. As the wind gains strength, the surface develops gradually from flat and smooth through growing levels of roughness. First, ripples form, then larger waves, called shop. The waves continue to build, their maximum size depending on three factors: wind speed, wind duration, and the area over which the wind is blowing, called the fetch."[1] Years ago, I was vacationing in Avalon, New Jersey, for the summer. Sitting on the beach, staring out at the ocean, I pondered how waves never stopped rolling in; they are incessant. Moreover, they could change direction, speed, and height in an instant. They were also influenced by the weather and other events. No wave is ever the same, but they share similarities. For example, I noticed the curve of a wave was not too different from any of the shells at my feet. Surfers love this curve, called the "barrel." While it seemed far-fetched at the time, I wondered if these patterns or cycles could be broken down into mathematical equations. I thought of how these waves were calm but could suddenly turn into rogue waves, not too different from the storms on

Wall Street, otherwise known as recessions or depressions. I was convinced that nature might teach us something about investing.

Financial waves exist on Wall Street and not every day is a sunny one. Financial storms happen and can be quite devastating, not too different from hurricanes or other natural storms by sea. Hurricanes can and will happen. Likewise, financial storms are beyond our control. Whether they are financial or not, storms can cloud our vision and lead us to make bad decisions while in a panic mode. Paradoxically, often the worst of times are the best of times to invest. Alternative investments all move in waves. Patterns, cycles, and trends occur with alternative investments. There are waves that exist with hedge funds, venture capital, commodities, real estate, LBOs, and managed futures.

After *Wave Theory for Alternative Investments* was released in 2010, I noticed a torrent of articles from newspapers and magazines covering different types of waves, figuratively and literally. One important non-finance wave that developed was one I call a "Protest Wave" or wave of protest exemplified by the movement, Occupy Wall Street. "In many cities (notably London, which has followed the example set by Occupy Wall Street in New York) the protesters have set up encampments that are meant to last indefinitely; in others they came and went. Defining where the wave of protests started is hard."[2] A current wave of animosity and distrust of large banks is transparent and will likely continue until all the shenanigans stop. When protestors gather in 900 cities around the globe, it signifies a real problem.

There also appears to be a mergers and acquisitions (M&A) wave forming amongst registered investment advisors (RIAs). According to industry-wide data compiled by Schwab Advisor Services, in the first quarter of 2013, RIA M&A activity recorded its highest number of deals since the first quarter of 2012, with 13 completed deals totaling $5.8 billion.[3] The following RIAs were involved: United Capital, Exencial, Silver Lane Advisors LLC, Luminous Capital Holdings LLC, Mt. Eden Investment Advisors LLC, Hanlon Financial Group, and LPL Financial, to name a few. Waves are prevalent.

Another powerful wave that seems to be forming is that of investors and financial advisors being more attracted to the model of an investment firm versus a "bulge bracket" firm, which was the basis behind Glass-Steagall years ago. I call this wave the Bank Wave. Former heads of the big banks that advocated large universal banks have changed their minds. "Critics of the bank expansions include Philip Purcell, former chairman and chief executive of Morgan Stanley, and Sheila Bair, former head of the Federal Deposit Insurance Corporation. John Reed, who ran Citicorp before it was merged with Travelers Group Inc. in the 1998 megadeal creating Citigroup, and recently retired Citigroup Chairman Richard Parsons have said it was a mistake to allow the creation of the big financial conglomerates."[4] Megabanks might be too unwieldy and cause additional problems. Citigroup grew too large and the US Government essentially broke up the bank and sold parts off after the Great Recession. The result was beneficial and Citigroup prospered. Many investment firms did quite well during the Great Recession and continue to attract top tier talent and investors looking for an alternative to the big banks or "bulge bracket" firms.

WAVES IN SCIENCE

Waves vary in each scenario. The patterns, cycles, or trends that I have identified with waves and alternative investments might actually be found on a much larger scale with the universe. Waves are found in numerous places and differ from one another, such as transverse (a disturbance sends waves perpendicular to the original wave) and longitudinal waves (a disturbance that sends waves in the same direction as the original wave). In mathematics and science, a wave is a disturbance that travels through space and time, usually accompanied by the transfer of energy.[5] Waves are repetitive. They move in cycles.

The question of how the universe commenced has been debated for millennia. Albert Einstein suggested that the universe was formed from a large explosion (the "Big Bang"). As we know, evidence of the Big Bang was discovered in 1965, ten years after Einstein's death. Scientists concluded that the Big Bang was the beginning of all space and time. The universe was thought to have begun with the Big Bang approximately 14 billion years ago and has expanded ever since. Another more recent belief is cyclical, where the Big Bang happened not just once but a myriad of times. Paul Steinhardt and Neil Turok describe a cyclical model of the universe:

> Which proposes that the big bang repeats itself every trillion years or so leading to the formation of new galaxies, stars, and planets each time. Instead of relying on inflation to smooth out the original fluctuations, the model has an ultra-slow phase of contraction leading up to each bang that smoothes and flattens the universe naturally. Hence, the cycles are interwoven. The events at the end of one cycle determine the large-scale structure in the cycle to come.[6]

Dr. Paul Frampton, Louis J. Rubin Jr., and Lauris Baum, all from the University of North Carolina, believe there are four parts to a cyclical universe: expansion, turnaround, contraction, and bounce.[7] It is possible that the universe moves in waves; there could be a pre-big bang alternative or cyclical model. Years ago I pondered whether or not alternative investments move in waves. As Carl Sagan states in *Broca's Brain*, "The universe forces those who live in it to understand it."[8] We learn new things about science just as we do with finance. For example, gravitational waves were found, shedding light on another type of wave: "One of the most exciting new developments in physics is the imminent advent of gravitational wave astronomy—viewing the cosmos not with light and its electromagnetic complements like radio, x-rays, infrared, microwaves and gamma-rays, but rather with ripples of gravity, or gravitational waves."[9] Studying various waves helped me with the premise that alternative investments move in waves. Antiquated theories or old beliefs should be replaced with new ones. New scientific studies replace old ones that are no longer applicable.

There are many different types of waves that we are oblivious to but they still exist. Sitting on a beach, once can observe "ocean" waves. "Light" waves from the sun help with a summer tan. When you head home from the beach and put something in the microwave oven, one is exposed to "microwaves." Microwaves are even used with executing trades on Wall Street. On your way to work in the morning, you turn on the radio to hear how your sports team did or to listen to some music. The sounds you hear involve "radio waves." Scientists are even working on T-waves or Terahertz

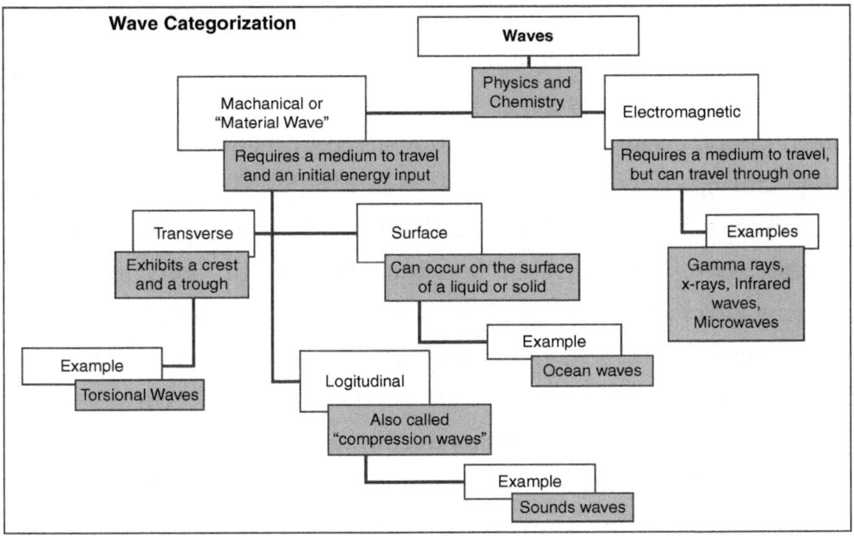

Figure 1.1 Types of Waves in Nature with Examples.
Source: Author.

waves that are in between microwaves and infrared light waves. For example, the California Institute of Technology is working on a chip that enables T-waves to penetrate a wide variety of non-conducting materials. One day, like Superman, it will be possible for us to use a cell phone to see through paper, plastic, wood, masonry, clothing, and ceramics. The bottom line is that there are different types of waves that surround us day to day. Figure 1.1 is a Wave Categorization chart that provides some of the examples and types of waves that exist in chemistry, physics, and mathematics.

OCEANIC WAVES

The best-known waves are ocean waves. The base substance, water itself, has many unusual properties, such as high surface tension and heat capacity, which are of tremendous significance to everything from the oceans' ability to support life to their stabilizing effect on the world's climate, and their ability to transmit waves.[10] Today there are even devices that monitor ocean waves. "Pennington-based Ocean Power Technologies Inc. last week announced the trial deployment of an autonomous wave energy device, part of the company's PowerBuoy product line."[11] By studying ocean waves, one might derive a better understanding of waves found with alternative investments.

In "Ocean Waves," there are numerous studies regarding wave height in the sea including during hurricanes: "It is of interest, however, to estimate the largest wave height in the long term when sea severity is changing. A typical example of this situation is the estimation of extreme wave height during a hurricane including the growing and decaying stages of the sea condition."[12] In 1973, Borgman developed an approach for estimating extreme wave height during a hurricane. However, in order to estimate extreme waves and sea states, it is necessary to gather enough data over a fixed time period. It does not appear that there is a perfect way to predict extreme values of waves and sea states. There is no theoretical basis for selecting any particular probability distribution to characterize significant wave height data.[13] Rogue waves were discussed in Wave Theory for Alternative Investments. "An unusually high single wave event observed offshore is commonly called a freak wave. This definition is somewhat obscure since neither the cause of the occurrence nor criteria to define freak waves have been clarified. Freak waves have been observed only rarely and these observations occurred under unexpected conditions: hence, only few measured data are available."[14] Freak waves or rogue waves can be seen in the financial markets, as recently witnessed in the Great Recession.

Naysayers believe that one cannot predict or forecast a wave, whether it is found in the ocean or on Wall Street. Yet one individual formed a company that actually predicted waves in the ocean. His name is Sean Collins, the surfing swami who developed a wave-prediction program called Surfline. "Sean Collins transformed the search for a perfect wave from a spiritual quest to something like a science."[15] Surfers swear by his program. Surfers want to find the best waves. Using undersea maps with satellite and buoy data, Collins became adept at predicting good surfing waves based on the weather.[16] It is not inconceivable that one day software will exist that guides investors to making better choices with alternative investments.

FINANCIAL WAVES

Just as there are different types of waves found in the ocean, there are financial waves such as IPO waves, M&A waves, equity waves, fixed income waves, cash waves, value waves, growth waves, foreign bond waves, and others. Securities called Credit-Default Swaps, which are traded amongst banks and various institutional investors, can move in waves and make waves. "But as with much of the Greek financial crisis, the tiny country could leave big waves in its wake."[17] Alternative investments move in waves. There are hedge fund waves, real estate waves, venture capital waves, managed futures waves, LBO waves, commodity waves, and many others. Regarding real estate, waves can be seen as prices decline after events such as World War I, the Great Depression, and World War II. This boom and bust is nothing new, as many investors in real estate surmised after the Great Recession when the real estate market imploded. Real estate continuously gets overvalued and then undervalued. It typically reverts to the mean. Figure 1.2 shows the "Annual change in home prices over 120 Years," where these patterns, trends, and cycles are more apparent.

Banks and investment firms packaged subprime loans into Collateralized Debt Obligations (CDOs) before the Great Recession. "The CDO is a structured investment vehicle with assets comprised of a large, diversified pool of debts (predominately mortgages, with a high proportion of subprime and Alt-A mortgages). The liabilities of a CDO are sold to investors with various levels of risk and return potential called 'tranches' (from the French word for 'slice')."[18] CDOs sound more complicated than

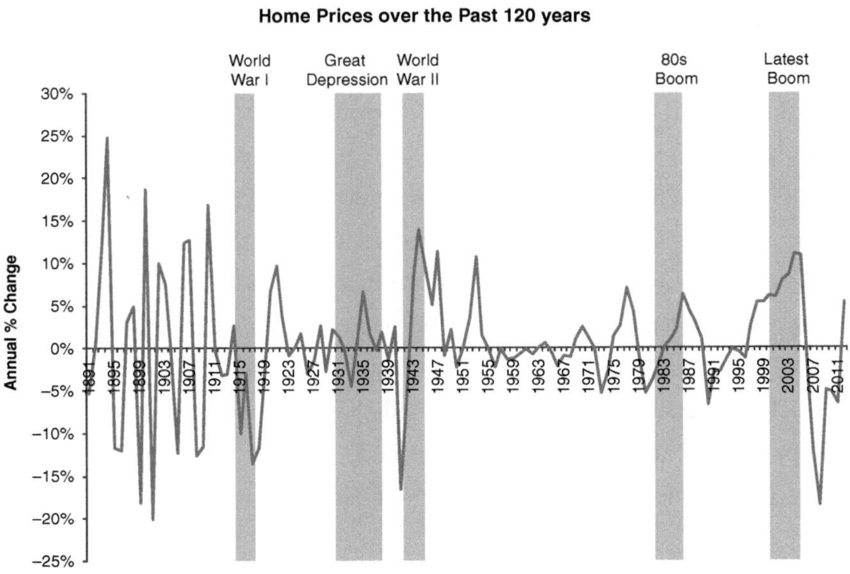

Figure 1.2 Fluctuations of United States Home Prices over the Past 120 Years, with Highlighted Periods of Economic Downturns and Recoveries.

Sources: Author, Robert Shiller.

they really are. "Banks and other financial firms typically create CDOs by wrapping together 100 or more bonds and other securities, including debt investments backed by home loans."[19] A number of these CDOs appeared to be problematic from the very beginning and might have been designed to fail. "In 2007, just as the housing market was about to crash, Citigroup cooked up a $1 billion collateralized debt obligation known as Class V Funding III. This mind-numbing concoction included other CDOs based on subprime mortgages. Once Citigroup sold it to investors, the bank bet against it and made a profit of at least $160 million. According to the SEC, the CDO was designed to fail."[20] CDOs were not just problematic in the United States. Banks around the globe offered them. Enforcement actions are coming to light years later: "U.S. securities regulators filed their first enforcement action tied to rosy credit ratings bestowed on thousands of mortgage-backed investments before the financial crisis erupted, accusing Mizuho Financial Group Inc. of rigging a 2007 bond deal... Mizuho agreed to pay $127.5 million to settle charges of negligence."[21]

Rating companies separate CDOs into tranches and assign ratings. Although quite risky, CDOs were given investment-grade ratings despite the risky underlying asset class. "CDOs are rated double- or triple-A. But these ratings can be misleading: CDOs can add highly speculative or even unratable debt to the highly rated tranches."[22] Rating agencies made a lot of money from throwing ratings on various CDOs: "CDOs have been a bonanza for the rating companies. In the past three years, S&P, Moody's and Fitch have made more money from evaluating structured finance—which includes CDOs and asset backed securities—than from rating anything else, including corporate and municipal bonds, according to their financial reports. The companies charge as much as three times more to rate CDOs than to analyze bonds, published cost listings show."[23]

The issuance of CDOs skyrocketed: "CDO issuance has soared over the past few years from $69 billion in 2000 to $476 billion in 2006."[24] Yet the sky-high pile of CDOs on the market began to falter:

> The fate of one exotic security may signal more trouble ahead for the credit markets. In early November, a collateralized debt obligation

> called Carina CDO apparently started liquidating its $450 million portfolio filled with bonds backed by subprime mortgages and pieces of other CDOs. These sales prompted credit rating agency Standard & Poor's to downgrade Carina's bonds from AAA to junk in a day.[25]

Rogue waves can cause huge short-term disturbances. "For shorter periods of time, the market as a whole can lose touch with fundamental laws grounded in economic growth and returns on investment...But in the long term, market data show that individual stocks and the market as a whole do follow these fundamental laws."[26] Meanwhile, hedge funds, insurance companies, banks, and non-institutional buyers such as retail investors lined up to buy to CDOs:

> CDOs are generally divided into different tiers, with the so-called equity portion sitting at the bottom of the pile. Investors in the part of the structure get higher returns, but they can be hurt badly if something goes wrong and borrowers can't make their payments. Those equity investors are the first to absorb any losses and can be wiped out because CDOs use a lot of leverage. The new vehicles buy those equity portions.[27]

Like any security, CDOs can be influenced by behavioral finance.

Equally troublesome, certain firms on Wall Street had vast exposure to CDOs. "Merrill Lynch and Citigroup led in sales of collateralized debt obligations—and racked up multibillion-dollar losses when they turned sour."[28] Morgan Stanley was involved with a US Probe: "Morgan Stanley arranged and marketed to investor pools of bond-related investments called collateralized-debt obligations, or CDOs, and its trading desk at times placed bets that their value would fall, traders said. Investigators are examining, among other things, whether Morgan Stanley made proper representations about its roles."[29] A number of deals were named after US presidents James Buchanan and Andrew Johnson that traders called "Dead Presidents." The bank helped design these deals and then bet against them.

The waves found with alternative investments are also triggered by events or what I call the "drivers." Some of these drivers are beyond anyone's control such as economic cycles, war, or violent storms such as a hurricane. In some cases, alternative investments are driven by behavior identified in a relatively new field called behavioral finance. "Recent Developments in fields such as behavioral economics, experimental economics and neuroeconomics have begun to revive the long-dormant relationship between economics and psychology."[30] Whether it is with an individual or a group trying to curb his or her own behavior, behavior can sometimes be influenced. Understanding our behavioral patterns can help us become better investors. After all, human beings are complex and very emotional:

> Every emotive experience we experience in life plays a role in paving new highways of thought in our brain. These patterns of thought circuitry, informed by electronic and chemical release and forming neural connections called synapses, are the chief catalysts for decision-making in life. Synapses allow neurons to form circuits that make up our central nervous system, that system which controls our physical and mental functions. By understanding these paths of thought and how they were formed, we can fairly well predict behavior in certain circumstances or situations.[31]

Recessions, depressions, and other financial storms occur on a regular basis. Recession and recovery analysis are "primarily designed to facilitate the evaluation of prevailing business conditions by comparing current contractions, or current expansions, with corresponding phases in the past. This is done by measuring changes of individual time series from their standing at cyclical turns and corn-paring current with past changes over a series of widening time spans. All comparisons are based on seasonally adjusted data, if such adjustment is warranted."[32] These storms can affect alternatives investments (just like other asset classes).

Given the regularity of these storms, is it feasible to predict when they might occur so that an investor might change their asset allocation to either profit or attempt to avoid a loss? Table 1.1 is a chart on bear market waves with two stock indexes.

Table 1.1 Bear Markets Form Waves

Nasdaq composite, 2000–2002	**Price: 5,132 to 1,108 (down 78%)**
First wave	March 2000 to May 2000 (down 41%)
Second wave	Sept. 2000 to April 2001 (down 62%)
Third wave	May 2001 to Sept. 2001 (down 40%)
Fourth wave	Jan. 2002 to Oct. 2002 (down 47%)
Follow-through day	Oct. 15, 2002 (up 5.1%)
S&P 500, 2008–2009	**1,576 to 666 (down 58%)**
First wave	Nov. 2007 to March 2008 (down 20%)
Second wave	June 2008 to Nov. 2008 (down 47%)
Third wave	Jan. 2009 to March 2009 (down 29%)
Follow-through day	March 12, 2009 (up 4.1%)

Source: "First Spot Three Sell Waves," IBD, p. B1, November 11, 2011.

UNDERSTANDING WAVES HELPS MAKE INFORMED DECISIONS

The pertinent question is whether one could use this information about waves to make better investment decisions. The answer is "yes" and perhaps even more so than publicly traded equities. Value versus growth investing has been shown to move in waves. Before 2009, Value did better than Growth. The Russell 1000 Growth then outperformed the Russell 1000 Value from 2009 to 2011. "From the beginning of 2009 through the end of 2011, the Russell 1000 Value Index—the stocks in the Russell 1000 index with the strongest value characteristics—returned 39%, versus their growth counterparts in the Russell 1000 Growth Index, which returned 64%."[33] Various studies with alternative investments indicate studying waves might help make better investment decisions. For instance, in "The Role of the Private Equity Sector Promoting Economic Recovery," Robert J. Shapiro in March 2009 contends that private equity aids companies in difficult times:

> Private equity can play a valuable role during recessions and early recoveries. This role arises from the core activities which produced strong returns during the recent period of low-cost financing and healthy overall growth: As the recession increases strains on many firms and reveals areas of weakness and under-performance, private equity expertise in focusing investments and organizational and strategic changes where they can produce the most positive results

> can prevent some firms from falling into bankruptcy and help turn around other companies which otherwise might languish through these perilous times.[34]

Regarding the Great Recession, Shapiro states, "For thirty years preceding this crisis, the private equity sector has achieved notable success in attracting investments and securing strong returns" and "companies held by private equity firms have generally outperformed averages for their industries."[35] I advise many clients, both institutional and individual. Many of these clients expressed an aversion to LBO funds because they viewed them as "too risky" when in reality they just did not understand them. The essence behind LBOs is that an investor is merely taking advantage of the economic cycle. Having an alternative investment such as a LBO fund can help a portfolio. Frequently, with investments that might not be the easiest to comprehend, they are often the ones that can make the most money. However, one must do their homework and be cognizant of when they are making the investment and to whom are they giving their money. One should never blindly invest in an alternative investment.

Alternative investments can have unusually high peaks and troughs just like the ones found in the ocean. Yet alternatives can sometimes reach a trough or peak irrespective of a recession. For example, silver, corn, gold, and cotton all reached highs after the Great Recession. Measuring or tracking performance results of all alternative investments collectively (both before and after recessions) might not be as revealing as observing them individually. Because there is no vehicle that investors can select that covers all alternative investments, it would be prudent to examine thoroughly each and every alternative investment one is considering adding to a portfolio before adding it. For example, if one wants to add oil to a portfolio, they should select an appropriate vehicle and then examine how it might add or detract from an existing portfolio.

Alternative investments appear to act independently of one another depending on the storm. Real estate and hedge funds did well during the market collapse from 2000 to 2002 (where the stock market dropped around 51 percent), but did not fare as well during the Great Recession. The housing bubble that burst led to a worldwide real estate collapse in prices and ultimately there was a credit crises that came about. The credit crisis affected hedge funds negatively because they were thwarted from borrowing in order to sell or short positions, which is the essence behind hedge funds. Since hedge funds have a number of styles, not all of them performed poorly. Some even did quite well, such as short sellers or global macro. To compare how different hedge-fund styles have performed on either a raw or a risk-adjusted basis, one can use the Bloomberg Active Indices for Funds (BAIF) function, which lets you rank return data for indexes that track asset-weighted composites of funds with similar characteristics.

Certain types of real estate, such as storage companies, also held up well, while residential real estate was decimated. The best time to buy real estate is when it gets decimated. For example, the period after the Great Recession was a phenomenal time to buy. Overall, real estate was one of the better-performing asset classes over the past decade despite the real estate collapse because it sprang back. A variety of investors including the Smart Money (large institutional investors) bought real estate. Hedge funds and private equity funds are attracted to the returns, such as with single-family homes. "Picking up those mortgages at rock bottom prices has delivered returns of 30% or more for savvy hedge funds this year. The other, and more intriguing, way of betting on rising house prices is to buy the houses themselves. KKR, Colony Capital, and Blackstone are among those amassing large portfolios of homes, mostly buying from banks' foreclosure auctions."[36] After the Great Recession, home prices began improving. Figure 1.3 is a chart showing how big pension plans performed with real estate compared to other asset classes.

Real estate even outperformed both equities and fixed income. Up until 2010, equity and fixed income provided some of the lowest returns for the big public pension funds. Bonds even went negative. "The Barclays U.S. Aggregate Bond Index, known as "the Agg"—which tracks the broader debt market the way the Standard & Poors-500 follows stocks—declined 0.12% in the first quarter, its first negative return in that period since 2006. And with many large investors yanking funds tied to the Agg, the index's flagging popularity is having repercussions for how hundreds of billions of dollars are allocated in fixed income portfolios."[37]

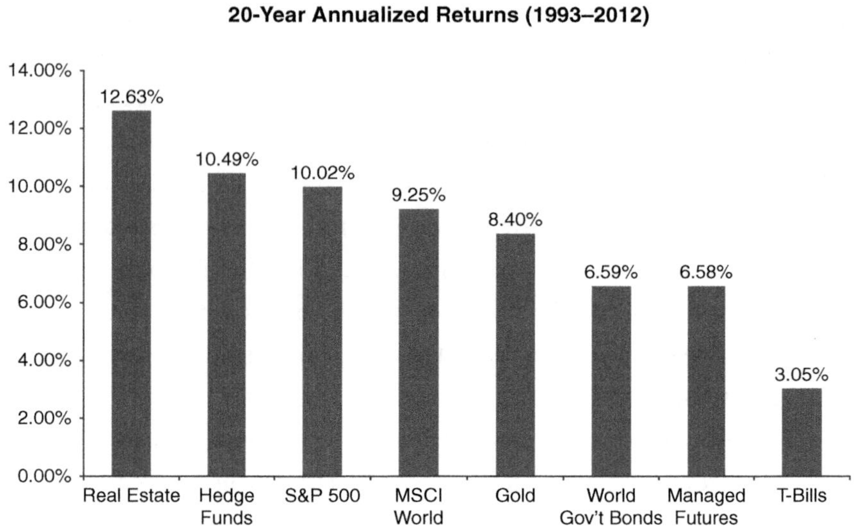

Figure 1.3 Comparison of Alternative Investments over 20 Years with Stocks, Bonds, and Cash.

Source: Author.

The goal of studying waves with alternative investments is to understand exactly where one is buying or selling in order to build better, more diversified portfolios. No one has a crystal ball. Yet it can be useful to see how an asset class has been performing. Are you investing at the peak or the trough? An investor interested in venture capital might be inclined to put money into the asset class after hearing how well it did over a number of years from 1994 to 1999. Yet this might not be the ideal time to put a lot of money to work in venture capital. The year 1999 was abnormally good for venture capital but it would have been devastating to invest at this juncture; the following three years were brutal for venture capital, with huge losses. Likewise, investors might have heard about a few social media companies where venture capitalists made a lot of money.

Any investor will acknowledge that securities can be overvalued or undervalued at times. Reversion to the mean, which is also referred to as regression to the mean, is essentially a statistical concept that the bigger the change of a random variable from its mean, the more likely the next variate will not change as much. Regression to the mean is used in statistics. "Regression to the mean (RTM) is a statistical phenomenon that can make natural variation in repeated data look like real change. It happens when unusually large or small measurements tend to be followed by measurements that are closer to the mean."[38] People in general have difficulty understanding regression toward the mean: The mathematical concept of mean reversion can be applied to stocks and other assets. "Using mean reversion in stock price analysis involves both identifying the trading range for a stock and computing the average price using analytical techniques taking into account considerations such as earnings, etc."[39] Alternative investments are no different; they frequently revert to the mean.

In particular, investors notice a change such as gold increasing in price. They observe that it is moving in one direction over time. They mistakenly believe it will continue moving in one direction only and that it will never reverse its direction. No consideration is made with regard to how far up or how far down the price has moved. Many times the investor has a myopic view and looks at a small time frame such as a month or two. A purchase or sale then transpires at an extreme when the alternative investment is way over- or undervalued. Sadly, the investor loses money when the wave reverses. I received many inquiries about whether gold was "cheap" at $1,800 after it went up for a decade. The time to buy is not after a huge run. Gold has had many waves over decades. When I was interviewed by a reporter for the Wall Street Journal, the reporter looked up gold on Yahoo and told me that it would keep going up. The price of gold was around $1,500. She told me that there were no waves and that gold would continue going up and never come back down again in price. Her belief was that ETFs made the market more accessible. Gold went past $1,800 and then plummeted to $1,200.

Potentially, alternative investments can be used to lower risk and increase returns. Alternative investments move in and out of favor, like ocean waves. In order to illustrate this notion, I developed a chart called *The Wave Chart*. In this chart, one can clearly see that alternative investments can move in and out of favor, similar to stock, bonds, and cash. This chart reinforces the idea that all securities move in waves. The chart includes a 20-year ranking of asset class returns for equities, fixed income, and alternative investments (Figure 1.4).

The Wave Chart uses the S&P500 for equities, NAREIT for real estate, HFRI Fund Weighted Composite for hedge funds, Cambridge Venture

The Wave Chart: 20-Year Ranking of Asset Class Returns for Equities, Fixed Income, and Alternative Investments

	1991	1992	1993	1994	1995	1996	1997	1998	1999	2000
Best Return	NAREIT Composite 35.68%	HFRI Fund Wghtd Composite 21.22%	Int'l Stk 32.94%	CAMB US Venture Cap 20.07%	CAMB US Venture Cap 47.81%	NAREIT Composite 35.75%	CAMB US Venture Cap 54.40%	CAMB US Venture Cap 35.89%	CAMB US Venture Cap 319.77%	S&P GSCI 49.74%
	HFRI Fund Wghtd Composite 32.19%	CAMB US Private Eqty 16.38%	HFRI Fund Wghtd Composite 30.88%	CAMB US Private Eqty 16.37%	S&P 500 Composite 37.20%	S&P GSCI 33.92%	CAMB US Private Eqty 39.63%	S&P 500 Composite 28.34%	CAMB US Private Eqty 50.51%	NAREIT Composite 25.89%
	S&P 500 Composite 30.23%	NAREIT Composite 12.18%	CAMB US Private Eqty 21.89%	Int'l Stk 8.06%	CAMB US Private Eqty 27.48%	CAMB US Venture Cap 30.18%	S&P 500 Composite 31.83%	Int'l Stk 20.33%	Average 44.55%	BarCap AggregateBnd 11.63%
	CAMB US Venture Cap 20.58%	CAMB US Venture Cap 10.61%	CAMB US Venture Cap 21.87%	S&P GSCI 5.29%	HFRI Fund Wghtd Composite 21.50%	S&P 500 Composite 23.82%	NAREIT Composite 18.86%	CAMB US Private Eqty 11.70%	S&P GSCI 40.92%	BARC CTA Index 7.86%
	BarCap Aggregate Bnd 16.00%	Currency 10.27%	NAREIT Composite 18.55%	Average 4.61%	S&P GSCI 20.33%	CAMB US Private Eqty 23.20%	Average 16.97%	BarCap Aggregate Bnd 8.69%	HFRI Fund Wghtd Composite 31.29%	Cash 5.96%
	Average 15.55%	S&P 500 Composite 7.49%	Average 13.06%	Cash 4.24%	Average 18.75%	HFRI Fund Wghtd Composite 21.10%	HFRI Fund Wghtd Composite 16.79%	BARC CTA Index 7.01%	Int'l Stk 27.30%	Average 5.49%
	Int'l Stk 12.50%	BarCap Aggregate Bnd 7.40%	BARC CTA Index 10.37%	HFRI Fund Wghtd Composite 4.10%	BarCap Aggregate Bnd 18.47%	Average 18.09%	Currency 11 35%	Average 6.43%	S&P 500 Composite 20.89%	HFRI Fund Wghtd Composite 4.98%
	Currency 10.94%	Average 7.35%	S&P 500 Composite 9.97%	S&P 500 Composite 1.33%	NAREIT Composite 18.31%	BARC CTA Index 9.12%	BARC CTA Index 10.89%	Currency 5.71%	Cash 4.74%	Currency 4.45%
	CAMB US Private Eqty 9.57%	S&P GSCI 4.42%	BarCap Aggregate Bnd 9.75%	NAREIT Composite 0.81%	Int'l Stk 11.55%	Currency 6.69%	BarCap Aggregate Bnd 9.55%	Cash 5.06%	Currency 3.12%	S&P 500 Composite −9.03%
	Cash 5.75%	Cash 3.62%	Cash 3.09%	BARC CTA Index10.89% −0.65%	Currency 11.49%	Int'l Stk 6.36%	Cash 5.25%	HFRI Fund Wghtd Composite 2.62%	BarCap Aggregate Bnd −0.82%	Int'l Stk −13.96%
	BARC CTA Index 3.73%	BARC CTA Index −0.91%	Currency 3.33%	BarCap Aggregate Bnd −2.92%	Cash 5.75%	Cash 5.25%	Int'l Stk 2.06%	NAREIT Composite −18.82%	BARC CTA Index −1.19%	CAMB US Private Eqty −14.24%
Worst Return	S&P GSCI −6.13%	Int'l Stk −11.85%	S&P GSCI −12.33%	Currency 5.96%	BARC CTA Index −13.64%	BarCap Aggregate Bnd 3.63%	S&P GSCI −14.07%	S&P GSCI −35.75%	NAREIT Composite −6.48%	CAMB US Venture Cap −17.75%

	2001	2002	2003	2004	2005	2006	2007	2008	2009	2010
Best Return	NAREIT Composite 15.50%	S&P GSCI 32.07%	Int'l Stk 39.17%	NAREIT Composite 30.41%	CAMB US Private Eqty 30.94%	NAREIT Composite 34.02%	S&P GSCI 32.67%	BARC CTA Index 14.09%	Int'l Stk 32.46%	NAREIT Composite 27.56%
	BarCap AggregateBnd 8.44%	BARC CTA Index 12.36%	NAREIT Composite 38.47%	CAMB US Private Eqty 24.20%	S&P GSCI 25.55%	CAMB US Private Eqty 29.73%	Int'l Stk 11.63%	BarCap AggregateBnd 5.24%	NAREIT Composite 27.80%	CAMB US Private Eqty 21.45%
	HFRI Fund Wghtd Composite 4.62%	BarCap AggregateBnd 10.26%	S&P 500 Composite 28.36%	Int'l Stk 20.70%	CAMB US Venture Cap 14.71%	Int'l Stk 26.86%	CAMB US Venture Cap 11.09%	Currency 3.50%	S&P 500 Composite 25.92%	CAMB US Venture Cap 18.51%
	Cash 4.09%	Currency 6.29%	CAMB US Private Eqty 26.96%	S&P GSCI 17.28%	Int'l Stk 14.02%	S&P 500 Composite 15.61%	CAMB US Private Eqty 10.83%	Cash 1.80%	CAMB US Private Eqty 21.74%	S&P 500 Composite 15.06%
	Currency 2.71%	NAREIT Composite 5.22%	S&P GSCI 20.72%	Average 12.24%	Average 10.32%	CAMB US Venture Cap 14.99%	HFRI Fund Wghtd Composite 9.96%	CAMB US Venture Cap −17.36%	HFRI Fund Wghtd Composite 19.98%	Average 11.55%
	BARC CTA Index 0.84%	Cash 1.70%	HFRI Fund Wghtd Composite 19.55%	CAMB US Venture Cap 11.06%	HFRI Fund Wghtd Composite 9.30%	HFRI Fund Wghtd Composite 12.89%	Average 7.80%	Average −18.12%	Average 14.05%	HFRI Fund Wghtd Composite 10.49%
	Average −6.33%	Average −0.76%	Average 18.21%	S&P 500 Composite 10.74%	NAREIT Composite 8.29%	Average 11.96%	BARC CTA Index 7.64%	HFRI Fund Wghtd Composite −19.02%	S&P GSCI 13.48%	S&P GSCI 9.02%
	CAMB US Private Eqty −6.74%	HFRI Fund Wghtd Composite −1.45%	Currency 11.08%	HFRI Fund Wghtd Composite 9.03%	S&P 500 Composite 4.83%	Cash 4.76%	BarCap AggregateBnd 6.97%	CAMB US Private Eqty −23.63%	CAMB US Venture Cap 6.28%	Int'l Stk 8.21%
	S&P 500 Composite −11.85%	CAMB US Private Eqty −7.59%	BARC CTA Index 8.69%	BarCap Aggregate Bnd 4.34%	Cash 3.00%	BarCap Aggregate Bnd 4.33%	S&P 500 Composite 5.48%	S&P 500 Composite −36.58%	BarCap Aggregate Bnd 5.93%	BARC CTA Index 7.05%
	Int'l Stk −21.21%	Int'l Stk −15.66%	BarCap Aggregate Bnd 4.10%	BARC CTA Index 3.30%	BarCap Aggregate Bnd 2.43%	BARC CTA Index 3.54%	Cash 4.74%	NAREIT Composite −37.84%	Currency 0.91%	BarCap Aggregate Bnd 6.54%
	S&P GSCI −31.93%	S&P 500 Composite −21.97%	CAMB US Venture Cap 2.18%	Currency 2.36%	BARC CTA Index 1.71%	Currency −0.12%	Currency 2.59%	Int'l Stk −43.06%	Cash 0.16%	Currency 3.05%
Worst Return	CAMB US Venture Cap −34.05%	CAMB US Venture Cap −29.63%	Cash 1.07%	Cash 1.24%	Currency −1.21%	S&P GSCI −15.09%	NAREIT Composite −17.83%	S&P GSCI −46.49%	BARC CTA Index −0.10%	Cash 0.13%

Figure 1.4 The Wave Chart: 20-Year Ranking of Asset Class Returns for Equities, Fixed Income, and Alternative Investments.

Source: Author.

Capital index for venture capital, Barclays Aggregated Bond for fixed income, International Stock, Barclay CTA for managed futures, Currency, Cash, and the S&P GSCI for commodities. A total of seven different alternative investments are used along with stocks, bonds, and cash.

All securities move in waves, including alternative investments; they are no different. For instance, venture capital did quite well from 1994 to 1999. It ranked first almost every year out of all asset classes. However, the tech bubble broke and venture capital was one of the worst performers from 2000 until 2003. Whereas there were plenty of angel investors before this time period willing to take risk, it was a different story after the tech bubble. Years later, angel investors emerged again from 2003 until 2007. The cycle repeated itself after the Great Recession and angel investing is on an upswing once again since 2009 (Figure 1.5).

Real estate has its ups and downs. During 1998 and 1999, real estate performed poorly, but reversed in 2000 until 2006. Investors as well as institutions (such as banks), not paying attention or investing too aggressively, lost money. An accredited investor or an investor with more than $1 million in net worth outside a home or an income of at least $200,000 willing to accept additional risk, might contemplate a limited partnership formed by real estate developers or invest in a bank real estate fund for high net worth clients. However, quite a few real estate funds did not live up to

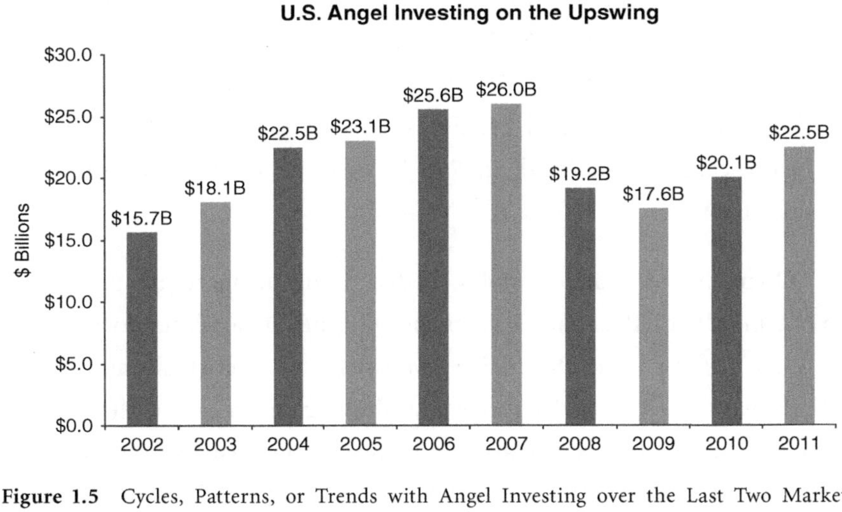

Figure 1.5 Cycles, Patterns, or Trends with Angel Investing over the Last Two Market Downturns.

Sources: Author, CVR, and UNH Center for Venture Research.

their expectations. For instance, Morgan Stanley had significant real estate losses. "Morgan Stanley recorded $700 million in charges tied to losses on investments in real estate. Problems in the real estate market began in 2007 with the value of residential real estate tumbling and sales declining. Now problems have emerged in commercial real estate as well."[40]

The real estate market crashed and performed horribly from 2007 to 2008. However, real estate led once again in 2009 and 2010. Real estate has had huge swings, as evidenced in the past two decades. A new wave of real estate appears evident. Private equity firms are moving into commercial real estate lending since banks are cutting back on lending. The gap appears to be getting filled by funds. Many real estate funds have started new funds in 2012. "Over the first three quarters of this year, global fund managers launched 14 real estate debt funds seeking $11.4 billion, according to a recent report by alternative asset researcher Preqin—and much of that was in recent months. In all of 2011, money managers launched 17 such debt funds seeking $4.1 billion."[41] REITs had a stellar performance in 2012:

> Double-digit returns and high yields, coupled with a gradually improving economy, are driving investment demand in commercial real estate investment trusts (REITs)...Almost all sectors of the REIT market produced double-digit total returns in the first nine months of 2012, according to the National Association of Real Estate Investment Trusts (NAREIT) in Washington, D.C. Commercial financing REITs gained 35.13%, industrial REITs gained 25.46%, shopping centers gained 24.65%, office REITs gained 14.08% and health-care REITs gained 13.67%. By contrast, the S&P 500 gained just 16.44%.[42]

Owing to the various styles, hedge funds in aggregate performed in the middle of the road. That is, hedge funds as a whole do not have huge swings like some alternative investments or even stocks and bonds. Many investors think hedge funds as a whole are more erratic than stocks. However, stocks are very volatile, as seen over the past two decades. The S&P500 did well from 1995 until 1999 and then did poorly from 2000 until 2002. Bonds performed poorly in 1999 but did well from 2000 to 2002.

Bonds performed poorly from 2003 until 2007 but then rallied in 2008 and dropped again in 2009 and 2010. As rising interest rates became a concern in 2013, there was a massive sell-off in bonds.

The Barclay CTA index for managed futures did very well in 2008 when stocks did poorly but flip-flopped the following year in 2009 when they were the worst performer. In 1999 when the stock market delivered healthy returns, the Barclay CTA index did poorly but then rallied the next few years from 2000 to 2002 when stocks crashed. If an investor were to put money into a number of alternative investments as indicated in *The Wave Chart* (real estate, managed futures, commodities, hedge funds, currencies, venture capital, and LBO) along with cash, equities, and fixed income, their portfolios would have performance that is quite compelling though one must keep in mind that past returns might not be indicative of future results.

By investing in alternative investments, an investor might also reduce the highs and lows commonly seen by holding solely stocks or bonds. A blend of investments in different asset classes, including alternative investments, can possibly help smooth out a portfolio. While one could argue that performance is no guarantee or indication of the future, an advocate of using alternative investments might counter with the fact that investors would be selecting actual managers and investments that they believe will outperform the indexes of various alternative investments. For instance, one cannot invest in a venture capital index like a stock index such as the S&P 500. One could select the Vanguard S&P 500 index, but there is no Vanguard venture capital index. Most venture capital investments are made by venture capital firms, a venture capital fund of funds, or making an investment directly into a private company with the expectation or hope that the investment will outperform the venture capital index. Hypothetically, if an investor elected a well-diversified portfolio seeking average returns from stocks, bonds, and alternative over the past 20 years, they would have achieved attractive returns and reduced volatility of their portfolio. If one invested 100 percent in stocks or 100 percent in fixed income, they would not have done as well as the investor that included alternative investments.

While my previous book is about patterns, trends, and cycles that alternative investments exhibit and defining alternative investments,

Understanding Alternative Investments takes it a step further. *Understanding Alternative Investments*, in other words, explains why it might make sense to add alternative investments to a portfolio, and the usefulness of including them. A new train of thought called "Modern Portfolio Allocation" is introduced. Modern Portfolio Allocation is a strategy regarding how alternative investments might be assigned or allocated to a portfolio in order to achieve further diversification. "Diversification can reduce risk to arbitrarily low levels. The reason is that with all risk sources independent, and with the portfolio spread across many securities, the exposure to any particular source of risk is reduced to a negligible level."[43] Using tactical and strategic asset allocation with alternative investments might help improve a portfolio. *Understanding Alternative Investments* explains why alternative investments move in waves, how institutions utilize both strategic and tactical asset allocation with alternative investments, and other useful strategies for investors as well as a number of vehicles one might consider possibly adding to a portfolio in a prudent manner depending on their goals and objectives.

2

NOT ALL FINANCIAL ADVISORS ARE CREATED EQUAL

A lot has changed in finance since the Great Recession, but the vast majority of financial advisors and wealth managers appear to not understand alternative investments and yet recommend them to clients. Buyer, beware! A study based on surveys amongst 1,643 retail investment advisors called "2011 Advisor Brandscape" that was done by Cambridge, Mass.-based Cogent Research showed that 78 percent of all retail advisors (primarily independent advisors) now allocate an average of 11 percent of their book to alternatives.[1] Investors that receive recommendations from advisors with little training or knowledge about alternative investments is a case of the blind leading the blind. In my opinion, such ignorance amongst financial advisors presents a moral hazard. If a consultant or financial advisor appears to know little about alternative investments, a red flag should go up. My advice is to not walk. Run. At the very minimum, ask how many years' experience they have with alternative investments, which ones they have worked with, and what professional training or degrees they have had to make them an expert. I would not take lessons from someone claiming to be a surf instructor who has never surfed before. Also, ask if they ever bought alternative investments themselves. A cook that refuses to taste their own cooking is not a cook.

Many of the big banks mistakenly think they can hire young employees and they will somehow instantly make a neophyte a star wealth manager.

Certain banks give tests in a given area and then assign managing titles, as though that really makes the junior advisor an expert. In my view, it does not. This practice is highly deceptive for investors. Many of the so-called tests are unsupervised and the answers are copied. Managers of these big banks are only fooling themselves. Obviously, the goal is for the big bank to make more money, but the reality is the seasoned wealth manager adds tremendous value and experience to the equation, which cannot be easily replaced. It takes years of experience to learn about alternative investments and it is not something one learns about on the Internet. The Internet provides an abundance of misinformation from people who think they know about alternative investments. As with many things in life, experience matters. Studies have been done that show high net worth clients desire wealth managers to be 45 years of age or older. Younger people (no matter how intelligent they might be) are not the first choice to experiment with someone's savings.

A large number of big banks in the United States (with thousands of advisors to sell products), as well as a number of foreign banks, focus on equity, fixed income, and cash. "Most investment professionals consider asset allocation the most important part of portfolio construction."[2] Oddly, a number of these big banks do not even mention alternative investments nor do they include them in any asset allocation model. For example, if one visits the Wells Fargo website, asset allocation is defined: "Asset allocation refers to how you choose to invest among asset classes like stocks, bonds, mutual funds, and cash."[3] Similarly, PNC bank on its website does not mention alternative investments for part of its asset allocation: "We believe asset allocation, or the process of investing your assets in the optimal mix of major asset classes, including stocks, bonds and cash, has been proven to contribute more to long-term investment results than any other strategy."[4] RBC does not mention alternative investments when it describes volatility of a portfolio: "The mix of equity, fixed income, and cash within a portfolio is a key determinant of the level of volatility a portfolio will experience."[5] Bank of America Merrill Lynch defines asset allocation as, "Asset allocation is a risk management strategy that can help reduce the effects of market fluctuations by recognizing and balancing the different characteristics of stocks, bonds and cash in relation to your goals and tolerance for investment risk."[6] Goldman Sachs Asset Management states, "Asset allocation strategically diversifies a portfolio among different asset classes, such as U.S. and international equities, bonds, cash equivalents, and real estate. Every investor has individual investing needs and objectives, so finding the right mix can be challenging."[7] The four portfolios that follow all have equities and bonds but no alternative investments. To Goldman's credit, they mentioned "real estate."

Almost every day during 2011–2012, negative news about big banks permeated the global air. Investors need to be cautious with any deal (not just in the United States and not just domestic banks but on a global basis). Due to the price of oil increasing, energy deals present both public and private opportunities on a global basis. Almost all banks offer some sort of investment opportunity but governments respond differently, especially with regard to a commodity such as oil: "Argentina plans to launch criminal and civil charges against companies involved in oil drilling off the disputed Falklands Islands, as well as those financing, servicing and even providing analysis for the exploration . . . The foreign minister singled out Royal Bank of Scotland Group PLC, Macquaire Group LTD, Credit Suisse Group AG, Morgan Stanley, Barclays PLC, and Standard Chartered Bank."[8] With all the flagrant disregard for investors and the general public, many argue that big banks should be broken up. Yet very large banks have an innate tendency to destroy themselves, such as Citigroup, which was forced to fire thousands of employees and have the government slice them up. Table 2.1 is a chart listing employees that were laid off between 2011 and 2012.

The numbers of employees that were terminated from banks were quite large. Tens of thousands of employees left the big banks. "Increasing regulatory constraints, rock-bottom interest rates and declining share prices have forced Wall Street institutions to pare back sharply on staff, pushing out as many as 230,000 finance professionals this year alone."[9] Banks, insurers,

Table 2.1 A Boom in Layoffs

Company	Layoffs	Year
Citigroup	11,000	2013
Bank of America	30,000	2013
UBS	10,000	2012
Morgan Stanley	1,600	2013
HSBC	30,000	2012
JP Morgan	17,000	2013

Source: Author.

and other investment managers fired so many people in 2011 that it was described as a new type of wave, a firing wave: "A wave of firings that will wash away more than 220,000 jobs in the global financial-services industry this year, eclipsing 174,000 dismissals in 2009, data compiled by Bloomberg show."[10] Bank employees, especially financial advisors, find the new atmosphere toxic and are looking for ways to jump ship. Former executives from Wall Street's so-called wire houses are betting that independent wealth managers are poised to dominate the business of caring for other people's money.[11] The bank wave of firing employees and employees quitting continues. While the stock market picked back up in 2012, there was no shortage of job reduction at the big banks: "Global financial companies are preparing to chop thousands of banking and trading jobs, signaling their latest retreat in the face of nervous markets, uneven economic growth, tougher regulations and slumping stock prices...As of June 30, the six largest U.S. financial firms by assets had cut over 18,000 jobs in the past year, or 1.6% of the total, according to an analysis by The Wall Street Journal."[12]

BANKS TODAY

Tough economic times means leaner banks. "Before the great crash of 2008, the universal banks swaggered around London, Hong Kong, and New York. Barclays, Citigroup, Credit Suisse, Deutsche, and UBS imagined they could be all things to investors in (almost) all corners of the globe. Five years on, in 2013, such ambitions will seem quaint as the American and European banks find themselves either shrinking further or increasingly marginalized."[13] Massive layoffs typically translates to worse service: "The drought means that investment banks will have to cut thousands more staff (on top of the 30,000 or so job cuts that have already been announced in the past year), as well as significantly reducing pay and bonuses for those staff left standing at the end of the year."[14] There is a definite trend with financial advisors moving away from large banks.

> Today, there are more than 16,000 RIAs collectively managing $2.7 trillion in assets (according to Cerulli Associates, company reports and Charles Schwab estimates). There are more than 500 firms

managing $1 billion or more, according to 2009 Schwab data. What's more, several RIAs are now extending their footprints beyond Main Street by expanding into multiple states and regions. The RIA model is also gaining popularity with advisors and investors overseas.[15]

Bulge bracket firms or the big banks noticed this mass exodus and are throwing a lot of money into lobbying: "So how do the wire houses and their bank/broker-dealer brethren respond to this growing sea change in the balance of power? The logical course of action would be for them to improve the value of their services, increase transparency, reduce conflicts and adopt a higher legal standard of care. Instead, they have chosen a more destructive route, using their influence and vast lobbying resources to hinder the RIA's ability to conduct business."[16] Instead of fixing the problem, money is poorly spent by many big banks. Even technology that can help an advisor is neglected and seems to have taken a backseat to many of the big banks. "You might think the most affluent investors would get the best tech tools. But surprisingly enough, experts say, most full-service brokers are behind the technological curve; their websites lack features that are standard among even run-of-the-mill discounters."[17] Sadly, most banks do not offer reporting technology for alternative investments.

Hypothetically, if one is an investor in alternative investments (which sometimes are tied to a bank that recommended them through an advisor), what is the likelihood that the advisor will be with you over the next ten years? And what happens if you do not follow the advisor to another firm? Will the information that the bank supplies to you be reliable and purely objective? Will you hear the actual truth or will it be a candy-coated apple with a razor blade hidden in it? Sadly, this might be the case where the investor will not receive objective advice. Objective advice is worth a lot these days. Many new risks associated with investing in alternative investments have evolved, which might not be apparent at first glance. The risk can be hidden. As a result, it is much more difficult today to find the crown jewels of the alternative investments world. "Investors need to think hard about portfolio construction and the risks they are taking in their portfolios, because the fact is that diversification is not as obvious as many may have thought, although it's also not abstruse."[18]

DODD-FRANK

With all its rules and regulations, Dodd-Frank appears to have missed many of the more crucial items it set out to fix. Dodd-Frank was written in the aftermath of the Great Recession. Its intentions were to curb financial excesses and misdeeds. Yet a number of the most egregious acts are untouched and completely overlooked; Sarbanes Oxley was overkill and Dodd Frank appears to be following closely in its footsteps. "The home of the deepest, most liquid capital markets in the world produced fewer than one-tenth of the IPOs around the globe in 2011...According to the SEC, the burden of complying with regulations such as Section 404(b) of Sarbanes-Oxley is more than seven times that imposed on large firms relative to their assets."[19]

New rules might very well make matters even worse than they already are, such as with Dodd-Frank harming small financial entities not labeled systemically important financial institutions (SIFIs): "The federal government's Financial Stability Oversight Council is now in position to designate certain nonbank firms as 'systemically important financial institutions' (SIFIs). Under the Dodd-Frank Act, that label can be attached to nonbank financial institutions—insurers, financial holding companies, hedge funds, finance companies, securities firms, perhaps even money-market mutual funds and private-equity firms—that will 'pose a threat to the financial stability of the United States' if they fail."[20] Competition would be severely harmed in the United States because the Too Big To Fail issue would be moved into other industries. Nonbank financial industries would likely go through an M&A wave because there would be an implicit guarantee like Freddie Mac or Fannie Mae with real estate loans. In other words, the federal government saying that it would give SIFIs unlimited financial support if they ran into problems (so nothing could ever happen to them) would result in a handful of government-run organizations acquiring smaller ones or putting them out of business, which would benefit no one.

Many view financial advisors merely as pawns manipulated by big banks. Advisors moving around result in nothing but an expensive version of adult musical chairs. Essentially, the Bonus Agreements and Promissory Notes are being used to recruit or snatch advisors from other banks in order to get more assets. Daily articles hit the market concerning advisors switching banks. "Morgan Stanley Smith Barney has lost six advisers overseeing more than $1 billion of client assets to competitors."[21] Once a big check is written, there is often pressure to push a product, which sadly includes alternative investments. Wall Street has a way of wrecking things that are good. "The largest retail brokerages in the nation may have ended last year on a high note with increased revenues, but brokers aren't finding themselves relaxing just yet. Instead, some say they are feeling the pressure to keep revenues up by promoting investment products with higher commissions and fees."[22] Because alternative investments are in demand, an abundance of new products is being sold. A lot of this product appears geared to charging high fees rather than generating good returns. Dodd-Frank completely misses this problem as well as many others. Hypothetically, if banks were made to pay off these loans and taxes were paid up front, it would not solve the deficit but it would reduce it.

Amongst other things, Dodd-Frank was intended to help investors by curbing big banks. However, it has had a rocky start. "The statute failed to change the balkanized nature of the financial-regulatory universe, which has been part of the problem leading up to the crisis. It did not curtail the leverage inherent in derivatives trading. Nor did it reduce the size or complexity of the existing mega-banks."[23] A terrific example of problems with big banks trading was JP Morgan's Michel Iksil: Bruno Michel Iksil had been selling protection on an index of 125 companies in the form of credit default swaps through most of January and February, which meant he was essentially betting on the improving credit of those companies in the index and would lose money if the market went the other way.[24] Except for those who wrote it, very few people in the United States have voluntarily read Dodd-Frank. "But Dodd-Frank is far too complex, and becoming more so. At 848 pages, it is 23 times longer than Glass-Steagall, the reform that followed the Wall Street crash of 1929. Worse, every other page demands that regulators fill in further detail. Some of these clarifications are hundreds of pages long."[25]

GOVERNMENT REGULATIONS

Government regulation can be unnecessarily excessive. The law firm, Davis Polk, formed a useful subscription service called The David Polk Regulatory

Tracker, which is an online service designed to aid market participants with more than 200 required rule makings and 70 required studies, and more than 1,000 other key provisions. Very few individuals have a grasp on the Volcker rule: "Take the transformation of 11 pages of Dodd-Frank into the so-called 'Volcker rule', which is intended to reduce banks' ability to take excessive risks by restricting proprietary trading and investments in hedge funds and private equity (Paul Volcker, a former chairman of the Federal Reserve, has argued that such activity contributed to the crisis). In November four of the five federal agencies charged with enacting this rule jointly put forward a 298-page proposal which is, in the words of a banker publicly supportive of Dodd-Frank, 'unintelligible any way you read it.'"[26] Increased regulation might not be a solution. Michael Porter and Jan Rivkin, co-leaders of Harvard Business School's United States Competitiveness Project surveyed approximately 10,000 Harvard Business School alumni and found regulation to be a major concern. Asked to identify the greatest impediment to investing and creating jobs in America, our survey respondents cited regulation more than any other problem."[27]

Increased government regulations might have good intentions but often create dilemmas. The Volcker rule already has caused problems especially with Europe and the Debt Crises. U.S. regulations could dissuade banks from trading European sovereign bonds and make matters worse. The rule was intended to restrict banks from making bets with their own money, but is viewed as excessive. Government regulation with alternative investments is frequently counterproductive. A KPMG survey amongst investors who buy alternative investments expressed that government response was not helpful. "The results of this survey show that the anticipated increase in regulation is not wanted by the majority of investors, managers or service providers. Despite regulation being widely promoted as a way to protect the investor, it is these investors who are most strongly against it. Few investors believe it will produce any tangible benefits."[28]

3

ACCESS TO ALTERNATIVE INVESTMENTS AND COMPETITIVE ADVANTAGES

Alternative investments are not generic products to procure or mass market to investors. A prudent investor will know the nuances between sellers. Sellers are not all the same. Figure 3.1 is a chart showing where an investor can find alternative investments through another party (as opposed to finding alternatives investments themselves).

While fluid and evolving, it appears that investment firms after the Great Recession have the best access and means to diversify with alternative investments. These midsized firms or regional firms have access, provide a lot of due diligence, charge reasonable fees, and offer objectivity. Not all banks are the same when it comes to alternative investments. I have been fortunate to have over 20 years of work experience with both banks (domestic and foreign) and investment firms. I have also worked with plenty of consultants. In *Registered Rep*, Diane Britton ranked firms on a scale from 1 to 10 for access to alternative investments (10 being the highest possible rating and 1 the worst): Edward Jones (7.6), Merrill Lynch (Bank of America) (8.4), Morgan Stanley (7.7), Raymond James and Associates (9.1), UBS (8.6), and Wells Fargo Advisors (8.2).[1] Raymond James, a full service investment firm, was ranked higher than most banks.

Access is important when buying alternative investments. Having two or three monolithic banks will not likely deliver the best of anything,

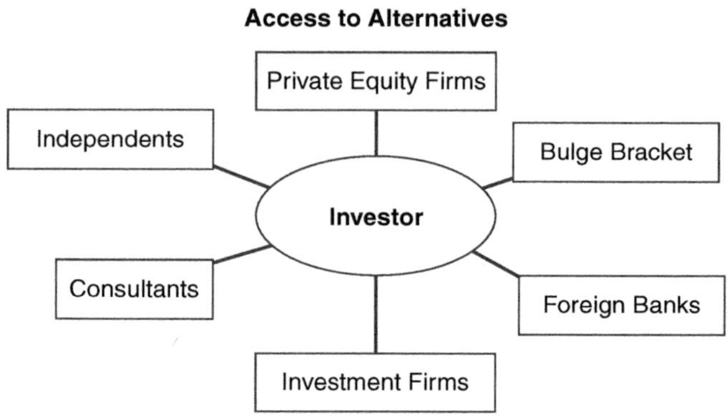

Figure 3.1 Sellers of Alternative Investments.
Source: Author

let alone attractive alternative investments. "A financial system composed of more banks, numerous enough to ensure competition in funding businesses and households but none of them big enough to put the overall economy in jeopardy, will give the United States a better chance of navigating through future financial potholes and precipices. As this more level playing field emerges, it will begin to restore our nation's faith in the system of market capitalism."[2] Big banks often copy one another. If one bank introduces a new product like a BDC (Business Development Corporation), other big banks will likely follow.

RESEARCH TO ALTERNATIVE INVESTMENTS IS CRITICAL

Besides access to alternative investments, it is prudent to find financial advisors with firms that have good investment research, asset allocation programs, range of products, access to in-house investing experts, ongoing training, and technology. If a firm ranks low in any of these categories, an investor might think twice before investing in alternative investments with them. While some banks have cut costs with research, the money spent on research is not wasted and can provide a valuable tool to help clients know which wave to consider when exploring alternative investments. "Investors often rely on information provided by financial analysts to form expectations about a company's future prospects."[3] Good research is helpful to advisors. It is likely that a new leader of the midsized investments firms will emerge and this will become the go-to place for high net worth investors seeking the very best alternative investments: "The flow of advisers out of the big brokerages isn't ebbing, to judge by the headcounts they revealed in their latest quarterly earnings reports...Advisers are defecting not only to join or start up their own registered independent advisory firms, which is considered the classic breakaway path. They also are headed to high-profile HighTower Advisors and Dynasty Financial Partners LLC, as well as to regional brokerage companies such as Raymond James Financial, Inc. (RJF) and Janney Montgomery Scott LLC."[4] Having more choices for investors to tap into for selecting alternative investments will be better than having fewer options. That is, more variety is a good thing to have, not a bad one.

Large banks offer research as well but it has substantially fallen in quality. JP Morgan and Barclays, however, continue to write good research which can be helpful when selecting alternative investments. One thing is certain and that is good advice is worth paying for and will not change. Banks that issue lousy research will most likely regret it down the road. Investors, especially institutional and high net worth, are not stupid. Several large banks provide shockingly lousy research that is borderline insulting to read.

Private equity firms have also changed and have become institutions that offer different types of funds. For instance, Bain Capital, Blackstone, Carlyle, KKR, TPG, Apollo, and few other buyout shops morphed into large companies with a variety of funds. Most of these firms offer alternative investments such as real estate, venture capital, commodities, and foreign LBO. It is unclear whether these private equity firms will master new areas beyond how they originally started with LBOs. In other words, will an organization that started with LBOs be able to do as well in real estate or commodities? Time will tell.

UNDERSTANDING FEES TO ALTERNATIVE INVESTMENT OPPORTUNITIES

Fees are more of an issue today with alternative investments. According to CalPERS CEO, Anne Stausboll, on April 4, 2011, CalPERS commissioned the "Special Review of placement agent activity," which involved alleged wrongdoing of its former CEO and several former board members.[5] With institutions, fees are an issue. The large dollars behind them frequently end up with lower pricing or more services. While quite a few individual investors, with a million dollars or less, think they should be treated like institutional investors, there is a marked difference. Nothing is free and sound financial advice should cost something. The problem is finding this advice; it is easy to lose money and much more difficult to make it. Quite a few investors fail to understand this fact. Cost is one thing while net returns are another. Retail investors should focus on net returns and not necessarily be obsessed with cost. "There are many other common behaviors of which we need to be mindful when investing. These include the tendencies to focus on historical costs, single securities instead of a diversified portfolio, and fees instead of net returns."[6]

Institutional investors can experience problems and are not immune. CalPERS, for example, had problems with fees, so the rest of the investor population will need to look two or three times under the hood. CalPERS has a tremendous amount of money and resources behind it, as opposed to a retail investor with far less money to invest and limited resources. Fees are not always transparent: "With respect to fees, the special review focused on whether, during its investment process, CalPERS was misled or made to overpay, resulting in increased expenses and, ultimately, harm to CalPERS' beneficiaries. The special review assessed the apparent arrangements, financial and otherwise, between CalPERS and its external money managers, and between those external money managers and third-party placement agents."[7] Full disclosure of fees is important not just for institutions but for individual investors as well. "CalPERS administers the largest state pension fund in the United States. Since 1985, the assets of the CalPERS investment portfolio have grown from about $29 billion to over $225 billion. The portfolio is held for the benefit of over 1.6 million California public employees, retirees and their families. Based in the California state capitol, Sacramento, CalPERS has over 2,300 employees, who are all civil servants."[8] CalPERS is the "smart money" or institutional money. It is also the marquis institutional investor with the most admired way to manage large amounts of money in a prudent fashion.

SIZE DOES MATTER

Historically, the vast majority of the bank mergers have been problematic. They have been especially irksome for the ill-conceived, poorly thought out, and hastily slapped together mergers during the Great Recession. Moreover, the changing financial landscape has made it a more arduous task to find decent alternative investments. Even before the ramshod financial mergers during the Great Recession, there were problematic financial mergers. I know because I was personally involved with a bunch of them. My first firm, Alex. Brown, was acquired by Banker's Trust after the Glass-Steagall Act was changed. BT Alex. Brown was then acquired by Deutsche Bank. I later joined Morgan Stanley after it merged with Dean Witter and then formed a joint venture with Citigroup called Morgan Stanley Smith Barney. The former head of Morgan Stanley, Phil Purcell, believes big banks have gotten too large and unwieldy: "From a shareholder point of view, it's crystal-clear these enterprises are worth more broken up than they are together."[9]

A handful of financial mergers have worked out while the vast majority have failed miserably. For example, Thomas Weisel was the former CEO of Montgomery Securities, which he sold to NationsBank in 1997 for $1.2 billon. A year later, he left and formed Thomas Weisel Partners. Thomas Weisel Partners was then acquired by the 119-year-old Stifel Financial Corp. in St. Louis in a fire sale. The merger was fairly successful. Stifel itself has an interesting history. It was formed in 1890 when plummeting commodity prices led to the panic of 1890.[10] After the downturn in 2008, Stifel bought 58 UBS offices in a $51.1 million deal. Revenue more than tripled from 2005 through 2008 and net income doubled to $55.5 million. Employees more than doubled as well to 4,335 during the same time period. Stifel remains strong despite big banks trying to limit advisors going to the firm. "Last year, an arbitration panel ruled that Stifel had to pay Wachovia a mere $166,964 out of its $36 million claim over allegations that Stifel systematically acquired its financial advisers, management personnel, administrative staff and client relationships on a national scale without compensation."[11] Investors need to be cautious about buying alternative investments when firms merge. Access and quality can be negatively affected.

Another well-known merger involved Hambrecht and Quist (H&Q), which was acquired by Chase. I had the privilege of meeting Dan Case.

Daniel H. Case III was the CEO of the high-tech banking boutique, H&Q,or Hambrecht and Quist in San Francisco. My former boss at Alex. Brown, introduced me to Dan and we had breakfast together in the 1990s. Dan Case told me (during our breakfast) that he firmly believed there were "IPO waves." When we met, the market was terrible. He said, "The stock market as well as the IPO market will come back. It is not the first time the market corrected (nor the last) but IPOs come back and there will be opportunity."[12] His astute comments helped me lay the ground work for Wave Theory. Dan's brother was Stephen M. Case, CEO of America Online Inc. (AOL), which Alex. Brown took public. "Started in 1985 by an ex-assistant brand manager by the name of Steve Case, America Online reached a $166 billion market cap in early 2000."[13] Alex Brown clients made a lot of money from AOL.

Although H&Q was a fabulous firm, Alex. Brown was known as the "Crown Jewel" of Wall Street and involved with many of the fastest-growing companies in the country, such as Microsoft, Amazon, Starbuck's, and Sam Adams (The Boston Beer Company). I introduced the Boston Beer Company to Alex. Brown, which led to the first publicly traded micro-brewery in America. The stock was originally $15.00 on the IPO but reached $265.1300 later in 2013. Alex. Brown, H&Q, Robertson Stephens, and Montgomery were collectively known as the "Four Horsemen." A lot of deals these that firms took public were technology companies. Investors interested in alternative investments had access to the best venture capital and IPOs anywhere. The majority were immensely successful and even responsible for the hiring of thousands of employees. While there are exceptions, successful emerging growth companies often grow into big, mighty corporations and the investor will likely benefit (Table 3.1).

Table 3.1 Companies Taken Public by the "Four Horsemen"

Company name	# of employees at inception	# of employees present
Oracle	(1984) 38	104,500
Domino's Pizza	(1983) 500	145,000
Microsoft	(1984) 342	89,403
Papa John's	(1991) 40	16,000
Go Daddy	(2004) 347	3,200
Qualcomm	(1991) 436	15,106
Jiffy Lube	(1985) 56	20,000
Cablevision	(1984) 293	14,471

Source: "20 Companies, 30 Years, 575,457 Jobs," *INC Magazine*, p. 77, September 2011

These and other fast-growing companies help propel job growth. AOL, for instance, grew to be one of the largest companies in the country. Venture capital creates jobs as one can clearly see. The United States was built by entrepreneurs and small businesses. It is the backbone of the nation and part of its DNA. IPOs are good for the economy.

Unfortunately, Dan Case passed away on June 26, 2002, after a 15-month battle with brain cancer. His demise was most unfortunate and symbolic of the demise of the mid-sized investment banking boutique that fueled American growth. "His talents were obvious from the start. Dan joined H&Q as an intern in 1979 and rose through the ranks quickly. For two decades, he provided technology startups with the cash they needed to flourish."[14] It is interesting to note that the old H&Q did not have tens of thousands of financial advisors. Rather, they focused on quality financial advisors. These advisors were not only very good at wealth management but they knew alternative investments inside and out. Today, clients seek quality not quantity (Figure 3.2).

As one of my ultra-high net worth clients commented when I was working for a large bank, "I do not give a rat's ass how many advisors your large bank has, I only care about what can be done for me." While

Figure 3.2 Financial Firms and the Number of Advisors Employed.

Note: *As of December 2010.

Source: Author.

this comment was crass, it also made sense and rang true. Later, after witnessing what happened with the Morgan Stanley Smith Barney sales force getting 25 percent of the Facebook IPO disaster to offer clients instead of 15 percent (which is common), it became much clearer. "Retail investor confidence and the underlying fairness of the IPO market have been badly damaged by Facebook's IPO."[15] A drop in Facebook stock after the May 17 offering fueled shareholder complaints, regulatory probes, and more than 40 lawsuits, with some investors claiming the social-network company's managers failed to disclose revised forecasts before the IPO, and others blaming underwriters or analysts.[16] Large banks profiting while investors lose money is problematic. The result of investors losing billions of dollars in an IPO will be less interest in buying a new offering of an emerging growth company. What goes around comes around. Amongst U.S. venture capital-backed companies after Facebook's listing on May 18, there were no IPOs for months.

The trend or new wave for financial advisors runs against big banks with armies of advisors. Quite a few financial advisors and wealth managers are unhappy with the big bank mergers. "A whopping 63 percent of MS advisors believe the integration had a negative impact on their business, up from 49 percent last year." One advisor wrote, "The wheels are coming off," and, "They have lost their way."[17] Banks continue to lose money and struggle with ill-fated attempts to make wealth management commoditized. "And like it or not, the financial advisor industry is going through its own evolutionary changes after the 2008 meltdown. Many firms have lost revenues over the past few years right at the same time they're about to come up against regulatory changes in the Dodd-Frank era."[18] Instead of spending money on items that will help investors, many banks have eliminated or cut costs in areas that will ultimately lose clients and decrease revenue. I know a lot of advisors at big banks. Very few are happy.

Most investors do not want a giant shopping market for investing: "As part of a continuing trend, financial advisors are increasingly bolting from traditional Wall Street brokerage firms and other financial service employers to become independent broker-dealers and advisors, according to Cerulli associates."[19] They want service and unbiased help selecting the best investments for a sound portfolio as opposed to just buying. Further, the volatile market does not dictate a buy and hold period so good advice is valuable. "As long as geopolitical and macroeconomic chaos rules the day, the investing train will zigzag in unpredictable ways."[20] Sanford Weill, who built Citigroup Inc. through a plethora of acquisitions, expressed his view that big banks should be broken up, not permitted to get larger: "After years of silence, banking's greatest living empire builder—who powered Citigroup's ascent to the top of the U.S. banking industry, and then watched from retirement as the New York company nearly collapsed in the 2008 financial crisis—joined the ranks of big-bank critics who contend that smaller is better. It was as if Napoleon had called for an end to military conquest."[21] So where does one go to find alternative investments?

Bigger is not necessarily better when one is referring to banks. The bank mergers stemming from the Great Recession made banks even larger. "Assets of the top 10 holding companies totaled $11.3 trillion at the end of Q1 2012, or 84% of GDP. Before the absorption of Merrill Lynch, Wachovia, Lehman Brothers, Bear Stearns, Washington Mutual, Countrywide, and others, the top 10 had $8.1 trillion at the end of Q2 2007, or 62% of GDP."[22] Boutique and middle market firms have even noticed a rise in stock prices while a number of big banks struggle, indicating a turning of the tide. Boutique and middle market firms will likely be the preferred go-to sources for alternative investments going forward. Investors in general are looking at the big banks with distrust. Trust needs to be rebuilt and trust is not easy to obtain nor can a big bank buy it. Roy Dilberto of RTD Financial Advisors Inc. described a recent client meeting: "Recently, we were told by some clients at their review meeting that they had been searching for years for an advisor who truly cared about them—who they were and what was important to them. Many have given them lip service; it was obvious that advisors were more interested in their money than their lives."[23] A bank's image can easily be tainted. Granted, certain banks have better images than others. But public image is not the only criteriona an investor should examine. Overall ethics and fee disclosure are extremely important when buying alternative investments from a bank or investment firm. According to The 22nd Annual Broker Report Card Survey, rankings can vary (Figure 3.3).

Bosses and Paperwork

Management and compliance are often sources of advisor discontent. This year, the overall ratings inched up for management performance (up to 7.6 from 7.5) and compliance (up to 7.6 from 7.2). Morgan Stanley and Raymond James & Associates were the only firms that saw their overall management and compliance scores decline from last year. At Morgan Stanley, ratings for morale, public image, and senior management dropped significantly from last year.

Management (scored 1–10, with 10 highest)	*Average Rating*	*Edward Jones*	*Merrill Lynch (Bank of America*	*Morgan Stanley*	*Raymond James & Associates*	*UBS*	*Wells Fargo Advisors*
Your branch manager	8.4	9.4	8	6.9	9.2	8.5	8.3
Senior management	7.6	9.2	7	4.1	9.3	8.4	7.5
Strategic focus	7.6	9.3	7	4.3	9.3	8.3	7.5
Overall ethics	8.3	9.7	8	5.5	9.6	8.5	8.5
Public image	7.6	9.6	6.6	4.3	9.4	7.1	8.4
Moral	7.4	9.4	6.8	3.6	9.4	7.9	7.4
Overall rating of performance	7.6	9.4	7	4.1	9.4	8	7.8
Compliance support (scored 1–10, with 10 highest)							
Risk management	7.6	9.4	7.6	5.8	9	7.3	7.7
Compliance-specific training	7.9	9.4	7.4	5.9	9	8	7.7
Reduction of administrative burden (time and effort)	6.7	9.1	6	3.8	8.5	6.6	6
Fee disclosure	8	9.6	7.8	5.7	9.2	8	7.9
Overall rating of compliance support	7.6	9.4	7.2	5.2	9	7.5	7.2

Figure 3.3 The 22nd Annual Broker Report Card Survey.

Source: Diana Britton, "Withering Wirehouses? Not Quite," *Registered Rep*, p. 30, December 2012.

As evidenced with Libor, a number of big banks violated trust in epic proportions. "Libor is used as a benchmark for trillions of dollars-worth of consumer and business loans and financial-market trading contracts. The rate is a measure of what banks pay each other for short-term loans."[24] Investors now question banks that handle money in a reckless fashion. Settlements with regulators over the misuse of Libor have been ongoing. For example, UBS reached a settlement with regulators about Libor: "Just when it appeared global banks' transgressions couldn't get worse, UBS has broken new ground. In its $1.5 billion settlement with various countries, UBS admitted to thousands of instances of interest-rate manipulation, involving more than 100 employees and managers, in currencies including the yen, the pound, the Swiss franc, the U.S. dollar, and the euro."[25]

A few investors feel that they know everything these days. However, most do not want to buy big bank product and many require more help than ever, which explains why big banks have to pay a lot of money hiring advisors from competitors. Bank of America Corp.'s Merrill Lynch Wealth Management unit has tweaked its recruiting deal to attract financial advisers from competitors, offering bigger upfront cash payments as well as an extra client-asset incentive to a larger pool of top-tier brokers.[26] The amount of money bulge bracket banks are paying to keep and attract financial advisors is staggering. "Building the biggest brokerage firm on Wall Street is proving costly to Morgan Stanley and Citigroup Inc., which are planning to pay brokers about $3 billion to keep them from being poached away from the joint venture, people familiar with the matter said."[27] The problems with big banks will not dissipate on their own and will likely take years to fix. "As investors shied away from stocks following the financial crisis, brokerage firms like Morgan Stanley Smith Barney have found it hard to expand. Meanwhile, the process of combining back-office systems, which was expected to be a major source of cost savings, has turned out to be more complicated than expected."[28]

WHERE DO THE BEST ADVISORS WORK?

Large banks are having difficulty keeping wealth advisors. Regardless of how much money big banks are paying financial advisors, there is a mass exodus. The model with many banks is flawed. The high volume indicates that these full service brokers are struggling. Market share has dropped around 5 percent for the big banks or "bulge bracket firms" between 2001 and 2010 (Figure 3.4).

Culture has a lot to do with where a financial advisor works today, which is why so many advisors are flocking from banks to RIAs or investment firms. "Stratos Wealth Partners announced today the addition of two former Morgan Stanley Smith Barney advisors, Craig P. Adams, CFP and Steve Beierlein to their newly created Utah office. This addition boosts the network of Stratos Wealth Partners to over 125 affiliated advisors managing over $4 billion in client assets under management."[29] Many financial advisors that are leaving big banks opt for regional firms. "Top regional firms like RBC, Oppenheimer, Robert W. Baird, Janney Montgomery Scott, Raymond James, and Stifel Nicolaus have a lot to offer advisors for whom firm culture is the top concern. These firms believe culture consists of both visible aspects of a firm such as structures and processes, and invisible aspects such as espoused beliefs, values, strategies, goals, philosophies, perceptions, thoughts and feelings within

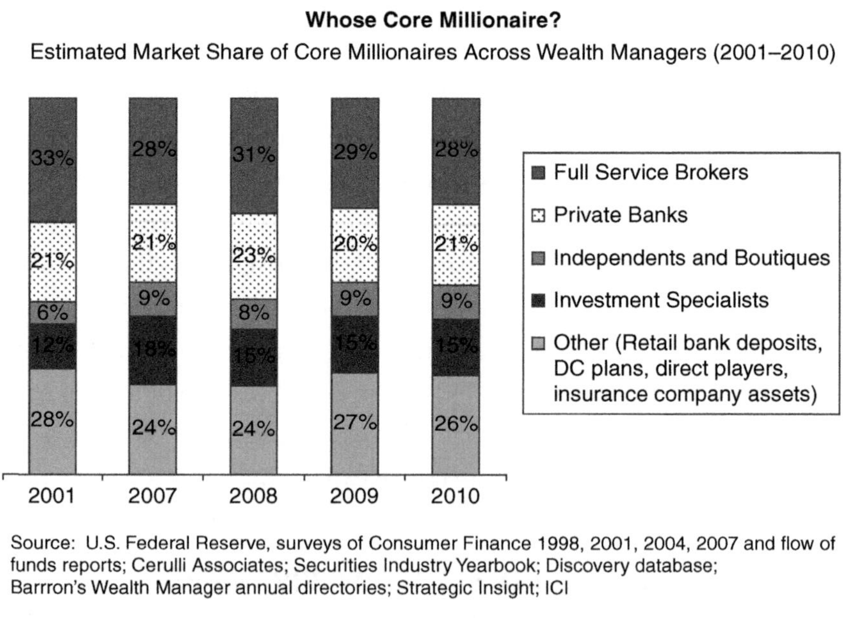

Figure 3.4 Market Share of Millionaires Across Wealth Managers.

Source: Kristen French, "Private Banks Could Eat Your Lunch," *Registered Rep*, p. 21, April 2012.

Table 3.2 Top 10 Regionals by Headcount
After years of being acquisition targets, many of the largest regional firms are surging back, growing their advisor count from 2007.

Rank	Firm	2007	2008	2009	2010	AUM (2010) ($ Bbillions)
1	Edward Jones & Co.	10,532	11,172	12,615	12,000	$572.60
2	Waddell & Reed	2,293	2,366	2,675	2,238	$33.90
3	Ameriprise	2,453	2,832	2,445	2,168	$84
4	RBC Wealth Management	1,810	2,085	2,200	2,078	$186.60
5	Stifel, Nicolaus & Company	564	1,142	1,719	1,871	$101
6	Oppenheimer & Co.	1,396	1,482	1,474	1,400	$73
7	Raymond James & Associates	1,070	1,184	1,274	1,266	$107.80
8	Morgan Keegan & Company	1,075	1,089	1,250	1,200	$80
9	Janney Montgomery Scott*	857	852	800	750	$50
10	Robert W. Baird & Co.	591	600	670	680	$63

*In April 2012, Raymond James acquired Morgan Keegan.

Source: Diana Britton, "A Regional Resurgence," *Registered Rep*, June 5, 2012.

the firm."[30] Table 3.2 depicts a clear trend or wave of advisors moving to regional firms.

Big banks, on the other hand, are losing advisors. The trend will likely continue. Money does not always purchase happiness.

Buying alternative investments involves careful consideration. Whom you are dealing with is crucial when selecting alternative investments. Companies like LPL Financial and Cambridge are attracting many talented advisors. LPL now has 13,600 financial advisors, as of February 2014. Both have made strides into offering clients advice on alternative investments. Neither offers investment banking which means there will be little to no conflict of interest.

4

THE CHANGING FINANCIAL LANDSCAPE

BIG BANK WOES

Financial mergers happen all the time. Some companies have even created businesses out of all these financial mergers and acquisitions such as Sandler O'Neill + Partners, "a full-service investment banking firm specializing in financial services companies."[1] There is a need for such firms considering that many financial mergers do not work out too well. Many have been colossal disasters and painful, like putting a dog to sleep. US Trust's acquisition by the discount broker, Schwab, in 2000 was doomed from the start: "The union of the two firms kicked off a clash between the populist Schwab and white-glove U.S. Trust. It also exposed long-term problems in U.S. Trust's business, notably the outdated state of its technology and its failure to serve investors' increasingly sophisticated demands."[2] Founded in 1853, US Trust's clients are high net worth, white glove, and somewhat demanding clientele, which is different from low-fee, self-serve, discount-paying Schwab clients. Merging a discount brokerage with a private wealth management platform was beyond mismatched. US Trust was then sold to Bank of America which appears to have been in better match.

The crises during the Great Recession led to a widespread bank M&A frenzy. Big banks were merged with other banks, which resulted in even larger banks, while Lehman was oddly left to fail. "In 1970, according to data from the Federal Reserve Bank of Dallas, the five largest U.S. institutions owned 17% of banking industry assets; in 2010 that share was

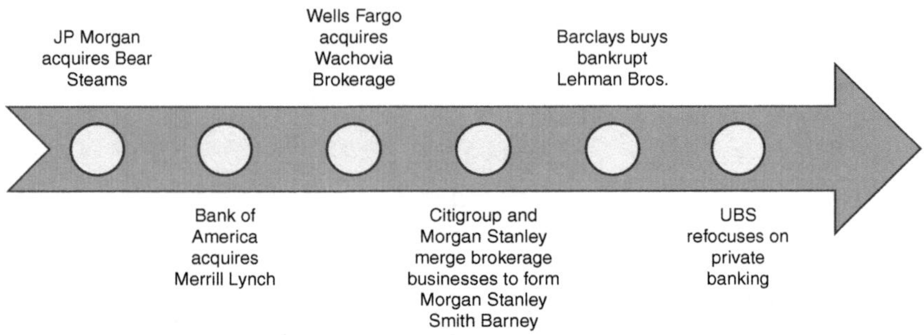

Figure 4.1 Great Recession Bank Mergers.
Source: Author.

52%. Their business has expanded well beyond the role as steward of the community's assets into riskier endeavors that chase supersized returns."[3] Figure 4.1 shows just how much the financial landscape changed in the United States after the 2008 stock market crash.

At first blush, one might feel a false sense of security having money at a big bank with thousands of financial advisors. But high net worth money continues to leave big banks. "The biggest brokerages should be worried about the decline in their market share in recent years, in which more people have taken their money to other types of financial advisors."[4] Most big banks were poorly run and almost collapsed, which was the contrapositive of small banks: "Many of the biggest banks have sputtered, their balance sheets still clogged with toxic assets accumulated in the boom years. In contrast, the nation's smaller banks are in somewhat better shape by some measures. Before the financial crisis, most didn't make big bets on mortgage-backed securities, derivatives and other highly risky assets whose value imploded."[5]

Ultra high net worth clients do not tolerate cumbersome trust departments nor like to be treated as one of the herd. For example, the Bank of America, Merrill Lynch, and US Trust combination caused some problems because of culture clashes and other troubles. Ironically, Sallie Krawcheck was let go by Bank of America for supporting advisors and trying to do the right thing for clients. Citi sold some products in 2007 and 2008 that lost money. As she recalls, "Instead of reading investors the fine print, the advisers pounded the management team to partially reimburse their clients for our stupidity. I advocated for that too, the bank eventually relented, and I subsequently lost my job."[6] Typically, one does not get let go for doing a good job. She was also well liked by financial advisors and I believe was very helpful integrating Merrill with Bank of America. Investors in alternative investments need to be wary when events such as the dismissal of Sally Krawcheck occur.

NEW FINANCIAL PRODUCTS

Wall Street continuously invents new products. These products can be esoteric and confusing. For example, Credit Default Swaps are not well understood and still unproven. Yet banks trade trillions of dollars worth of them. The world market for Credit Default Swaps is substantial. "Total notional amounts outstanding of OTC derivatives amounted to $639 trillion at end-June 2012."[7] Individual banks can trade trillions of dollars worth of credit default swaps. JP Morgan was by far the biggest seller of protection on an index tracking corporate credit known as CDX.NA.IG.9.[8] JP Morgan's index of credit defaults swaps was creative but also unproven, with banks and hedge funds betting billions of dollars. Credit Default Swaps are thought by a number of investors to serve as a gauge for market health or weakness of a particular company. "While the swaps can help investors hedge risks and bet on market trends, the thin trading underlines a key shortcoming of an instrument that has a huge influence on risk perceptions. During periods of stress, the actions of a few traders can have an outsize impact on delicate market psychology."[9] As with any new financial product, the unexpected can happen. This time was no different. "JP Morgan's heavy selling of protection earlier this year had caused the cost of credit protection on the index to diverge from the cost of insuring the individual companies in the index from defaults. Many banks and hedge funds took the opposite position, expecting the prices to converge, which they eventually did."[10] Alternative investment products can be misunderstood and problematic for investors, especially new ones.

A BDC, or Business Development Company, is a form of publicly registered company in the United States that invests in small to mid-sized businesses. It was created by Congress in 1980 as an amendment to the Investment Company Act of 1940. BDCs are securities that are relatively new and marketed by many firms as alternative investments. There are pros and cons to any investment. A BDC offers liquidity and income to investors.

A BDC can fluctuate in price. There is not a lot of data to analyze how these structures might do in a down market or in a rising interest rate environment. To an extent, an investor will need to rely on due diligence from the bank or investment firm selling the BDC. The majority of BDCs distribute a large portion of their taxable income to avoid corporate taxation. Among other factors, evaluating the management team of a BDC is prudent, just like with any other investment. By 2013, the general public had been conditioned to hearing about billion-dollar errors like the trading problems with JP Morgan or trillions needed by governments to bailout banks. The London Whale cost JP Morgan billions in losses, not to mention a huge fine. As banks get bigger, they will be forced to mass market more products, which includes alternative investments. By nature, alternative investments are not fruitful being mass marketed. It is a paradox. The problem might get further out of hand, promoting even bigger banks: "Large banks are both too complex to understand and too big to fail…Having overly complicated banks makes it all the more imperative to resolve the TBTF dilemma: how to wind down a large institution without forcing taxpayers to bail it out and destroying the financial system."[11] Contagion risks amongst big banks is a valid fear since the dollar amounts keep getting larger and the average investor will have little to no knowledge on what is going on behind the scenes: "For countries such as Germany, France and the Netherlands, JP Morgan said it had a net exposure of nearly $150 billion, yet didn't disclose hedges or gross exposures. Muddying the waters further: Major country exposures in JP Morgan's quarterly report are based on its 'internal risk management approach.'"[12] J.P. Morgan has made a concerted effort to fix these and other complications since the Great Recession.

Federal Reserve presidents have expressed concern about the possibility of another crisis if one or more big banks were to fail. "As the financial crisis of 2008 showed, the very diversification, structure and size of most of our largest banks put the community's assets at tremendous risk. They had become 'too big to fail,' and the government—really the American taxpayers—had no choice but to keep their colossal mistakes from bringing down the economy."[13] The haphazard bank mergers after the Great Recession were not just the fault of the banks. Rather, it was a combination of regulators and banks problems. The government made the decision to combine the banks and make them bigger: "On complexity, regulators should shoulder part of the blame. During the crisis, the Treasury Department and the Federal Reserve encouraged banks to buy each other—J.P. Morgan gobbled up securities firm Bear Stearns Cos. and the banking operations of Washington Mutual Inc., which was felled by bad mortgages."[14]

J.P. Morgan helped the financial system by buying these companies. Unfortunately, it acquired additional problems that needed to be fixed. While alternative investments have not caused a crisis and near collapse of the banking system, the dollars flowing into the space is rampant. "The top 100 alternative asset managers, ranked by total AUM, managed USD 3,108.4 bn on behalf of their investors in 2012."[15] Alternate investments might very well eclipse both equities and fixed income someday to dominate the asset allocation pie chart for institutional and individual investors. Regardless of the structure, whether it is a bank, regional firm, RIA, or consultant, investors' interests must always be placed first. Based on the growing interest shown by investors in alternative investments and the mergers that transpired, a number of large banks will have to recruit experts in alternative investments to provide education about financial advisors, types of products to be offered, applicable research, complaints, monitoring conflicts of interest, improving technology for reporting, and other services. The challenge for these banks is that there are very few experts who are knowledgeable in alternative investments and can overlook any or all of these needed changes.

FINANCIAL NOMADS

The worry or concern about big banks has led many investors and financial advisors to head for the exit. Given all the problems with bank mergers, the plight of the financial advisor is undetermined. The turnover and upheaval amongst financial advisors with big banks has been unprecedented. There appears to be a mass exodus of advisors racing to go independent or join a regional firm. Websites now track advisors leaving the big banks. A number of advisors are also discovering the merits of joining large private equity firms or hedge funds interested in wealth management instead of big banks. In short, big banks will have a lot of trouble keeping financial advisors especially those whose clients desire attractive alternative investments. Even members of the Federal Reserve have expressed concern. "In recent weeks, at least four current Fed presidents—Esther George of Kansas City, Charles Plosser of Philadelphia, Jeffrey Lacker of Richmond, and Richard Fisher of Dallas—have voiced concern about the risk of another crisis if one or more of the big banks were to fail. Giant institutions sheltered under an invisible government umbrella pose a clear and present danger to the U.S. economy," the Dallas Fed's annual report cautioned last month.[16]

Bigger banks might not be a panacea and could very well exacerbate the problem. Because financial advisors are switching firms trying to find a secure home, it can be troublesome for the end user, the investor. Not all alternative investments can be moved. Many alternative markets are illiquid. When an advisor moves and a client follows, sometimes not all the investments leave. In other words, they might have purchased long-term, proprietary alternative investments that cannot be transferred. Quite a few investors realize the dilemma with immobility after they sign ACAT transfer papers. Unfortunately, it is too late by then, which does not help them.

The client's assets that can be moved will move, but the alternative investments might have to stay with the old firm or bank especially if they are illiquid and/or proprietary. I once had a new client that handed me four brokerage statements of alternative investments at banks he used in the past but we could not move them over. If an investor is not paying attention, they will most likely fail to accomplish their goals or worse, lose money. A lack of attention can result in losses in any investment, regardless of whether it is a municipal bond or alternative investments. Investors would be wise to fully investigate where they buy alternative investment products and should ask plenty of questions if an advisor should request that they move with the advisor to another firm or bank.

INVESTMENT BANKING HAS CHANGED

Another new trend emerging is that top-tier investment bankers are leaving bulge bracket firms and joining smaller firms or starting their own boutique firms. Both financial advisors and investment bankers are moving around. Investors, however, might benefit from top-tier investment bankers forming boutiques or going to regional firms. In other words, they might help investors find compelling investment opportunities. Investment bankers are the ones that structure or package the opportunity for investors. Top investment bankers want to be compensated and no good banker works for free. Studies have been done that show it can be more lucrative for an investment banker to work for a mid-sized or boutique firm than the big banks. "According to SNL Financial today, the smaller pure investment banks paid their employees the highest percentages of the banks' total revenue. Goldman Sachs and Morgan Stanley handed out the slimmest percentages to their employees."[17] Private equity or venture capital frequently leads to an IPO. Gaining access to these opportunities is not a simple task, and certain firms have better performance than others (Table 4.1).

One might incorrectly conclude that the largest banks have the best performance regarding IPOs but this is not true. In fact, two of the top three underwriters having high average returns happen to be regional firms (June 16, 2011–June 15, 2012): William Blair and Jefferies. The trend will likely continue if not outright favor boutique or regional investment firms. Big banks are firing investment bankers even as they are fleeing because of the regulatory changes. "Wall Street's latest problem: too many bankers

Table 4.1 Underwriter Rankings: June 16, 2011–June 15, 2012

Rank	Underwriter	Average return
1	William Blair	51.00%
2	Jefferies & Co./Deutsche Bank Securities	26.50%
3	Deutsche Bank Securities	26.50%
4	Citi	24.10%
5	JP Morgan	23.40%
6	Credit Suisse	18.00%
7	Stifel Nicolaus Weisel	17.80%
8	Oppenheimer & Co.	15.30%
9	BofA Merrill lynch	9.80%
10	Goldman Sachs	9.50%
11	Morgan Stanley	4.40%
12	Maxim Group LLC	0.00%
13	RBC Capital Markets	−0.30%
14	Raymond James	−1.20%
15	Barclays	−1.70%
16	Johnson Rice & Co.	−10.70%
17	Wells Fargo Securities	−11.00%
18	Goldman Sachs (Asia)	−11.40%
19	UBS Investment Bank	−11.40%
20	Roth Capital	−21.90%
21	FBR Capital Markets	−26.80%
22	Broadband Capital	N/A
23	EarlyBird Capital, Inc.	N/A
24	Rodman & Renshaw	N/A

Source: "Underwriter Rankings," IPO investment advisory firm Renaissance Capital LLC, p. 1, June 15, 2012. www.renaissancecapital.com.

and not enough deals. Amid new regulation, lower profits and a dreary market for mergers and acquisitions, several banks are planning to trim investment-banking units that were built for an era of deals aplenty."[18]

ALTERNATIVE INVESTMENTS REQUIRE MORE EDUCATION

Whereas foundations and endowments allocated 25–40 percent of their assets to alternative investments (according to Thomas Strauss, former president of Salomon Brothers and currently a founder of Ramius, LLC), the large distributors committed only 2–3 percent, a paltry $100 billion out of the $4.5–5 trillion Ramius estimated they had under advisement—and the platforms were looking to significantly increase that.[19] Banks realize the institutional attraction toward alternative investments but have a dilemma with retail investors. Marketing a complex investment to the masses with thousands of advisors who have little to no training with alternative investments is problematic and a potential legal quagmire. Speaking with a couple presidents of the largest banks in the United States, they admitted to me that roughly 80–90 percent of their financial advisors had little clue about alternative investments. Generally, the blind leading the blind seldom produces positive results. Yet, the top advisors (mostly in the remaining 10 percent of the rest of the advisors) realize the importance of adding alternative investments to a portfolio regardless of whether or not they work for a large bank. Barron's indicated that the top wealth advisors allocate around 20 percent of client portfolios to alternative investments.[20] Some of these high-end, experienced advisors and wealth managers already know how to add alternative investments to create a well-diversified portfolio while others are quickly studying them in order to move up the learning curve and be able to answer client questions. Investor demand will not subside any time soon so any advisor refusing to become well versed with alternative investments would be well advised to seek another line of employment. Alternative investments are here to stay. They will likely become a bigger part of the asset allocation pie. Investor intent is quite apparent, as evidenced by the large amount of dollars flowing into the space.

KNOWLEDGE REALLY IS POWER

True wealth management is highly specialized. For example, high net worth individuals value good research. Good research can aid selecting the best alternative investments. While there were problems with research stemming back to the Tech Bubble, the US Government's attack on research years ago by Wall Street was harsh: "In a pact that could change the face of Wall Street, 10 of the nation's largest securities firms agreed to pay a record $1.4 billion in penalties to settle government charges involving investor abuses during the stock-market bubble of the late 1990s."[21] The settlement concerned overly optimistic research reports. The result was not positive and failed to accomplish what was intended (to improve research). A number of big banks let their research departments deteriorate, which is evident in reduced coverage and lack of quality with today's research. The proportion of sell ratings on Wall Street remains under 5 percent, despite the fact that any first-year MBA student can tell you that 95 percent of the stocks cannot be winners.[22]

If one invests in alternative investments, research is important. Research can help show trends. For example, most banks or firms have research analysts that cover oil or gold. Oil and gold are commodities, which are alternative investments. Research analysts write research on information technology. Information technology is part of the venture capital world and IPO market. Almost every firm writes research on real estate or REITs. Besides some of these alternative investments, research departments typically offer technical and fundamental research that can help an investor decide when it is a good time to buy or sell. However, budgets for research went out the window at the big banks and the results of these cutbacks were quite visible. Some large banks provide no technical analysis for advisors.

One issue that was not well defined by regulators was pre-IPO research: "Bans on pre-IPO research have existed since the 1930s, but the current problems stem from the post-Internet bubble attempts to clean up banks' conflicts of interest. In 2003, the then New York State Attorney General Eliot Spitzer spearheaded a 'global settlement' with banks aimed at stopping analysts from colluding with bankers to drum up investor interest in favored companies. As part of that regulatory wave, the ban on pre-IPO research was tightened."[23] Regulators banned written research before an IPO but not verbal or phone conversations with companies, which was used in Facebook. Frequently, when the government cracks down on something, costs just get shuffled around and the little guy gets whacked. Ultimately, the result of less money going to pay for research meant that less research would be available and firms would fire analysts and reduce coverage.

RESEARCH, REGULATION, AND WHERE TO FIND THE BEST REPORTS

The government will most likely crack down again on research since it was not clearly defined a decade ago with new regulation. History repeats itself, especially with Wall Street. Goldman Sachs was one bank to get fined. "Goldman Sachs Group Inc. agreed to pay $22 million to securities regulators to settle claims it inappropriately funnelled trading ideas to preferred clients in meetings known as 'huddles.'"[24] Others followed suit shortly after. Morgan Stanley and other big banks face problems with pre-IPO research with Facebook. Citigroup was fined $2 million when a junior analyst improperly disclosed information before the Facebook IPO according to the Massachusetts Secretary of the Commonwealth, William Galvin. "The SEC's focus is on whether Facebook information was leaked selectively to privileged investors, not on whether analysts were improperly disclosing their own research, as in the Citigroup censure, the person said. If sales people attached to the underwriting group led by Morgan Stanley (MS) were telling wealthy investors to stay away, while encouraging retail investors to buy all the shares they could, that might constitute illegal misrepresentation, the person said."[25]

Historically, big banks dominated the research scene and all the household names ranked high in the research rankings. By the end of 2011, the research rankings were dominated mostly by small- to mid-sized firms or foreign banks (other than Standard and Poor's, which has great research but is viewed neither as a bank nor as an investment firm). These regional firms and foreign banks tend to write excellent research. None of the big banks in the top five in 2003 even appeared in the top five in 2011. The tide turned in 2011 and small- to mid-sized firms dominated the research rankings. For instance, Raymond James, Robert Baird, William Blair, and BMO Capital were in the top five for 2011. A number of big banks, on the other hand, moved downstream. For instance, Morgan Stanley was ranked 74th out of 86 firms by *The Wall Street Journal*, Tuesday, May 10, 2011 in Firm by Firm: Tally of Awards Won by 86 Research Firms. It appears as though research changed somewhat for Morgan Stanley after the merger with Smith Barney. In 2003, Morgan Stanley was number 1. The small- to mid-sized firm, Raymond James (which was 10 in 2003), moved to second place in 2011 (Figure 4.2).

BEATING the BULGE BRACKETS

The New Trend: Better Research with Small/Mid-sized Firms

Bold = Small/Mid-sized firms; * Market Capitalization as of 7/15/11; **Division of McGraw-Hill Company

Rank	2003	2009	2010	2011	Market Cap.*
1	Morgan Stanley	Goldman Sachs	***Stifel Nicolaus***	Standard & Poor's Equity Research	$12.95 billion**
2	Standard & Poor's	Standard & Poor's	Credit Suisse	***Raymond James Financial***	$3.93 billion
3	Merrill Lynch	Merrill Lynch	Deutsche Bank	***Robert W. Baird & Co.***	private
4	Credit Suisse First Boston	Morgan Stanley	UBS	***William Blair & Co.***	private
5	Smith Barney	J.P. Morgan Chase	J.P. Morgan Chase	***BMO Capital Markets***	$34.73 billion
6	UBS Warburg	Citigroup	Wells Fargo Securities	Credit Suisse	$44.17 billion
7	Deutsche Bank	***Oppenheimer & Co***	***Raymond James***	***Morningstar***	$3.04 billion
8	***A.G. Edwards***	***Raymond James***	Bank of America Merrill Lynch	Wells Fargo Securities	$144.03 billion
9	Lehman Brothers	***Stifel Nicolaus***	***KeyBanc Capital Markets***	Deutsche Bank Research	$48.62 billion
10	***Raymond James***	Credit Suisse	***Keefe Bruyette & Woods***	J.P. Morgan Chase	$158.23 billion
11	Bear Stearns	UBS	***Oppenheimer & Co***	***Needham & Co.***	private
12	***McDonald Investments***	***BMO Capital Markets***	Citigroup	***Stifel Nicolaus***	$1.95 billion
13	***Banc of America Securities***	***Cowen & Co.***	Barclays Capital	UBS Investment Research	$63.78 billion
14	RBC Capital Markets	***Robert W. Baird***	Standard & Poor's	***Canaccord Genuity***	$0.958 billion
15	Prudential Securities	***Argus Research***	***CL King & Associates***	***D.A. Davidson & Co.***	private
16	***CIBC World Markets***	***Sandler O'Neill***	***JMP Securities***	***Gabelli & Co.***	$1.10 billion
17	***Robert W. Baird***	***Sterne Agee & Leach***	***Sanford C. Bernstein***	***Jefferies & Co.***	$4.15 billion
18	***Legg Mason***	***SunTrust Robinson Humphrey***	***Cowen & Co.***	***JMP Securities***	$0.158 billion
19	Goldman Sachs	***Stephens***	***BMO Capital Markets***	***Keefe Bruyette & Woods***	private
20	***BMO Nesbitt Burns***	RBC Capital Markets	***William Blair***	***Northland Capital Markets***	private
	Credit Lyonnais				
	Fahnestock				

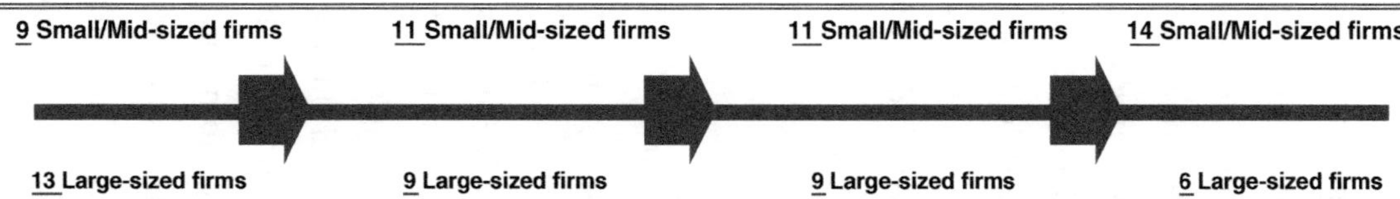

"Wall Street Journal – The Best on the Street." *The Wall: Journal.* May 12, 2003. "Wall Street Journal – The Best on the Street." *The Wall Street Journal.* May 26, 2009. "Wall Street Journal – The Best on the Street." *The Wall Street Journal.* May 25, 2010. "Wall Street Journal – The Best on the Street." *The Wall Street Journal.* May 10, 2011.C13.

Figure 4.2 Changing Trends in Research with Banks and Investment Firms.

Source: Author.

On January 18, 2012, Citigroup was fined for disclosure lapses, which was similar to a problem in 2010 whereby they failed to disclose certain conflicts of interest: "Regulators said the lapses, which exceeded 9,000 instances, were 'largely the result of programming and technical errors and deficiencies.' The fine is the third for New York-based Citigroup on a research-disclosure lapse in the past decade and comes on the heels of a similar disclosure mishap in 2010 at Morgan Stanley for failing to make public disclosures governing research analyst conflicts of interest. Morgan Stanley declined to comment."[26] Research plays a very important role, especially for alternative investments. For instance, an investor might want to invest in a private placement for a new promising medical device. Does the bank he or she is dealing with have a good medical device analyst to help evaluate the offering? Analysts compare private companies with public corporations. The bottom line is that analysts can not only cover individual companies but also offer valuable insight and help investors.

RESEARCH QUALITY

Analysts vary in caliber. Because research is very time consuming and labor intensive, quality can range widely or be inconsistent. Besides fines, another main point behind the settlement was that Wall Street firms needed to make available third-party research or provide "Independent Research" for investors at no charge. The US Government's solution to making big banks use third-party research was typical of government response in that they meant well but the solution was ill conceived, hasty, and had negative ramifications. In short, the third-party research idea failed to work. Eager to grab some of the $432.5 million that firms had to pony up for research, many small research boutiques surfaced, only to provide mediocre research. Unfortunately, investors did not benefit and it reinforced the idea that government actions can adversely affect investors. Research regarding commodities, real estate, and other alternative investments is helpful in making investment decisions.

Risk appears to go way up for investors when a government intervenes, no matter what country an investor examines. "During good economic times, the equity-risk premium is compensating investors almost entirely for economic risks because government policy is unlikely to change. But during bad times, political risks comprise more than half of the equity-risk premium."[27] Politics can affect alternative investments in a number of ways and an election can especially wreak havoc. "Political dysfunction will continue to feed market volatility. The US economy is now facing a sizeable fiscal drag just as the economy is showing renewed signs of life. Election-year politics will only add to the uncertainty."[28] While some firms are fearful about political commentary, others find it helpful. Politics can influence the market and alternative investments. I have found it to be most useful for one that invested in alternative investments to hear the view of an analyst with regard to politics. Government action can create political waves that affect alternative investments.

Uncertainty scares the market. A new president will likely change the way a country is run, especially if they are from a different party or have diametrically opposed views. The incumbent might like solar energy while the non-incumbent(s) prefer oil, nuclear, natural gas, or coal. The incumbent might support health care and banks while the non-incumbents might like technology, consumer, or energy companies. Depending on the individual that is elected, the landscape could change quickly. An investor that puts funds directly into a private natural gas company or a private equity energy fund might be affected adversely if an elected official is devoted to solar energy and opposed to natural gas. Certain industries could be heavily taxed while others are given government funds, bailouts, or even subsidies. During the Great Recession, certain banks were allowed to fail while others received inordinate amounts of support. Political risk with alternative investments has become much more acute. "Polarization has become a pervasive and much-noted feature of American politics. The two major parties are sharply divided over issues ranging from taxation to gun control to climate change, and much political discussion is characterized by considerable acrimony."[29]

The market has become increasingly volatile. During the past decade, investors (most likely because of the changes that transpired) act differently. "Conservatism is extremely suggestive of the underreaction evidence... Individuals subject to conservatism might disregard the full information content of an earnings (or some other public) announcement, perhaps because they believe that this number contains a large temporary component, and still cling at least partially to their prior estimates of earnings."[30] Earnings announcements used to play a bigger role with investors. Today, investors tend to underreact and overreact, creating immense volatility in the public market. "Recent empirical research in finance has uncovered two families of pervasive regularities: under reaction of stock prices to news such as earning announcements, and overreactions of stock prices to a series of good or bad news."[31] Behavioral finance is a driver for alternative investments and helps explain waves of buying or selling.

5

I HATE TO SAY IT, BUT I TOLD YOU SO

VOLATILITY

Based on a *Morningstar* poll (912 responses; poll taken November 10, 2009), "More Advisors Are Reporting that 76–100% of their Client Groups are Using Alternative Investments than Last Year,"[1] both finance experts and investors clearly see the merits of diversifying with alternative investments. In *Smart Money's* "Own More 'Alternatives,'" "The financial crisis did more than just shred the mystique of the buy-and-hold era; it also left many investors skeptical of the idea that stocks, bonds and cash were enough to see them through to the finish line. After all, stocks and bonds both took huge tumbles simultaneously, and low interest rates during the recovery made most people's cash holdings about as profitable as a pet rock. Those trends are fueling demand for a wider array of assets—from long-short funds, which can improve their returns by betting against stocks, to commodities, which tend to rise when stocks fall."[2]

Stocks and bonds have historically had huge swings in total return and averaged below 10 percent. Over the past 75 years, equities averaged 9.9 percent compared with fixed income that averaged 5.5 percent and cash with 3.8 percent. Volatility ranged from -41.1 percent to 60 percent with equities. Equities can have high returns but with that comes bad years not too dissimilar from living in Florida. Florida is known for nice weather but it can quickly change as evidenced by all the hurricanes. The weather is better than most states such as those found in the northeast but when a storm or hurricane hits, the downside is big. Hurricane Andrew in 1992 caused $23.4 billion in damages, while Wilma in 2005 caused $9.4 billion and Charley in 2004 caused $8.6 billion.[3] While bonds had good returns nearly 30 years ago with 42.1 percent during 1982, more recently they had their worst year in 2009 and lost -12.2 percent. Most would think T-Bills would be at the lowest during the past few years but long ago T-Bills were actually 0 percent in 1940. Stocks did the best in 1935, with a return of 60 percent but did the worst in 1931, with a return of -41.1 percent. Stocks also carried the highest standard deviation of 19.20 percent from 1926 to 2010 compared to bonds with a standard deviation of 7.40 percent and 0.90 percent for T-Bills.[4] Total annualized returns from 1926 to 2010 for stocks were 9.90 percent, 5.50 percent for bonds, and 3.80 percent for T-Bills.[5]

The majority of financial planners use alternative investments to even out the bumps in a portfolio, opting for investments that zig when stocks or bonds zag.[6] Managed futures, for instance, zig when the market zags; they tend to do well when equity markets are doing poorly. "Managed futures have historically exhibited low correlation to traditional investments, generating strong absolute returns across market cycles. This stems from managed futures' ability to utilize multiple trading disciplines to create opportunities for managers to potentially profit from both positive and negative developments across multiple markets."[7]

The Journal of Financial Planning published an article I wrote on April 5, 2012 titled "Riding The Right Wave with Managed Futures." Institutions, from small to large, are allocating more to alternative investments: "From SWFs to corporate and public pension funds, all are focused on alternatives," said Christopher Kojima, managing director and head of alternatives investments and manager selection at Goldman Sachs Asset Management. "Alternatives have become a critically important ingredient…investors are increasingly looking at the connection between alternatives and the broader portfolio."[8] A lot of whales are floating around these days. "The whales of our current economic society swim mainly in financial market oceans."[9] Whales are part of the "smart money" and they can influence the market. Sometimes the influence leads to problems such as JP Morgan paying approximately $900 million in fines for the "London Whale." While not invincible, CalPER's returns are better than the market as well as many

Table 5.1 CalPERS vs. S&P 500 Historical Rates of Return

Year	CalPERS year end, December 31	S&P year end, December 31
1991	23	30.2
1992	6.5	7.5
1993	13.4	10
1994	−1	1.3
1995	25.3	37.2
1996	12.8	23.8
1997	19	31.8
1998	18.5	28.3
1999	16	20.9
2000	−1.4	−9
2001	−6.2	−11.8
2002	−9.5	−22
2003	23.3	28.4
2004	13.4	10.7
2005	11.1	4.8
2006	15.7	15.6
2007	10.2	5.5
2008	−27.8	−36.6
2009	12.1	25.9
2010	12.6	15.1

Sources: Author; CalPERS; and S&P

other pensions. CalPER's is a real whale. Table 5.1 shows CalPER's returns from 1990 to 2010.

A century ago, stocks were viewed as aggressive investments and had far fewer investors. "Stocks were less common in the portfolios of individual investors a century ago than in today's portfolios, and they were considered more risky than they are considered today."[10] Alternative investments are viewed by many as aggressive investments. However, times change as seen with equities. There are different types of alternative investments, with different risk profiles. Some are higher risk while others are lower risk. There is a spectrum of alternative investments with different degrees of risk. Alternative investments might even act as a core component for asset allocation one day, with smaller allocations to equities and fixed income.

THE MARKET AND ALTERNATIVE INVESTMENTS

A large number of the wealthiest individuals in the United States made their money from alternative investments. Nearly 43 percent of the Forbes 400 list derived their fortunes from alternative investments (Figure 5.1).

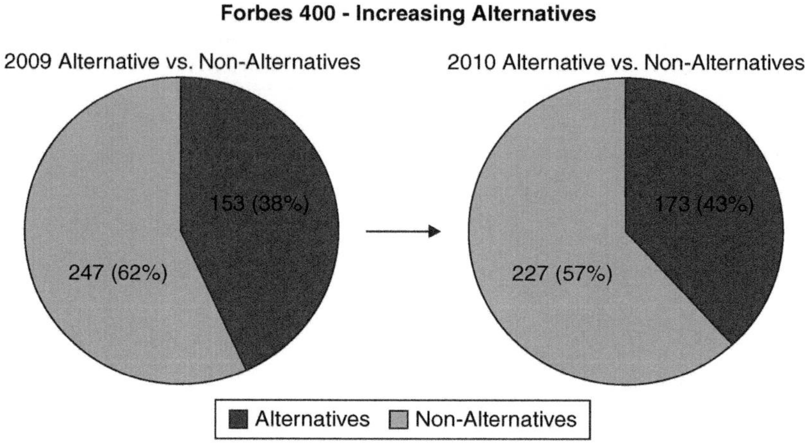

Figure 5.1 Wealth from Alternative Investments vs. Non-Alternative Investments.
Source: Author, "The 400," *Forbes*, 2010.

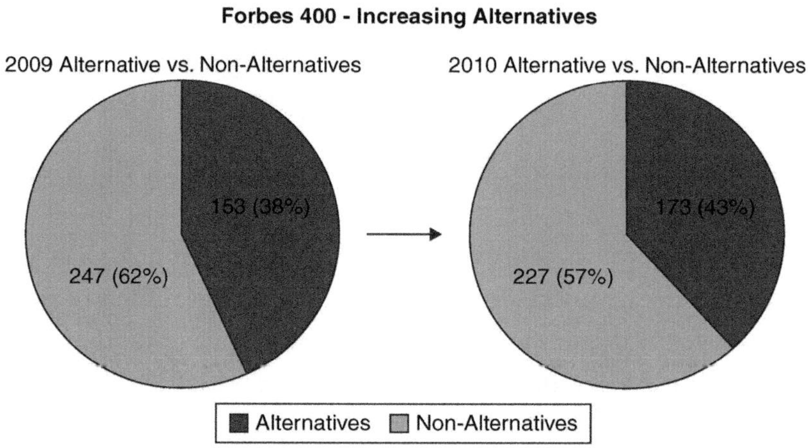

Figure 5.2 Growth in Alternative Investments.
Source: Author, "The 400," *Forbes*, 2010.

More and more fortunes are being made with alternative investments. A number of hedge funds and IPOs helped increase the number of billionaires from 2009 to 2010 (Figure 5.2).

Any serious investor is exploring the world of alternative investments. Alternative investments are being used not just in taxable accounts but for retirement accounts as well. I sat on a panel at Pensions and Investment East Coast Defined Contribution Conference 2011 where we were the first to discuss the possibility of adding alternative investment to a 401(K) plan. In "Retirement Ready," April–May 2011, *Worth* states: "And while old-school portfolios were divided between stocks and bonds, now advisors make room for a healthy dose of alternative investments. Commodities and real estate have a place even for investors with modest asset levels. For those with bigger portfolios who can handle illiquid investments and stiff minimums, hedge funds, private equity, master limited partnerships and other alternative investments should be included."[11] Those investors not paying attention to the world of alternatives are similar to a surfer sitting on the beach not paying attention to the waves in the ocean or a surfer paddling around without noticing a bunch of fins circling around. But the astute investors, who are paying attention, will be much more likely to be surfing than those not even in the water. Alternative investments are gathering more interest from investors these days. For instance, Morningstar noted a clear and distinct move toward the use of alternative investments with investors from 2008 to 2009: "More advisors than in 2008 report that at least three fourths of their client groups are using alternative investments."[12]

While the alternative investments space is growing rather quickly, it is by no means reaching capacity. That is, there is room for growth with alternative investments. An annual survey estimated that the combined wealth of the world's 10.9 million rich people stood at $42.7 trillion in 2010, more than in 2007, the year the financial crisis began.[13] "Household net worth—the difference between the values of households' assets and liabilities—was $77.3trillion at the end of the third quarter of this year, about$1.9 trillion more than at the end of the second quarter."[14]

ETFS AND MUTUAL FUNDS

Alternative investments are becoming one of the most sought-after investments to add to a portfolio. Investors in alternative investments are not just institutional. Years ago, alternative investments were the private beach for institutions but today the beach party is for the most part open to everyone: individuals, mass affluent, high net worth, and institutional investors (see "Heavier Use" chart). Minimums and access are still hurdles but even they have changed. Mutual funds are a large market. "Total worldwide assets under management in mutual funds—including offshore funds and unit trusts—totaled $16.797 trillion as of Dec. 31, an increase of 15.3% from the end of 2009. That was the first year in which *P&I* collected data that included the offshore and unit-trust figures." However, ETFs are growing faster. "Total worldwide assets under management in ETFs rose to $1.171 trillion as of Dec. 31, up 36.9% from the previous year. That figure itself was an increase of 45.2% from Dec. 31, 2008, nearly doubling worldwide ETFs in the span of two years."[15]

Mutual funds and ETFs are focusing more on alternative-like offerings. They are not true alternative investments but rather versions of real alternative investments. For instance, a private equity fund specializing in timber is not the same as an ETF that invests in publicly traded companies involved with timber. Yet it can give an investor some exposure as well as easy access to areas similar to actual alternative investments. ETFs are generally composed of publicly traded companies and are liquid as opposed to illiquid. I call these mutual funds or ETFs "Alternative Like Investments." ETFs, focused on alternative like investments, have grown dramatically since 2006. As of July 2011, there were approximately 368 alternative-like investment ETFs. According to *Research Magazine*, US ETFs as a whole grew in number to 1,241 ETFs by year end 2012.[16] Since these funds are relatively new compared to the actual alternatives or mutual funds, not a lot of data is available. Table 5.2 shows a comparison between ETFs and mutual funds. I sat on a panel for Index Universe where we discussed ETFs and alternative investments.

Likewise, past performance is not readily available since many ETFs are new. While one can examine a ten-year track record of a real estate fund, index, or private real estate, these funds do not go back that far so performance cannot be measured. Yet the recent performance of a number of ETFs with a flavor for alternative investments was good in the beginning of 2012 (Table 5.3).

Table 5.2 ETF And Mutual Fund Asset Growth

Year	Mutual fund assets	ETF assets
2004	$8.1 trillion	$228 billion
2005	$8.9 trillion	$301 billion
2006	$10.4 trillion	$423 billion
2007	$12.0 trillion	$608 billion
2008	$9.6 trillion	$531 billion
2009	$11.2 trillion	$777 billion
2010	$11.8 trillion	$992 billion
2011	$11.6 trillion	$1.04 trillion

As of 8/31/11. Source.
Source: "Investing," Wealth Management, *Financial Advisor Magazine*, p. 104, December 2011; and Investment Company Institute, as of August 31, 2011.

Table 5.3 Top-performing ETFs, Ranked by January 2012 Price Gains

ETF name	Ticker	% change
VS Inverse VIX Short Term	XIV	31.03%
Global X Uranium	URA	28.71%
E-Tracs Long Platinum ETN	PTM	27.54%
EG Shares India Infrastructure	INXX	26.96%
Market Vectors Solar Energy	KWT	23.85%
Guggenheim Solar ETF	TAN	22.67%

Source: Author.

EXCHANGE TRADED PRODUCTS

A new phrase for ETFs has evolved, called "exchange-traded products." Exchanged traded products include ETFs, exchange-traded commodities (Europe), and exchange traded vehicles (US) (Figure 5.3). Active domestic equity as of December 31, 2010 was $1.78 trillion while active domestic bonds were $2.49 trillion. Alternative investments were $591 billion, which includes real estate equity, venture capital, buyout funds, infrastructure, private securities, timber, energy, distressed debt, mezzanine debt, commodities, currency, and hedge funds, but does not include REITs, mortgages, inflation protected securities, collateralized debt obligations, and convertibles. If one added this latter group, one would be adding another $244 billion to the alternative investments pool, which would equate to a total of $835 billion. Alternative investments compared to worldwide assets are still small depending on how one views the market. For example, corporate cash is in the trillions.

PUBLIC AND PRIVATE ALTERNATIVE INVESTMENTS

Some view a portion of public companies as alternative investments based on what the company does to generate revenue or if it is listed on an exchange. For instance, if you own a hotel, it might be considered an alternative investment given it is private real estate. Yet a group of hotels assembled to go public as a hotel REIT may or may not be viewed by investors as an alternative investment. The hotel REIT would be a publicly traded stock but some would still argue that because it is real estate, it should be an alternative investment. I view this as Classic Coke versus Diet Coke; you are still drinking a soda. Gold serves as another example. If the entity is a

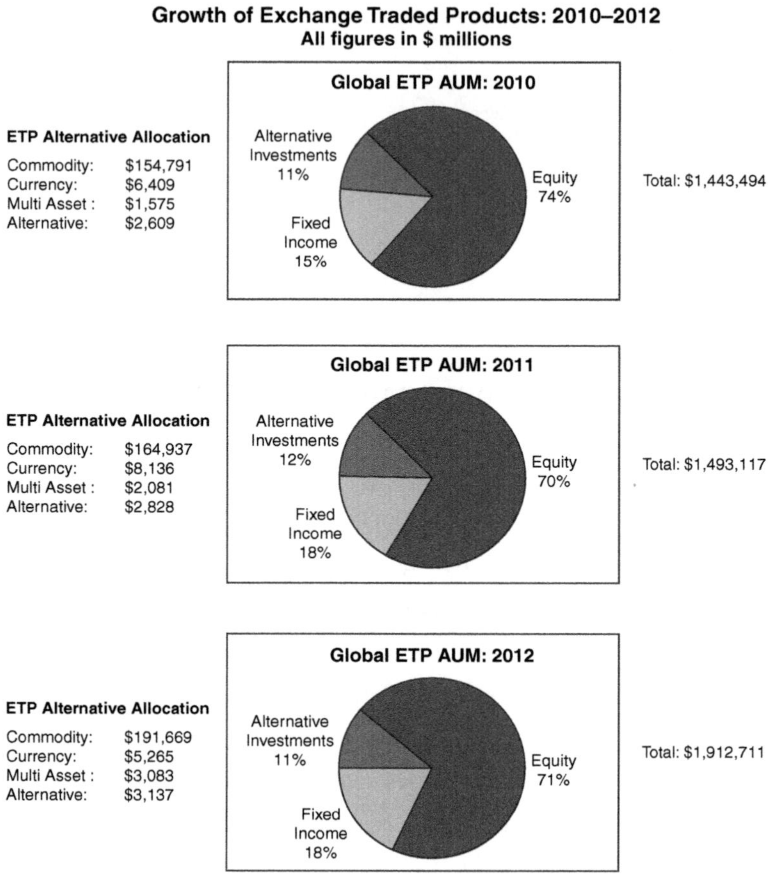

Figure 5.3 Growth of Exchange Traded Products (All figures in $ millions).
Source: Author.

gold miner or gold ETF that is offered on an exchange, one could view the security as a stock while others might see them as alternative investments in gold. Facebook might serve as another example when it was a private company. Shares of the company had been sold through private exchanges. High net worth investors, venture funds, and hedge funds invested in Facebook when it was private. As a $100 billion publicly traded company, it is no longer an alternative investment but rather a large publicly traded company. Further, many companies, such as natural gas and oil companies, are not always viewed as alternative investments once they are public, even though they involve commodities that fall under the spectrum of alternative investments. Investments in private companies involve venture capital, which is an alternative investment. It is the Classic Coke. Investments in publicly traded companies might involve similar areas as private companies but are not technically alternative investments. These investments can be viewed as Diet Coke. Both have advantages as well as disadvantages. Investors can have one or the other. Some investors, depending on their net worth or preferences, own both.

DIVERSIFICATION IS NOT LIMITED

There are three legs to a financial stool: fixed income, equities, and alternative investments. Investors limiting diversification to just stock and bond portfolios felt the repercussions during the Great Recession. Equities were annihilated. The MSCI EAFE Index was -43.25 percent, Russell 2000 Growth -38.54 percent, and the SP500 Index -37 percent for 2008. Very few equity investors were happy. "The behavior of the world's key stock markets since the mid-1990s has confused and frustrated investors and managers. It has led many to question whether the stock market is anything more than a giant roulette table essentially unconnected to the real economy shaped by inflation rates, interest rates, growth in gross domestic product (GDP), and corporate profits."[17] The Great Recession appeared to be reminiscent of past financial hurricanes, with equities ultimately going into a sideways market.

Wild swings with equities have frequently led investors (depending on when they entered the market) to end right where they started: "After a crash, a long bull run, another crash, and a lightning-fast doubling, the S&P 500 is hovering around the level that it did in late 1999. So all that stocks have given you thus far in the 21st century is motion sickness and a dividend yield that didn't keep up with inflation. That's not much to believe in, and judging from the money that's pouring out of mutual funds, these Job-like trials have a lot of folks rethinking their commitment to stocks."[18] The 1970s, as an example, was a sideways market. Hypothetically, if my parents got excited when I was born in 1966 and invested in the Dow Jones, they would not have made money until after I went to college in 1984. Bonds were also pummeled and did not offer the protection they had in the past. Municipals were -2.5 percent, Corporate bonds -4.9 percent, Emerging Market Debt -14.7 percent, and High Yield -26.2 percent.

A number of bond mutual fund managers lost as much as or more than equity managers, perturbing investors further.

Alternative investments in 2008 were not a panacea but did fairly well compared to other asset classes. The MBS index was 8.3 percent; TIPS -2.4 percent. Hedge funds varied but on average did far better than equities. Market Neutral 1.1 percent; HFRI Macro 4.83 percent; Short Selling 24.72 percent; CTA Global 12.78 percent; HFRI Fund Weighted Comp -19.02 percent; HFRI FOF -21.36 percent; Managed Futures 14.1 percent; Real Assets 5.8 percent. Adding alternative investments to a fixed income and equity portfolio can possibly lower risk and increase returns, which is why the smart money is focused on alternative investments. "The focus on alternatives reflects institutional asset allocation trends, according to consultants and managers. The market recovery in 2010 firmly put investors on more solid ground as they reassess their portfolios, with many focusing on finding the right balance in their desire to lower volatility without sacrificing returns."[19]

As we know, volatility is a measure of risk. "Market volatility to some degree is inevitable. The VIX measures the near-term expected volatility of the markets and may be a good indicator as to the expectation of how certain investments may perform in various market volatility environments."[20] Investors learned more about volatility in the Great Recession than in almost any other time period since the Great Depression. Economic cycles repeat themselves in boom and bust (Figure 5.4).

Standard deviation is calculated as the square root of variance, which measures the variability (volatility) from an average. Standard deviation is a statistical measurement which that is also known as "historical volatility" and is used as a means to measure the amount of expected volatility. Alternative investments, having long been viewed as "too risky," performed reasonably well compared to their counterparts, stocks and bonds. It was an eye-opener as to what is risky and what is not so risky. Assets generally considered risky, such as managed futures (along with a number of other select alternative investments), performed well. Just by the name, "managed futures" sounds risky. Before the market crashed during the Great Recession, a prospective client (who had no knowledge of managed futures) looked at me with a blank stare when I raised the topic of managed futures.

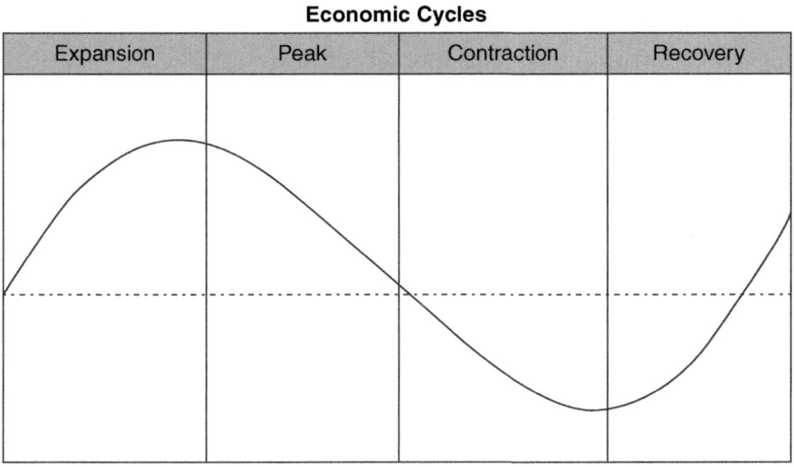

Figure 5.4 Economic Cycles.
Source: Author.

What are managed futures? "Managed-futures funds invest in futures, swaps, options, and other contracts whose values are tied to the movement of various markets or market indicators, including stock indexes, interest rates, commodities, precious metals, and currencies. A given contract's value might depend on the price of gold relative to that of copper, for example, or the likelihood that spreads between short-term and long-term interest rates will narrow."[21] Using Wave Theory, managed futures might be an alternative investment to consider especially for declining or bear markets. Managed futures utilize futures. "Futures contracts are standardized, transferable exchange traded contracts which allow an investor to take a directional (long or short) position in a wide range of underlying assets including currencies, fixed income, equity indices, commodities, energy, etc. The current futures price is the price today for delivery of the underlying asset at a pre-specified date in the future."[22] In the past, mainly institutions invested in managed futures. However, a number of vehicles such as mutual funds have made managed futures easy to obtain and at lower minimums. "Most extreme bear or bull markets have not happened overnight, but instead have occurred as the result of continued deterioration or improvement in economic conditions. In bear markets managed futures strategies position themselves short as markets begin to decline and profit if markets continue to fall. Similarly, in bull markets, managed futures strategies position themselves long as markets begin to rise and can profit if the rise continues."[23] Managed futures will likely gain more attention, especially through volatile markets or down markets.

A market crash typically brings down the value of many assets. Individual equities, or those found in mutual funds, indexes, ETFs, UITs, or separately managed accounts, tend to plummet and some never recover. Years after the Great Recession, quite a few investors abandoned equities due to their volatility: "The unhappy combination of tumbling and volatile stock prices turned up the volume of stock-fund redemptions. Investors withdrew a net $61.3 billion from U.S.-stock funds in the third quarter, through Sept. 21, according to estimates from the Investment Company Institute trade group."[24] Many alternative investments, however, did not fall as much and some even had positive gain, which was an eye-opener for investors after the Great Recession took place. Assets considered safe or conservative became more volatile and did not perform well such as municipal bonds or corporate bonds. The otherwise liquid market of ARPS completely dried up and investors could not sell what they thought were short-term, liquid municipal bonds. Even money market funds performed poorly. "The issue is simple-yet-frightening: Money-market funds have become 'systemic' institutions, whose size, interconnectedness and behavior have the potential to cause serious damage to companies, investors and the economy."[25] Those who never owned alternative investments started asking questions about how to add them to their portfolios while investors who already owned alternative investments, sought more after the market started to recover.

INSTITUTIONAL ASSETS

Regardless of an investor's risk appetite (conservative, moderate, or aggressive), adding alternative investments can possibly lower risk and increase returns. "Executives at public pension plans looking to enhance their investment returns should pay more attention to reducing risk, using alternative investments to boost returns and cutting costs, according to pension and investment executives."[26] For instance, Dr. Everett M. Ehrlich in his paper "The Changing Role of Hedge Funds in the Global Economy" suggested that by "Allocating 10% to hedge funds has the potential to add $13.67 billion to public pension plan returns annually."[27] If one is not an executive at a pension plan, they can select alternative

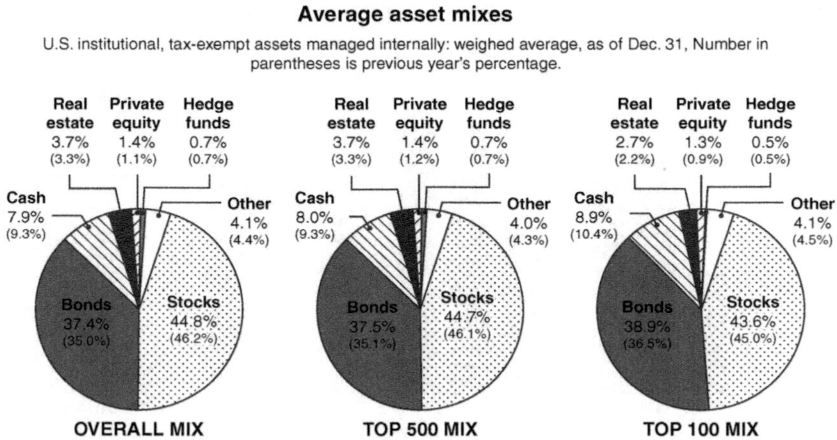

Figure 5.5 Institutional Assets Managed Internally (Weighted Average, as of Dec. 31. Number in Parentheses is Pervious Year's Percentage).

Source: *Pensions and Investments*, p. 32, May 28, 2012.

investments themselves, or hire an advisor. Newspapers and magazines such as *Pensions and Investments* provide detailed information on alternative investments. Figure 5.5 shows US institutional, tax-exempt assets managed internally as of December 31, 2011.

Both institutions and individuals are looking for help with collaboration investments. Institutions, however, have large staff and resources, unlike most individual investors. Further, they can negotiate terms that would generally be unavailable to a high net worth individual. It is interesting to see which alternative investments institutional investors need help in to identify and select alternative investments to add. The allocation to bonds, stocks, and alternative investments changes when one examines an allocation including advisors to these institutions for selecting alternative investments. The bottom line is institutional investors see value in hiring experts to guide them when selecting alternative investments. Quite a few institutions made horrific investment decisions with alternative investments as well as had terrible timing or made poor tactical asset allocation decisions. From Figure 5.5, it appears that institutional investors are slightly more comfortable in picking out real estate investments themselves than hedge funds. Commodities are not even listed. There are a number of websites devoted to alternative investments, such as http://Altnews.com or conferences such as http://AlternativeInvestmentsConferences.com.

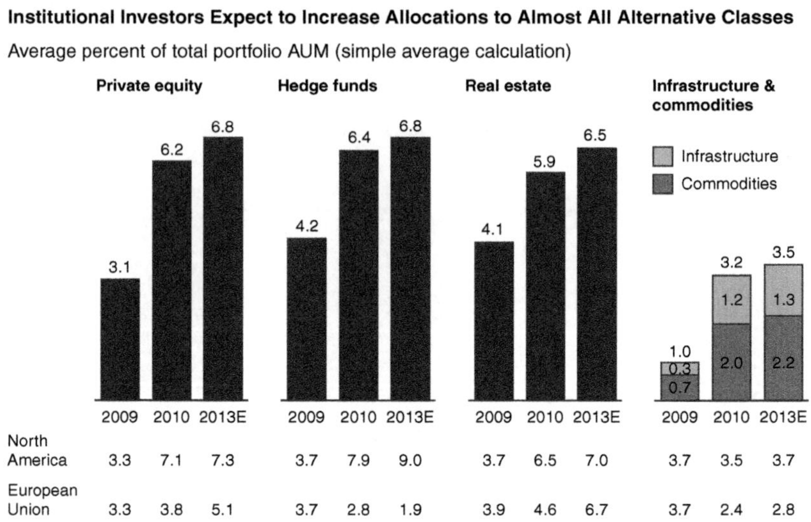

Figure 5.6 Allocation of Institutional Investors' Assets.

Source: The Mainstreaming of Alternative Investments: Fueling the Next Wave of Growth in Asset Management," McKinsey & Company, p. 6, June 2012.

While institutions have historically invested in alternative investments a lot more than high net worth or retail investors, the tide is not changing. In fact, institutional investors intend to devote more assets to alternative investments mainly to private equity, hedge funds, real estate, and maintaining infrastructure and commodities in the future (Figure 5.6).

Institutional investors are also increasing dollars to alternative investments, not just domestically but globally. Allocations to private equity, real estate, hedge funds, infrastructure, and commodities have increased. Alternative investments are global. Because of institutional and individual demand, the global marketplace will continue to grow and present new opportunities. Similarly, certain areas of the globe, such as Asia, will likely foster growth in alternative investments. "While many investors based in North America and Europe find themselves contending with increased financial regulation, emerging markets around the globe are opening up to private equity and hedge fund investment... 18% of investors in alternatives are currently based outside North America [51%] and Europe [31%], a figure which will likely increase in the coming years as investors based in these regions become more active in alternative assets."[28]

6

THE "SMART MONEY" IS GLOBAL

Large pensions have done quite well by adding alternative investments to equity and fixed income; big public pension funds with a total market value greater than $5 billion did well using alternative investments. Figure 6.1 is a performance chart of alternative investments (real estate, hedge funds, and private equity), equity, and fixed income, with annualized returns over ten years ended December 31, 2012. Over the past decade, the "Smart Money" increased returns with alternative investments. Pension plans continue to find merit with alternative investments and have increased allocations. Table 6.1 shows the top 200 pension plans in 2011 and how much they increased their exposure to alternative investments.

In *The Wall Street Journal's* "Pensions Leap Back to Hedge Funds," the article states: "On average, hedge funds as a class have delivered for large pension funds that have dabbled in them for overtime, data show. Large pension funds scored median annualized returns of 6.8% investing in hedge funds in the past decade, compared with 5.7% from stocks and 6.1% from bonds, according to Wilshire Associates, an investment consultant in Santa Monica, Calif. Private equity delivered 6.7%."[1] Adding alternative investments to an equity and fixed income portfolio might possibly lower risk and increase returns. I noticed this benefit approximately two decades ago before alternative investments were popular. Now there is data to illustrate this observation.

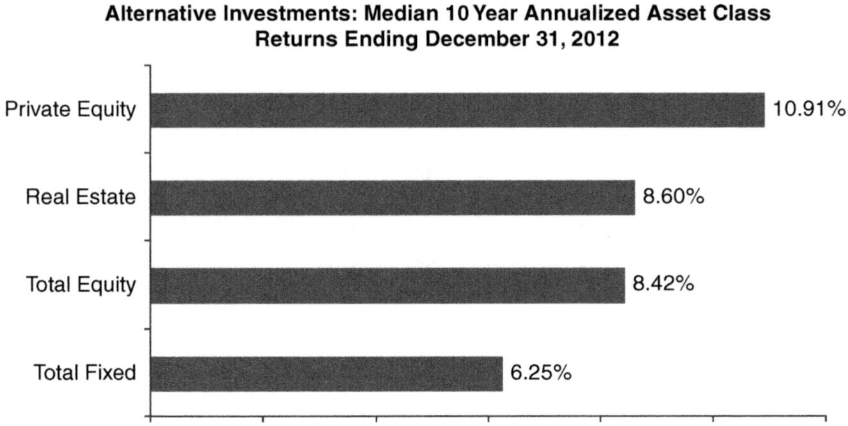

Figure 6.1 Performance of Alternative Investments Compared to Equities and Fixed Income.
Source: Wilshire Associates.

Hypothetically, if an investor wanted to add alternative investments to a stock and bond, portfolio, they should diversify with more than one alternative investment. Equities have different sectors, which have also changed over time. During the past century, in fact, many sectors that were once in big demand are not as popular today, such as railroads. Railroads had a sector weighting of 62.8 percent in 1899, but only 0.2 percent in 2000.[2]

The United States has fallen behind: "Between 1999 and 2009 America's share of world exports fell in almost every industry: by 36 percentage points in aerospace, nine in information technology, eight in communications equipment and three in cars. Some loss of market share is inevitable as China and other economies emerge. But even in absolute terms, there is cause for worry."[3] Many times, a naïve investor or uninformed financial advisor will add just one alternative investment such as a single commodity ETF or buy a mining company stock. Erroneously, the investor will conclude that such a purchase makes them well diversified. Typically, if an investor buys stocks, mutual funds, money manager, indexes, or ETFs, they will add foreign or emerging markets. Few investors limit themselves to investing in just one country. Alternative investments are no different.

While data is not available for alternative investments over the past 100 years, one can now see annualized returns with stock, bonds, and bills in a number of countries around the world for the past century (Table 6.2).

Table 6.1 Alternative Investments by P&I Top 200 Pension Plans in 2011

Investment	% growth	Amount invested
Real estate equity	26%	$212 billion
Private equity	16%	$313 billion
Venture capital	26%	$34.8 billion
Buyouts	15%	$71.4 billion
Commodities	13%	$20.6 billion
Infrastructure	25%	$6.4 billion

Source: "Funds Still Carrying Torch for Alternatives," P&I, February 6, 2012, p. 24.

Table 6.2 Annualized Real Returns on Major Asset Categories Around the World, 1900–2000

Country	Equities	Bonds	Bills
Australia	7.5	1.1	0.4
Belgium	2.5	−0.4	−0.3
Canada	6.4	1.8	1.7
Denmark	4.6	2.5	2.8
France	3.8	−1	−3.3
Germany*	3.6	−2.2	−0.6
Ireland	4.8	1.5	1.3
Italy	2.7	−2.2	−4.1
Japan	4.5	−1.6	−2
The Netherlands	5.8	1.1	0.7
South Africa	6.8	1.4	0.8
Spain	3.6	1.2	0.4
Sweden	7.6	2.4	2
Switzerland**	5	2.8	1.1
United Kingdom	5.8	1.3	1
United States	6.7	1.6	0.9

*Bond and bill figures for Germany exclude the years 1922–1923;
**Swiss equities from 1911.
Sources: Elroy Dimson, Paul Marsh, and Mike Staunton, *Triumph of the Optimists: 101 Years of Global Investment Returns*, New Jersey: Princeton University Press, 2002, p. 52. Estimates for a larger number of countries, and updated to the most recent year-end, are available in Elroy Dimson, Paul Marsh, and Mike Staunton, *Global Investment Returns Sourcebook*, Zurich: Credit Suisse Research Institute.

The United States was not ranked first for the top ten performing stock markets by annual total return from 2002 to 2011. In fact, the United States appeared only once during this time period where it was ranked 7th in 2011. Other than that, the United States was not a top ten performer during any year for these ten years. No accurate data exists for alternative investments over the past 100 years. However, one can now see both nominal and real returns for stocks, bonds, and cash on a global basis. Nominal returns do not include inflation. Real returns after inflation are much lower percentages. US inflation nominal return (geometric) was 3.2 percent. The real return for US Bills from 1900 to 2000 was 0.9 percent, 1.2 percent for bonds, and 5.8 percent for equities. The dispersion of returns varied widely over this time period. For example, US Bills were 0.0 percent in 1938 but 14.7 percent in 1981, bonds were –14.4 percent in 1919 but 34.4 percent in 1985, and equities were –18.8 percent in 1919 but 29.5 percent in 1933. One hundred years from now, someone will likely make a chart covering 2000–2100 with stocks, bonds, and alternative investments.

Markets change. Few investors are aware that the United States was not the dominant player with equity in the past and for a long time the US was ranked second to Europe. "At end-1899, 783 companies had their shares traded on the London Stock Exchange. This was over six times as many as were then quoted on the NYSE. At the end of 1899, just 123 NYSE stocks are listed in the *Commercial and Financial Chronicle*, the most authoritative data source on the NYSE."[4] Yet the tide changed one hundred years later and the United States dominated the global landscape. "By the end of 2000, there were 6,340 US stocks quoted on the NYSE, Amex, and Nasdaq, with a total capitalization of $14.4 trillion. This compares with a value of $2.7 trillion for the 2,140 companies, including Alternative Investment Markets stocks, traded on the London Market."[5] China and other countries in Asia listed many new companies as described in *Wave Theory for Alternative Investments* during the first decade of the twenty-first century and might be the dominant player over the next century. "By 2030, China's share of global economic power will match America's in the 1970s and Britain's a century before."[6] A global IPO report from Ernst and Young showed Asia-Pacific with a large portion of both number of deals and capital raised in 2011 (Figure 6.2).

A review of IPOs for the third quarter of 2010 and 2011 showed that China had the top dollar volume worldwide. In the first nine months of 2011, China had $43.1 billion in IPOs versus the United States, with only $26.3 billion. In the first nine months of 2010, China had $75.6 billion versus the United States, with an anemic $11.2 billion. By the end of 2010, China was ranked second for the largest market capitalization according to the Economist.[7] "Chinese issuers continue to lead the global IPO nationality rankings, with $4.5 billion raised via 48 IPOs in 2012 YTD, despite

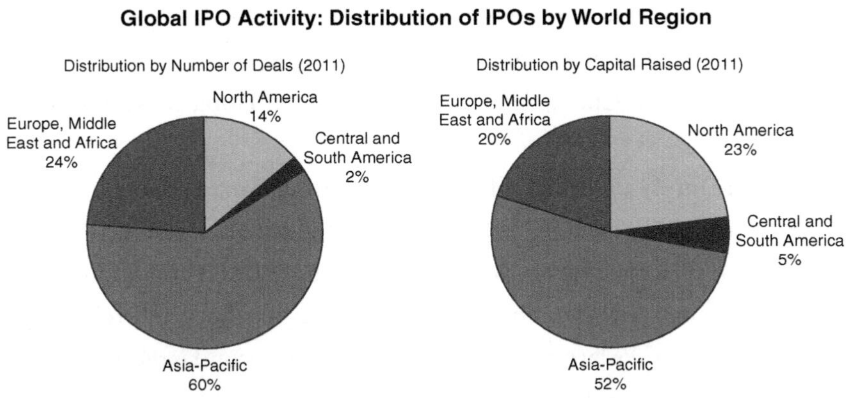

Figure 6.2 Distribution of IPOs by Location.
Sources: Author; "2012 Global IPO Update," E&Y, December 2012, pp. 28–29.

the volume being less than a third of the $14.7 billion priced in the same period last year. China has been top issuer nationality for global IPOs every year end but one (2008) since 2006. In all other years since 1995 the US has topped the rankings."[8]

China is not without its own problems in 2011. However, China has a lot of cash: "China, like Europe and the U.S., has a debt problem. On May 31 China agreed to provide as much as $436 billion to cover bad loans made to local governments, an amount equal to about half of the U.S.'s Troubled Asset Relief Program of 2008. But China also has a trump card that others don't: $3.2 trillion in cash reserves, by far the biggest hoard in the world."[9] If China deployed more cash toward venture capital, at this rate, one might not need to wait 89 years till the end of the century to see China fly by the United States. "China, Singapore and other command economies are directing increasing resources to human-capital development."[10] There appears to be an abundance of private equity and venture capital deals in China. It is likely China will open the floodgates, which will benefit not only Chinese investors but the rest of the world needing fuel for growth. Allowing this flexibility would be mutually beneficial. Chinese investors could diversify and perhaps gain access to faster exits. Likewise, there are plenty of other countries around the globe with talented entrepreneurs looking for investors. For example, Canada, South Korea, Brazil, India, Turkey, Israel, and many others.

China has opened new exchanges as well and has greatly improved its prowess in private equity. Astute domestic VCs and LBO firms were quick to notice and formed partnerships. "Preqin's extensive database shows that there are over 230 venture firms investing in China. 37% of these venture firms are based in China, 29% in the US, 11% in Hong Kong and 5% in the UK."

Hedge funds and other alternative investments are attracting interest. New commodities such as rare earth gained popularity and now there is even a new ETF for rare earth. China and commodities go hand in hand. As China grows, the demand for commodities has been unprecedented. China is the world's largest energy consumer and second largest consumer of oil behind the United States, but its demand for oil is growing rapidly, accounting for half of the world's oil consumption growth in 2011; China produced an estimated 4.3 million barrels per day of total oil liquids in 2011 and this was projected to rise by approximately 170 thousand barrels per day by the end of 2013.[11] A lot will transpire in China going forward and alternative investments will play a major role. "It is now a foregone conclusion that China's economy will become the biggest in the world sometime very soon. According to the World Bank, the size of China's economy is $10.1 trillion, compared with $14.6 trillion for the U.S., based on purchasing power parity."[12] One hundred years from now the landscape might be very different from today. The world's population is around 7 billion and China has a sizeable headcount. According to the Chinese government as of January 2013, its population exceeds 1,354,040,000 people.[13] Investors who think outside the box and explore alternative investments will most likely benefit.

There are different types of alternative investments, and they will have different risk as well as return profiles to examine. Investing in one alternative investment, therefore, does not mean one is well diversified. I have even seen boards of pension plans with well-educated members have similar provincial thinking. As shocking as it sounds, most do not know how to diversify with alternative investments. Buying shares in a mining company does not exactly make one diversified with alternative investments. There are different types of alternative investments as well as a plethora of investment options one can select to gain exposure to the world of alternative investments (Figure 6.3).

When you add up all alternative investments, it might be a larger space in terms of number of choices than the equity or fixed income markets. For

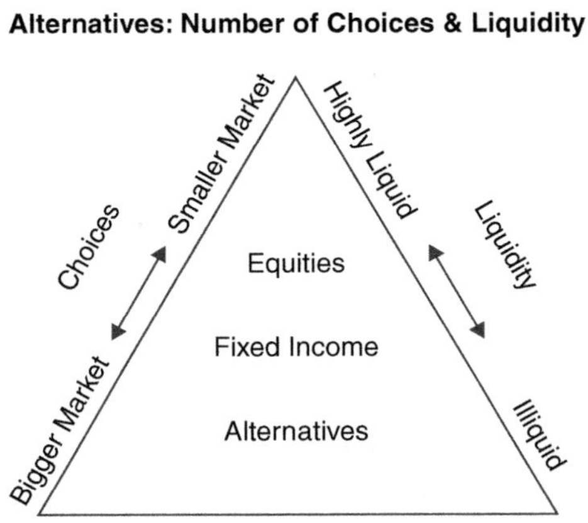

Figure 6.3 Number of Choices and Liquidity of Alternative Investments.
Source: Author.

example, if there are slightly more than 10,000 publicly traded domestic companies, the number of private companies dwarfs public companies by around 10 to 1 so there are over 100,000 private companies that one could select just from the United States. But alternative investments are (for the most part) illiquid, unlike stocks that are highly liquid. However, illiquidity can also happen with securities that are liquid. "Illiquidity can arise if volatility rises or if more agents face reduced risk-bearing capacity—for instance, because of investor redemptions, losses, or increased risk aversion."[14] Having a liquid security that becomes illiquid can be more troublesome to a lot of investors, as opposed to owning something illiquid from the start such as alternative investments. Any decision to invest in an alternative investment should not be made whimsically or by simply following the herd. It is irrelevant what one hears. Your 401(k), personal account, the pension plan you represent, or whatever situation you might find yourself in regarding alternative investments, needs to be carefully considered so you make the best possible choice. Selecting the right alternative investment is not easy.

As mentioned in *Wave Theory for Alternative Investments*, I wanted to cover three primary alternative investments and cover them well: hedge funds, commodities, and venture capital. While I covered three main types of alternative investments, there are still plenty of other alternative investments one could utilize. Some institutions have dominated their asset allocation with alternative investments. A manager named Jack Coates took over management of the underfund pension plan for U.S. forest products firm Weyerhauser in 1985 to 2010 and allocated substantially all of the fund's assets in opportunistic alternative investments which generated annualized returns of 15.3%.[15] While an investor might not typically replace equities and fixed income with alternative investments, they might be remiss in avoiding them altogether. Each decade, the alternative investments space grows larger, stemming back to the 1970s where a stock and bond approach was the norm to invest (Figure 6.4).

Modern Portfolio Theory (MPT) was started in the 1950s before anyone knew what alternative investments were, and over time, other asset classes as well as alternative investments grew. "The main organizing principle of MPT is efficient diversification. The basic idea is that any investor who is averse to risk, that is, who requires a higher expected return in order to increase exposure to risk, will be made better off by reorganizing the portfolio so as to increase its expected return without taking on additional risk."[16] MPT primarily revolves around stocks, bonds, and cash. Many investments that are commonplace today were unheard of back then or not available. For example, one could invest in real estate 60–70 years ago but REITs were not in existence till much later. "A REIT is similar to a closed-end mutual fund. REITs invest in real estate or loans secured by real estate. Besides issuing shares, they raise capital by borrowing from banks and issuing bonds and mortgages. Most of them are highly leveraged (debt-financed) with a typical debt ratio of 70%."[17] The playing field has opened up and alternative investments are now part of the investment world. As evidenced over time through both good and bad markets, adding alternative investments can possibly lower risk and increase returns (Figure 6.5).

In Morningstar Advisor, December/January 2010, "No Alternative But to Diversify," the editor Jerry Kerns states: "So-called alternative investments are getting a boost nowadays from investors scrambling to figure out what went wrong in their portfolios in 2008. Many investors who thought they were properly diversified actually weren't, and they took it on the chin hard. It was a wake-up call, and the rush to find strategies and investment vehicles that promise to offer truer diversification than mainstays such as emerging markets, commodities, and REITs is on."[18] The "smart money" or large institutional buckets of money are big believers in diversification.

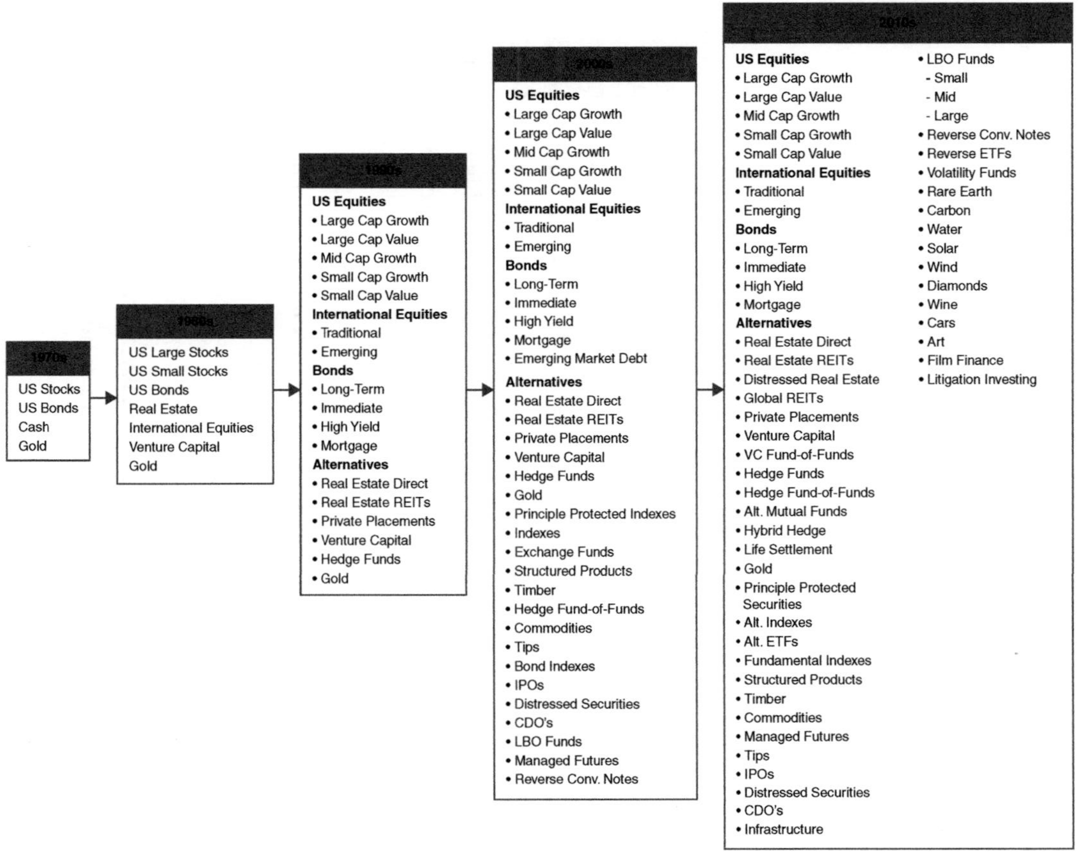

Figure 6.4 Growth of Alternative Investments.

Source: Author.

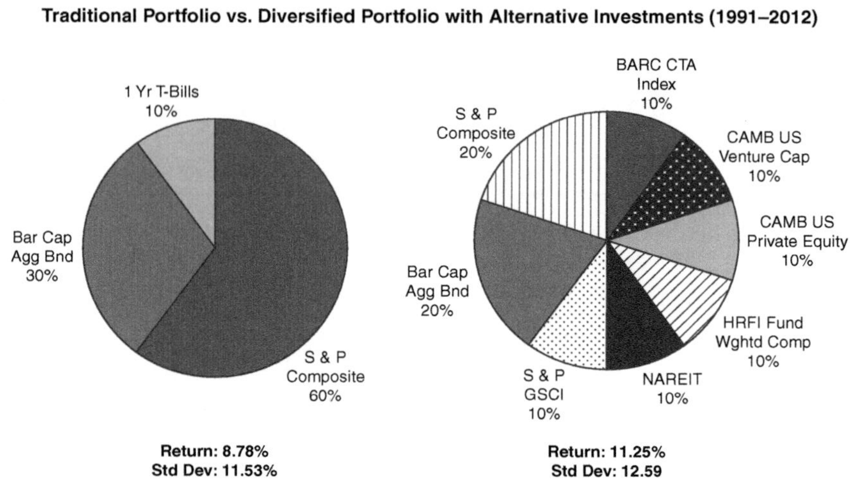

Figure 6.5 Traditional Portfolio vs. Diversified Portfolio with Alternative Investments.
Source: Author.

"Diversification reduces variability."[19] Even in the thick of the storm, the majority of the "smart money" never abandoned alternative investments. Some institutions were tied to schools that needed funds because the stock and bond part of their portfolios dropped so much that they needed to explore any and every way of seeking liquidity. A number of high net worth investors inquired or tried to pull money from alternative investments. However, they had lockups or would have exit fees so they left the money alone, which turned out to be a good thing. Panicking and selling blindly are two excellent ways to lose money. In fact, the antithesis transpired with a lot of the "smart money" and they added to their allocations rather than sold or withdrew funds (Figure 6.6).

The largest corporate pension plans have more than 20 percent invested in alternative investments. Virtually all smart money invests in alternative investments. Sovereign wealth funds (SWFs) diversify with alternative investments. For example, Middle Eastern SWFs have remarkably diverse investment portfolios. In Monitor's "Testing Time Sovereign Wealth Funds in The Middle East & North Africa and The Global Financial Crises," May 2009, showed that institutional funds (that include alternative investments as opposed to ones that do not or have very little allocated to alternative investments) do better:Since they have not needed to persuade stakeholders to agree to increased exposure to risk and illiquid assets, such as real estate, Middle Eastern SWFs could diversify their portfolios early

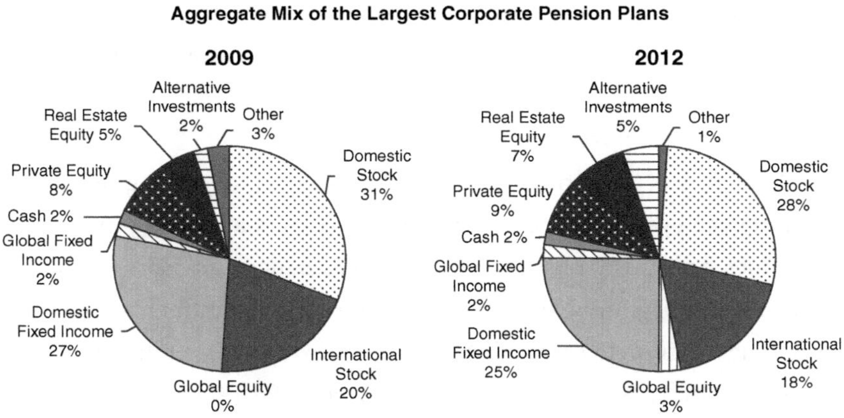

Figure 6.6 Large Pension Plans and Alternative Investments.

Sources: "Aggregate Asset Mixes," *Pensions and Investments*, February 7, 2011, p. 27, February 6, 2012, p. 20, February 4, 2013, p. 28.

on, and thus deliver high returns from the outset. Since its establishment in 1976, ADIA has delivered an annual return of about 10 percent, compared with the 3.94 percent gained by Norway's Government Pension Fund—Global, the most transparent SWF, since its foundation in 1998.[20] SWFs consider utilizing different asset classes, especially alternative investments. In Wharton's "The Brave New World of Sovereign Wealth Funds," two Middle Eastern SWFs were described as having success with alternative investments: "KIA and ADIA, with their long track record and expertise, followed a very prudent strategy in achieving safe investments. They have also built their internal teams and have learned institutionally from their mistakes. No asset class was excluded over time, including real estate, private equity, hedge funds, listed equities and direct investments."[21]

By adding alternative investments to a traditional stock and bond portfolio, risk is often lowered and returns are increased. I ran hundreds of models and collected a large amount of data from 1994 to 2010 that illustrates this fact. An investor limiting investment selection is nothing short of being remiss; a wide range of investments should be considered. "Another means to control portfolio risk is diversification, by which we mean that investments are made in a wide variety of assets so that the exposure to risk of any particular security is limited."[22] No asset class should be automatically excluded. Investors with bias and closed minds typically do not fare well. As SEI and Strategic Insight explain in the Executive Summary of "Exotic to Mainstream," "Respected investment strategists have concluded that diversification remains a valid approach although it has become more difficult to achieve and warrants incorporation of a broader set of risk exposures and asset classes, both long and short, in investor portfolios."[23]

Evidence of how the alternative investments space is growing and catching the eye of both investors and advisors is appearing in a variety of venues previously unseen. For instance, financial advisors and wealth managers are beginning to be tested on alternative investments. The three-year-long program to earn a CFA now covers extensively a number of alternative investments. In each Level of the 2014 CFA Program Curriculum, an entire session is devoted to Alternative Investments. Alternative investments are different from bonds and equities. They might possibly help lower risk and increase returns. The CFA program covers real estate, private equity (LBO and venture capital), commodities, and hedge funds. It is now possible to earn a designation with CAIA (Chartered Alternative Investment Analyst). "The CAIA designation is recognized globally as the benchmark for the analysis, application, and standards of practice in the alternative investment arena."[24]

The majority of mutual fund companies now offer alternative investments such as market neutral, absolute-return, unconstrained, long/short, all asset, commodities, short selling, real estate, distressed debt, merger-arbitrage, Treasury Inflation Protected Securities, and many others. For instance, PIMCO, which is a leading global investment management firm founded in 1971 and known for its prowess with fixed income, now has a total of 13 alternative investments funds out of 57 mutual funds in 2011. Mutual funds adding alternative funds is both good and bad. On the one hand, investors have more selection and more diversification. On the other hand, mutual fund companies are expanding and going into a new area with alternative investments. Unchartered waters with investing can lead to losses and sometimes very large losses that might never be recovered. Mutual fund companies are struggling with adding alternative investments. The largest mutual fund company in the United States, BlackRock, offered the iShares Diversified Alternative Trust (ALT) on October 6, 2009. Performance was lackluster and the mutual fund company shut it down in 2013. "iShares expects the liquidation of ALT to be completed and a final distribution of the cash proceeds to be made to its shareholders on or about June 4, 2013."[25] More troubling is that iShares rarely shuts down ETFs. "ALT's closure may come as a shock to some investors, as iShares has a reputation for not closing ETFs. The firm has not closed an ETF since 2002."[26] Another large mutual fund company, Nuveen, has also experienced difficulty offering alternative mutual funds. Nuveen Investments, known for fixed income, bought part of Gresham Investment Management LLC. Gresham is the commodity sub-advisor for a closed-end commodity IPO called the Nuveen Long/Short Commodity Total Return Fund on October 25, 2012, which was priced at $25 per share but the fund dropped -24.68 percent by July 31, 2013.[27]

The CEO of one of the largest mutual fund companies in the world told me that alternative investments were his "number one priority." Alternative mutual funds saw $87.6 billion in inflows, bringing total assets in that category to $125.7 billion.[28] Mutual fund companies will likely continue to cater to the growing demand of investor interest in alternative investments both domestically and abroad. SEI and Strategic Insight report, "Alternative mutual funds and UCITS are attracting significant flows. In 2009, investors poured $110 billion into alternative mutual funds, with the largest flows going into long/short, market neutral, commodity, and currency funds."[29] Barron's reported on April 11, 2011, a total of 82 new alternatives funds with $40.4 billion in net flows and 14 commodities funds with $26.1 billion in net flows since the beginning of 2009. Investors are especially "drawn to products that act like hedge funds, taking both long and short positions in stocks."[30] Figure 6.7 is a chart showing US mutual funds/ETF assets.

Toward the beginning of 2013, I had breakfast with Jack Bogel, the founder of Vanguard. While Jack literally started the industry for low-cost mutual funds for equity and fixed income, he recognizes the importance of alternative investments. In his most recent book, *Don't Count On It!*, Jack begins to explore using alternative investments with stocks and bonds or as he states, "alternative classes." It is also no coincidence that Vanguard has added numerous low-cost indexes and funds devoted to alternative-like investments. His book acknowledges waves with equities (large cap versus small cap and value versus growth), and he even praises Benjamin Franklin

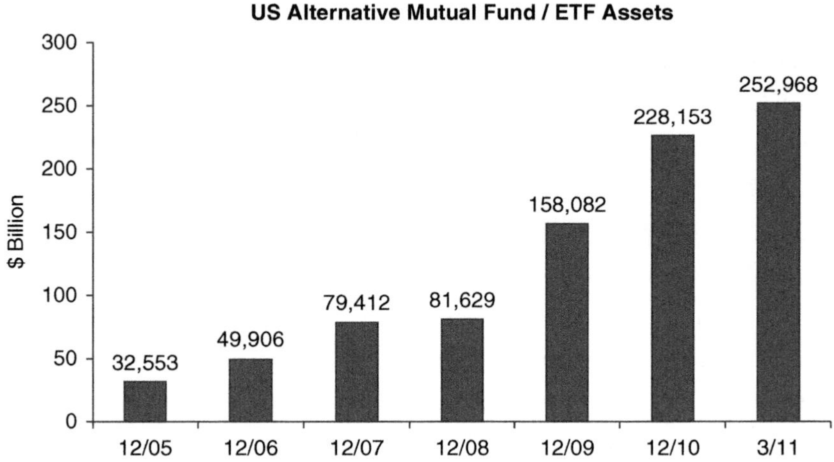

Figure 6.7 Domestic Alternative Mutual Fund/ETF Assets.
Sources: Author; Strategic Insight Simfund.

as an entrepreneur: "Let's begin with Franklin's entrepreneurship. It was not only remarkable for his era; it was remarkable for any era."[31] Benjamin Franklin was one of the greatest entrepreneurs ever.

I noticed a trend starting in 2006 and I gave a presentation on alternative investments at The Merion Cricket Club. Mutual funds were becoming more hedge fund-like and hedge funds started to act more like mutual funds. While my presentation was prescient at the time, not until 2012 did this trend become visible: "The Morningstar and *Barron's* Alternative Investment Survey of U.S. Institutions and Financial Advisors aims to capture trends in alternative investing. Judging by this year's responses, advisers are increasingly using mutual funds to get at alternative strategies and asset classes."[32] At the time of my presentation in 2006, there were no such funds. I was the first to outline the model which I nicknamed, "The Hybrid Hedge." The model was later published by McGraw-Hill in my book, *Wave Theory for Alternative Investments*. Today, there are many mutual funds utilizing alternative investment like strategies. "Managed futures and currency mutual funds recorded inflows of $3.6 billion and $3.4 billion, respectively, in 2011, despite the fact that managed futures lost 6.9% that year, while currency funds lost money every year since 2008."[33] Hedge funds are changing. The Hybrid Hedge, which utilizes the best of both worlds between alternatives and mutual funds, is now a reality. Several fund companies and banks attempted to copy my idea with the Hybrid Hedge model since 2006. "Alternative investments and mutual funds have historically existed in separate realms—where high-net-worth and institutional investors have been the beneficiaries of access to the former, and a broader range of investors have taken advantage of the strengths of the latter. However, recent years have seen a blurring of the lines between the two worlds—and that shift has gathered momentum in the wake of the financial crisis."[34]

There are negatives to both hedge funds and mutual funds. The downside of hedge funds is that they can be costly, not very transparent, illiquid, and unregulated. Because hedge funds used to be for institutions and high net worth individuals only, the mutual fund industry identified a marketing opportunity for retail investors by offering mutual funds with hedge fund like strategies. "Investor interest in hedge-fund strategies has never been higher—but it's the mutual-fund industry that seems to be benefiting."[35] Mutual funds are not hedge funds and it has been a difficult task for mutual funds to create funds that resemble hedge funds; they are different vehicles. Certain mutual fund organizations took existing funds and tried to market them as alternative or hedge fund like mutual funds with little success. The ideal vehicle would be a combination of the two vehicles (hedge funds and mutual funds) seeking the least amount of negative characteristics while attempting to maximize the positive attributes of both. The hybrid hedge has many of the positive attributes of both hedge funds and mutual funds but without the negatives (Figure 6.8).

BUSINESS SCHOOLS CATCH ON TO ALTERNATIVE INVESTMENT STRATEGIES

Business school classes are also covering alternative investments. Yale, UVA, Stanford, Wharton, and other fine schools have been early adopters. Years ago, there were entrepreneur classes or M&As. Today, entire classes are devoted to alternative investments. Wharton, for example, offered a class called "Advanced Seminar on Private Equity" in the spring of 2011.
A number of cutting-edge, top-notch business schools such as Wharton have even expanded related courses such as Behavioral Finance, taught by Professor Yu Yuan, where the syllabus starts, "Over the past several

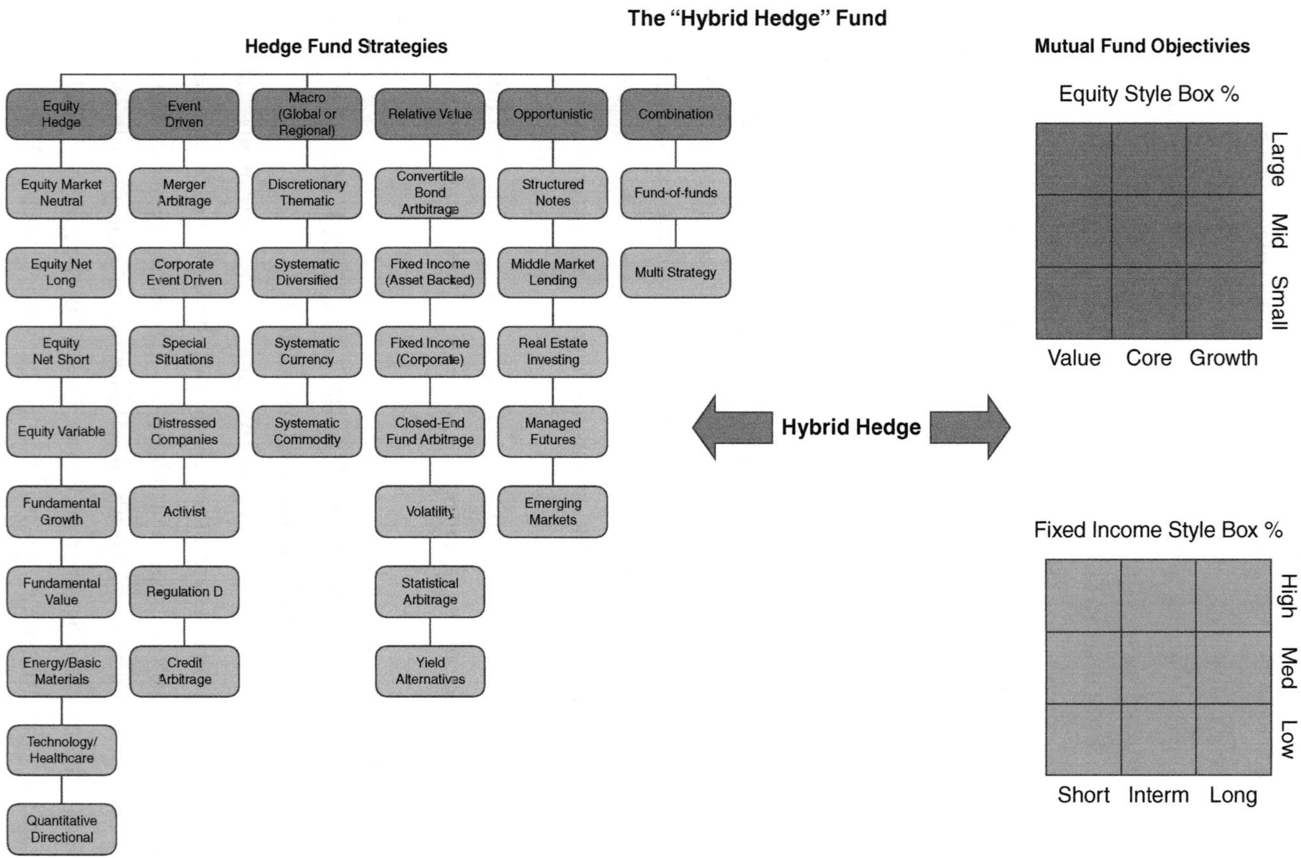

Figure 6.8 The "Hybrid Hedge" Fund.

Source: *Wave Theory for Alternative Investments*, McGraw-Hill, Stratosphere, LLC, p. 342.

decades, the field of finance has developed a successful paradigm."[36] But many business schools are having problems and fail to see the significance of alternative investments, which is a tremendous disservice to students. "Yet, privately at least, some business schools are worried that a two-year decline, along with a level of applications from American students lower than it has been this century, is more than just a response to the economy. They fear that the established model of business education may be in trouble, if not for all schools, then definitely for mid-ranking American institutions offering a traditional two-year MBA."[37]

There is a definite need for education with alternative investments. While many business schools have received substantial donations from those involved with alternative investments, few offer classes on the subject. Only a handful of top-tier schools in the United States offer courses on alternative investments, such as venture capital, real estate, IPOs, entrepreneurship, M&As, and others. Yet a growing number of schools outside the United States have seen value to adding courses devoted to alternative investments and are quickly embracing the subject matter with alacrity. As part of our DNA, we tend to cling or gravitate to what we are familiar with, not the unknown. As human beings, we are naturally afraid of the unknown. Investors tend to initiate avoidance behavior, like an ostrich sticking its head in the sand when faced with something new. For example, certain investors prefer to invest in their own countries and have a strong bias that where they live is superior to the rest of the world. "People simply prefer to invest in the familiar" and "Each investor is most optimistic about his own country's equity returns."[38] Even sports teams tend to play better at home hence the name, "home court advantage." Alternative investments are global, not just for the United States. The growth potential with alternative investments is likely with unchartered waters in areas of the world not known presently for alternative investments. When I started my financial career in the early 1990s, trend-setting advisors were just adding some foreign exposure to asset allocation models. The models at best had 5 percent of foreign exposure. Virtually no advisor or clients were examining alternative investments in the early 1990s.

Getting investors to understand what lies on the other side of the fence is somewhat daunting, which might also explain why US business schools have been slow to adapt to the world of alternative investments. Alternative investments involve a space that is not that well known compared to the commonplace classes concerning accounting, marketing, finance, human resources, and other topics that are standard at every business school. Most investors and business schools do not think outside the box. Only the forward-thinking ones do and they have been rewarded by higher rankings, smarter students, and bigger donations.

Business schools slow to catch on with alternative investments, let alone relevant topics such as Behavioral Finance, will invariably fall further behind and hurt themselves; they will miss the education wave. What does missing the wave mean for business schools? Less donations. After all, some of the largest donors for business schools made fortunes with alternative investments. Donald Trump, Carl Icahn, Leon Black, Stephen Schwartzman, and Ronald Perelman all earned a lot of money from alternative investments. Incidentally, they all went to Wharton. Other schools are receiving large donations as well. Henry Robert Kravis, one of the partners of KKR, pledged $100 million to Columbia Business School in October 2010 to help pay for an expansion of the school.[39] Education in the United States is struggling but continues to escalate in cost. Overall, per-pupil spending has risen from $5,671 in 1970 to $12,922 in 2007–2008—a 128 percent rise—and public school employment has been ten times the rate of student enrollment while school district administrative staff per pupil has doubled.[40] Because of the high cost, students are taking out even more loans:

> The cost of university per student has risen by almost five times the rate of inflation since 1983, making it less affordable and increasing the amount of debt a student must take on. Between 2001 and 2010 the cost of a university education soared from 23% of the median annual earnings to 38%; in consequence, debt per student has doubled in the past 15 years. Two-thirds of graduates now take out loans.[41]

Schools will invariably need to justify the increased cost to parents and students. In the United States, there is an education crisis. Tuition costs have skyrocketed. Focusing on alternative investments will likely be prudent for many schools as a useful tool to provide to students as well as a source to attract meaningful gifts. A 9-foot-tall (2.7-meter-tall) bronze spider sculpted by Louise Bourgeois sits in front of the Black Family Visual Arts Center, built with $48 million from buyout billionaire Leon Black, who graduated from Dartmouth in 1973.[42] Rising tuition costs and a poor job market, along with a surplus of graduates, puts pressure on schools to differentiate themselves and show a value proposition. Median pay was down in 2012 and it is much harder for newly minted graduates to get hired. Studying something useful will likely pay off. I will always remember a business school class that I had about entrepreneurs, and that was a really time long ago.

7

HEDGE FUNDS: EVIL OR ANGELS IN DISGUISE?

Often the best time to invest is when it appears to be the worst time, when market conditions are deplorable. Smart Money typically has good timing. "The number of public pension plans investing in hedge funds has leapt 50% since 2007 to about 300, according to Preqin. State pension systems had $63 billion invested in hedge funds as of their fiscal 2010 and are expected to invest another $20 billion in hedge funds in the next two years, according to a recent report by consultant Cliffwater."[1] Hedge funds became better not worse after the Great Recession, as so many mistakenly predicted. Hedge funds have become more attractive to investors, both on an institutional and on a retail level. The landscape for hedge funds has ultimately become more competitive. Hedge funds have even lowered their fees. "The overwhelmingly majority of investors interviewed, both large and small, are united in the belief that the industry's 2 and 20 fee structure is not sustainable—and that a number of the practices in the alternative investment industry (such as gates, side-pockets, etc.) will not endure."[2] One of the best-known hedge funds, Paul Tudor Jones, lowered fees. Hedge funds were also shown to add value, as evidenced by studies done on institutional investors in hedge funds. Returns also improved. Everett M. Ehrlich in "The Changing Role of Hedge Funds in the Global Economy" examined various institutional investors and "found that reallocating 10 percent of pension portfolios to hedge funds has the potential to add approximately $13.67 billion in returns yearly. Our analysis found similar potential for university endowments, which stand to add more than $1.73 billion in expected returns per year by shifting 10 percent of assets to hedge funds."[3]

Taking a contrarian view after the Great Recession when it appeared perilous to invest in hedge funds and going against the grain is easier said than done. It takes both courage and discipline. Likewise, discovering and exploring areas that might not necessarily be well understood or are off the beaten path can sometimes lead to the best returns. "A glimpse into the secretive world of large U.S. endowment funds reveals strong, benchmark- and index-topping returns of their hedge fund portfolios. Just six of the 25 largest U.S. endowments provided publicly available, detailed financial information for June 30, the fiscal year-end for many endowments. In examining that information, *Pensions & Investments* found the six had a collective $89 billion in assets as of June 30, of which $18.4 billion was in hedge funds."[4] All assets should be considered when investing and the greater the selection, the more likely an investor will lower risk. The smart money did not abandon hedge funds. Hedge Fund Research (HFR), which tracks hedge funds, showed hedge funds increasing from 1990 to YTD Q2 2013 (Figure 7.1).

The hedge fund industry concluded 2010 with the largest quarterly increase in assets in its history, according to data released today by HFR,

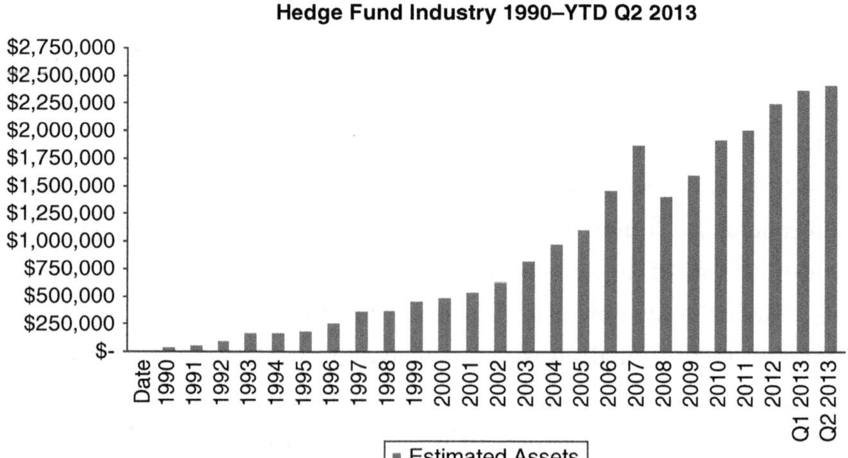

Figure 7.1 Hedge Fund Growth of Assets.

Source: HFR Global Hedge Fund Industry Reports, © 2013 HFR Inc., www.hedgefundresearch.com

the leading provider of hedge fund industry data. "Analysis of asset class returns shows that, after extraordinarily good or bad performance, a reversal of fortunes occurs more often than not."[5] Flash forward to 2013 and the hedge fund industry grew to approximately $2.5 trillion. What happened? For starters, institutional investors even began investing directly into hedge funds. "New and experienced institutional investors are more comfortable investing directly in hedge funds either with the assistance of a specialist hedge fund consultant or through a customized hedge fund portfolio managed by a hedge fund-of-funds manager thanks to lessons of the recent past."[6] The Massachusetts state pension fund, governed by the Pension Reserves Investment Trust, in April 2011, said they would invest directly into hedge funds.[7] The Ohio Public Employees Retirement System (PERS) stated it was investing directly in hedge funds in 2011.[8] "The Fire & Police Pension Association of Colorado, which manages roughly $3.5 billion, now has 11% of its portfolio allocated to hedge funds after having no cash invested in these funds at the start of the year."[9] "New Jersey's State Investment Council, which sets investment policy for the state's pension, voted last week to raise the target allocation for hedge funds to 10% from 6.7%, which would make hedge funds the $73 billion fund's largest alternative investment asset."[10] Figure 7.2 is a chart of inflows versus outflows.

The "smart money" sought hedge funds like never before. Bridgewater, one of the largest hedge funds with assets around $100 billion, raised a new fund. "Bridgewater Associates is nearly finished launching

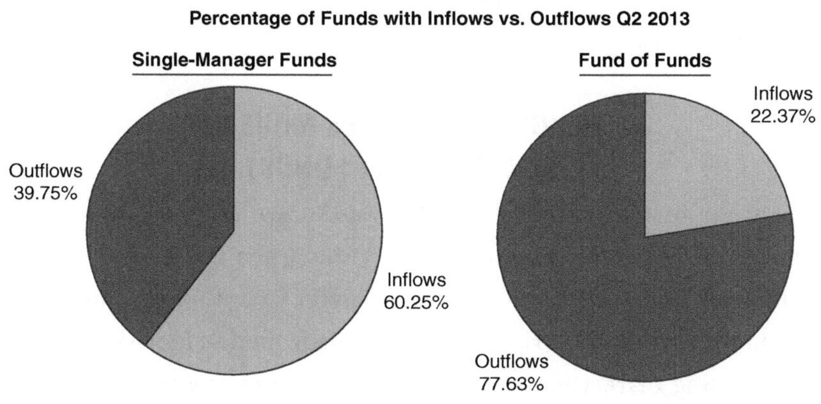

Figure 7.2 Hedge Fund Inflows and Outflows.

Source: HFR Global Hedge Fund Industry Reports, © 2013 HFR Inc., www.hedgefundresearch.com

a $10 billion fund, the latest sign of the hedge-fund industry's rebound from the 2008 financial crisis."[11] However, these flows went to single manager hedge funds as opposed to hedge funds of funds. Hedge funds of funds were almost the polar opposite with monthly outflows as opposed to inflows. Growth of defined benefit assets reached an all-time new high.

Total industry assets grew to $1.917 trillion, reflecting a quarterly increase of nearly $149 billion, topping the previous record increase of $140 billion in Q2, 2007.[12] "Hedge fund assets rose to 1.6% from 1.3% of total worldwide assets compared to the previous year."[13] Pension funds like to invest in hedge funds; they are one of the preferred alternative investments. Hedge funds have compelling risk and reward ratios.

Over the decade that included two horrendous market collapses, hedge funds exhibited better returns, with lower risk than both the S&P 500 and the MSCI World Index.

Hedge funds are likely to continue to grow: "Total industry assets rose to $2.02 trillion, up $102 billion in the first quarter. The total tops the pre-crises record of $1.93 trillion set in the second quarter of 2008."[14] Hedge fund assets were only $38.9 billion in 1990. As of the end of third quarter 2011, hedge fund assets were $2.04 trillion. According to *Pensions and Investments* analysis of reported hedge fund search and hiring activity, "This year is shaping up to be the strongest for institutional investment in hedge funds since 2007. Institutional investors, especially U.S. public pension plans, have been pouring new money into hedge funds to the tune of $39.9 billion of net inflows and pending searches year-to-date through Nov. 10."[15]

HEDGE FUND STYLES MOVE IN WAVES (QUANT FUNDS)

One of the first styles of hedge funds was known as quant funds. Quant funds initially became popular in the 1990s when PhDs headed toward Wall Street. Essentially, a quantitative analyst ("quant") uses numerical or qualitative techniques. Originally, quants made models for risk assessment or predicting market movements. Today, the term applies to individuals involved in almost any application of mathematics in finance. Statistical arbitrage and market neutral are two types of popular quant funds. Computers do the trading as opposed to humans. Complex mathematical models analyze large amounts of data and decide which investments should be bought or sold. Many quants follow a momentum strategy; they buy securities rising in price or sell ones dropping in price. They might buy equities with accelerated earnings.

In 2009 most of the securities that did well were high risk and not conservative. For example, high yield (junk bonds) did well. Companies with little or no profits rose in price faster than good companies with earnings, which hurt the quant models. What happened was not supposed to happen and therefore the models failed. 2009 and 2010 were years that caused quant funds trouble: "The assets of a broader universe of quant hedge funds have dwindled by about $50 billion. One in four quant hedge funds have closed since 2007, according to Lipper Tass."[16] Many of the models went askew and seemed unprepared for a rogue wave where the majority of securities all plunged at once. Not only did various asset classes plummet at the same time but markets such as the ARP market evaporated, creating a liquidity crises. In essence, the market experienced the perfect storm.

Yet quantitative funds have an important attribute. Whereas human nature can interfere with prudent investment decisions, quant funds are run by computers that show no emotion. "Quantitative trading still has many advantages over its chief competitor, the human brain. From the individual who holds on to losing stocks for too long to overconfident money managers who mistakenly think they can predict financial trends, human nature is capable of placing bad bets time and time again. Psychology and raw emotion often rules the stock market."[17] Waves change with alternative investments and hedge fund styles. "Welcome to the Age of Quant. As high-speed trading continues to define the markets, quantitative strategies are all the rage, and quants are Wall Street's hottest stars."[18] As the hedge fund industry evolved over time, different styles formed.

HEDGE FUND WAVES

Hedge funds as a whole move in waves as exhibited by all alternative investments. As more data became apparent over time, it became evident that styles change and move in waves, not too dissimilar from the equity with large cap versus small cap or growth versus value investing. Table 7.1 shows how hedge funds styles changed over the years.

What was popular in the 1990s (Equity Hedge and Macro) was not as popular in 2010. Likewise, what was not in favor in the 1990s (Relative Value and Event Driven) was attractive to investors in 2010. Relative Value attracted more assets from 2010 to 2013 (Figure 7.3).

Increasing assets and number of funds tend to correlate with better performance. As performance did well for Relative Value, new funds were created and more assets were attracted. Relative Value gained more market share. Figure 7.4 is an estimated sub-strategy composition for Relative Value, Q2—2013 with regard to number of funds and assets.

Table 7.1 Estimated Strategy Composition by Assets under Management

	Q4 1990	Q4 2010
Relative Value	13.88%	24.44%
Equity Hedge Driven	37.07%	29.76%
Event Driven	9.75%	25.94%
Macro	39.30%	19.86%

Source: HFR Global Hedge Fund Industry Reports, © 2013 HFR Inc., www.hedgefundresearch.com.

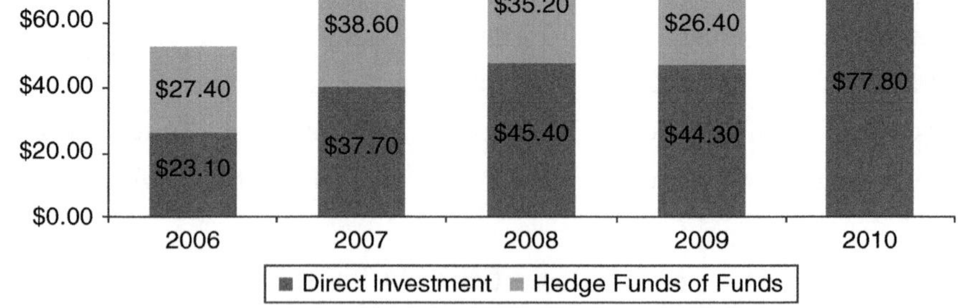

Figure 7.3 Defined Benefit Investments in Hedge Funds.

Source: HFR Global Hedge Fund Industry Reports, © 2013 HFR Inc., www.hedgefundresearch.com

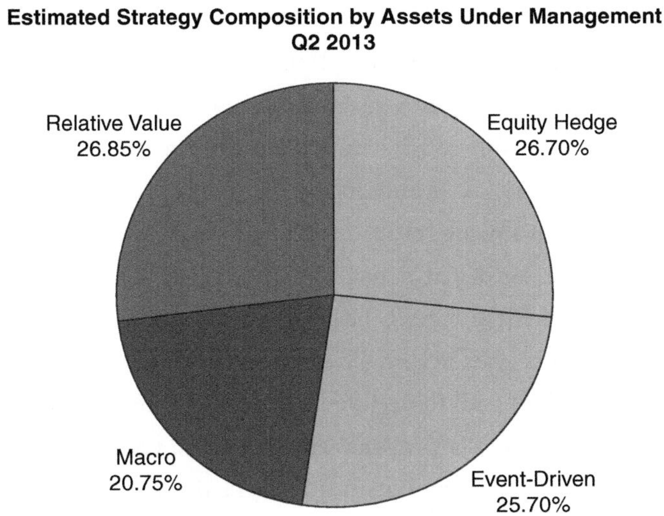

Figure 7.4 Hedge Fund Assets by Strategy.
Source: HFR Global Hedge Fund Industry Reports, © 2013 HFR Inc., www.hedgefundresearch.com

Global Macro dropped to around half of the assets under management. "Macro-focused managers have been tripped up by whiplash-inducing swings in stocks, currencies and commodities, often brought about by the latest twists and turns of impossible-to-time political developments. Stubbornly low U.S. Treasury yields have been a trap for managers worried about inflation and the deteriorating U.S. fiscal outlook. Making matters worse is a tendency of markets around the world to move in lock step."[19] The European debt crises and problems along with the US Treasuries receiving a downgrade would appear to benefit Macro funds. However, that was not the case and it became increasingly difficult to find special opportunities. "Macro funds generally hunt among global financial markets in search of opportunities created by big-picture economic, fiscal and political trends."[20]

Global macro was a hedge fund style that performed quite well in 2007 and 2008 when the stock market was hammered. As the stock market turned around in 2009 with the S&P 500 going up 26.47 percent and 2010 (15.08 percent), Global Macro did not fare as well. Global Macro outperformed the S&P 500 in 2000, 2001, and 2002 when the S&P 500 was down -9.09 percent in 2000, -11.85 percent in 2001, and -22.09 percent in 2002. The S&P 500 then outperformed Global Macro in 2003 and 2004. While there can be an anomaly, certain patterns, trends, or cycles (Wave

Theory) can be evidenced with hedge funds and hedge fund styles. When the stock market performed well in 1998 and 1999, the S&P 500 outperformed Global Macro in both years. It is also of interest that the HFRI Wghtd Comp outperformed the HOF Composite every year from 1998 to 2010 except two years (2002 and 2007).

Ideally, the funds being selected for a hedge fund of funds will outperform the index because of active management. The bank or consultant selecting the hedge funds should ideally be picking better hedge funds and buying/selling when appropriate. Presumably, they add value. Hedge funds focusing on Emerging Markets tend to decline the most at the break of a market collapse but they tend to rally the quickest. This trend happened in 2003 and after 2010. Many investors and institutions still afraid of hedge funds claim they do not like the volatility and the wide swings they perceive embody hedge funds. Yet equities exhibit more volatility than the HFRI Fund Wghtd Comp. Returns are more reliable than the wide range exhibited by stocks. A group of hedge funds with different styles will not have as many highs and lows as the S&P 500 Index. For instance, in 1998, the S&P 500 was the best performer. Similarly, it performed the best in 2010. However, during 2001 and 2002, the S&P 500 was the worst performer. A key difference is the ability for a hedge fund to short. Shorting protects on the downside. Figure 7.5 shows the HFRI Indices annual investment returns (2000–YTD Q2 2013).

Hedge fund strategies move in waves, as depicted by the HFRI Indices Annual Investment Returns. Investors, similar to mutual fund investing,

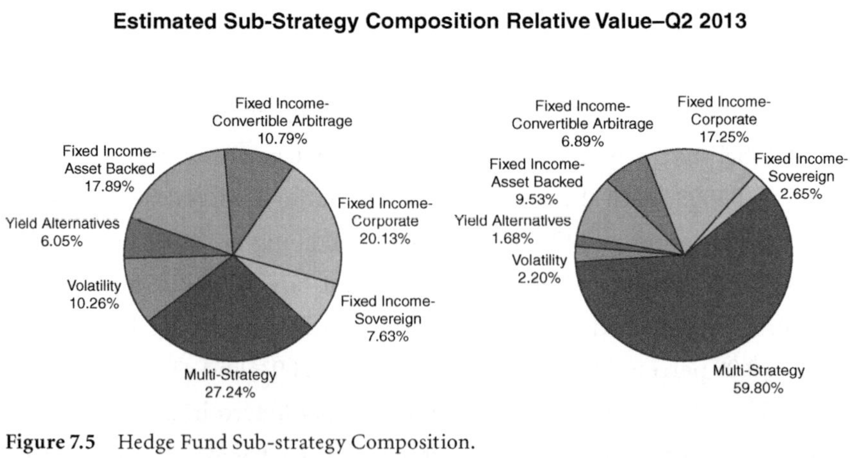

Figure 7.5 Hedge Fund Sub-strategy Composition.

Source: HFR Global Hedge Fund Industry Reports, © 2013 HFR Inc., www.hedgefundresearch.com

frequently chase returns of the best-performing hedge fund strategy. However, hedge fund strategies can move in and out of favor just like stocks or bonds. "The class of hedge fund strategies termed *arbitrage strategies* has historically produced stable, modest returns punctuated by intervals of dramatically poor performance. The weakness stems from an important oversight in modeling: hedge fund returns and their underlying risks factors can have a nonlinear relationship."[21] In terms of number of hedge funds, Equity Hedge was almost half of all hedge funds by 2013 (Figure 7.6).

A number of the funds cited in *Wave Theory for Alternative Investments* continue to grow and prosper. Ray Dalio's Bridgewater Associates LP has scored gains of more than $3.5 billion in its flagship hedge fund and the $71 billion fund now is up more than 20 percent this year, making it among the best performers in the hedge fund business.[22] Below are net returns of single-manager hedge funds by strategy (Table 7.2).

As of June 2013, Relative Value was at the top of the charts. Charts like these can be useful for an investor to see signs of a particular hedge fund style coming back in vogue. Preqin and HFRI offer excellent charts. Global Macro moves in waves like the other hedge fund styles, and hedge funds as a whole move in waves. As seen by the HFRI Indices Annual Investment Return 2000–TYD Q2 2013, Relative Value was trading higher as well as Distressed Hedge Fund Event Driven. Macro continued to slide.

Table 7.2 Hedge Fund Waves by Strategy

Apr-13	May-13	Jun-13	Q1 2013	Q2 2013
Event Driven 1.14%	**Event Driven** 2.02%	**Relative Value** −0.59%	**Event Driven** 4.17%	**Event Driven** 2.30%
CTAs 0.98%	**Long/Short** 1.33%	**Event Driven** −0.85%	**Long/Short** 4.15%	**Relative Value** 0.82%
Relative Value 0.94%	**Multi-Strategy** 0.85%	**Ctas** −1.26%	**Relative Value** 2.56%	**Long/Short** 0.32%
Long/Short 0.68%	**Relative Value** 0.47%	**Multi-Strategy** −1.49%	**Multi-Strategy** 2.13%	**Multi-Strategy** −0.26%
Multi-Strategy 0.39%	**Macro Strategies** 0.06%	**Macro Strategies** −1.51%	**Ctas** 1.24%	**Macro Strategies** −1.42%
Macro Strategies 0.02%	**Ctas** −2.02%	**Long/Short** −1.66%	**Macro Strategies** 1.14%	**Ctas** −2.30%

Source: "The Preqin Quarterly Update: Hedge Funds," Preqin, July 2013, p. 3.

HFRI Indices Annual Investment Returns (2000 – YTD Q2 2013)

2000	2001	2002	2003	2004	2005	2006	2007	2008	2009	2010	2011	2012	YTD Q2 2013
HFRI ED: Merger Arb 18.02%	HFRI RV: ConvertArb 13.37%	Barclays Gov't/Credit 12.10%	HFRI Emerging Markets 39.36%	HFRI ED: Distressed 18.89%	HFRI Emerging Markets 21.04%	HFRI Emerging Markets 24.26%	HFRI Emerging Markets 24.92%	Barclays Gov't/Credit 6.09%	HFRI RV: ConvertArb 60.17%	S&P 500 15.08%	Barclays Gov't/Credit 9.24%	S&P 500 15.99%	S&P 500 13.82%
HFRI EH: Eq Mrkt Ntrl 14.56%	HFRI ED: Distressed 13.28%	HFRI RV: ConvertArb 9.05%	HFRI ED: Distressed 29.56%	HFRI Emerging Markets 18.42%	HFRI Equity Hedge 10.60%	HFRI ED: Distressed 15.94%	HFRI Macro 11.11%	HFRI Macro 4.83%	HFRI Emerging Markets 40.24%	HFRI RV: ConvertArb 13.07%	S&P 500 2.09%	HFRI Relative Value 10.59%	HFRI ED: Distressed 6.79%
HFRI RV: ConvertArb 14.50%	HFRI Event-Driven 12.18%	HFRI Macro 7.44%	S&P 500 28.67%	HFRI Event-Driven 15.01%	HFRI Fund Wghtd Comp 9.30%	S&P 500 15.78%	HFRI Equity Hedge 10.48%	HFRI ED: Merger Arb -5.36%	HFRI ED: Distressed 28.13%	HFRI Emerging Markets 11.96%	HFRI ED: Merger Arb 1.48%	HFRI Emerging Markets 10.37%	HFRI Event-Driven 5.65%
HFRI Relative Value 13.41%	HFRI Emerging Markets 10.36%	HFRI Relative Value 5.44%	HFRI Event-Driven 25.33%	S&P 500 10.86%	HFRI ED: Distressed 8.27%	HFRI Event-Driven 15.33%	HFRI FOF Composite 10.25%	HFRI EH: Eq Mrkt Ntrl -5.93%	S&P 500 26.47%	HFRI Relative Value 11.73%	HFRI Relative Value 0.15%	HFRI ED: Distressed 10.12%	HFRI Equity Hedge 5.34%
Barclays Gov't/Credit 13.27%	Barclays Gov't/Credit 9.40%	HFRI ED: Distressed 5.28%	HFRI Macro 21.42%	HFRI Fund Wghtd Comp 9.03%	HFRI FOF Composite 7.49%	HFRI ED: Merger Arb 14.24%	HFRI Fund Wghtd Comp 9.96%	HFRI Relative Value -18.04%	HFRI Relative Value 25.80%	HFRI Event-Driven 11.53%	HFRI ED: Distressed -1.79%	HFRI Event-Driven 8.89%	HFRI RV: ConvertArb 4.35%
HFRI Equity Hedge 9.09%	HFRI Relative Value 8.92%	HFRI Emerging Markets 3.70%	HFRI Equity Hedge 20.54%	HFRI Equity Hedge 7.68%	HFRI Event-Driven 7.29%	HFRI Fund Wghtd Comp 12.89%	HFRI Relative Value 8.94%	HFRI Fund Wghtd Comp -19.02%	HFRI Event-Driven 25.04%	HFRI ED: Distressed 11.26%	HFRI EH: Eq Mrkt Ntrl -2.12%	HFRI RV: ConvertArb 8.58%	HFRI Fund Wghtd Comp 3.55%
HFRI Event-Driven 6.74%	HFRI Macro 6.87%	HFRI FOF Composite 1.02%	HFRI Fund Wghtd Comp 19.55%	HFRI FOF Composite 6.86%	HFRI Macro 6.79%	HFRI Relative Value 12.37%	Barclays Gov't/Credit 7.75%	HFRI FOF Composite -21.36%	HFRI Equity Hedge 24.55%	HFRI Equity Hedge 10.58%	HFRI Event-Driven -3.30%	HFRI Equity Hedge 7.41%	HFRI FOF Composite 3.32%
HFRI Fund Wghtd Comp 4.98%	HFRI EH: Eq Mrkt Ntrl 6.71%	HFRI EH: Eq Mrkt Ntrl 0.98%	HFRI FOF Composite 11.61%	HFRI Relative Value 5.58%	HFRI ED: Merger Arb 6.25%	HFRI RV: ConvertArb 12.17%	HFRI ED: Merger Arb 7.05%	HFRI Event-Driven -21.82%	HFRI Fund Wghtd Comp 19.98%	HFRI Fund Wghtd Comp 10.49%	HFRI Macro -4.16%	HFRI Fund Wghtd Comp 6.36%	HFRI Relative Value 3.12%
HFRI FOF Composite 4.07%	HFRI Fund Wghtd Comp 4.62%	HFRI ED: Merger Arb -0.87%	HFRI RV: ConvertArb 9.93%	HFRI Macro 4.63%	HFRI EH: Eq Mrkt Ntrl 6.22%	HFRI Equity Hedge 11.71%	HFRI Event-Driven 6.61%	HFRI ED: Distressed -25.20%	HFRI ED: Merger Arb 11.63%	HFRI Macro 8.61%	HFRI RV: ConvertArb -5.16%	Barclays Gov't/Credit 5.07%	HFRI EH: Eq Mrkt Ntrl 2.77%
HFRI ED: Distressed 2.78%	HFRI FOF Composite 2.80%	HFRI Fund Wghtd Comp -1.45%	HFRI Relative Value 9.72%	Barclays Gov't/Credit 4.54%	HFRI Relative Value 6.02%	HFRI FOF Composite 10.39%	S&P 500 5.49%	HFRI Equity Hedge -26.65%	HFRI FOF Composite 11.46%	Barclays Gov't/Credit 6.99%	HFRI Fund Wghtd Comp -5.25%	HFRI FOF Composite 4.79%	HFRI ED: Merger Arb 1.31%
HFRI Macro 1.97%	HFRI ED: Merger Arb 2.76%	HFRI Event-Driven -4.30%	HFRI ED: Merger Arb 7.47%	HFRI EH: Eq Mrkt Ntrl 4.15%	S&P 500 4.91%	HFRI Macro 8.15%	HFRI RV: ConvertArb 5.33%	HFRI RV: ConvertArb -33.71%	Barclays Gov't/Credit 4.81%	HFRI FOF Composite 5.60%	HFRI FOF Composite -5.73%	HFRI EH: Eq Mrkt Ntrl 2.98%	HFRI Emerging Markets -0.10%
S&P 500 -9.09%	HFRI Equity Hedge 0.40%	HFRI Equity Hedge -4.71%	Barclays Gov't/Credit 5.07%	HFRI ED: Merger Arb 4.08%	Barclays Gov't/Credit 2.55%	HFRI EH: Eq Mrkt Ntrl 7.32%	HFRI EH: Eq Mrkt Ntrl 5.29%	S&P 500 -36.99%	HFRI Macro 4.37%	HFRI ED: Merger Arb 4.60%	HFRI Equity Hedge -8.38%	HFRI ED: Merger Arb 2.76%	HFRI Macro -0.53%
HFRI Emerging Markets -10.71%	S&P 500 -11.85%	S&P 500 -22.09%	HFRI EH: Eq Mrkt Ntrl 2.44%	HFRI RV: ConvertArb 1.18%	HFRI RV: ConvertArb -1.86%	Barclays Gov't/Credit 4.07%	HFRI ED: Distressed 5.08%	HFRI Emerging Markets -37.26%	HFRI EH: Eq Mrkt Ntrl 1.43%	HFRI EH: Eq Mrkt Ntrl 3.16%	HFRI Emerging Markets -13.99%	HFRI Macro -0.06%	Barclays Gov't/Credit -2.81%

Figure 7.6 Hedge Fund Indices.

Source: HFR Global Hedge Fund Industry Reports. © 2013 HFR Inc., www.hedgefundresearch.com

BEHAVIORAL FINANCE AND HEDGE FUNDS

One key element that helps hedge funds in a down market is the ability to short unlike mutual funds, which historically were only long. Shorting is not necessarily bad for an investor. As Professor Yu Yuan from Wharton explains, "One of the industrial fields where behavioral finance is the most applied is the hedge fund industry. Many hedge fund managers use behavioral finance knowledge or at least follow behavioral finance spirit to create their trading strategies. Managers also raise capital with consideration of investors' behavioral rules (or biases)."[23] Part of the phobia or fear of hedge funds is due to the aversion with selling short any security. By nature, we want securities to go up and have a hard time relating to shorting a security. Shorting does not appear to be part of our investment DNA. "Individual investors, due to limited knowledge or behavioral biases, are reluctant to take short positions."[24] Investors by nature are fearful. Fear sometimes perpetuates fear. The negativity toward hedge funds even transferred to popular strategies such as the quant funds. Because of this, even the beloved quant funds got the cold shoulder from investors.

INCREASED REGULATION

Increased regulation helped raise the cost of doing business with hedge funds, particularly small ones. The result was both positive and negative. For instance, many small hedge funds could not afford to stay in business, with costs rising especially after the loss in 2008. The way hedge funds are structured, a loss can affect future earnings. While they are trying to make back money for these losses, adding additional costs or expenses, such as with Dodd-Frank, was devastating to a number of hedge funds. Dodd-Frank makes it extremely difficult to start a new hedge fund:

> Title IV of the Act, among other things, (i) alters the Securities and Exchange Commission ("SEC") registration criteria applicable to hedge fund managers and other investment advisers, materially changing the composition of the pool of registered investment advisers, (ii) significantly increases the record-keeping and reporting obligations applicable to registered and unregistered advisers to hedge

> funds and private equity funds, (iii) raises the "accredited investor" standard for individual investor eligibility to participate in private offerings (including offerings by hedge funds and private equity funds), and gives the SEC broad authority to adjust the "accredited investor" standard going forward, and (iv) applies inflation indexing to the "qualified client" standard under which registered advisers are permitted to charge performance-based compensation.[25]

If it is not lucrative for the manager of the fund or any person managing your funds, it is almost certain it will not be for you. No one works for free. "Managers are now more concerned with regulation and governance than they are with investment performance (75% respondents noted that this is one of their most significant challenges)."[26] The Volcker Rule made it even more expensive for hedge funds and private equity funds. The Volcker Rule is also global, not domestic. "Regulation is coming to the alternative asset management industry on both sides of the Atlantic. The impact of various US regulatory and legislature initiatives, including the so called 'Volcker' rule, which proposes a ban on proprietary trading by banks, will likely be considerable for the alternative investment industry, as talent migrates towards boutiques."[27]

The new rules and regulations are so confusing that law firms developed helpful flowcharts to explain some of the countless changes. For instance, Davis Polk put together the flowchart in Figure 7.7.

Small hedge funds that existed before the new regulation are hurting. Because of all the new regulations, it has become increasingly expensive to operate a small hedge fund: Gone are the days of the two-man shop or business school roommates with a clever ideas of managing money.

Hedge funds will most likely move location if they are under siege in a particular country. If government regulation is onerous for hedge funds, they will likely pack up and leave. There have been many situations around the globe where hedge funds were forced to relocate because governments where they were based, became hostile to them: "As of early November, the number of funds located in Malta had grown to more than 500 with 8 billion Euros ($10.7 billion) under management…The island has benefited

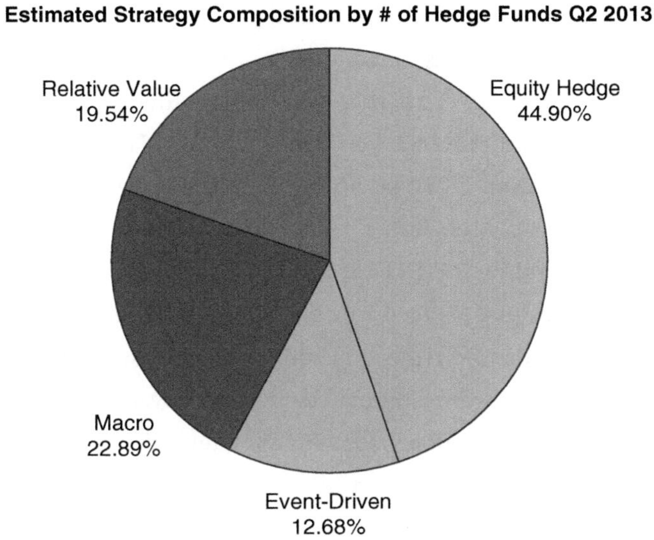

Figure 7.7 Hedge Fund Strategy Composition by Number of Funds.
Source: HFR Global Hedge Fund Industry Reports, © 2013 HFR Inc., www.hedgefundresearch.com.

from a growing demand by investors for transparency as well as from fear among hedge funds that the EU was becoming increasingly hostile to firms based out of it."[28] When an investor sees hedge funds turning into family offices, small funds closing shop or selling, and moving to other countries, it is not a good sign. Government regulation can be excessive and have the opposite effect of what it intended. "There is an ever-more-apparent risk that the harm done by the massive cost and complexity of its regulations, and the effects of its internal inconsistencies, will outweigh what good may yet come from it."[29] Small investors typically get hurt the most by excessive government regulation. Investors should be cautious when they see surges such as these.

HEDGE FUND-"LIKE" STRATEGY

A number of new ETFs, indexes, and mutual funds developed hedge fund-like strategies. Traditional hedge funds are available to accredited investors while mutual funds with hedge fund-like strategies are available to anyone and typically have low minimums. "Many mutual-fund companies have taken a page straight from the hedge-fund playbook and are offering funds that can profit when stocks and bonds fall. Others trade currencies and use complex derivatives."[30] There are even some innovative ways to track the whole hedge fund universe. For instance, the IQ Hedge Multi-Strategy Tracker is a replication ETF that attempts to track the whole hedge fund universe.

Both mutual funds and ETFs are adding offerings that include various hedge fund strategies. "Hedged mutual funds, also known as long-short equity mutual funds, offer more liquidity and transparency than traditional hedge funds but their returns tend to be lower."[31] The growing list of mutual funds that resemble hedge funds (alternative mutual funds) will likely continue because of investor demand. Instead of alternative mutual funds (mutual funds with similar objectives to a hedge fund), Fidelity Investments in a partnership with Arden Asset Management now offers a mutual fund of hedge funds. The objective is lower fees and liquidity. However, illiquidity is not a necessary evil, as evidenced by Harvard's endowment not being able to sell alternative investments at the bottom of the Great Recession. Investors, when the market drops, tend to pull out like a rabbit that gets its foot caught in a trap. The rabbit will tear its foot off to get away and so will the average retail investor. Institutional investors can panic as well. Harvard had liquidity issues. Fortunately, they did not sell their alternative investments and the value went back up again. Hedge fund managers also can be adversely affected by large amounts of money leaving with no restrictions.

ALTERNATIVE MUTUAL FUNDS

Alternative mutual funds are typically less expensive than the classic hedge fund. Investors also demanded more transparency and liquidity, paving the way for vehicles such as the Hybrid Hedge. A Hybrid Hedge resembles a hedge fund but has some of the positive attributes of mutual funds: liquidity, transparency, lower fees, and regulation. Investors, both institutional and retail, will likely seek the Hybrid Hedge model because its features essentially cover the best of both worlds from hedge funds and mutual funds. The Hybrid Hedge model also offers full transparency unlike a model with a number of hedge funds thrown in it. Transparency will continue to be important to investors and hedge funds will most likely need to adopt. The Statement of Financial Accounting Standards No. 157 (SFAS 157) was introduced as a guide to measuring and reporting fair value of assets. The present structure causes some concern. "Their research shows valuations that hedge funds report for their stocks in quarterly filings with the Securities and Exchange Commission are sometimes at odds with actual share prices."[32] The Hybrid Hedge model also is more diversified than a fund selecting a handful of hedge funds. Monitoring hedge funds is not easy. Just because they are thrown in a mutual fund does not reduce all the due diligence needed and ongoing monitoring.

Hedge fund replication strategies began to flourish and attract more interest since the Great Recession. Companies like Natixis, Goldman Sachs, Deutsche Bank, Credit Suisse, Rydex/SGI, Index IQ, and others offer a number of options for investors to examine. "These strategies rely on computer programs that essentially drive looking in the rear-view mirror. Computer models evaluate past returns of hedge funds, either across the entire industry or by specialty."[33] Replication strategies for hedge funds are in essence passive or index-like strategies, as opposed to hedge funds that incorporate active management. While an investor can gain exposure to different types of hedge fund strategies, replication strategies are not perfect. "Replicator funds, unlike hedge funds, are essentially passive, index-based strategies."[34] Following in a hedge fund's footsteps (by assembling investments that would have produced similar returns or buying after they do) might not equal or beat the hedge fund's performance. Hedge funds have a lot of resources. As a result, performance might not be the same, or worse, might suffer.

BUYING RESEARCH OR TROUBLE

The settlement in 2003 that the New York Attorney General Eliot Spitzer forced with Wall Street to spend $460 million on independent stock research for their clients led to more use with their hedge fund clients as opposed to retail investors: "Less than 2% of Goldman Sachs Group Inc.'s Private Wealth Management clients likely downloaded a report each month, according to data from the public reports."[35] The US government started prosecuting a number of hedge funds and employees in 2010 for obtaining research viewed as "insider trading." Here lies a paradox. The US government changes research on Wall Street in order to help investors. Hedge funds seek investment knowledge outside of Wall Street research in order to earn higher rates for investors. Investors pay hedge funds a lot of money and expect the hedge fund manager to have a competitive advantage. Hedge funds were the biggest buyers of independent research, since they wanted to gain an edge and they paid for it. After a number of hedge funds produced stellar returns, the US government accused them of wrongdoing. There is a fine line of whether this should or should not be viewed as insider trading. In certain cases, there appears to be wrongdoing. But in others, it appears to be a witch hunt or political vendetta. "There is no insider-trading statute. Most modern-day, insider-trading prosecutions are brought under the general federal statue forbidding securities fraud. Fraud involves lying, deception, or trickery. But most stock sales occur over exchanges, where the buyer and seller never meet, let alone mislead each other."[36]

As an investor in hedge funds, it is prudent to note trends such as government intervention. Is a given government favorable to hedge funds or anti-hedge fund? Is a government increasing taxes concerning hedge funds or lowering them? Is a government filing lawsuits against a particular hedge fund manager that it believes harmed investors or is there some other political agenda lurking in the background? For instance, a politician might be accused of being lax toward hedge funds. As a result, they take a hard line against hedge funds. There is the mentality of "shoot first, ask questions later." Here are a number of hedge funds that the US government pursued: SAC Capital (Steve A. Cohen); Galleon Group (Raj Rajaratnam); Harbinger Capital (Philip Falcone); Millennium Global Emerging Credit Fund (Michael Balboa); and Magnetar Capital (Alec Litowitz/Ross Laser).

The US government attack on hedge funds was quite transparent. Rajaratnam was convicted and this also led to another conviction with a Goldman Sachs' board member and former head of McKinsey, Rajat Gupta. Other investigations took place. Steve Cohen had his hedge fund, one of the largest in the world, destroyed because of insider trading though there was never any evidence implicating Cohen personally. Falcone had his fund destroyed. After much struggling, Chapter 11 seemed the only option left for LightSquared. "Mr. Falcone's LightSquared Inc., a wireless-networking venture, filed for Chapter 11 bankruptcy protection Monday. The move, which came after the company failed to reach an agreement with its lenders to avoid a default, further clouds the future for Mr. Falcone and his signature investment."[37] Besides making every new hedge fund manager timid, the approach of finding bad guys through data analysis is completely and utterly unreliable. Multiple fraud cases were filed against hedge funds by the SEC during the later part of 2011 and in 2012, which appears to be a "shoot first then ask questions" mentality. The mentality that if you are successful, you must be doing something wrong, appears to prevail. Investors in hedge funds can be affected by these actions. For example, a hedge fund manager might likely be focused on defending himself as opposed to the performance of the fund.

Due diligence and diversification is essential for selecting hedge funds. Even the smart money or institutional investors such as hedge funds themselves can get burned. For example, quite a few hedge funds, including those in New York that employed the well-regarded detective firm Kroll, lost money with Scott Rothstein for discounted legal settlements.

> Unlike Bernie Madoff or Allen Stanford, who mostly hurt individual investors, the 49-year-old Rothstein sucked in a billion dollars from sophisticated investors—including New York hedge funds that employed the well-known detective firm Kroll and an onsite inspector at Rothstein's Fort Lauderdale law firm, from which he sold discounted legal settlements with annualized returns as high as 437%. Sadly, the settlements didn't exist.[38]

There is smart money but there is also what I call the "Foolish Money." If an alternative investment sounds too good to be true, it usually is and one should walk. An interesting and peculiar trend occurred with a few hedge funds, despite the difficulty they had during the Great Recession. As the market picked up again in 2010–2011, a small minority of hedge funds started making investments in venture capital. Falcone, for instance, invested in a start-up, LightSquared. His idea was not a bad one and likely would have worked if the Federal Communications Commission (FCC) did not take away his license rights after giving it to him. Historically, hedge funds have not put a lot into venture capital because of the illiquidity. When Falcone invested, his hedge fund was $26 billion in 2008 but this dropped to less than $5 billion in 2011. The investment in LightSquared was not excessive because of all the assets Falcone had under management at the time. Redemptions make it difficult to manage money regardless of the vehicle, which is why investors in alternative investments should pay attention if there is trouble. Mutual fund redemptions can also be problematic for a manager. What might have appeared to be a small investment at the time for Falcone soon became his largest by far. Falcone clearly was invested for the long haul and most likely allocated assets based on $26 billion in assets.

HYBRID HEDGE MODEL

The Hybrid Hedge model is a strategy that evolved to essentially combine both hedge fund and venture fund investments. Hedge funds can invest in venture capital through vehicles known as "side pockets." Side pockets are used to separate and distinguish investor ownership of illiquid assets purchased by hedge funds. Historically, the alternative investment market was segregated. LBO funds did not invest in real estate, venture capital, commodities, or other alternative investments. They stuck to their knitting as firms grew and the market changed. Most of the large LBO funds are now firms that specialize in a variety of alternative investments. They have all sorts of offerings for alternative investments. In fact, they have expanded so much they are now investing or building capabilities in fixed income and equity. For example, Carlyle Group, which was originally a LBO fund, has morphed into a much larger publicly traded company with real estate, venture capital, and other alternative investments. Carlyle bought a controlling interest TCW, which is known for fixed income like corporate bonds, US Treasuries, municipals, etc. In a sense, the larger private equity firms are becoming similar to mutual fund companies, with huge menus or investment options. For instance, Crosslink offered a type of hybrid option. "Stark's Carbonite investment is quintessential

Crosslink. The firm, with $2.15 billion under management, tries to make money from a hybrid strategy of providing venture funding for private companies and hedge fund investments to profit from public ones."[39] A hybrid model will most likely become more attractive to allow managers optimum flexibility and to make the best possible investments.

Consultants tend to favor cookie-cutter models for clients because it is easier to direct venture capital funds in one part of an allocation and hedge funds into another. However, this might not be the best method. It is the same nonsensical advice as the old style box that consultants stuck to, no matter what happened with the market. Years ago, a money manager that shifted assets was depicted as a "style drifter," but things changed after the technology bubble and managers were allowed more flexibility. It is now acceptable to "drift." There is no logical reason why one should not explore a hybrid model of investing for alternative investments.

After LinkedIn and Pandora went public, the race was on to find the next social media company to back, with the hopes of a quick exit strategy such as an IPO. "LinkedIn's rather gargantuan valuation suggests that investors eager to play the stunning growth, popularity and near-ubiquity of Facebook are grabbing at anything that faintly resembles it, even if that means paying up for a far more limited opportunity in a site whose user aren't remotely as engaged as Facebook's."[40] Bankers were delighted by the sky-high valuation of LinkedIn. LinkedIn went public at $45 in May, quickly jumped to as high as $122, and now trades at $68, or 240 times projected 2011 profits, and 127 times 2012 estimates.[41] Hedge funds and investors sought a piece of this action. "Tiger Global Management LLC, a hedge fund founded by Chase Coleman, paid $20 million for a stake in LinkedIn Corp., valuing the professional-networking website at more than $2 billion, said two people familiar with the matter."[42] A number of hedge funds backed a competitor of Groupon called LivingSocial. "When daily-coupon website LivingSocial Inc. said it raised $400 million in April, the firms putting up cash included hedge funds Tiger Global Management, Lone Pine Capital, and Brookside Capital, people familiar with the matter say."[43] It was almost as though one took a time machine and went back to the late 1990s when the Internet was the Wild West. LivingSocial, however, did not jump right into the public market prematurely. "Asking for a huge valuation on a questionable business model proved troublesome for Groupon. Hopefully, by staying out of the public market for longer, LivingSocial will give itself time to mature."[44] Ironically, Sarbanes-Oxley meant to help small investors but opened the door for hedge funds to buy venture capital. "Some call it 'regulatory arbitrage': well-meaning but inherently flawed laws such as Sarbanes-Oxley that were designed to protect small investors from the next Enron have imposed such heavy costs on public companies that many private ones are delaying their initial public offerings."[45] Hedge funds by nature move in and out of investments. If they invest in venture capital, an investor needs to pay careful attention to what the hedge fund is doing. "It's unusual for hedge funds to dabble in venture capital."[46]

COMPETING WITH HEDGE FUNDS (VENTURE CAPITAL AND IPOS)

High net worth and sometimes smaller institutional investors get the faulty idea that they can do what a hedge fund is doing and attempt to buy the same investments. In most cases, this is a disaster. Hedge funds are difficult to compete with and hard to follow. The amount and frequency of hedge funds buying venture capital has picked up quite a bit from being virtually nonexistent before Sarbanes-Oxley when hedge funds seldom invested in venture capital. "Hedge funds, private-equity firms and mutual-fund companies, facing a dearth of initial public offerings, are taking bigger stakes in private technology companies to benefit when they go public."[47] Prudent investors in alternative investments will examine all the players when competing. Hypothetically, if one invests in LinkedIn while it was private, who are the other investors? Are they long- or short-term investors? Hedge funds can also set up numerous vehicles to invest like side pockets. Because of changes in the law, it is much more cumbersome for individual investors to understand who the other investors are or what their motives really are. Are they there to help the company or make a quick buck?

Another important question to ask is, "Who are the underwriters?" Do the underwriters have pre-existing relationships with any of the institutional investors? Is there favoritism? Do they get preferential treatment? How much of the company do they own? Whether you are a retail investor, ultra high net worth investor, or another hedge fund, one might ask why a certain hedge fund was offered pre-IPO shares or IPO shares of a hot deal while others were excluded. Is the ownership buried in a massive prospectus? The new environment for investing in alternative investments, such as venture capital or hedge funds, requires a lot of due diligence. That is, an inordinate amount of due diligence is needed today. One almost needs to be a detective or forensic accountant. Jose Miguel Mendoza, a corporate law lecturer at Oxford University studying IPO investing, claimed in 2010 that venture capitalists were responsible for most of the stock changing hands in pre-IPO markets but last year hedge funds bought 70 percent.[48] There is a reason these shrewd investors are called the smart money. Are there conflicts that one should be aware of before making an investment that might have been disclosed by either the underwriters or the company? Buying IPOs shares is not the same as investing in the company while it is private. An individual investor needs to decide whether it is better or not for them to invest in private shares or public shares like an IPO. However, an investor can easily get burned if they are not paying attention. Investors that own private shares in a company might be selling shares in an IPO while some retail investors are buying.

If an investor is a retail investor, it is generally a good idea to take note of what institutional investors are doing. Buying IPO shares as well as stock in the aftermarket after a company just went public can be dangerous for a retail investor especially when lockups come off and large investors can dump shares. Hedge funds and other institutions buy percentages of a company with ease. It requires a lot of experience and know-how concerning IPOs and the purchase of shares in the aftermarket. For example, the hedge fund Tiger bought shares of LinkedIn. It is difficult if not impossible to follow what a hedge fund is doing. Discovering buyers before, during, and after an IPO can be a challenge. "While we knew Coleman was buying up shares of LinkedIn, we didn't know it was to the tune of over $75,000,000 and Coleman himself now owns a little

Table 7.3 LinkedIn and Tiger Global

December 21, 2009– August 10, 2010	PIP V acquired shares of preferred and common stock of the Issuer (which were later exchanged for Class B Common Shares) in a number of secondary transactions, pursuant to which PIP V purchased 2,436,001 shares of preferred and common stock of the Issuer (which were later exchanged for 2,436,001 Class B Common Shares) for an aggregate amount of $31,740,600.70.
August 10, 2010–April 15, 2011	LinkedIn Holdings acquired shares of common stock of the Issuer (which were later exchanged for Class B Common Shares) in a number of secondary transactions pursuant to which LinkedIn Holdings purchased 1,306,927 shares of common stock of the Issuer (which were later exchanged for 1,306,927 Class B Common Shares) for an aggregate amount of $29,796,007.50.
May 24, 2011	Post-IPO, Tiger Global Management LLC reported a purchase of 300,000 Class A Common Shares at the IPO price of $45.00 per share for an aggregate amount of $13,500,000.

Source: Form 3 (Initial Statement of Beneficial Ownership), LinkedIn Corp, Reported by Coleman Charles P III, Securities and Exchange Commission, Edgar Online, June 3, 2011, 2.

over 4 percent of LinkedIn, according to the filing."[49] Table 7.3 contains Tiger Global's interest in pre-IPO and post-IPO LinkedIn shares:

Tiger did quite well with its various vehicles buying shares of LinkedIn. LinkedIn's IPO was priced at $45 per share but started trading at $83 per share.

THE FACEBOOK FIASCO

Institutional and individual investors are interested in alternative investments. However, rushing into these vehicles without proper due diligence can be a mistake. Facebook is a wonderful example of how things can go horribly wrong as well as how investors can easily get burned if they are not paying attention. Facebook involves two main types of alternative investments (venture capital and hedge funds) as well as other vehicles such as IPOs and mutual funds that invest in private companies as well as IPOs. Further, it involves mutual funds invested in IPOs. Lastly, Facebook illustrates both private and public exchanges. Early in 2011, Facebook hinted at going public in early 2012. A reporter called me and asked if there was a lot of upside to Facebook at $100 to $200 billion valuation. Facebook was private at the time. A number of institutions and investors were investing and valuations appeared excessive. I put the phone on mute and laughed. There are many finance books on the market that cover valuation but none of them have chapters called Hype.

The purpose behind venture capital is to invest early, not when values are in the stratosphere. For instance, Accel Partners invested a lofty $12.7 million in Facebook in 2005 when the company was priced around $100 million and could reap a 1,000 times return with its stake potentially worth as much as $9 billion.[50] Accel did not invest at a $100 billion valuation. Timing is important when investing in alternative investments such as venture capital. Are you investing early or are you late to the party? Many investors show up after the party. Likewise, the vehicle or means an investor selects to invest in a private company can be equally challenging. For instance, a number of funds that bought shares of Facebook as a private company bought at the wrong time. "As initial valuations go, $100 billion is a big number to ask. But at least Facebook has a business model to buy into . . . Facebook collects loads of information about its users that can be used to target advertisements. That should help it capture a bigger share of advertising dollars."[51] By the end of 2011, Facebook was planning an IPO in the first half of 2012.

The split of fees between banks for taking Facebook public was unusual. "Morgan Stanley got 38.5% of the fees, while J.P. Morgan got just over 20% and Goldman Sachs got 15%, not exactly the typical split for a deal with three underwriters."[52] Further, Morgan Stanley increased both the amount of shares and the dollar price shortly before the Facebook IPO. "Facebook and Morgan Stanley, its lead underwriter, faced criticism for boosting the number of shares sold in the IPO by 25 percent to 421.2 million in the days before deal."[53] The bigger the IPO deal, the more lucrative it is typically for a bank. The IPO for Facebook ended up being the second largest IPO ever and also held the record for most amount of venture capital ever raised for a company. "Facebook originally filed to sell 337 million shares at a price range of $28 to $35, but this week hiked that expected range to $34–$38."[54] Prudent investors will examine the financial landscape and market before buying alternative investments. The landscape can quickly change.

Most CEOs or entrepreneurs elect not to sell on the IPO and cash out. It is viewed negatively by investors. The sentiment is, "Why should I buy shares if the person running the company is selling?" Similarly, many venture capital firms decide to hold as opposed to sell if they truly believe in the company. With regard to Facebook, the well-known and respected venture capital firm, Greylock, did not sell as nearly as much percentage-wise as other sellers at the IPO price of $38.00 despite the long-term investment and guidance they gave the company. "Other investors, including Tiger Global Management, Goldman Sachs, DST Global and Mail.ru group, all decided to sell significantly larger amounts of their holdings than they had previously indicated they would. In some cases it was almost double the amount and represented half their shares."[55] Right before the IPO, it was announced that selling shareholders would sell more at $36.00 per share (which ended up being $38.00, with Morgan Stanley setting the price at the very high end of the range):

> The company itself will not float extra stock, Facebook said in a Wednesday filing with the U.S. Securities and Exchange Commission. But early investors like venture capital firm Accel Partners; Tiger Global Management, the hedge fund; Goldman Sachs; PayPal co-founder Peter Thiel; and companies tied to Russian tycoon Yuri Milner are cashing out with additional sales to the tune of as much as $3.8 billion…Milner's Digital Sky Technologies Global Ltd will unload an additional 19 million shares, bringing the value of its sale to more than $1.6 billion. Mail.ru, another firm controlled by the Russian mogul, will sell a stake worth $705 million.[56]

Accel Partners, another venture capital firm, filed to sell more shares. Hedge funds, which historically do not invest in venture capital, might have a different objective from investors in an IPO. "But the most winning trade of the week, month, and no doubt the year, belongs to Charles "Chase" Coleman, the 36-year-old hedge fund manager who runs Tiger Global Management. Coleman on Wednesday indicated that he intends to sell a big chunk of his firm's holdings in Facebook in the big social network IPO that is about to take place."[57] Investors should always be observant of the smart money. A few of the funds and what their stakes are worth in Facebook are as follows: DST Global led by Yuri Milner had 131.3 million shares worth $5 billion; Mail.ru Group (also run by Milner) had 56.3 million shares worth $2.14 billion; and Tiger Global Management had 53.8 million shares worth $2 billion (selling approximately 50 percent of its shares in the IPO).[58]

The majority of Facebook shares sold on the IPO came from existing shareholders, followed by the CEO. "Facebook Inc. sold 180 million of its shares in its initial public stock offering. Another 241.2 million came from existing stockholders, including the company's earliest investors and CEO Mark Zuckerberg."[59] The IPO enabled existing shareholders to cash out a staggering sum of money. Existing shareholders walked away with $9.2 billion while the company received less. Facebook received only $6.8 billion. With the green shoe, existing shareholders could cash out even more. "At the $38 offer price, Facebook itself will raise nearly $7 billion. Add cash already on its balance sheet, and it begins life as a public company with about $11 billion total. If underwriters exercise their option to sell extra stock, about 60% of the cash raised in the IPO is going straight to selling shareholders, not to the company."[60] Smart money tends to win over foolish money (frequently known as the retail investor), which is the loser. Competing with smart money is most difficult. For example, Tiger Global's investment into Facebook: "Coleman is known to shy away from press and avoid discussing stakes in private companies, however, his investment in Facebook has gathered a lot of media attention as most believe his stake in the social networking site currently valued at $50 billion gives him access to private information about the company financials."[61] The importance for an investor is to be cognizant of what an institution or the smart money is doing. Are they buying or selling? Hedge funds have always sought hot IPOs to flip but primarily at the time of the offering because the shares are publicly traded and highly liquid; they can quickly sell them. However, hedge funds are now investing privately and then selling on the IPO:

> The shareholders stepping up most aggressively to sell stock include Tiger, Thiel, Accel, but also DST Global and Mail.ru, according to the May 16 filing. Greylock Partners also modestly increased its allotment... Tiger Global Management sold 23.4 million shares, a 596% increase from the 3.4 million it anticipated selling as of the May 3 filing. The firm was the most aggressive seller. It still holds 30.4 million shares... Goldman Sachs sold 28.7 million shares, a 117% increase from the 13.2 million it expected to sell as of May 3. Goldman still holds 37.3 million shares.[62]

Since IPOs can frequently have an initial pop in price, it is essentially free money to buy and flip an IPO. Investors bought into the Facebook IPO to make money. Strangely, the CEO of Morgan Stanley, Jim Gorman, admonished investors in Morgan Stanley's Facebook IPO during an interview with CNBC: "The group of people that thought they were buying this stock so they could get an enormous pop were both naive and bought [shares] under the wrong pretenses."[63]

Rarely have hedge funds bought shares pre-IPO like Tiger; hedge funds typically buy liquid investments. Buying private companies has not been their bailiwick. Retail investors would be wise to proceed with caution when hedge funds start plowing large amounts of money into private deals. If the deal has strong demand they will wait to sell on the IPO. "Many institutional investors seek allocations of supposedly hot IPOs because they want to make money, not because they want to own the stocks. Access to hot IPOs is one way Wall Street rewards profitable clients. If the deals don't trade well initially, institutions often sell quickly to lock in whatever profits that they can."[64]

It is not easy for the average retail investor to outwit the smart money, especially an institutional investor that invested large amounts of money into a company far before a retail investor. "While the ability to allocate IPO shares is seen as a strength of so-called wirehouses like Morgan Stanley Smith Barney, the 'value proposition seems a bit weaker' following Facebook's disappointing debut."[65] Facebook changed its S-1 before going public. An S-1 that gets changed so quickly and last minute is difficult to evaluate. It would not enable an investors to find how the deal changed unless of course they were a securities attorney or an extremely sophisticated purchaser of IPOs. In other words, virtually no average investor would be able to piece together everything going on behind the scenes. The urgency by Morgan Stanley, the lead manager for the IPO, appears somewhat peculiar, especially considering the information disseminated as well as the details about the company which were not clearly explained. As reported by PrivCo, on "May 9, 2012: Facebook's underwriting team offers a bare minimum disclosure and amends its S-1 stating simply that daily active users are increasing at a faster rate than deliverable ads due to mobile and potentially decreasing revenues," and on "May 15–16,

2012: Underwriters encourage institutional and retail investors to request more shares than they may want. Investors are told demand for Facebook IPO shares is so robust that they will only receive a fraction of their allocation requests."[66] It is doubtful that investors would have invested as much as they did in Facebook if they studied all the risks involved.

The Facebook IPO was pitched to many retail investors as a "gift" when in reality it was as far from a gift. "The Facebook IPO was supposed to be the kind of opportunity that customers of Wall Street wirehouses could look forward to receiving. Instead, it has turned out to be another blemish on Wall Street's already tarnished image with retail investors."[67] Increasing the amount of shares last minute can harm an IPO. "Facebook initially set out to sell 337.4 million shares to the public, according to an S-1 the company filed with the SEC on May 3. Two days before the IPO, it increased the amount to 421.2 million, with the additional shares coming from shareholders, not the company, according to the May 16 SEC filing. The company's contribution to the offering—180 million shares—stayed unchanged."[68]

One year before Facebook went public, reporters asked if the valuation for Facebook at $100 billion was a good deal. "A group of Facebook shareholders is seeking to offload $1 billion worth of shares on the secondary market, a sale that would value the company at more than $70 billion, according to five sources with direct knowledge of the situation...It is questionable whether new investors would realize the exponential growth that early-stage investors got in Facebook."[69] Interestingly enough, the IPO was priced at $38.00, making the company worth in excess of $100 billion. After the IPO, the share price came right back down to the valuation of $70 billion. Valuing a private company is never easy. Private companies that set an IPO price too high, can run into a number of problems. Owing to the tens of billions of lost dollars in the Facebook IPO during its first two months, regulators are looking into the Facebook IPO's disappointing results:

> Regulators are looking into a report that Morgan Stanley, the lead underwriter for Facebook's initial public offering last week, shared a negative assessment of the social network with major clients ahead of the IPO. Rick Ketchum, head of the Financial Industry Regulatory

> Authority, an independent regulatory body, acknowledged an article from Reuters saying that a Morgan Stanley analyst reduced his revenue projections for Facebook shortly before the offering and shared this with institutional investors. The report has raised questions about whether certain investors received privileged information ahead of the offering that should have been disseminated more widely.[70]

During the road show for Facebook, certain investors appeared to get favoritism with regard to useful financial information. "Massachusetts Secretary of the Commonwealth William Galvin has subpoenaed Morgan Stanley over questionable actions surrounding its role as lead underwriter of Facebook's IPO. The subpoena accuses Morgan Stanley of discussing Facebook's lower revenue projections with certain institutional investors—a move which possibly violates Massachusetts state securities law."[71]

CONFLICTS OF INTEREST

Conflicts of interest can harm investors. For example, naïve investors jumped at the opportunity even though many had no idea what they were doing. For instance, Morgan Stanley mutual funds bought private shares of Facebook. A question then arises: how can the bank be objective when they were also an underwriter getting a fee for an IPO and representing the company? Investors bought Morgan Stanley funds, which received a lot of publicity that they were buying pre-IPO Facebook shares. Mutual funds appeared to be a viable way to gain access. "By getting in ahead of the crowd, the funds position themselves for potentially big gains if companies go public."[72] Quite a few questions come to mind. Did those investors buying the Morgan Stanley funds ultimately get a good deal? Did they do better than the Morgan Stanley clients who bought the IPO shares? Did neither do well? Morgan Stanley made millions but what about the retail clients of the bank? What price did the fund pay for the pre-IPO shares and at what price did they sell? Were the shares bought in the funds just to land the Facebook deal at the expense of the fund shareholders? Did they sell on the IPO with other institutions or not? Either way, there is an inherent conflict of interest when you sit on both sides of the table, on top of the table, and underneath it as well. Other mutual funds lost money—funds not even affiliated with Morgan Stanley. "Facebook's disastrous stock-market debut sheds new light on the hazards of investing in funds that invest in private companies. GSV Capital and Firsthand Technology Value, two funds designed to give retail investors exposure to tech companies before their initial public offering, have lost 37% and 32% of their values, respectively, since Facebook went public."[73]

Initial finger pointing was focused at Nasdsaq, "In the wake of the botched offering—Facebook has shed $22 billion in market value since the May 18 deal—much of the focus has been on the chaotic first day of trading, which was marred by technical problems on the Nasdaq Stock Market. But interviews with Wall Street bankers, brokers, investors and Silicon Valley executives reveal that Mr. Grimes, his firm and Facebook made several decisions in the weeks leading up to the offering that contributed to the rocky ride."[74] No matter what the excuse is from an underwriter, when investors buy high such as retail investors purchasing Facebook IPO shares, they tend to take a dim view of it:

> To anyone outside of Wall Street, this whole arrangement seems like a giant conflict of interest. Just days before the IPO, Morgan agreed to allow Facebook to sell more shares than it originally proposed. Morgan also set the IPO price higher than originally expected. That, in part, set the stock up for the fall, creating the trading gains for Morgan. Wall Street, of course, doesn't see it that way. In fact, Facebook's own prospectus says that the underwriters 'may sell more shares than they are obligated to purchase under the underwriting agreement, creating a short position.'[75]

Billions of dollars were lost by individual investors with the Facebook flop. The Facebook IPO created mistrust. "Public perception seems to be that Morgan Stanley favored institutional customers rather than the retail clients who make up the bulk of business for its 17,000 advisers. Published accounts claimed that many of Morgan Stanley's big clients got phone calls informing them that the firm's technology analyst had reduced his estimates for the company."[76] The question to ask is, "What next?" Facebook is a well-known entity and was virtually impossible to have botched an IPO. After the Facebook IPO, the former CEO and chairman of Morgan Stanley, Phil Purcell, argued for big banks to be broken up including Morgan Stanley:

> Right now the market valuation of too-big-to-fail institutions is too low because of the earnings volatility inherent in investment banking and trading. There is also a mismatch between the cultural values that infuse investment banking and those of asset management, retail banking, and private wealth management. The financial giants have mixed profitable and client-centric services with the higher risk, more volatile and opaque investment banking and trading.[77]

The bottom line is that the retail investor got annihilated with the Facebook IPO and the reason why is quite clear; the retail investor's interest seemed to be put last not first. "One reason Morgan Stanley got the Facebook mandate was its wide retail distribution network. Yet many of the firm's retail customers—who got an estimated 25% of the firm's allocation—are sitting with losses on their Facebook shares and steaming that some institutional customers were warned of problems with the deal while they were told nothing."[78]

The poorly handled Facebook IPO might have an adverse effect on the entire IPO market, venture capital, alternative investments, and banks that offered these shares. Any IPO that craters will likely spook investors due to Facebook's size. It might adversely affect future IPOs. Venture capital moves in waves and the way that Facebook was handled could have severe repercussions for the whole market. "With just four IPOs on the calendar for next week, June 2012 US listed IPO activity could be the lowest since June 2003 (3 IPOs). Average June IPO activity since 1995 is 29 deals making it the third highest month on average over the 18 year period."[79] Regulators will examine Facebook and might impose more regulation. Rep. Darrell Issa, R.-California, on behalf of the House Oversight and Government Reform Committee, suggests the rules for pricing IPOs and disseminating information need to be updated: "The Facebook IPO taught us that, at a minimum, the IPO process suffers substantial flaws. In fact, it appears the entire IPO regulatory framework, based on an outdated Securities Act of 1933, fails to provide a market-based solution to IPO pricing."[80]

In December 2012, Morgan Stanley paid a $5 million fine concerning Facebook. "Massachusetts said that Morgan Stanley's senior investment banker on the deal 'orchestrated' phone calls from Facebook to analysts in a way that favored large investors over small ones and that violated restrictions on bankers' role in the IPO process."[81] With the M&As of many banks due to the Great Recession, the financial landscape has forever changed. For example, initial public offerings must be large enough now for banks to make money. This need can create conflicts and problems, especially for those investing in alternative investments.

HEDGE FUNDS IN THE FUTURE

Hedge funds are not all evil. Granted, there have been quite a few standout nefarious characters, but this is the exception rather than the norm. There will be some rotten eggs out of ten thousand hedge fund managers. It is inevitable. The objective for every investor (including the banks, consultants, and other alleged experts that failed to guard clients against Bernie Madoff) is to perform proper due diligence. The experts clearly failed here. It is no use for an investor to realize after the fact when there is a blow-up or the manager is thrown in jail. Bernie Madoff is a learning lesson for everyone. When a fraud is discovered, investors typically lose money. What happened to all the investors who lost money with Bernie Madoff? Fortunately, it turns out that quite a bit of money is being recovered. "Irving Picard has collected $7.6 billion for victims of Bernard Madoff's Ponzi scheme, and he's aiming much higher. Investors were lucky. The trustee liquidating Madoff's firm, Picard has filed more than 1,000 lawsuits that he calculates would bring in $100 billion, far more than the $19 billion that he estimates disappeared."[82] When the news broke about Madoff at the end of 2008, it could not have occurred at a worse time in the market, causing even more fear with hedge funds. In fact, Madoff ran a ponzi scheme rather than a hedge fund. There was so much deception, many investors thought they were investing in a hedge fund. As a result, virtually every investor questioned or examined any alternative investment.

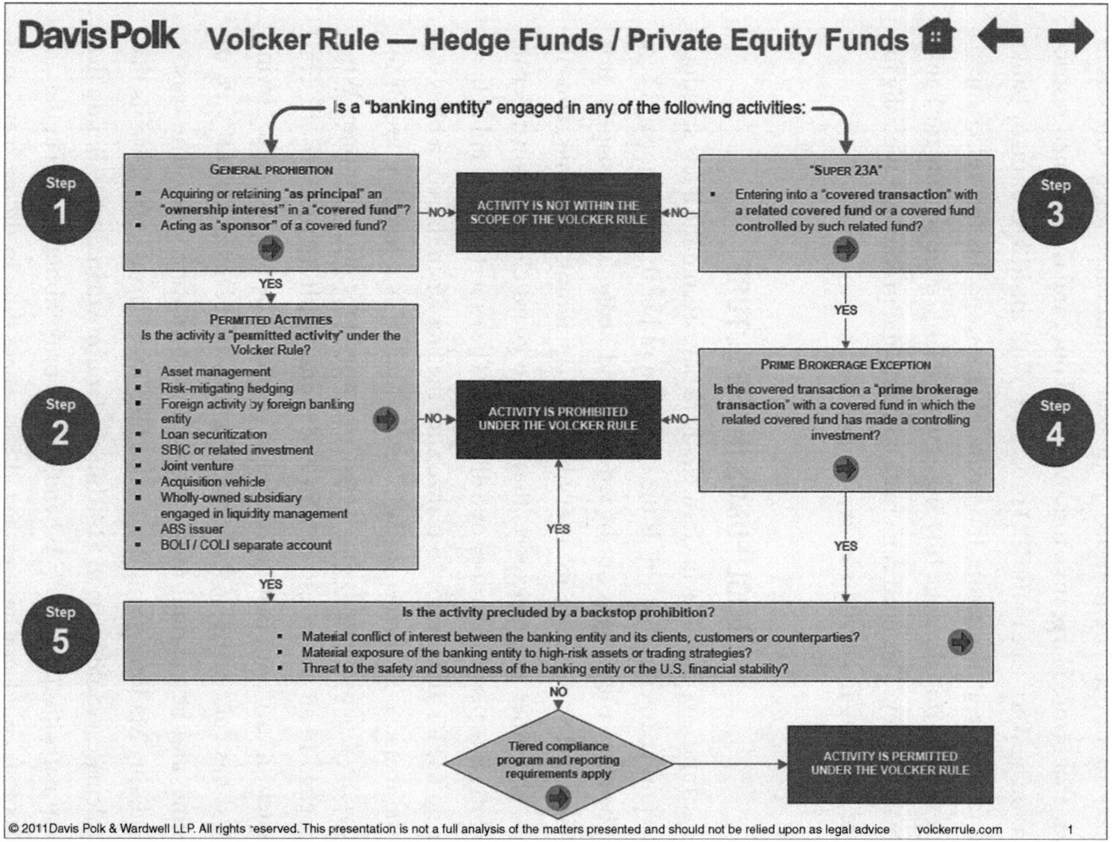

Figure 7.8 Volcker Rule Proposed Regulations for Hedge Funds / Private Equity Funds.

Source: Davis Polk & Wardwell LLP, "Volcker Rule Proposed Regulations: Hedge/PE Funds Summary," http://www.davispolk.com/files/Publication/58f87d88-c7d7-4b7a-af28

Despite the fact that there was extreme pessimism about investing and a negative sentiment about hedge funds, the circumstances in 2008 and 2009 were unusual. Wave Theory shows that if the hedge fund market keeps growing the way it has since the Great Recession, it is not inconceivable that the hedge fund market doubles by 2015. Hedge funds came roaring back dispelling all the naysayers. "We find that global sentiment is a statistically and economically significant contrarian predictor of market returns."[83] Hedge funds are likely to continue attracting assets. It is predicted that U.S. allocation to hedge funds will increase 28 percent of total portfolio assets by the end of 2013.[84] Rogue waves or Black Swan events frequently distort value perceptions. Closed-end funds illustrate this point:

> The problem of accounting for price changes on the basis of fundamental values is not confined to the overall stock market. Studies of price behavior in setting where fundamental values can be measured directly have similar trouble in explaining prices. The classic example is closed-end mutual funds, discussed by Malkiel and Firstenberg (1978). These funds have traded at both discounts and premiums relative to their net asset value during the last twenty years. At any moment, the cross-sectional dispersion in discounts is substantial and difficult to link fundamental factors.[85]

Closed-end funds can offer exceptional buying opportunities since investors tend to throw the baby out with the bath water. Unlike open-ended funds where there is no limit of shares, closed-end funds have a set amount of shares and trade on an exchange. Since they trade on an exchange, prices can fluctuate. Case in point, one can examine NAV or net asset value compared with the stock price of the closed-end fund to see how much above or below the price should actually be worth.

8

THE FOOLS' GOLD OR THE REAL DEAL?

REVERSION TO THE MEAN

Gold moves in waves like other commodities. For example, gold went from a trough to a peak (April 20, 2001–September 5, 2011) and then from a peak to a trough (September 6, 2011–December 19, 2013). I call this Gold Wave VI since this was the sixth time that gold exhibited a clear cycle, pattern, or trend. Many self-proclaimed gold experts mistakenly forecasted that gold would surpass $2,000 per troy ounce. It did not happen. Any naysayers of Wave Theory were proven wrong again. Yet a reversion to the mean was inevitable. Amongst other dilemmas, the stock market collapsing from the tech bubble and then again from the real estate bubble drove scared investors to this precious metal. Gold looked like it was going straight into the sky. Eventually, however, a wave will reverse. Trees do not grow to the sky. Gold reached a nadir in August 2011 at $1,888.70. By April 2013, gold dropped to $1,361.10 per troy ounce. Gold plummeted to $1,195.00 by December 19, 2013 and lost -29 percent year-to-date. Hedge funds and other "smart money" investors began selling. Besides institutional investors, governments stockpiled the yellow metal for years, which also helped drive the price higher. As the United States and other economies recovered, investors turned to equities and focused less interest on gold. Recent sales occurred with gold ETFs during the first quarter of 2013. The reversal of the gold wave was not a surprise.

SUPPLY AND DEMAND

Like all commodities and other alternatives, gold revolves around supply and demand. Two market collapses, uncertainty in the market, war, and other turmoil helped sustain this wave. The real estate blowup and credit crises helped drive investors to gold. After the oldest and one of the biggest money market funds, the high-profile Reserve Primary Fund, "broke the buck" (its net asset value dropped below $1), gold appeared to be the security blanket of choice. The "Great Recession" caused a lot of interest in gold because some investors thought the world was coming to an end. Historically, investors flock to gold and other commodities when there are catastrophic or cataclysmic events that lead to uncertainty.

Fear of inflation, the growing deficit in the United States, sovereign debt, a likely double-dip recession, political stammering, and the tsunami in Japan along with their nuclear plants imploding all created a somewhat negative environment, which led investors to seek solace owning gold: The benchmark 100-troy-ounce Comex gold contract for December delivery has rocketed up 11 percent since August 2011 to a recent record of $1,817.60 a troy ounce, as investors across the globe scrambled to shield their wealth from the fears roiling the stock and bond markets.[1] Each of these global dilemmas includes other ramifications. For example, Greece's inability to pay its debts is wreaking havoc across Europe. "As the climate gets more poisonous and elections approach in France, Germany and Greece itself, the risk of a disastrous accident—anything from a disorderly default to a currency break-up—is growing."[2] If Greece failed, many other countries in the European Union might follow, causing even bigger problems.

Fear has a way of feeding upon itself. The fear of a government having difficulty will create more fear, which can drive investors further to gold. Gold went up in value to $1,800 when investors thought France would get downgraded. Typically very stable, France unexpectedly added to the European nightmare. The fear became real and the inevitable occurred.

France was downgraded, which resulted in the number of AAA-rated countries dropping once again.

Central banks have also helped lift the price of gold by buying an unprecedented amount of gold in 2010–2011: "From 1989 to 2008, the world's central banks disposed of a net 190 million ounces at an average price of about $398 each, according to data from the World Gold Council. Since then, they have bought back a net 28 million ounces—at nearly three times the price. If the world's central banks were a single entity, this sell-low-buy-high approach would be perverse."[3] Gold or any other alternative will be affected by institutional investors or the smart money. "Retail investors do not qualify, because they rarely matter when it comes to influencing a company's share price. In spite of collectively holding around 40 percent of U.S. equity, they do not move prices, because they do not trade very much. The real drivers of share prices are institutional investors, who manage hedge funds, mutual funds, or pension funds and can hold significant positions in individual companies."[4] The price of gold trended up but experienced a lot more volatility because of the smart money flowing in and out of it.

While Greece's debt obligations looked ominous and threatened Europe as a whole, the United States also raised concern with its own pending debt obligation; an August 2, 2011 payment that was due and the question of whether or not Congress would or would not raise the federal government's $14.29 trillion borrowing limit remained unanswered, causing more concern. "Gold futures have marched higher for 10 consecutive sessions as investors stocked up on the metal amid wrangling over the U.S. debt limit and amid worries about the European Union's ability to stave off a default by one of its debt-laden members, Greece."[5] Possible defaults with government debt were now on both sides of the Atlantic during 2011 and 2012. Historically, the United States has had the highest rating of AAA since 1941. Yet the United States faced a possible downgrade in US Treasury securities whether or not the default actually occurred. A lower rating translates to higher costs for the United States and forced debt reduction. A downgrade would invariably lead to investors demanding a higher interest rate because of increased risk. When investing, anything can happen. No security or market is invincible. "At $9.7 trillion of securities outstanding,

Treasuries are one of the most liquid markets in the world. Treasury debt made up 95% of total issuance of fixed-income securities in the U.S. in 2010 and make up the bulk of U.S. triple-A rated assets, according to data from Barclays Capital."[6] If investors believe the dollar and US debt are not as safe as they thought, they will flock to precious metals like gold. As a result, gold exceeded $1,600 a troy ounce and reached $1,602.10 on Monday, July 18, 2011.

Once again, gold was a safe haven for investors. Bad news such as the United States getting downgraded will motivate people to buy even more gold. "Gold's long rally has bolstered that belief. Bullion futures rose 2% to $1,888.70 per troy ounce on Monday in New York trading, up for the sixth consecutive trading day and 16% this month. Prices have risen for each of the past 10 years, and are up 32.9% in 2011, which would make this year the biggest percentage gain of the long bull market in gold if the gain holds."[7] Gold reserves increased globally. "So far this year (2011), a net 6.7 million ounces have been added to official reserves world-wide, according to the World Gold Council. That is more than all of last year and almost 2.5 times this year's net inflows to physically backed exchange-traded funds."[8] Economic turmoil causes investors to rush to gold and other precious metals. Gold's sibling, silver, also went up and rallied to a 31-year high of around $50.00 in April, 2011.

GLOBAL GOLD

Gold bugs (as those diehard fans of buying gold are described) are not just domestic. Jewelry continues to be the dominant holding of gold rather than ETFs, mutual funds, and other forms of gold. Gold is desired everywhere. Investors around the world seek protection in gold, especially during trying times or economic upheaval. India is a large buyer of gold for jewelry. India is one of the biggest markets for gold jewelry. Close to India, with regard to gold consumption, is China. The demand from both countries is great: "The data show that gold's ascent is being driven by extraordinary demand from India and China, where rising prosperity is making it easier for millions of people to buy gold in all its forms, particularly jewelry."[9] Total demand in China was 294 tonnes in the first quarter of 2013, a rise of 20 percent on the same quarter the previous year, and total demand in India was 257 tonnes, up 27 percent on the same quarter

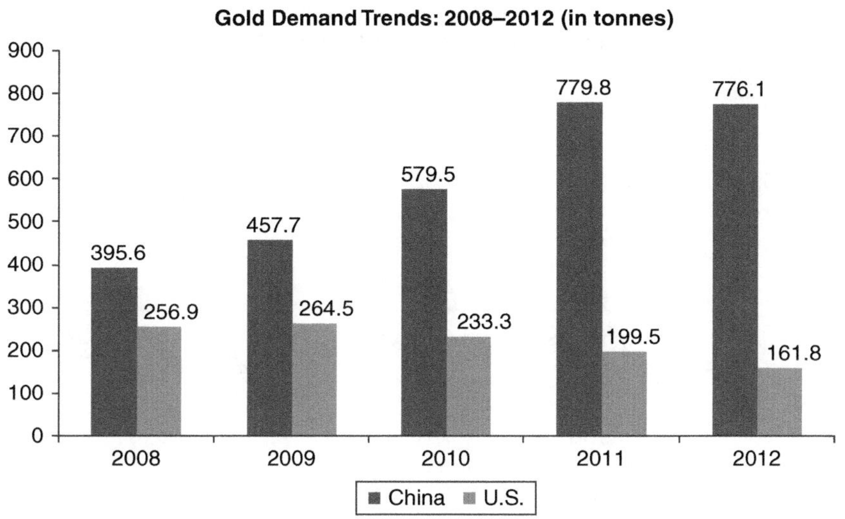

Figure 8.1 Trends in Gold Demand (in tonnes).
Source: "Global Demand Trends," World Gold Council, 2008–2012.

in 2012.[10] China now dwarfs the United States with regard to buying gold (Figure 8.1).

China was the main driver behind gold going up early in 2012: "The Chinese have been loading up like never before on gold ahead of the Lunar New Year, which falls on January 23 this year. It is a time of gift-giving that takes place during family dinners, with the older generation giving money to younger members."[11] War, natural disasters (such as tsunamis, cyclones, hurricanes, fires, tornados, or earthquakes), political upheaval, financial storms, health-care epidemics such as the plague, or any other large-scale calamity causes investors to invest in gold. In troubled times gold can act as a safety blanket. Jewelry is easily carried out of one country into another and the precious metal carries value everywhere.

The United States clearly holds the most gold but other countries are adding to their stockpiles as well. Figure 8.2 is a chart of gold held by various countries throughout the world. According to the World Gold Council, the United States has 76.1 percent of its reserves in gold holdings (8,133.5 tonnes) as of December 2012.

WAVE REVERSAL

What happens when the wave reverses? Commodities move in waves, like all alternative investments. When the world's problems subside, gold may

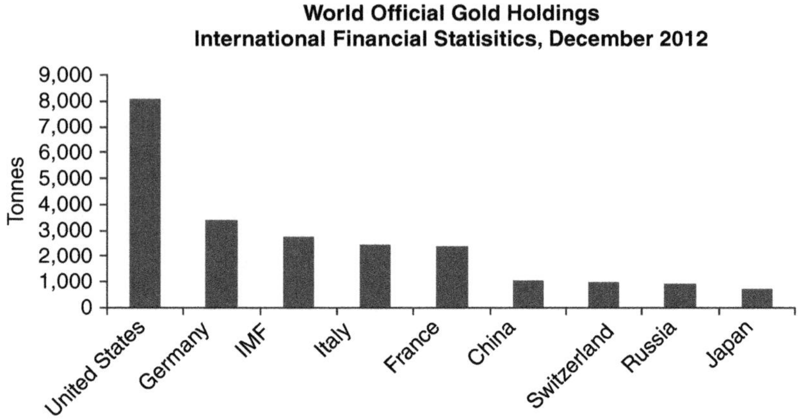

Figure 8.2 Gold Holdings Across Countries.

Source: "World Official Gold Holdings," International Financial Statistics, World Gold Council, December 2012.

reverse directions. Which country will start selling first? Will smaller countries like Cyprus exaggerate any problems they have in order to unload gold supplies first? Like a retail investor, no government wants to look stupid and left holding the bag. Even toward the end of 2011, the demand for gold was weak. Even with all of Europe's woes, gold declined in value. "The problem for gold is that demand for Treasuries is leading to a rising US dollar. That hits gold, which is priced in dollars, by making it more expensive for buyers who hold other currencies."[12]

Numerous investors and reporters told me that they thought gold just went straight up and that there were no gold waves. However, this myopic thinking is erroneous. Gold has historically had many waves. Gold has had not just one but many waves and I believe there have been around six different domestic waves. Gold and other alternatives exhibit short- and long-term waves, which one should explore before making an investment. It is not inconceivable that gold will experience another correction. It has been a long time since gold had a major correction and those corrections tended to be infrequent. From 1999 to 2011, gold experienced three declines greater than 20 percent, but snapped back each time. But this time around might be different.[13] The more information one has, the better it is to make a prudent decision. Some investors look at price while others look at weight. Others use both.

Alternatives typically revert to the mean when they are overvalued or undervalued, similar to the tech bubble in 2000 or the real estate bubble in 2007. Market peaks and bubbles ready to burst typically present danger signs, like having numerous companies filing to go public in a particular sector. The gold wave will likely reverse, as it has in the past. Commodities typically revert to the mean.

WAVE PEAK SIGNALS

Amongst other things, when a commodity or sector dramatically increases or decreases in price, M&A follows. However, not all of these M&A deals are successful. For instance, gold miners did poorly compared with gold over a couple of years from 2010 to 2011 despite the run-up in the underlying commodity, gold. "It's true that mining stocks can magnify gold's moves. That's because of the enormous influence the metal's market price has on a company's earnings. Once bullion advances beyond its production cost, price changes flow directly to the producer's bottom line. But investors and advisors should remember that while this may happen, there's no guarantee it will."[14]

Investors should also be wary of numerous companies going public in one sector. Frequently, this is a sign that they might have poor performance. How many search engines exist today when there were at least ten around the time of the tech bubble? Typically, there are only 1–3 leaders. Not every company can be a leader in a particular sector. For example, a total of 12 global mining companies were priced during the first week of June in 2011. Glencore International PLC's IPO, which raised $10 billion on May 19, 2011, was one of the largest. However, Glencore dropped after its IPO: "The IPO immediately propelled Glencore, with a market value of $59 billion, into the FTSE 100 Index, which tracks the U.K.'s biggest companies, although the stock had fallen 28.2 percent from its initial price as of Aug. 8."[15] Figure 8.3 is a chart of year to date global mining volume, January 1–June 9.

"Many big deals have performed poorly—most notably Glencore, whose shares are down about 31% since its May IPO. At one point in August, of the 20 European IPOs this year larger than $200 million, 19 were either trading lower than their issue price or had been pulled."[16] Arch

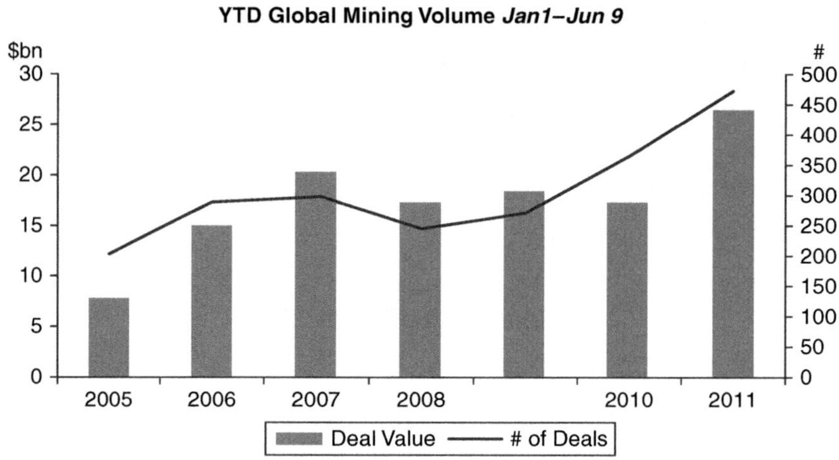

Figure 8.3 Gold Mining Volume: 2005 to 2011.

Source: Vidushi Gupta, "Two Largest 2011 Global Mining ECM Deals Price in Q2," Dealogic, June 10, 2011.

Coal Inc. priced a follow-on offering, raising $13 billion and was the largest US mining company since CONSOL Energy.

BUBBLE TROUBLE

Investors sometimes find themselves in a bubble and tell themselves, "This time is different. It will only go higher and I might miss out." However, thinking such as this is often wrong. "When investors have been experiencing some years of abnormally high or low returns, they begin to believe that those returns probably will not return to the long-term mean returns for that asset class. They also generally lose sight of the fact that those long-term average returns imply that the asset will at some point produce returns as far (and sometimes as often) below the mean as above the mean."[17] It is easy for someone to think gold will just go straight to the moon and never correct. Negative news helps drive investors to gold and make them fearful. The more negative news, the more investors flock to gold. Investors tend to overreact to negative news.

Buying gold is not the same as purchasing a growth company like Microsoft. One can buy gold miners, which is different from buying the actual commodity. Gold, as we know, can fluctuate in value. It also pays no dividend. Commodities such as gold are traded with futures: "A future contract is an order that you place in advance to buy or sell an asset or commodity. The price is fixed when you place the order but you don't pay for the asset until delivery date. Futures markets have existed for a long time in commodities such as wheat, soybeans, and copper."[18] Commodities have risk including unforeseen risk. For example, there is risk where an investor buys or sells futures. "The failure by regulators to detect allegedly falsified bank statements at Peregrine for at least two years has again raised questions about their ability to protect customers of futures brokerages. Last fall, futures regulators failed to detect problems that led to the implosion of MF Global Holdings Ltd."[19] Those who bought gold in 1973 paid approximately $106.48. By 1979, gold prices were around $459.00, more than a four-fold increase over six years. Just like today, gold was a hot topic back then and investors wondered whether or not to jump in, wait, or take a pass. Hypothetically, if one invested at the beginning of 1980, how did they do? Gold continued its ascent to $594.90, but then the wave crested, and from 1981 on there was a reversal and the beginning of a decline for gold. By 2001 gold dropped to $271.04. Those who jumped in at the high got burned. Investing in gold is by no means risk-free, as evidenced by those who lost more than 50 percent over this time period. What happened after 2001? Gold formed a new wave (Gold Wave VI), abandoning its trough to reach a new high over the next nine years. Gold reversed its course more than a decade later after hitting an all-time high. In August 2011, gold started to correct.

THE GOVERNMENT AND GOLD

Government action can affect any commodity or alternative investment including gold. Moreover, various governments buy and sell gold as well as can write or create new laws. "The CFTC was once seen as sleepy and toothless, but the Dodd-Frank law handed the agency arguably more power than any other regulator. Under the law, the CFTC is supposed to police the derivatives market and force once-private transactions onto open exchanges, in full view of regulators."[20] Gold was not so much a target with new rules as oil. Oil shot straight to the sky and regulators were concerned that it was because of market manipulation. As commodities play a larger role with investors, ETFs and mutual funds are facing increased regulations. ETFs were viewed negatively by regulators for a period of time but there was no evidence of any foul play or misuse. ETFs are liked by investors and are not going away. In other words, the market is growing for ETFs and they are competition for actively managed mutual funds: "Exchange-traded funds are posing a new threat to the $7.8 trillion market for active mutual funds by challenging the notion ETFs are only good for tracking benchmarks."[21]

While the search for the oil manipulators proved fruitless, an even larger problem developed called MF Global. MF Global was a firm specializing in commodities that caused problems for both investors and customers. One of the most astute self-made billionaires in the United States, Michael Flowers, and his private equity firm, J.C. Flowers & Co., had an investment in MF Global: "The fallout from the collapse of MF Global, which had hundreds of thousands of customers, is already being felt in Washington, where regulators on Friday vowed to crack down on some of the practices that enabled the firm to place risky bets."[22] The entity as well as the advisor where one buys alternative investments is extremely important. One might successfully invest in gold or other commodities but then be thrown a curve ball if the company they entrust goes under and their money is lost, stolen, or tied up in bankruptcy. Michael Flowers and many less sophisticated investors were duped. Oddly, the US government failed to find anyone culpable.

GOLD CORRELATIONS

Alternative investments tend to hold up reasonably well in down markets compared with equities and bonds. By diversifying alternative investments, one can possibly lower risk and increase returns. Typically, there is a low correlation between alternative investments (such as commodities or hedge funds) and stocks or bonds. "Portfolios of less than perfectly correlated assets always offer better risk-return opportunities than the individual component securities on their own. The lower the correlation between the assets, the greater the gain in efficiency."[23] Gold is another fine example of an alternative investment with a low correlation to equities. It is important to know your assets so they are not too highly correlated. One might add one type of alternative investment, thinking the assets are not correlated but there might be more in common than the investors believe. For instance, a hedged equity, macro, event driven, and commodities asset allocation has low correlation with fixed income. On the other hand, US Equity has low correlation with macro and commodities but a higher correlation with hedged equity and event driven/relative value.

9

VENTURE CAPITAL

VENTURE CAPITAL IS BACK!

While venture capital appears to have not been affected as adversely as publicly traded stock markets, it is somewhat deceiving because venture capital is private and usually lags the stock market either on the way up or down. A healthy IPO market is essential to US venture capital. IPOs, like commodities, revolve around supply and demand. Bernie Marcus cofounded Home Depot during a recession back in 1978 and took the company public in 1981. The company prospered, growing into one of the largest in the United States. Home Depot created thousands of jobs. Even Google, which was one of the best companies to emerge from the last recession (though public now), had a precipitous drop in stock price. Yet Google's stock price went back up with the market rather quickly. And how is Google doing? "Google has done quite well without its own social network. Its online search engine accounts for two-thirds of queries made in the U.S., and even more in parts of Europe. Its revenue is expected to surpass $36 billion this year."[1] Google and other technology companies amassed massive amounts of cash. "Google, which has $39 billion in cash, and Apple, which holds $76 billion including long-term investments, don't pay dividends."[2]

US companies are flush with cash. By mid-2011, US companies were sitting on a record cash hoard of more than $2 trillion.[3] These cash hoards tend to bode well for mergers and acquisitions because companies will look at both internal and external growth. Venture capital leads to growth. "Our research highlights that the existence of VC financing likely is a facilitator of high-revenue growth."[4] While it is hard to believe, I remember when

Google was a small private company struggling to get venture capital. "Nike is setting up a venture capital off-shoot to back startups focused on alternative energies and efficient manufacturing. The technologies could help Nike produce its products more sustainably and cheaply. The move takes a page from Silicon Valley, where technology companies have started venture arms."[5] Companies in the United States are sitting on billions in cash, and venture capital is a means to help them grow. Venture capital can be quite beneficial for individuals as well as companies.

Venture capital is fundamental to the economy. Jobs are created by the entrepreneurs building these fast-growing companies fueled with venture capital. According to the Kauffman Foundation, start-ups have been holding up since the Great Recession. "According to the 'Kauffman Index of Entrepreneurial Activity,' a leading indicator of new business creation in the United States, 0.34 percent of American adults created a business plan per month in 2010, or 565,000 new businesses, a rate that remained consistent with 2009 and represents the highest level of entrepreneurship over the past decade and a half."[6] Job creation remained an issue into 2011. According to the SBA, small employers have generated 65 percent of net new jobs over the past 17 years.[7] Government support for small businesses was lackluster. Funds that should have gone to help small business ended up being used by banks just to pay back TARP.

At the bottom of the stock market, investors lost anywhere from 40 to 80 percent depending on the country and the type of investment made. By 2009, the number of funds and capital committed had rapidly declined. The number of deals and median amount raised prior to an IPO peaked in 2007 and continued a downward spiral until 2009 (see Figure 9.1). Venture funds that invested during the Great Recession are likely to do well, especially if they reserved their cash and took time selecting the best companies they could find. A fund Union Square raised in 2008 was half invested as of March (2010), when it was generating a 23 percent net internal rate of return.[8] It took until 2010 for the Venture Capital wave to reverse. See Table 9.1, which shows venture-backed IPOs increasing in 2010.

VENTURE CAPITAL WAVES

There are three primary exit strategies for venture capital: M&A, IPO, or the private market. Even though it appears to be a short period of time,

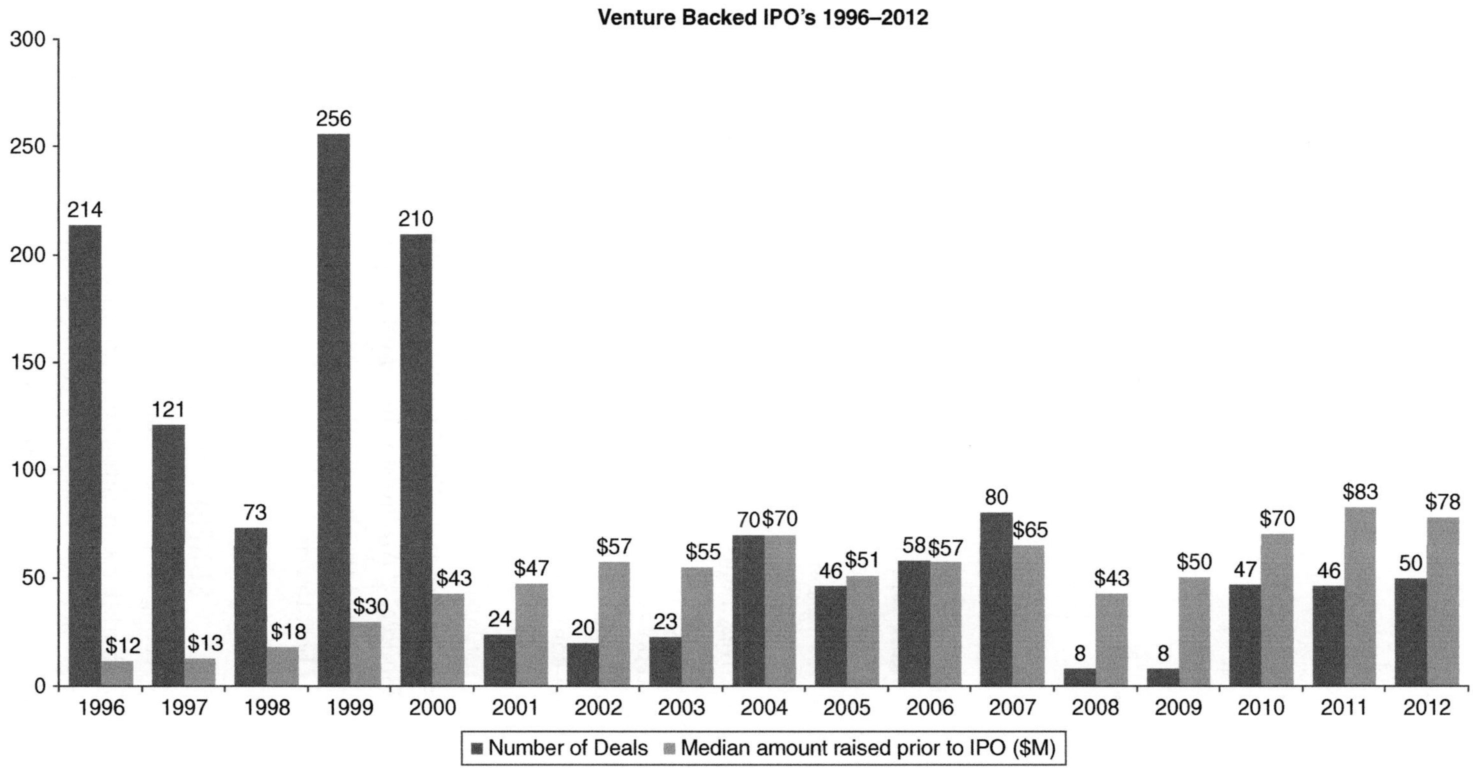

Figure 9.1 Number of Deals and Amount Raised Prior to IPO of Venture-backed IPOs.

Source: Author, using data from Dow Jones VentureSource.

Table 9.1 Fundraising by Venture Funds

Year	Number of funds	Venture capital ($M)
2003	160	$9,144.71
2004	212	$17,826.28
2005	234	$30,080.75
2006	236	$31,161.40
2007	235	$29,378.09
2008	215	$25,073.93
2006	161	$16,175.90
2010	174	$13,436.80
2011	187	$19,045.73
2012	189	$19,448.46
2013	35	$4,053.25

Sources: Author; Thomson Reuters and NVCA.

the time period from 2006 to 2010 shows both IPO and M&A waves. Waves were apparent with deal flow and equity into US venture-backed companies. Venture capital flowed back in during 2010, 2011, and 2012.

By way of comparison, $41 billion was raised in 2007 while only $11.6 billion was raised in 2010. "Hit by the financial meltdown and recessions, many venture capitalists scrambled in 2009 to shut down their weaker investments and conserve cash. New investment activity declined, and profits from IPOs and acquisitions were few and far between."[9] Deal flows for 2009 included insider rounds, which artificially made the year appear better than it was because the same people who invested in the companies were investing again and these were not new deals. "In the second quarter of 2009, VC's nationwide did 53 percent of their deals as insider rounds, not bringing in any new investors to participate in the funding, according to a data mash-up provided by Dow Jones VentureSource."[10] An investor in venture capital should pay attention to both M&A and IPO waves. There are times to sell and periods of time where it is best to wait.

SURFING IN A HURRICANE

The idea of investing in private equity in 2009 was about as attractive as surfing in a shark tank or throwing yourself off an ocean liner while strapped to an anchor. 2009 was Armageddon for investors. News articles during this time period were pessimistic, using words such as "triage, ailing, plunged, slump, or bad." As one can plainly see in Figure 9.2, during 2008

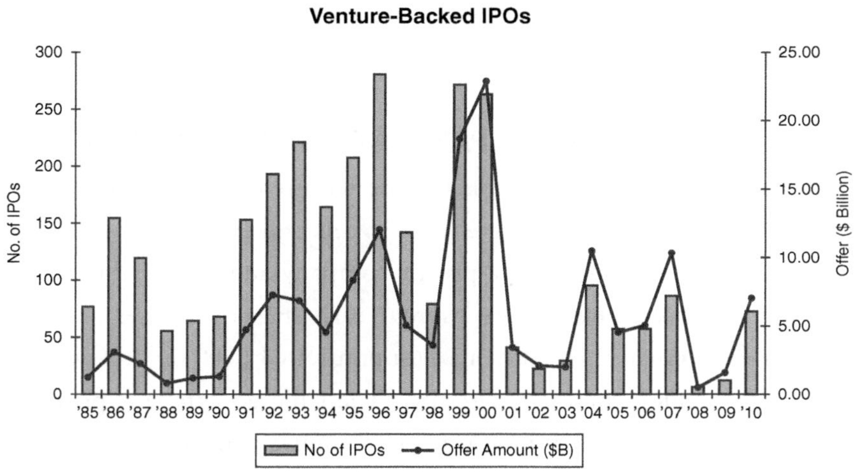

Figure 9.2 Number of IPOs and Offer Amount of Venture-backed IPOs.
Source: "National Venture Capital Association Yearbook," 2011, p. 14.

and 2009, venture-backed IPOs were not too popular. Some even thought venture capital was over. However, Wave Theory tells us that this was precisely the best time to invest. Despite the negative media, Eric Lefkofsky seeded Groupon with $1 million in 2008, which might have appeared dubious considering the market collapse.

Those who bet the farm can make a lot of money. "In asset markets, the richest individuals may well be those who placed large bets on very risky gambles and won. Their success would naturally tend to reinforce their confidence in their own hunches whether or not such confidence is justified."[11] Placing a million-dollar bet on any company is extremely risky. Even if you feel that you know the business or your background gives you an edge, it is still risky.

While good companies will grow regardless of market conditions, venture capital can offer exceptional buying opportunities in bad times. For example, Groupon was founded in 2008 and offers subscribers coupons with email. When I first reviewed the company, I thought it was one in a few that would bode well in the middle of a recession. There are "daily deals" for services such as massages at a spa, goods such as clothing at GAP, or even dinner at a local restaurant. Yet Eric knew precisely what he was doing, as any experienced surfer in the VC waters knows. Groupon was neither the first company he invested in nor the last. Rather, it was one of many investments. Lefkofsky is listed as the largest shareholder, with

21 percent of the shares, and earned a seat on the Forbes 400 list for his venture capital investment.

NEVER BE LATE TO A PARTY WITH VENTURE CAPITAL

Groupon is an excellent example of how venture capital can be lucrative for investors, a lesson to observe when to sell, and distinguishing the difference between investing in a private company and buying IPO shares. Buying IPO shares gives you exposure to early stage companies but is not buying an alternative investment. Groupon raised $700 million with the sale of 35 million shares (5 percent). "The Chicago company priced its IPO at $20 a share, according to people familiar with the matter, above the range of $16 to $18 a share that it set two weeks ago. At $20, Groupon would be valued at nearly $13 billion before its Friday debut on the Nasdaq Stock Market."[12] Valuation of a private company is never easy but pricing an IPO too high can often lead to poor results.

In less than one year, Groupon lost half its value. Yet Groupon was not the only Internet company that filed to go public. Investors were drawn to a handful of Internet names in 2011. A number of Internet IPOs hit the market: Pandora, LinkedIn, Groupon, and Zynga. Mutual funds bought shares of companies like Zynga. "In February 2011, heavyweights Morgan Stanley Investment Management, Fidelity Investments and T. Rowe Price Group Inc. together invested $490 million in the maker of games including 'FarmVille' and 'Words with Friends,' valuing Zynga at $10 billion. The investors paid $14.03 per share, according to Securities and Exchange Commission filings."[13] Figure 9.3 is the stock performance of the Morgan Stanley and Goldman Sachs lead managed IPO for Zynga.

Decent IPOs will continue despite some of the flaws found with certain troubled IPOs. Though it has not yet filed to go public, Dropbox, with only 70 staffers but 50 million users generating $240 million in revenue for 2011, grosses nearly three times more per employee than even Google, which might explain why the company was able to raise a whopping $250 million on a $4 billion valuation.[14] Yelp filed an S-1 on November 17, 2011 for $100 million. The company is a leading website for online local reviews and has been growing at around 80 percent each quarter of the year.

Zynga IPO: Morgan Stanley and Goldman Sachs Joint Bookrunning Managers

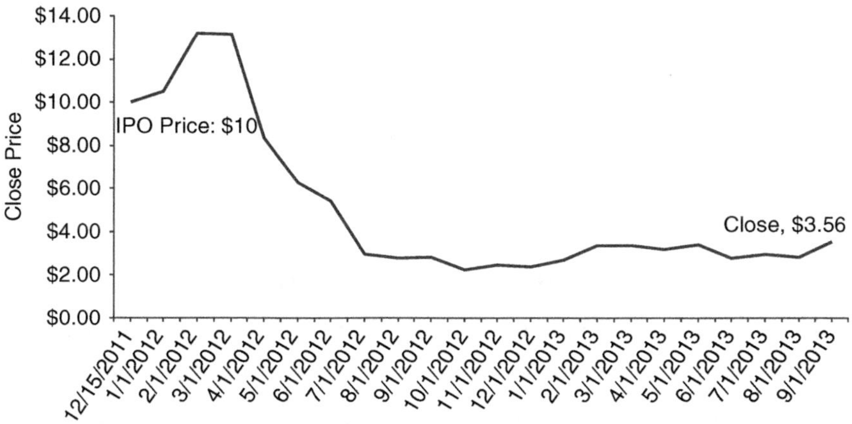

Figure 9.3 Morgan Stanley and Goldman Sachs Joint Booking Running Managers of Zynga IPO.

Source: Author.

GLOBAL VENTURE CAPITAL AND IPOS

Internet IPOs are not just domestic. They are global. For example, Russia appears to be making quite a bit of progress with the Internet as well as giving investors the opportunity to participate in new and attractive IPOs. Russia overtook Germany as the market with the highest number of unique visitors online.

Russia also merged two stock exchanges, which might become a financial hub. "Clearly, internet investing is going global and the West is losing its monopoly, not just in thinking up clever ideas for web businesses but in financing them."[15] Russia appears to have learned from the United States with regard to how venture capital works and how companies go public (before Sarbanes-Oxley and other regulation). "Another factor favoring investment in start-ups is the level of government support for foreign and domestic investment in private equity: at the federal and regional levels, the Russian state is investing tens of billions of dollars in innovation."[16] Russia supports Internet companies going public and is very much pro-business. Yandex raised $1.3 billion on Nasdaq in May 2011 and Mail.ru raised more than $900 million in London in November 2010. As of 2011, Internet users in Russia exceed that of Germany, France, Britain, Italy, Turkey, Spain, and Portugal.

While Russia is dependent (or at the mercy of) on US banking techniques, they will likely continue to learn the IPO process. "Direct state financing is also provided through the Russian Venture Company, which has launched 12 hi-tech funds in Russia and abroad. Three years ago, fewer than two dozen funds were operating in the country, but now there is more money in Moscow than in many other innovation hotspots."[17] Areas in which the United States stumbled could easily be avoided by other nations.

LEARNING WHERE TO SURF

Prudent investors with venture capital know when to buy or sell. Frequently, a new area will spawn other ideas and new companies will emerge. In 2013 and the beginning of 2014, venture dollars flowed into a number of interesting new areas such as Sustainability, Big Data, 3D Printers, Virtual Realty, Bitcoin, Cardio Companies, Storage Companies, Medical Marijuana, and Cloud Computing. It is impossible to predict the size of a new area but all of these areas appear to have potential. Sometimes new areas for venture capital can run into problems and fizzle out of favor. Two controversial areas attracting investors are Bitcoin and Medical Marijuana.

Bitcoin advocate Charlie Shrem was arrested and charged with a money-laundering conspiracy. Bitcoin is a virtual currency that started as an experiment and gathered not only a lot of support but also investors such as Cameron and Tyler Winklevoss known for Facebook. Bitcoin also lost over $5 billion in value when a bug affected some of the exchanges. One of the exchanges, Mt. Gox, an exchange in Tokyo, halted withdrawals. On February 14, 2014 about $2.5 million was apparently stolen from Silk Road 2.0, a website that is used to trade mainly illegal drugs.[18] The virtual currency shows the perils of getting in too early. Mt. Gox filed for bankruptcy in Japan, saying it lost nearly half a billion dollars' worth of the virtual coins due to hacking into its faulty computer system.[19] While Bitcoin might ultimately be successful, regulation is needed because it is an exchange. The bankruptcy and other early dilemmas hurt investors in any private companies devoted to the virtual currency as well as those who bought the currency on an exchange. Early investors must always be cautious, especially with controversial companies.

Another controversial area is Medical Marijuana, which has led to many new companies and attracted investors. More than 20 states allow the sale of medical marijuana. Colorado and Washington have even legalized the drug for recreational use. Entrepreneurs are starting companies that make equipment to grow marijuana, vending machines to sell marijuana, and other innovative ideas. Bloomberg BusinessWeek describes these entrepreneurs: "A whole new pot economy has grown up, complete with cannapreneurs and even private equity financers."[20] Investors put so much money into penny stocks involved in this area that it created a billionaire on paper according to the LA Business Journal. However, this area is very high risk. Federal law is different from state law. Federal law still prohibits possessing, using, or selling marijuana according to the 1970 Controlled Substance Act, which classifies marijuana as a Schedule I drug. Early in February 2014, the Treasury and Justice Department issued guidance for banks concerning marijuana-related businesses. "The Financial Crimes Network ("FinCEN") is issuing guidance to clarify Bank Secrecy Act ("BSA") expectations for financial institutions seeking to provide services to marijuana-related businesses. FinCEN is issuing guidance in light of recent state initiatives to legalize certain marijuana-related activity and related guidance by the U.S. Department of Justice ("DOJ") concerning marijuana-related enforcement priorities."[21].

One wave that is clearly gaining momentum is Cloud Computing. "Cloud Computing is a sharp departure from the status quo. Today most companies own their software and hardware and keep them 'on premise' in data centers and other specialized facilities. With Cloud Computing, in contrast, companies lease their digital assets, and their employees don't know the location of the computers, data centers, applications, and databases that they're using."[22] Waves can vary in size and Cloud Computing appears to be quite large. Cloud providers have their customers access data and software off their servers via the web. In 2011, IBM introduced its Hadoop-based Infosphere BigInsights cloud software with big data-processing capabilities including scalability and flexibility in handling fast-growing and non-relational data such as social network comments, weather data, log files, genomic data, and even video.[23] The growth potential for Cloud Computing is mind boggling. A small, fast-growing company that went public, Salesforce.com, reached a stock market value of $13.3 billion as of December 16, 2011. By January 2013, Salesforce.com exceeded $24 billion in market cap. No only is there competition amongst Amazon, Apple, Microsoft, and other 800-pound guerillas, but numerous smaller companies are working on the cloud. "As with any online or hosted service, security, reliability, availability, and performance are the biggest concerns."[24] One of the reasons Cloud Computing has become of so much interest is because it ties into mobility. Cloud Computing is necessary for all the data storage generated by cell phones.

There are many new Cloud Computing companies filling needs. For example, "Cloud Computing startup enStratus Networks Inc. raised $3.5 million in venture capital in a round led by El Dorado Ventures."[25] The start-up enStratus offers cloud governance by leveraging existing IT policies and procedures. Also, cloud networks have emerged, which essentially serve as cloud backups. "Don't look now, but as telecom companies acquire Cloud Computing vendors, we're seeing the beginning of cloud networks: chains of linked data centers owned by one company that let two or more data centers back up one another."[26] Even the CIA is getting into Cloud Computing with private clouds. "The CIA is now working toward general-purpose data center architecture—a private cloud—in which any of the servers could host a variety of workloads. And it's working with others in the intelligence community to create shared computing resources that all intelligence agencies can access."[27] The Pentagon has the largest IT budget out of any organization in the world and will spend approximately $38.4 billion in fiscal 2012. Security for the cloud is needed. A private company called Gazzang provides security solutions and operational diagnostics that help enterprises protect sensitive information and monitor performance in cloud environments. Cloud Computing companies are going public, such as Fusion-io, a data storage company, went public on June 9 at $19.00, raising $234 million. Fusion-io helps speed up storage for the cloud. As an example, the company helps power the iCloud for Apple and provides higher information density with Facebook. Similarly, FusionStorm Global Inc. filed for an IPO in August,2011 to raise $175 million. In 2010, they had gross profit of $123 million on revenue of $727 million. FusionStorm offers integrated IT solutions, including data storage, network optimization, and cloud services to businesses and local governments. Another cloud company, Guidewire Software, provides a core system suite for the global property-and-casualty insurance industry covering underwriting, policy administration, billing, claims, and reinsurance management. The software produces savings and faster response to claims.

BEHAVIORAL FINANCE AND FUNDS RAISING CAPITAL

Strong venture firms can raise money even in difficult times to pursue new venture capital developments. Behavioral finance is revealing more about various alternative investments. For instance, papers have been written about venture capital such as "Specialization and Success: Evidence from Venture Capital" by Paul Gompers, Anna Kovner, Josh Lerner, and David Scharfstein on how organizational structure affects behavior and outcomes. "We find that venture capital firms with more experience tend to outperform those with less experience, and that both firm and person level industry experience matters for investment success."[28] Knowledge is power with venture capital. Investors in venture capital must carefully consider the organization they choose to invest with since they vary.

Battery Ventures closed its eighth fund in July at $750 million. Another well-respected name in venture capital, NEA, raised a venture capital mega-fund in 2009: "NEA's $2.48 billion fund is 20 times the size of the average venture fund raised last year and is the largest launched since the financial crisis."[29] Later, in May 2012, NEA announced the closing of another giant venture fund. By mid-2012, NEA closed on a $2 billion fund. Union Square, which raised a venture fund in 2008 during terrible market conditions, might raise a new fund in 2011. "Twitter Inc. investor Union Square Ventures is laying the groundwork to raise another $150 million to $200 million that it could plow into new technology companies, people familiar with the plans said."[30] Summit Partners raised a fund that exceeded the last raise they had. "Boston-based Summit Partners has closed its third venture capital fund, at $520 million, well above the firm's prior VC fund."[31] Overall, despite the new wave of venture capital, few funds were able to raise funds as reported by *Pensions and Investments*: "Venture capital is gaining a little love and some new money from institutional investors following a decade-long stretch of poor returns and client withdrawals. Only a select few managers are benefiting."[32]

NEW AREAS

Timing with alternative investments is something a prudent investor should not neglect. Finding a new wave with the right venture capital fund can make a world of difference with performance. Performance with venture capital continues to favor the successful venture firms with established track records. "Forty-one percent of venture fund managers managing a top quartile fund go on to produce another top quartile fund with their next effort, with a total of 73% of managers performing above the median benchmark with their successor fund."[33] However, a number of new venture firms entered the picture with compelling stories. These firms are likely to raise assets and prosper. Some are run by successful entrepreneurs with skin in the game. Others are highly specialized. Like all other alternative investments, venture capital moves in waves. See Figure 9.4, comparing the IPO market with increased unemployment. In 2009, there were just 12 IPOs and 2008 had an anemic 6 IPOs. When the stock market plummets and the going gets tough, innovation flourishes and entrepreneurs build great companies.

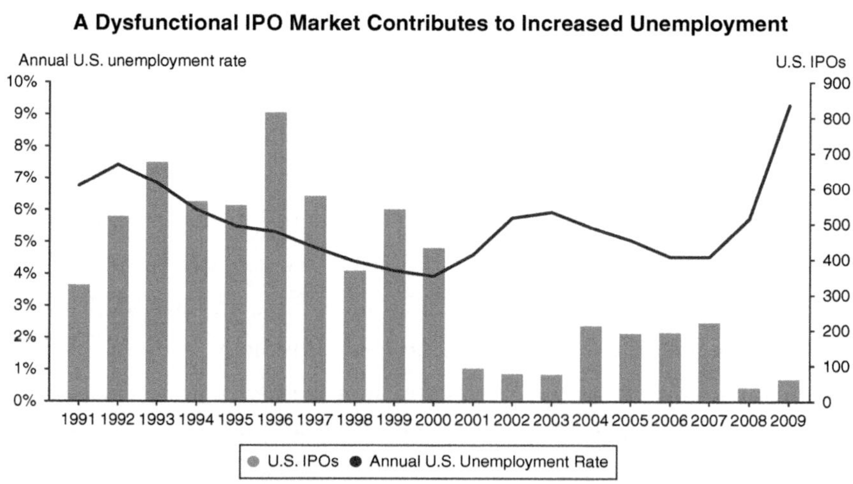

Figure 9.4 IPO Market and Unemployment.

Source: David Weild and Edward Kim, "Market Structure Is Causing the IPO Crisis – And More," Capital Market Series, IssuWorks and Grant Thornton, June 2010, p. 1.

Technology companies typically account for almost 30 percent of IPOs in a given year and IPOs are key to job growth. For instance, A123 Systems went public in September 2009, the only VC-backed company to go public. A123 is a smart-battery company. This alternative energy makes lithium-ion batteries for electric cars and is part of a segment of tech companies called clean technologies or cleantech. While cleantech looked like it was finished when the market collapsed in 2008, I pointed out in my previous book that it very likely would come back and possibly be stronger. I believe now there is a second wave of cleantech, or Cleantech 2.0.

Disruptive market forces could, over many years, enable clean technologies to supplant fossil fuel the way the PC replaced the mainframe. Two high-profile VCs, John Doerr and Vinod Khosla, are dedicated to clean technologies: "Now the former colleagues are competing to fund the most promising startups in clean technology, a potentially lucrative but risky field many believe could lead to Silicon Valley's next boom."[34] Khosla raised a large fund dedicated to clean technology. Khosla Ventures closed a billion-dollar fund by the end of 2011.

Government support or lack of it can affect next-generation technologies: "Governments have long been central in advancing the development of next-generation technologies . . . Government support is most effective when it's directed not just at nascent technologies but also at nascent business models."[35] The US Department of Energy (DOE) helped support both Tesla Motors and Fisker Automotive in 2009. As described by the Wall Street Journal in "Venture Capital: New VC Force": "The DOE hopes to lend or give out more than $40 billion to businesses working on 'clean technology,' everything from electric cars and novel batteries to wind turbines and solar panels. In the first nine months of 2009, the DOE doled out $13 billion in loans and grants to such firms."[36] Fisker won loans from the federal government for approximately $528 million while Tesla Motors got a $365 million DOE loan to build electric cars. "Fisker has raised more than $1 billion in funding since it was founded in August 2007, and last year it bought a former General Motors Co. assembly plant in Wilmington, Del., for $18 million. That's where it will manufacture Project Nina, as well as future vehicles such as a hardtop convertible coupe and possibly a crossover vehicle."[37]

SURFING WITH THE GOVERNMENT

Government intervention with venture capital can be positive. In-Q-Tel, the U.S. Government's venture arm, was run by Buzzy Krongard, the former CEO of Alex. Brown, which undoubtedly explains why the venture was successful not only in helping the United States achieve a lead in technology for national security, but also in the performance of its investments. Under Buzzy, many companies that the U.S. Government invested in, went public or were sold. As a Director at Alex. Brown, I worked with numerous technology companies that went public. However, there is a wrong way for government to be involved with venture capital. The most obvious is when politicians force an agenda or meddle with the venture capital process. The legendary venture capitalist Tom Perkins forecasted that all solar companies like Solyndra would fail. "Government venture capital can't 'conjure up the 'animal spirits' of capitalism: 'Let's make money!' Perkins said. Instead, government has social objectives or, in the case of the Solyndra loan guarantee, lofty goals like reducing the need for oil. But the biggest reason, Perkins said, is that government VC investing in 'done by people who are not qualified. I almost said 'incompetent.'"[38]

While too early to tell, one interesting attempt by the U.S. Government to encourage investment in early private stage companies is called the JOBS Act (Jumpstart Our Business Startups)."When Congress, in an almost unheard-of display of bipartisanship, passed the JOBS Act in April, crowdfunding seemed poised to boom. In 2011 alone, crowdfunding platforms helped raise about $1.5 billion for start-ups and other projects, according to Massolution, a research firm covering the space."[39] Yet no guidelines were put in place. Rules cannot be followed if they are not clearly disseminated. The most significant bits of the act are bottled up at the SEC, which is responsible for transforming laws into rules that can actually be implemented, and the SEC is swamped with rule-writing duties: the JOBS Act adds to an in-tray already bulging after the passage of the Dodd-Frank act in 2010.[40] Meanwhile, quite a few websites were started to benefit from the new law and it appears that thousands of companies are seeking funds:

> Many crowdfunding sites have been cropping up to cash in on the new law. Once the JOBS Act rules are in place, at least 100 crowdfunding companies are expected to launch, says Kevin Berg Grell,

> who runs an accreditation program for the professional association Crowdsourcing.org. By the end of 2013, that number could double, he says. But these new companies have found themselves running headlong into a regulatory thicket.[41]

In some cases, shares are purchased but with others, one will receive merely a product or service for free, not too dissimilar from a donation where one gets a dinner or complimentary gift bag."Kickstarter doesn't give the funder a stake in the project. Equity crowdfunding allows funders to buy shares in small startups. Venture capital is limited to individuals with $1 million net worth."[42] Kickstarter is not a company for those looking for venture capital type investments. "For all the buzz about Kickstarter—it has raised more than $230 million for 23,000 'projects' since 2009—it does not sell equity... Instead, the public makes donations and gets some sort of premium reward."[43]

Not much transpired with regard to rules. "In short, all legislative affairs activity and regulatory inactivity has occurred in the equity-based crowdfunding space. As a result, micro-finance and debt-based crowdfunding has, to date, been able to flourish without the promotion and attendant scrutiny of the Administrative Branch."[44] Like a lot of government regulation, there are areas that will be overlooked or not well thought out. "A second JOBS Act provision will allow widespread advertising and marketing of private offerings, formerly restricted to wealthy investors."[45] While it is too early to tell, the JOBs Act might be destined for trouble. "For small investors it will be either a great "level-the-playing-field" opportunity to get in on the ground floor of promising startups or a federally sanctioned invitation to fraud on a scale not seen since the boiler-room days. Or both."[46] Table 9.2 is a useful chart differentiating the three types of crowdfunding.

Table 9.2 Types of Crowdfunding

	Types of Crowdfunding
1. Lending-based crowdfunding	• Investors are repaid over time • Investment is usually in proportion to risk
2. Donations/gift-based crowdfunding	• Money is given to a business, with no expectation of ownership or a return on investment • Company might give a product to investors
3. Equity-based crowdfunding	• Accredited investors receive a percentage of the company in return for investment

Source: Author.

The JOBS Act might also affect other alternative investments besides investment going into private companies. For example, the JOBS Act involves commodities. Like venture capital, commodities are an alternative investment. Commodity pools are often called managed futures funds and marketed as privately placed limited partnerships. "Finra, an independent regulator for all U.S. exchange markets and brokers, also was required under the JOBS Act to set its own equity crowdfunding rules. But unlike the SEC, it wasn't given a deadline."[47] If an investor does not understand the venture capital or IPO process, it will be that much more difficult; they will most likely fail to comprehend the ramifications and ultimately lose money.

Government involvement with business can adversely affect alternative investments. While venture capital waves are transparent and the market has improved, it is also evident that the governments' idea for Glass-Steagall and Sarbanes Oxley were somewhat ill-conceived. Solyndra is a classic example. "The White House this month made final a $197 million guarantee for SolarPower Inc., a maker of lightweight solar panels in San Jose, Calif. Two more guarantees for solar manufacturers valued at combined $425 million are due to be approved before a Sept. 30 deadline."[48] The US administration made the decision to keep giving billions of dollars to solar projects regardless of the outcome. The US Government allocated tens of billions for these futile solar projects. In 2009, over $60 billion was allocated for the stimulus package specifically for renewable energy and transmission projects. In September 2011, the "Energy Department completed a $737 million loan guarantee to Tonopah Solar Energy and an additional $337 million for Sempra Energy. Tonopah Solar is a wholly owned subsidiary of SolarReserve."[49]

Cleantech showed signs of life in 2011. As the SF Business Times stated in "Cleantech VC funding bounces back," "Venture capital investing in clean technology companies rebounded in the first quarter with solar, biofuel and other 'green' firms garnering $2.6 billion from investors."[50] Cleantech spread across the country and appears to be a viable movement not just on the west coast. For example, Greentown labs, a nonprofit incubator for clean-technology startup companies started in Boston mid 2011. Cleantech has morphed into new businesses as well as created jobs in areas like San Francisco: "The San Francisco metropolitan area, which includes Oakland and Fremont, ranks No. 1 out of the top 100 metropolitan areas for the number of cleantech jobs it has, with 13,917."[51]

It is important for investors to be cognizant of what direction a government is taking with a certain sector or industry. A government can destroy or help an area. However, a government might wade into an area they should not be in or have no clue about. Therefore, an investor should be very careful about investing in the footsteps of a government. Solar energy is a good example. Previously, the White House touted Solyndra as a leader with its green jobs program: The $535 million government loan guarantee so prized by the solar-panel maker may have ultimately contributed to the company's undoing, say investors with knowledge of the company's operations. The new factory built with DOE funds foisted fixed costs.[52] Taxpayers lost $535 million and the ordeal was labeled Solargate after executives pleaded the Fifth Amendment. Many venture capital firms and other investors backed solar companies following in the government's footsteps. Some were burned.

The US Government has made quite a few business blunders over time. "Politicians make political decisions, not economic ones. Thus history is littered with government investment disasters. The Clinch River Breeder Reactor, authorized in 1970, was estimated to cost $699 million. The project ran through $8 billion before, unbuilt, it was canceled in 1983."[53] There were numerous repercussions to Glass-Steagall being repealed. Many former heads of large banks have concluded the act was problematic. "The former Citigroup chairman now believes it was a mistake to scrap the Glass-Steagall separation of commercial and investment banking. As stunning as this admission was, he was only catching up with what markets already think."[54] While there is a long list, research and IPOs was an area that suffered.

Going against a wave is fruitless, similar to driving the wrong way down a number of one-way streets. Investing in solar was hopeless, like driving in the opposite direction on a one-way street. Evergreen Solar Inc. filed for bankruptcy in August 2011 after receiving state and local subsidies. Competition from China as well as new technologies made the space immensely competitive. Politicians steering money blindly, to profit themselves or gain political contributions, will rarely produce meaningful results. In other words, the companies they support will most likely fail. One does not need to be Descartes to know that if you build a house or anything else using a weak foundation, the result will be lackluster. Politicians made green jobs a political agenda. "President Obama has made green jobs a centerpiece of his economic policy. But plunging prices and the August bankruptcies of Evergreen Solar, SpectraWatt, and the now-infamous Solynda raise doubts whether made-in-America solar products can compete with Chinese rivals."[55] It would be ill-advised to discount China for improving upon their technology prowess. "As more US tech startups see China as an essential place to do business, increasing numbers of Chinese investors are funding them and helping them expand to the mainland. Chinese venture capital firms backed 28 US companies in 2011, nearly double the number two years earlier, according to Dow Jones VentureSource."[56] While the United States is the global superpower, China has been making great strides in many fronts involving technology. For example, China is working toward a permanent space station and made great progress in November 2011 when the Shenzhou-8 spacecraft docked with the Tiangong-1 laboratory module. Years ago, an investor could make an investment in venture capital here in the United States without observing the rest of the world. However, that is no longer the case. Venture capital is global. Presently, there are signs of a new wave of global venture capital. The wave that is forming is domestic but has the potential of expanding abroad.

RIDING THE RIGHT WAVE

After the repeal of the Glass-Steagall Act, which had separated commercial from investment banks, banks did not need to provide as much support like research and liquidity to attract underwriting business. IPOs in the United States are way down from their historic high of 4,085 deals in 2007: "But IPOs are still out of reach due to the high cost of public-company reporting introduced by Sarbanes-Oxley legislation, as well as the lack of sell-side analysts to pump up IPOs for investors since Wall Street's settlement with former New York Attorney General Elliot

Spitzer."[57] Compared to the year 2000, where there were 8,039 deals and $99,223,690,200 invested, 2011 is anemic. The US listings are down 43% since the peak in 1997 (Table 9.3).

Venture capital plays an important role in any economy. Venture capital is evolving and helps find new areas that one might have little knowledge about and presents a huge growth opportunity. One of these new areas, which I call "Cardio Companies," involves the heart and cardiovascular disease. Over one million Americans die from cardiovascular disease, which represents around 40 percent of all deaths for those 35 and older. Heart disease is not just domestic, it is a problem everywhere. Heart disease is the world's biggest killer, claiming 7.3 million lives in 2008. The majority of Americans are overweight. Obesity is a problem in the United States. The condition is associated with cardiovascular disease and other ailments. In New York the number of major steakhouses featured in the Zagat guides has increased sevenfold over the past 30 years, to about 125 today.[58] Every 34 seconds a heart attack occurs and every 60 seconds a death occurs because of heart disease.

Table 9.3 Number of Venture Capital Deals by Year

Year	Number of deals	Amount invested
1995	1897	$8,012,866,300
1996	2642	$11,348,442,100
1997	3223	$14,982,750,400
1998	3733	$21,510,506,900
1999	5605	$54,966,243,300
2000	8044	$105,223,794,400
2001	4590	$40,975,854,300
2002	3201	$22,140,744,500
2003	3019	$19,677,047,200
2004	3216	$23,235,111,700
2005	3299	$23,604,559,200
2006	3879	$27,588,487,900
2007	4211	$31,882,616,100
2008	4163	$29,920,614,800
2009	3140	$20,380,904,900
2010	3622	$23,314,765,100
2011	3937	$29,462,811,000
2012	3698	$23,524,895,000

Sources: Author; PricewaterhouseCoopers/National Venture Capital Association Money Tree Association Report, Data: Thomson Reuters and National Venture Capital.

Venture capital flows to areas with growth potential. Cardio companies fit this description.

One day we might see a venture fund focused on health care and perhaps even has a focus just on cardiovascular disease. "Venture capital will most likely become highly specialized again."[59] Behavioral finance concurs with this sentiment. "We find that generalist firms tend to *underperform* specialist firms. Generalist firms do not appear to allocate capital as well across industries, and may also underperform in their investments within an industry."[60] The risk for venture firms specializing in an area such as cardiovascular disease is that the matter is highly complex and there is no cure. "Coronary heart disease, which affects 16.3 million Americans, refers to a range of conditions caused by fat build-up in coronary arteries that can lead to chest pain, heart attacks and death. It kills more than 405,000 people a year, including about 189,100 women, according to the National Heart, Lung, and Blood Institute."[61] The market potential is vast but finding a solution is complicated. Currently, there is no easy solution to remove plaque from blocked arteries, like Drano unclogging pipes for a sink.

A lot of venture capital deals involve new technology. Cardio companies involve new technology. While a stress test might reveal a problem with the heart, a heart imaging test called computed tomographic (CT) angiography or coronary computed tomographic angiography (CCTA) is much more detailed and helpful in revealing a complication. CT angiography is a fast-growing technology for identifying cardiovascular problems. Technology is evolving rapidly in this area. The Wall Street Journal reported a new strategy to revive victims of heart attacks, which would improve a patient's odds of survival. "The capnograph, which measures carbon dioxide being expelled from the mouth of the patient, can tell rescuers when further efforts at cardiopulmonary resuscitation, or CPR, are futile or whether they should be continued."[62] Joshua Smith and Pramod Bonde developed the first wireless-powered, driveline-free heart pump called the Free-Range Resonant Electrical Energy Delivery System, or FREE-D. Many people with heart attacks fail to get help right away and many are reluctant to go to a hospital, which is a mistake.

While high risk, small companies frequently merge or get acquired. Selecting the leader can be rewarding for investors. An emerging area such as cardio companies can lead to many new small companies being formed. Careful selection is important, especially in a new area.

A sampling of ten private cardio companies I have observed might illustrate how a new area of venture capital can be formed are as follows:

1. *Infraredx*, Burlington, Massachusetts, analyses plaques. Infraredx is the only company with an "intravascular imaging system that is FDA-cleared for the detection of lipid core plaques, which are known to complicate stenting."[63]
2. *Corventis* is a company in San Jose, California, that makes wireless heart-monitoring and found a way to put sophisticated monitoring technology into patches. "The company, backed by venture-capital firms such as Kleiners Perkins Caufield & Byers, makes a waterproof Band-Aid-like patch that patients wear on their chests for up to a month. The device monitors their heart rate, fluids and respiratory activity. It can detect heart problems such as arrhythmias and transmit data wirelessly over a cellular network."[64]
3. *CardioVax LLC* is a start-up company based in Princeton, New Jersey, run by CEO Oye Olukotun. The company is dedicated to advancing technologies from discovery to routine clinical practice, and specifically to developing novel treatments for cardiovascular disease caused by atherosclerosis, an accumulation of fatty deposits in the walls of blood vessels.[65] CVX-210-H has reduced the progression of atherosclerosis by more than 60 percent in treated animals versus untreated animals.
4. *Sunshine Heart Inc.*, situated in Eden Prairie, Minnesota, and run by Dave Rosa, is developing medical technology to treat heart failure. Rosa has completed a clinical study that puts it closer to launching the next generation of its product. The start-up's C-Pulse system wraps a pulsating cuff around the aorta, improving blood flow in patients suffering from heart failure.[66]
5. *InterValve* raised $4.7 million to finance clinical trials. The Minnetonka, Minnesota, based company aims to tap into the growing market for so called transcatheter valve technology, which surgeons use to replace heart valves without cracking open a patient's chest.[67]

6. *Ikaria Inc.*, a critical care-focused biotechnology company based in Hampton, New Jersey, is developing a product designed to be administered by injection within 90 minutes of acute myocardial infarction.[68] The injection might limit muscle damage after a heart attack. "CardioMEMS is a medical device that has developed and is commercializing proprietary wireless sensing and communication technology for the human body. The company's technology platform is designed to improve the management of severe chronic cardiovascular diseases such as aneurysms, heart failure, and hypertension. CardioMEMS miniature wireless sensors can be implanted using minimally invasive techniques and transmit cardiac output, blood pressure, and heart rate data, which are critical to the management of patients."[69]
7. "*CircuLite*, in Saddle Brook, New Jersey, is transforming heart failure treatment with the development of minimally invasive devices for long-term partial circulatory support (PCS). CircuLite's Synergy® Pocket Micro-Pump system is designed to expand the treatment options for chronic heart failure patients and offers potentially broad commercial potential."[70]
8. *Osprey Medical*, a company in Eden Prairie, Minnesota, is another interesting cardio company that made a catheter device for cardiology patients who also suffer from kidney disease. "Physicians typically inject dye in a patient to X-ray the heart prior to cardiology procedures, such as placement of a stent. The dye doesn't harm most patients, but can cause significant damage to those who already suffer from kidney disease. Osprey's product, called Cincor, removes dye from the heart so it doesn't reach the kidneys."[71]
9. *Cellular Dynamics*, situated in Madison, Wisconsin, is the first company known to use iPS technology to make mass quantities of high-quality heart cells.[72]
10. *AliveCor*, located in San Francisco, California, has developed an iPhone ECG—a device that measures your heartbeat rhythm—that during a clinical study warned a cardiologist about a participant's impending heart attack.[73] Cardio companies have a tendency to get

acquired before going public, but not always. Cardio companies appear to be forming a new wave with venture capital. Larger cardio companies will most likely seek the route of an IPO.

Another growing area for venture capital is nanotech. Nanotechnology has evolved since 2004 and appears to be forming another wave. Nanotech is basically the science of making things smaller. A number of years ago, no one ever heard of Cleantech or Social Media. With venture capital, growth comes from fast-growing companies typically in a new area. Within various medical groups, investors can select many different health-care stocks from the various medical groups such as managed care, biomed/biotech, systems, medical devices, and others. New areas can evolve. Sometimes technology can even overlap. For instance, The Children's Hospital of Philadelphia spun off its first start-up company called Vascular Magnetics Inc., which has a therapy for treating peripheral artery disease. Vascular Magnetics Inc. combines two venture areas in one: cardio companies and nanotech. Magnetically guided nanoparticles are used to deliver drugs to blood vessels that are diseased and have blockages.[74] Companies such as Vascular Magnetics have growth potential, especially if they can help save lives of those diagnosed with heart disease.

Nanotech is here to stay. Just ask anyone who used one of the first cell phones that looked like a brick. Technology is getting smaller and smaller. Flat screen televisions can be mounted on a wall, as opposed to the ones a few years ago that were three feet deep. Liquid-crystal display (LCD) screens are almost as good as viewing the real thing. Yet, the next-generation televisions might be even better through nanotechnology using structures called quantum dots. Keyboards are now wafer thin. Canatu Ltd., for example, is a leading developer of a new class of versatile carbon nanomaterial-based components.[75] Not only is the keyboard as thin as a piece of paper, but it bends and can be rolled up.

NEW WAVE

The year 2010 was validation that a new venture capital wave was on its way. Venture-backed IPOs saw a run-up in IPOs toward the end of 2010,

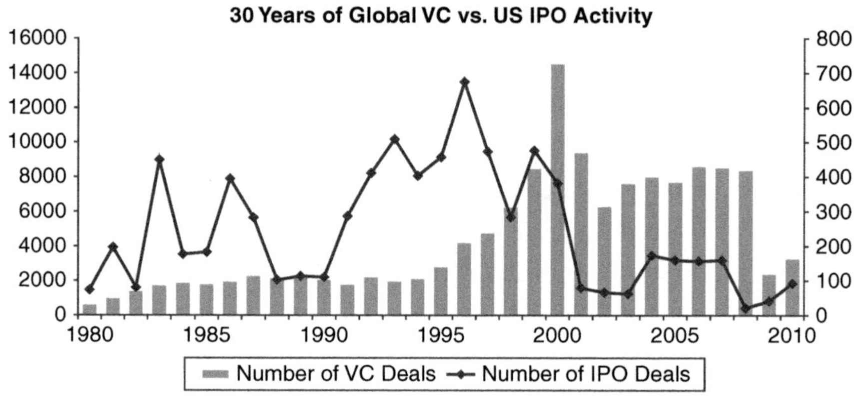

Figure 9.5 Global VC vs. Number of IPOs
Source: Author.

which had not been seen since the tech bubble. Exit activity increased. There were 32 venture capital-backed IPOs in Q4 2010, which was the most since Q3 2000 when there were 89. For the year, there were 72 venture-backed IPOs during 2010, the most since 2007 when there were 86. Some $1.2 billion was invested by venture capital firms in New York in 2010, which overtook Massachusetts in venture-capital funding for Internet and tech start-ups, making it second only to Silicon Valley. Figure 9.5 is a wave chart showing 30 years of global VC vs. US IPO activity.

The year 2011 was no slouch either. "After a May that one tracker says recorded the most U.S. IPOs since November 2007, and with what another tracker calls the biggest IPO backlog in three years, initial public offerings seem in recovery from three weak recession years."[76] M&A also picked up. PricewaterhouseCoopers LLP tallied 1,276 announced transactions with a total value of $454 billion during the first five months of 2011, and 36 percent of the deals struck have been for less than $1 billion, or transactions involving smaller companies.[77] There are both M&A and IPO waves associated with venture capital.

Though varying from quarter to quarter, M&A involving venture-backed companies increased. There were more M&A transactions with venture-backed companies for 2010. The primary exit strategies for venture capital (IPO or M&A) both picked up and appeared to move in tandem, as Figure 9.6 shows.

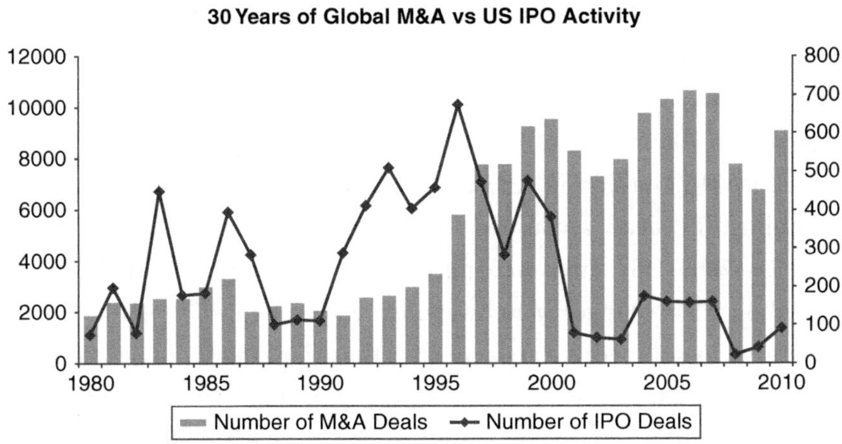

Figure 9.6 M&A Activity vs. Number of IPOs.
Source: Author.

The third exit strategy for venture capital, private exchanges, also flourished and directly became a bona fide exit. Private exchanges might one day become formidable competition with the old exit strategies, IPO and M&A. Owing to the Sarbanes-Oxley Act and other regulatory changes to capital markets over the past decade, the IPO is less attractive for many companies: 72 venture-backed start-ups went public in 2010—up from a mere 12 that made it in 2009 but far below the go-go 1990s before the tech bubble.[78] There are now around four primary private exchanges: SharesPost, SecondMarket, PortalAlliance, and Nyppex. A number of investors are using private exchanges. SharesPost's members include a variety of investors: venture capitalists, angel investors, mutual funds, high net worth individuals, family offices, and employees.[79] The extended period of time it took to go public helped drive interest in private exchanges. "Venture-backed firms, which in the go-go '90s were all too eager to tap public markets, are taking longer and longer to go public these days. That has provided quasi-stock exchanges, such as SharesPost and competitor SecondMarket, with a business in matching sellers looking for an exit with investors desperate to get in on the action."[80] The private exchanges are growing so much that their valuations have increased and some have even received venture capital themselves.

A fourth exit strategy also emerged: bankruptcy. Bankruptcy became a popular exit during the Great Recession. "When bankruptcies began to abate midway through 2009, they were replaced by a far more encouraging sign—the return of the IPO. In H2 2009, PE-backed companies raised US$15.9 billion in IPOs, more than in all of 2008 and H1 2009 combined. PE deals accounted for more than 14% of all IPO dollars raised in 2009. US listings were particularly PE-heavy; 33% of all dollars raised on US exchanges were by sponsored companies."[81] NOLs or "net operating losses" became attractive for those looking for losses to offset gains. NOLs can be used by a healthy company in order to reduce taxes. Sadly, a number of privately based companies were worth more dead than alive. Therefore, bankruptcy became an option.

As the stock market picked up again, venture capital followed. Not only did the number of venture-backed IPOs surge, but billions went into venture capital in 2010. The first quarter of 2011 was also robust: "Thirty-six US venture capital funds raised more than $7 billion in the first quarter of 2011, according to Thomson Reuters and the National Venture Capital Association (NVCA). This level marks a 76 percent increase, by dollar commitments, compared to the first quarter of 2010, which saw 44 funds raise $4.0 billion during the period. The first quarter marks the strongest quarter for US venture capital fundraising since the third quarter of 2008 and the best annual start for fundraising in the US since 2001."[82] Wave Theory, despite all the naysayers and those adamant that venture capital had plunged to the bottom of the sea after the financial shipwreck alternatively known as the Great Recession, is a valid theory. Venture capital bounced back and was forming a new wave.

BUBBLE TROUBLE

Post bubble, it took approximately 10 years (2001–2010) to equal the amount of venture capital raised during the bubble that lasted 5 years (1996–2000). That is, post bubble, it took double the amount of time to raise the same amount of venture capital raised during the bubble. Easy money can be a bad signal (Figure 9.7).

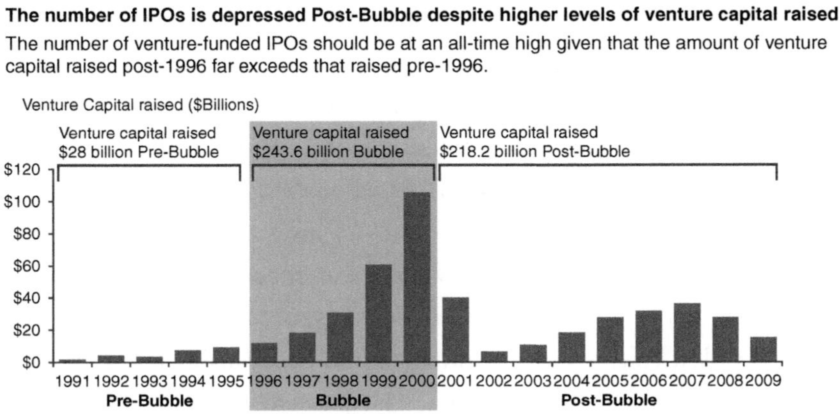

Figure 9.7 Raising Venture Capital Before, During, and After a Bubble.

Source: David Weild and Edward Kim, "Market Structure is Causing the IPO Crisis," GrantThornton, October 2009, p. 6.

It is most interesting to note that venture capital progressed and started a new wave despite unfavorable politics toward venture capital and a languid economic recovery in the United States. Figure 9.8 is a chart of US venture-backed IPOs pre and post the Great Recession.

Figure 9.8 shows the power behind a wave. Just like ocean waves, one cannot stop them; they are inevitable.

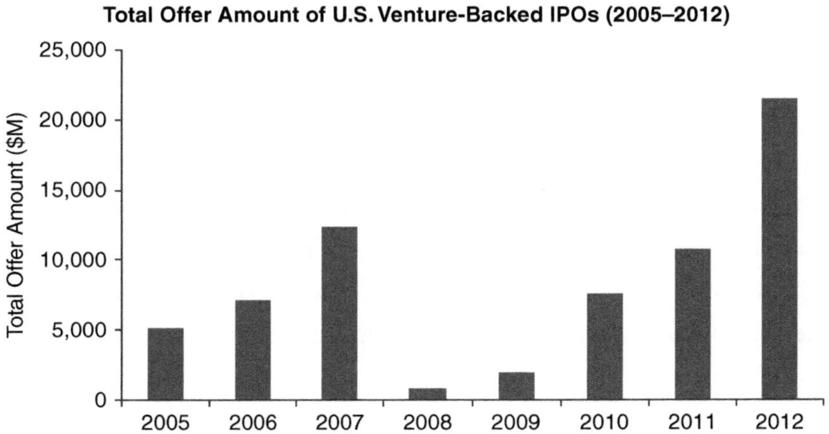

Figure 9.8 Total Offer Amount of Venture-backed IPOs.

Sources: "Global Economic Crisis Weighs Heavily on Venture-Backed Exits in 2008," Thomson Reuters, National Venture Capital Association, January 2, 2009, p. 2; "Venture-Backed Exits Enjoyed Higher Average Values on Lower Total Volumes in 2012," Thomson Reuters, National Venture Capital Association, January 2, 2013, p. 2.

By Q2 2011, venture capital investments rose 19 percent in Q2 2011 to $7.5 billion in 966 deals. Venture capital was back: "Venture capitalists invested $7.5 billion in 966 deals in the second quarter of 2011, according to the MoneyTree™ Report from PricewaterhouseCoopers LLP (PwC) and the National Venture Capital Association (NVCA), based on the data provided by Thomson Reuters. Quarterly venture capital (VC) investment activity increased 19 percent in terms of both dollars and the number of deals compared to the first quarter of 2011 when $6.3 billion was invested in 814 deals."[83] The investment level was not only coming back, it was reaching levels that were the same before the Great Recession. "The quarterly investment level represents the highest total in a single quarter since the second quarter of 2008. The deal count for the first half of 2011 (1,780 deals) is nearly identical to that seen in the first half of 2010 (1,784 deals), while the $13.8 billion invested in the first half of 2011 represented a 12 percent increase over the $12.3 billion invested in the first half of 2010."[84] By the year end, venture capital was the best-performing asset class, proving both that venture capital was not dead and more importantly the merits behind Wave Theory (Figure 9.9). A new wave was formed with venture capital. Dealogic showed venture capital-backed SEC registered IPOs from 1Q 2003–1Q 2012 (Figure 9.10).

VENTURE CAPITAL SECTORS

Some of the sectors supported by venture capital, such as biotech, came back with a vengeance. "Life sciences enterprises were among the big winners in the second quarter. Investment in biotechnology companies jumped 46 percent to $1.24 billion in the second quarter from $847 million in the first quarter."[85] Cleantech, however, showed signs that it might be slowing down. "VC funding of clean technologies—a category consisting of alternative energy, pollution and recycling, power supplies and conservation—showed a mixed pattern in the second quarter. The number of deals increased from 73 in the first quarter to 81 in the second quarter, but the amount of funding dropped by nearly a quarter to $942 million. For the first half of 2011, however, both the number of deals (154) and investment dollars ($2.2 billion) are about the same as the first half of 2010."[86] Yet, venture capital as a whole was increasing. "When the first three quarters of 2011 are combined, nationally VC firms invested $21.2 billion in 2,725 deals, representing 20 percent

The Wave Chart: 20-Year Ranking of Asset Class Returns for Equities, Fixed Income, and Alternative Investments

	1992	1993	1994	1995	1996	1997	1998	1999	2000	2001
Best Return	HFRI Fund Wghtd Composite 21.22%	Int'l Stk 32.94%	CAMBUS Venture Cap 20.07%	CAMBUS Venture Cap 47.81%	NAREIT Composite 35.75%	CAMBUS Venture Cap 54.40%	CAMBUS Venture Cap 35.89%	CAMBUS Venture Cap 319.77%	S&P GSCI 49.74%	NAREIT Composite 15.50%
	CAMBUS Private Eqty 16.38%	HFRI Fund Wghtd Composite 30.88%	CAMBUS Private Eqty 16.37%	S&P 500 Composite 37.20%	S&P GSCI 33.92%	CAMBUS Private Eqty 39.63%	S&P 500 Composite 28.34%	CAMBUS Private Eqty 50.51%	NAREIT Composite 25.89%	BarCap AggregateBnd 8.44%
	NAREIT Composite 12.18%	CAMBUS Private Eqty 21.89%	Int'l Stk 8.06%	CAMBUS Private Eqty 27.48%	CAMBUS Venture Cap 30.18%	S&P 500 Composite 31.83%	Int'l Stk 20.33%	Average 44.55%	BarCap Aggregate Bond 11.63%	HFRI Fund Wghtd Composite 4.62%
	CAMBUS Venture Cap 10.61%	CAMBUS Venture Cap 21.87%	S&P GSCI 5.29%	HFRI Fund Wghtd Composite 21.50%	S&P 500 Composite 23.82%	NAREIT Composite 18.86%	CAMBUS Private Eqty 11.70%	S&P GSCI 40.92%	BARC CTA Index 7.86%	Cash 4.09%
	Currency 10.27%	NAREIT Composite 18.55%	Average 4.61%	S& P GSCI 20.33%	CAMBUS Private Eqty 23.20%	Average 16.97%	BarCap AggregateBnd 8.69%	HFRI Fund Wghtd Composite 31.29%	Cash 5.96%	Currency 2.71%
	S&P 500 Composite 7.49%	Average 13.06%	Cash 4.24%	Average 18.75%	HFRI Fund Wghtd Composite 21.10%	HFRI Fund Wghtd Composite 16.79%	BARC CTA Index 7.01%	Int'l Stk 27.30%	Average 5.49%	BARC CTA Index 0.84%
	BarCap Aggregate Bond 7.40%	BARC CTA Index 10.37%	HFRI Fund Wghtd Composite 4.10%	BarCap Aggregate Bond 18.47%	Average 18.09%	Currency 11.35%	Average 6.43%	S&P 500 Composite 20.89%	HFRI Fund Wghtd Composite 4.98%	Average –6.33%
	Average 7.35%	S&P 500 Composite 9.97%	S&P 500 Composite 1.33%	NAREIT Composite 18.31%	BARC CTA Index 9.12%	BARC CTA Index 10.89%	Currency 5.71%	Cash 4.74%	Currency 4.45%	CAMBUS Private Eqty –6.74%
	S&P GSCI 4.42%	BarCap AggregateBnd 9.75%	NAREIT Composite 0.81%	Int'l Stk 11.55%	Currency 6.69%	BarCap AggregateBnd 9.65%	Cash 5.06%	Currency 3.12%	S&P 500 Composite –9.03%	S&P 500 Composite –11.85%
	Cash 3.62%	Cash 3.09%	BARC CTA Index –0.65%	Currency 11.49%	Int'l Stk 6.36%	Cash 5.25%	HFRI Fund Wghtd Composite 2.62%	BarCap AggregateBnd –0.82%	Int'l Stk –13.96%	Int'l Stk –21.21%
	BARC CTA Index –0.91%	Currency –3.33%	BarCap AggregateBnd –2.92%	Cash 5.75%	Cash 5.25%	Int'l Stk 2.06%	NAREIT Composite –18.82%	BARC CTA Index –1.19%	CAMBUS Private Eqty –14.24%	S&P GSCI –31.93%
Worst Return	Int'l Stk –11.85%	S&P GSCI –12.33%	Currency 5.96%	BARC CTA Index –13.64%	BarCap Aggregate Bond 3.63%	S&P GSCI –14.07%	S&P GSCI –35.75%	NAREIT Composite –6.48%	CAMB US Venture Cap –17.75%	CAMB US Venture Cap –34.05%

	2002	2003	2004	2005	2006	2007	2008	2009	2010	2011
Best Return	S&P GSCI 32.07%	Int'l Stk 39.17%	NAREIT Composite 30.41%	CAMBUS Private Eqty 30.94%	NAREIT Composite 34.02%	S&P GSCI 32.67%	BARC CTA Index 14.09%	Int'l Stk 32.46%	NAREIT Composite 27.56%	CAMBUS Venture Cap 13.81%
	BARC CTA Index 12.36%	NAREIT Composite 38.47%	CAMBUS Private Eqty 24.20%	S&P GSCI 25.55%	CAMBUS Private Eqty 29.73%	Int'l Stk 11.63%	BarCap AggregateBnd 5.24%	NAREIT Composite 27.80%	CAMBUS Private Eqty 21.45%	CAMBUS Private Eqty 10.90%
	BarCap Aggregate Bond 10.26%	S&P 500 Composite 28.36%	Int'l Stk 20.70%	CAMBUS Venture Cap 14.71%	Int'l Stk 26.86%	CAMBUS Venture Cap 11.09%	Currency 3.50%	S&P 500 Composite 25.92%	CAMBUS Venture Cap 18.51%	NAREIT Composite 7.28%
	Currency 6.29%	CAMBUS Private Eqty 26.96%	S&P GSCI 17.28%	Int'l Stk 14.02%	S&P 500 Composite 15.61%	CAMBUS Private Eqty 10.83%	Cash 1.80%	CAMBUS Private Eqty 21.74%	S&P 500 Composite 15.06%	BarCap Aggregate Bond 4.62%
	NAREIT Composite 5.22%	S&P GSCI 20.72%	Average 12.24%	Average 10.32%	CAMBUS Venture Cap 14.99%	HFRI Fund Wghtd Composite 9.96%	CAMBUS Venture Cap –17.36%	HFRI Fund Wghtd Composite 19.98%	Average 11.55%	Currency 2.33%
	Cash 1.70%	HFRI Fund Wghtd Composite 19.55%	CAMBUS Venture Cap 11.06%	HFRI Fund Wghtd Composite 9.30%	HFRI Fund Wghtd Composite 12.89%	Average 7.80%	Average –18.12%	Average 14.05%	HFRI Fund Wghtd Composite 10.49%	S&P 500 Composite 2.11%
	Average –0.76%	Average 18.21%	S&P 500 Composite 10.74%	NAREIT Composite 8.29%	Average 11.96%	BARC CTA Index 7.64%	HFRI Fund Wghtd Composite –19.02%	S&P GSCI 13.48%	S&P GSCI 9.02%	S&P GSCI 2.07%
	HFRI Fund Wghtd Composite –1.45%	Currency 11.08%	HFRI Fund Wghtd Composite 9.03%	S&P 500 Composite 4.83%	Cash 4.76%	BarCap AggregateBnd 6.97%	CAMBUS Private Eqty –23.63%	CAMBUS Venture Cap 6.28%	Int'l Stk 8.21%	Average 2.02%
	CAMBUS Private Eqty –7.59%	BARC CTA Index 8.69%	BarCap AggregateBnd 4.34%	Cash 3.00%	BarCap Aggregate Bond 4.33%	S&P 500 Composite 5.48%	S&P 500 Composite –36.58%	BarCap Aggregate Bond 5.93%	BARC CTA Index 7.05%	Cash 0.08%
	Int'l Stk –15.66%	BarCap Aggregate Bnd 4.10%	BARC CTA Index 3.30%	BarCap Aggregate Bond 2.43%	BARC CTA Index 3.54%	Cash 4.74%	NAREIT Composite –37.84%	Currency 0.91%	BarCap Aggregate Bnd 6.54%	BARC CTA Index –3.09%
	S&P 500 Composite –21.97%	CAMBUS Venture Cap 2.18%	Currency 2.36%	BARC CTA Index 1.71%	Currency –0.12%	Currency 2.59%	Int'l Stk –43.06%	Cash 0.16%	Currency 3.05%	HFRI Fund Wghtd Composite –5.56%
Worst Return	CAMB US Venture Cap –29.63%	Cash 1.07%	Cash 1.24%	Currency –1.21%	S&P GSCI –15.09%	NAREIT Composite –17.83%	S&P GSCI –46.49%	BARC CTA Index –0.10%	Cash 0.13%	Int'l Stk –11.73%

Figure 9.9 The Wave Chart: 20-Year Ranking of Asset Class Returns for Equities, Fixed Income, and Alternative Investments.

Source: Author.

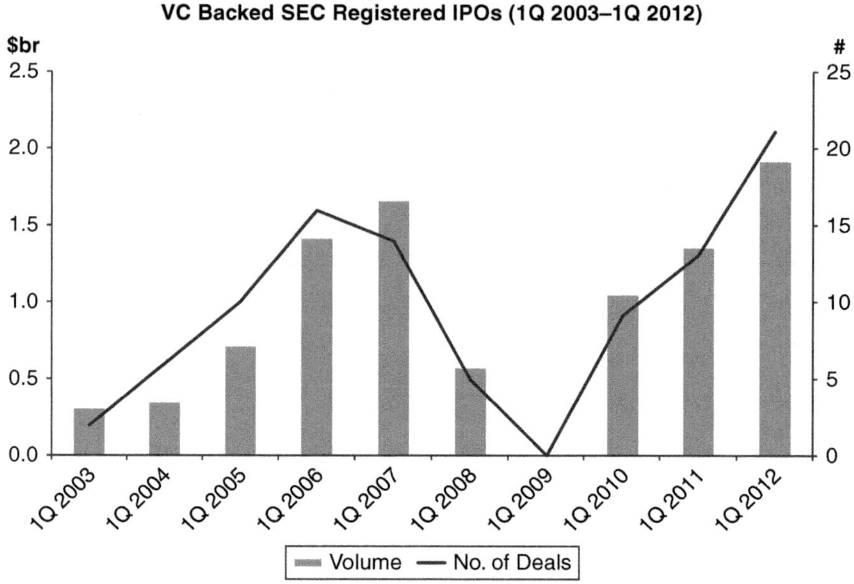

Figure 9.10 VC-backed SEC registered IPOs.

Source: "2012 VC-Backed SEC Registered IPO Volume Sees Highest First Quarter since 2000," Dealogic, April 3, 2012, p. 1.

more money and 3 percent more deals than the first three quarters of 2010."[87] "Nationally, according to the report, the number of deals also rose, from 1,005 in Q3 last year to 1,015 in this year's third quarter. Dollar volume also climbed nationally from $7.17 billion to $7.88 billion."[88] Besides biotech deals, software was the leader for 2011. Figure 9.11 lists the top industries by deals funded in 2011.

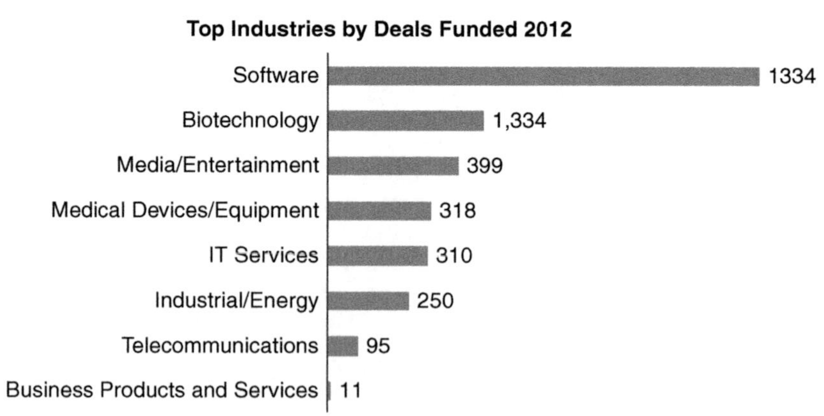

Figure 9.11 Deals Funded in Top Industries in 2012.

Source: PricewaterhouseCoopers/National Venture Capital Association MoneyTree™ Report, Data: Thomson Reuters.

Interestingly enough, the Internet, which was supposedly dead and never going to come back after the tech bubble burst in 2000, was the new all star. When the tech bubble burst and Nasdaq crashed, investors ran from technology. Internet companies went bankrupt daily. News reports claimed it was highly doubtful ecommerce would ever amount to anything. Anyone who bought shares or invested in the market was too embarrassed to admit it. Strangely, venture capital markets and Internet IPOs came back in vogue after the Great Recession, more than a decade after the Tech Wreck in 2000–2002. "Investments in Internet-specific companies also rose considerably to the highest quarterly level since 2001."[89] Internet led by year end 2012 (Figure 9.12).

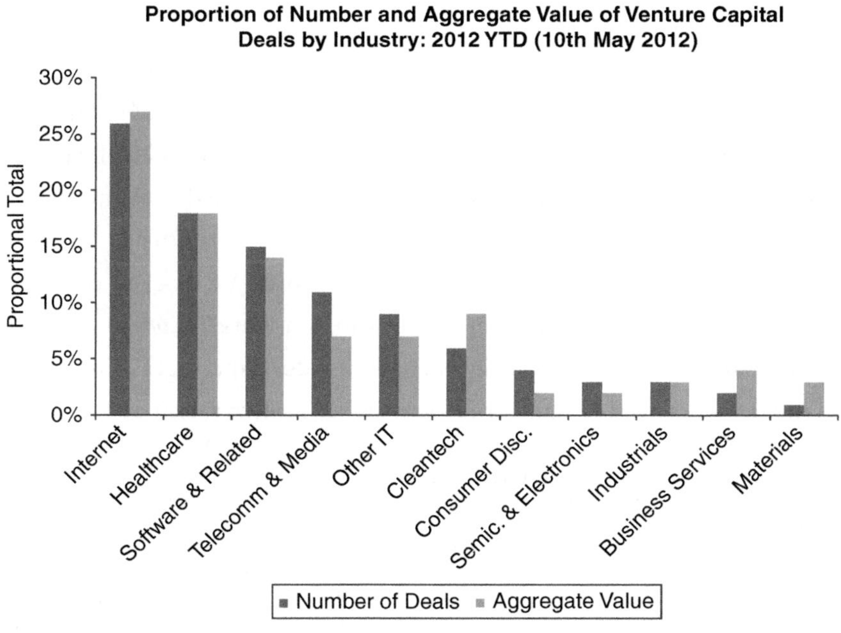

Figure 9.12 Number and Value of VC by Industries.

Source: "Venture Capital Deals by Industry, Stage, and Size," Preqin Special Report: Venture Capital, Preqin Venture Deals Analyst Online Services, May 2012.

VALUATION AND VENTURE CAPITAL

Many Internet companies such as Tumblr had little to no revenue. "Tumblr has scant revenues and a nascent business model, but the fast-growing blogging service said it raised $85 million in venture capital. The investment values the company at $800 million, said people familiar with the matter."[90] Yet the business model and the founder attracted interest from VCs. The company was started by a young entrepreneur who saw a need to help the arcane world of blogging. "Tumblr was founded in 2007 by Mr. Karp, a high-school dropout who was then 20 years old and who launched the site to simplify the blogging process. The name stems from tumblelog, which is a short-form mixed-media blog."[91] Blogging never existed during the tech bubble; it was new. The vast majority of the largest venture capital deals done in 2011 were Internet related and the top three deals were all Internet companies (Table 9.4).

Young entrepreneurs that helped create and develop the Internet, such as Marc Andreessen, came back and helped the next wave of Internet companies involved with social media: "After moving to Silicon Valley, he started Netscape Communications when he was 22 years old. Its stock market flotation in 1995 marked the beginning of the dotcom boom and made Mr. Andreessen a celebrity in the business world...Mr. Andreessen's own experience as practicing entrepreneur makes him ideally placed to counsel the bosses of startups that his firm has funded."[92] A number of private companies mentioned in *Wave Theory for Alternative Investments* went public since its release. For example a private VC-backed company situated in San Francisco, Twitter, was featured in *Wave Theory for Alternative Investments*. The company lets people broadcast messages of up to 140 characters known as "tweets." Mid-year 2011, Twitter raised $800 million

Table 9.4 The Top 10 Largest Venture Capital Rounds of 2011

Rank	Company	Industry	Amount
1	Zynga, Inc.	Online games	$490,000,062
2	Twitter Inc.	Social media	$400,000,000
3	LivingSocial, Inc.	Online coupon retail	$400,000,000
4	Reata Pharmaceuticals, Inc.	Pharmaceuticals	$300,000,000
5	LightSquared	Wireless communications	$265,000,000
6	Dropbox	Communications, networking, & storage technology	$250,000,000
7	Hibernia Atlantic, Inc.	Long-distance carriers	$250,000,000
8	BrightSource Energy, Inc.	Solar systems	$201,000,000
9	Adknowledge	Online advertising	$200,000,000
9	Plastic Logic Ltd.	Semiconductor, circuits, & other electronic components manufacturing	$200,000,000
9	True Car, Inc.	Online market places	$200,000,000
9	InMobl	Mobile advertising	$200,000,000

Source: "The Top 10 Largest Venture Capital Rounds of 2011," PrivCo, January 10, 2012.

in an investment round that valued the micro-blogging service at $8.4 billion after the deal.[93] Twitter is no longer a start-up since its founding in 2006 and now stands at 100 million users strong, and they tweet 230 million times a day.[94] Unlike the 1990s where hundreds of small Internet companies were going public, there were fewer IPO candidates this time around. Most were involving the social media wave. A major difference is that the next-generation Internet companies are much larger and have far more revenue than the ones during the tech bubble. For example, Twitter is growing rapidly. It is a technological marvel:

> Twitter, on the other hand, is intended to handle a huge daily volume of information, with scalability, polyglot persistence, and restricted search and archiving capabilities. For tweets, analytics, and other data, Twitter uses multiple data storage and retrieval approaches, including Cassandra, Hadoop, Hive, Pig, Vertica, and MySQL. As of December, Twitter was storing 250 million tweets per day with a data store built using MySQL.[95]

Twitter's growth continues amongst the other social media companies as it becomes more readily used around the globe: "Facebook dominates the social networking landscape in terms of overall users and time spent per user. But other firms, such as Twitter, LinkedIn, and Tumblr, are growing faster."[96] Twitter even played a role during the 2012 presidential debates: there were over ten million messages over a time period of one and a half hours.

Buying shares of an IPO is no easy task. Investors in the Facebook IPO lost money soon after the IPO. Twitter investors, on the other hand, did well. Twitter learned from the Facebook debacle. Management hired Goldman Sachs to be the lead underwriter for its IPO instead of Morgan Stanley, which took Facebook public. Shares of the Twitter IPO were priced at $26.00 per share, which ultimately leaped more than 70 percent the first day. By contrast, the Facebook IPO dropped in half during its first couple of months of trading. It took nearly one and a half years for investors to follow the stock back up again from around a low of $18.00 to the IPO price of $38.00. Management of Twitter and Goldman Sachs appeared to do the opposite of whatever was done for the Facebook IPO; they were determined to not make the same mistakes. For example, preferential disclosures with institutional buyers were avoided. Twitter was listed on the NYSE instead of NASDAQ. Twitter's management wanted to avoid any technological issues that occurred with Facebook. Early investors in Twitter were not eager to unload shares. There were no hedge funds planning on cashing out billions of dollars as retail investors bought shares. Venture firms that backed Twitter, such as Benchmark Capital Partners, Spark Capital, and Union Square Ventures, were not inclined to sell massive amounts of stock on the IPO. The filing made no mention of VCs selling. Founders and other early investors were not selling vast quantities of stock. Proceeds from the Twitter IPO were primarily for operating expenses and making acquisitions that were strategic to the company. The bankers for Twitter also did not boost the number of shares for sale of Twitter at the last minute before the offering while simultaneously raising the price of the IPO too far above the high end of the range. The Twitter IPO was priced on November 6, 2013, valuing the company more than $10 billion. At the time, there were 230,000,000 users. Facebook has a market cap of around $123 billion of 12 times that of Twitter. The valuation at the time of the Twitter IPO was considered reasonable by investors.

Valuation is still a concern amongst many of the next-generation Internet companies involving social media. "Zynga's new filing, an amended S-1 document for its initial public offering, also disclosed how the company has been valued in the past, prior to the recent market tumult. In March, Zynga said a 'third-party valuation report' indicated Zynga's worth was $11.5 billion, according to its filing. Just one month earlier, another third-party valuation report indicated Zynga's value was less than half that, at $4.98 billion."[97] The current wave of social media companies looks promising but valuations appear to be all over the place.

A popular company that started with an app for the iPhone called Angry Birds, developed a viable business model and then expanded into other areas. In addition to games, Angry Birds offers books and toys. The Internet companies that were popular in 2010–2011 were very different from those in the dot-com era. "Unlike dot-com companies a decade ago, however, the new crop of Web companies has attracted a large base of users and is generating revenue through online advertising and other means.

Their valuations have climbed rapidly lately and also triggered share trading on private exchanges."[98]

Another venture-backed company that set records for high valuation was WhatsApp. After Facebook's ascent almost one and a half years after its troubled IPO, it paid $19 billion to acquire this messaging startup. The deal was for both cash and $3 billion in restricted stock. WhatsApp's purchase price ranked the private company as the largest-ever for a venture-backed company. "The deal marks the coming-of-age of messaging apps, which let people send text messages and share photos and other stuff without incurring charges from telecoms firms."[98] As Apple, Facebook, Amazon, Microsoft, Priceline, Google, and others compete with one another and wander into each other's backyards, attractive new start-ups will likely get gobbled up and some might even get exorbitant offers like WhatsApp. These large publicly traded companies are sitting on record amounts of cash and have become quite acquisitive and entrepreneurs know it. For instance, the founder of Snapchat turned down a $3 billion offer from Facebook's Zuckerberg.

SURFING ALONE

While a number of the private companies mentioned in *Wave Theory for Alternative Investments* ended up being home runs (three out of five of the private companies that were featured did well), Energy Recovery has compelling technology but struggled. Energy Recovery Inc. is involved with cleantech; it is a leader in the design and development of energy recovery devices for desalination. Desalination may provide an inexpensive way to prepare seawater for consumption. The market for a technique to remove salt from ocean water is large given the size of the ocean. The Earth consists primarily of water: Earth's oceans contain about 324 million cubic miles (1.36 billion cubic kilometers) of sea water. Dissolved in this are some 53 million billion tons (48 million billion metric tons) of salts, gases, and other substances.[100] The global desalination market struggled during the recession. As with all venture capital investing, investing in a handful of private companies is likely to bring a mixed bag of results. The objective of course is to have more winners than losers, which is not an easy feat by any stretch of the imagination. A tremendous amount of research at due diligence is required for investing in private companies.

Sometimes a new area takes time to develop. Venture capital seldom turns a profit overnight; it takes time to develop an idea or product. A company in a new area is also helped if it is not the only one. In other words, it helps the process if others join the bandwagon and your company is not the sole company attempting to penetrate a space. Owning the Lone Ranger can be risky. Several companies competing in an area is preferable, especially if there are technology hurdles. Drinking water from the sea, for example, sounds great but it is a difficult process. "To make seawater fit for human consumption its salt content of approximately 3–5% must be cut to 0.5% or less. Existing desalination plants do this one of two ways. Some employ distillation, which needs about 10 kilowatt-hours (kwh) of energy per cubic metre of seawater processed. Brine is heated, and the resulting water vapor is condensed. Other plants employ reverse osmosis. This uses molecular sieves that pass water molecules."[101]

As with any technology, there is competition with desalination. The technology is evolving and there are several new players involved, not just one. For example, Siemens came out with a new system and demonstrated that it achieves 1.8 kWh/m^3 per cubic meter, which researchers might be able to lower further to 1.5 kWh/m^3, with a few minor improvements. Conventional consumption is typically 3.4–4.8 kWh/m^3. The Siemens system uses a process called electrodialysis. One day, it will be feasible to drink ocean water without salt. This is the essence of venture capital—making the impossible possible. Solving a difficult problem or an idea that appears wishful thinking might be possible. Venture capital helps render dreams reality; the borderline impossible or unlikely can become a reality. "As salt-filtering technologies replace boiling and reduce the price of desalinated water, governments in Australia, China, Israel, the United Arab Emirates and the U.S. are tapping the oceans."[102] In 2011, the global capacity of desalination plants reached 66.5 million cubic meters per day, with 15,988 plants in operation led by programs in Saudi Arabia, the United Arab Emirates, and Spain.[103]

VENTURE CAPITAL IS GLOBAL

While the United States struggled with IPOs after the Great Recession, the rest of the world was more proactive and favorable toward IPOs. Asia saw the value in both venture capital and IPOs. "As has been the case since 2009, Asia continued to dominate the global market, accounting for 53% of the total deals priced."[104]

China and India are both waking up to the world of alternative investments. Regarding venture capital, both countries are shifting into higher gears: "China and India have in recent times asserted themselves as key venture capital hubs. In 2011, there were 203 venture capital deals in China, an increase of 6% in comparison to the previous year."[105] However, they are also moving not just into venture capital and IPOs but real estate, commodities, hedge funds, LBO funds, and many others. Both countries are growing very rapidly. The gross domestic product is expected to grow 9 percent in India and 8.9 percent in China in 2011, according to an April 2011 poll by the *Economist* magazine, and last year, India won by a nose, registering GDP of 10.4 percent to China's 10.3 percent.[106] Interest in alternative investments will likely grow in both countries.

India is probably in second gear right now but in the future it is more likely the country switches to a higher gear. In fact, certain industries have completely turned around. India's economy is one of the world's most dynamic and some industries, such as media and aviation, are unrecognizable from ten years ago.[107] Population has a lot to do with India's progress. India's large population is both a blessing and a curse. For example, India's former capital, Kolkata (Calcutta) used to be its pride and joy. The former growth engine, however, lost its luster. Images of the plague, starvation, and extreme poverty come to mind at the mere mention of the name. But Kolkata is making a comeback and has potential to be turned around. Not only does India have a large population, which can be advantageous by having a huge workforce, but they are nurturing different types of private companies from small to large besides technology.

The number of billionaires in India has also increased during the past few years. In the past, India has had virtually no billionaires but the pace has picked up rapidly in the most recent years. IPOs can generate enormous amounts of wealth for entrepreneurs. Figure 9.13 is a chart of IPOs listed on various stock exchanges from around the globe as well as total value.

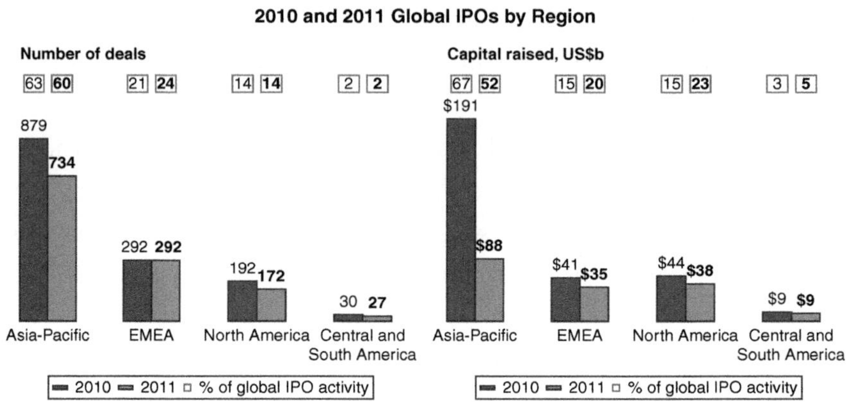

Figure 9.13 Global IPOs by Region.

Source: "Global IPO Trends 2012," E&Y, 2012, p. 5.

Dealogic, EY. 2012 Global IPO Update, EY, December 2012, pp. 28–29.

China has also changed and is now considered a superpower. Besides owning a large amount of US debt, China has been churning out public companies left, right, and sideways. Some of the IPOs are quite large. One Chinese brokerage, Citic Securities Co., listed a $1.7 billion IPO in October of 2011. Asian stock exchanges have grown. Mergers will invariably make some of the exchanges much larger. The RTS (Russian Trading System) and MICEX (Moscow Interbank Currency Exchange) exchanges merged in 2011, with the hope of becoming a leading global exchange.

ONE CAN SURF ANYWHERE (NO ONE HAS A MONOPOLY ON GOOD IDEAS)

The United States is in the lead right now but that could change some day. "The result is some 3,800 fewer companies trade on the U.S. exchanges today than in 1997, according to consulting firm Capital Markets Advisory Partners."[108] "Abroad, there are nearly eight times as many listings as in the U.S., with Hong Kong, China, and India among the leading venues."[109] Despite the doom and gloom that affected venture capital, the industry was similar to a Phoenix, rising from the ashes. According to the National Venture Capital Association, venture capital fundraising rose to $18.16 billion in 2011, up 31 percent from $13.77 billion in 2010, with the same number of funds raised in 2011 as the year before—169.[110]

The United States is known for its entrepreneurs and this cultural DNA is hard to break. "Penalizing the risk-takers by trying to 'level the playing field' through excessive regulation, taxation or antitrust threats will simply sap the entrepreneurial spirit from the marketplace, limit technological innovation and diminish the possibility of progress over the long haul."[111] There is a value to human capital. "Unleash the energies of entrepreneurial people and they will change the world. What we face today is not a space race but a race toward what can be a new American Century."[112] Venture capital will prevail again and new technologies will emerge. Andreessen Horowitz, a VC firm based in San Francisco, believes personal technology is changing. "They believe that networking and storage technology is about to go through the same kind of fundamental transition that the server business experienced in the late 1990s, when expensive, proprietary servers were replaced by much cheaper ones that used new technology."[113] A number of noteworthy private companies attracted funds during the difficult but rebounding venture capital market. The United States continues to be dominant with venture capital despite the rocky road from the Great Recession. However, it is in jeopardy of falling in the ranks similar to how it has fallen in education.

U.S. corporations have been hoarding cash, hesitant about investing in growth. Many reports of large amount of cash are being issued. As companies became leaner and meaner in 2011, earnings improved. "Better earnings—and record profits in some recent quarters—have helped fill the coffers of nonfinancial companies with what the Federal Reserve said was $2.05 trillion in cash and other liquid assets as of the end of June, the most since 1963."[114] A number of large publicly traded technology companies started making acquisitions. While a fair amount went to tech, life sciences companies also began showing promise. Interesting energy companies also surfaced. Table 9.5 lists the noteworthy venture capital deals that were able to prosper and raise funds.

Attractive early companies will always get seeded and new groups have evolved that help with this process. "In this torpid economy, it can be hard to find seed money for a new product, company, or artistic venture. Many are turning to Kickstarter, the two-year-old fundraising site that currently passed the million-donor mark. Entrepreneurs and creators

Table 9.5 Noteworthy Venture Capital of 2011–2012

Company	Amount	Date	Company	Amount	Date
6 Waves Lolapps	$35,000,000	Aug-11	Living Social	$176,000,000	Dec-11
Actifio	$33,500,000	Dec-11	Opera Solutions	$84,000,000	Sep-11
Agilyx	$22,000,000	Mar-11	Qwiki	$8,000,000	Jan-11
AppDynamics	$20,000,000	Jan-12	Smule	$12,000,002	Oct-11
Cram Worldwide	$2,000,000	Oct-11	Sonian	$9,000,000	Jan-11
DropBox	$250,000,000	Oct-11	Spotify	$100,000,000	Feb-11
Fisker Automotive	$218,433,421	Jan-12	Survey Monkey	$65,000,000	Jan-12
Four Square	$50,000,000	Jun-11	Tumblr	$85,000,000	Sep-11
General Fusion	$19,500,000	May-11	Vice Media	$50,000,000	Apr-11
Gilt	$137,999,857	May-11	Workday	$85,000,000	Oct-11

Source: Author.

used Kickstarter to raise $8.8 million in September, and those 50 projects exceeded their goals by the most."[115] Early stage incubators and "accelerators" have flourished. Some incubators have helped hundreds of early stage companies.

Likewise, quite a few companies set up venture arms including BMW. "BMW also created a $100 million venture capital fund, BMW i Ventures, to invest in start-ups like MyCityWay and ParkatmyHouse, which offers mobility services for crowded cities."[116] Colleges and universities became more active with venture capital. For example, the University of Minnesota also set up venture funds. "The University of Minnesota plans to launch two venture capital funds next year, one of which will invest in startup companies that license university technology. The fund backing university startups will total $20 million in size and will make seed-stage investments over a 10 year period. A separate $50 million fund will invest in startups nationwide."[117] Quite a few schools set up vehicles to invest in companies. It should be noted investing in initial public offerings is not identical to investing in venture capital. However, many venture-backed companies go public and an investor can obtain attractive returns (Figure 9.14).

SURFING IS COMPETITIVE AND SO IS VENTURE CAPITAL

Receiving a decent allocation is another stumbling block for IPO shares because basically who would not want shares of a hot deal? Everyone does. Unless one gives millions of dollars to a bank to invest as well as generating

Mean First-day Returns and Money Left on the Table, 1980–2012

The sample is IPOs with an offer price of at least $5.00, excluding ADRs, unit offers, closed-end funds, REITs, partnerships, small best efforts offers, banks and S&Ls, and stocks not listed on CRSP (CRSP includes Amex, NYSE, and NASDAQ stocks). Proceeds excludes overallotment options, but includes the global offering size. The amount of money left on the table is defined as the offer price to closing market price on the first-day of trading, multiplied by the number of shares offered (excluding overallotment options) on a global basis.

Year	Number of IPOs	Mean First-day Return: Equal-weighted	Mean First-day Return: Proceeds-weighted	Aggregate Amount Left on the Table	Aggregate Proceeds
1980	73	13.9%	19.7%	$0.18 billion	$0.92 billion
1981	197	6.2%	6.1%	$0.14 billion	$2.37 billion
1982	80	10.9%	13.2%	$0.13 billion	$1.01 billion
1983	449	10.0%	9.5%	$0.84 billion	$8.75 billion
1984	177	3.2%	1.9%	$0.04 billion	$2.28 billion
1985	183	6.3%	5.2%	$0.22 billion	$4.36 billion
1986	395	6.1%	5.0%	$0.68 billion	$13.69 billion
1987	283	5.7%	5.7%	$0.66 billion	$11.52 billion
1988	102	5.7%	3.5%	$0.13 billion	$3.72 billion
1989	113	8.2%	4.7%	$0.24 billion	$5.20 billion
1990	110	10.8%	8.1%	$0.34 billion	$4.27 billion
1991	287	11.9%	9.7%	$1.50 billion	$15.36 billion
1992	411	10.3%	8.1%	$1.82 billion	$22.58 billion
1993	509	12.7%	11.3%	$3.52 billion	$31.28 billion
1994	403	9.8%	8.4%	$1.46 billion	$17.30 billion
1995	457	21.2%	15.3%	$4.41 billion	$28.88 billion
1996	675	17.2%	16.1%	$6.80 billion	$42.25 billion
1997	473	14.1%	14.4%	$4.54 billion	$31.58 billion
1998	283	21.7%	15.6%	$5.25 billion	$33.66 billion
1999	476	71.0%	57.0%	$36.94 billion	$64.77 billion
2000	381	56.4%	45.8%	$29.69 billion	$64.86 billion
2001	79	14.2%	8.7%	$2.97 billion	$34.24 billion
2002	66	9.1%	5.1%	$1.13 billion	$22.03 billion
2003	62	12.1%	10.5%	$1.00 billion	$9.53 billion
2004	174	12.3%	12.4%	$3.87 billion	$31.31 billion
2005	160	10.2%	9.3%	$2.64 billion	$28.27 billion
2006	157	12.1%	13.0%	$3.95 billion	$30.48 billion
2007	160	13.9%	13.9%	$4.95 billion	$35.69 billion
2008	21	6.4%	24.8%	$5.65 billion	$22.76 billion
2009	41	9.8%	11.1%	$1.46 billion	$13.17 billion
2010	92	9.2%	6.1%	$1.83 billion	$29.85 billion
2011	81	13.3%	12.0%	$3.23 billion	$26.97 billion
2012	94	17.7%	8.9%	$2.78 billion	$31.12 billion
1980-1989	2,052	7.2%	6.1%	$3.28 billion	$53.85 billion
1990-1998	3,608	14.8%	13.0%	$29.64 billion	$227.17 billion
1999-2000	857	64.5%	51.4%	$66.63 billion	$129.62 billion
2001-2012	1,187	12.2%	11.2%	$35.45 billion	$315.42 billion
1980-2012	**7,704**	**17.9%**	**18.6%**	**$135.01 billion**	**$726.06 billion**

Figure 9.14 Mean First-day Retunrs and Money Left on the Table, 1980–2012.

Source: "Initial Public Offerings: Tables Updated Through 2012," Prof. Jay Ritter, p. 2, January 4, 2013.

a lot of commissions, an investor will not get a lot of shares if any. Ultra high-net worth clients get IPOs, not regular retail clients. Allocations are beyond the control of a financial advisor. Good clients can receive decent allocations but it is dependent on a lot of different factors such as the underwriter. Is the firm you bank with also an underwriter of IPOs? Are they the

Table 9.6 IPOs with At Least $50 Million in LTM Sales (2005 purchasing power) from 1980 to 2009 Categorized by Private Equity (Buyout Fund) Backing

Buyout-backed or not	Number of IPOs	Average first-day return	Average 3-year buy-and-hold return		
			IPOs	Market-adjusted	Style-adjusted
Buyout-backed	814	8.50%	36.10%	7.10%	2.80%
Non-buyout-backed	2,636	13.00%	40.30%	−4.80%	3.90%
All	**3,450**	**12.00%**	**39.30%**	**−2.00%**	**3.60%**

Source: "Initial Public Offerings: Tables Updated Through 2010," Prof. Jay Ritter, p. 25, June 1, 2011.

Table 9.7 IPOs from 1980 to 2009 Categorized by Venture Capital Backing

VC-backed or not	Number of IPOs	Average first-day return	Average 3-year buy-and-hold return		
			IPOs	Market-adjusted	Style-adjusted
VC-backed	2,577	28.10%	23.20%	−12.90%	0.02%
Non-VC-Backed	4,777	12.70%	19.90%	0	−0.12%
Non-VC and non-buyout	3,858	13.60%	16.7	−30.00%	−0.15%
All	**7,354**	**18.10%**	**21.00%**	**−19.60%**	**−0.07%**

Note: The non-VC- and non-buyout-backed IPOs do not include a minimum sales screen.

Source: "Initial Public Offerings: Tables Updated Through 2010," Prof. Jay Ritter, p. 25, June 1, 2011.

lead manager or a co-manager? If not, are they in the selling group? Are they even in the selling group?

Who is getting you the shares? Is it the top producer in the branch or a guy who just started his budding young career? And how much does the advisor know about syndicate? Buying IPOs is tricky and not for everyone. Hypothetically, if one purchased every IPO in a given year, Table 9.6 shows the average first-day returns on an annualized basis since 1980. Buying IPO shares can therefore be short term. However, one can hold the shares for the long haul. An average three-year buy-and-hold strategy for IPOs (whether they are VC-backed or non-VC-backed) appears in Table 9.7.

10

ASSET ALLOCATION AND ALTERNATIVE INVESTMENTS

Asset allocation is simply what you have invested in and the weightings an investor assigns to each asset class. "The goal of asset allocation is to get the best possible expected return/risk profile."[1] The majority of professionals in the world of finance believe that asset allocation will affect returns. By diversifying your assets, an investor will presumably lower risk and increase returns. For example, hedge funds can be used to reduce risk and/or possibly increase returns with a foreign or domestic equity index (Table 10.1).

In particular, macro hedge funds during recessionary periods have had high Sharpe Ratios and compelling returns. The Sharpe Ratio (sometimes referred to as the reward-to-volatility ratio) is a ratio of portfolio excess return to standard deviation. The objective is to not have all your assets highly correlated; risk can be reduced by owning different types of asset classes that are not highly correlated. If an investor is a founder of a life sciences company and it is acquired by a publicly traded health-care company and the entrepreneur is given shares of this public company, they will have a large single stock position in one sector, health care. Further, they will have just one stock and not a group of stocks. The risk lies in the individual company, the health-care sector, and the overall market. There are other risks as well such as management (the entrepreneur no longer runs his or her company but turned it over to another CEO when they sold their company). Investors view risk differently. By diversifying into other assets, whether it be municipal bonds or hedge funds, the investor will be

Table 10.1 Risk/Return With Hedge Funds vs. Equities, 2001–2010

Risk/Return with Hedge Funds vs. Equities 2001–2010		
	Annualized return (%)	**Annualized standard deviation (%)**
HFRI Equity Hedge (Total) Index	5.52	8.45
S&P 500 Total Return Index	1.41	16.38
MSCI World Index Gross (USD)	2.82	17.13

Source: Author

Alternative Investment 10 Year Correlation Matrix

		Equity				Fixed Income			Alternatives			
		Large Cap	Small Cap	EAFE	EME	Core Bonds	Corp. HY	EMD	Cmdty.	REITs	Hedge Funds	Eq. Market Neutral
Equity	Large Cap	1.00										
	Small Cap	0.94	1.00									
	EAFE	0.90	0.86	1.00								
	EME	0.79	0.74	0.91	1.00							
Fixed Income	Core Bonds	−0.26	−0.32	−0.17	−0.06	1.00						
	Corp. HY	0.77	0.73	0.77	0.81	−0.03	1.00					
	EMD	0.60	0.55	0.67	0.79	0.34	0.85	1.00				
Alternatives	Cmdty.	0.52	0.46	0.60	0.66	−0.18	0.56	0.48	1.00			
	REITs	0.79	0.85	0.73	0.63	0.01	0.72	0.65	0.40	1.00		
	Hedge Funds	0.82	0.77	0.88	0.89	−0.24	0.77	0.64	0.71	0.58	1.00	
	Eq. Market Neutral	0.59	0.55	0.74	0.61	−0.09	0.43	0.40	0.51	0.49	0.59	1.00

Indexes used -- Large Cap: S&P 500 Index; Small Cap: Russell 2000; EAFE: MSCI EAFE; EME: MSCI Emerging Markets; Bonds: Barclays Capital Aggregate; Corp HY: Barclays Capital Corporate High Yield; EMD: Barclays Capital Emerging Market; Cmdty.: DJ UBS Index; Real Estate: NAREIT Equity REIT Index; Hedge Funds: CS/Tremont Multi-Strategy Index; Equity Market Neutral: CS/Tremont Equity Market Neutral Index.

All correlation coefficents calculated based on quarterly total return data for period 6/30/03 to 6/30/13.

Figure 10.1 Alternative Investment 10-Year Correlation Matrix.

Source: Author, Tony Murphy.

spreading the risk. It is rare that all investments will be adversely affected simultaneously (Figure 10.1).

Envision taking a trip to Seattle for a friend's wedding where the weather frequently changes and the wedding party does not keep you well informed of the weather conditions or what to bring along. Do you take a sweater? Do you take a suit, dress, or jeans? The weather is unreliable (especially in Seattle) but you want to be prepared. You do not know if you will be on a boat taking a tour of the Peugot Sound in the rain or indoors in formal attire. Bringing a bathing suit when others have tuxedos might be most embarrassing. The prudent thing to do is mix it up and bring some casual and some formal attire to be prepared. How assets behaved in the past is based partially on statistical relationships such as variance and correlation. It is more or less a forecast but there is no guarantee that past performance will continue into the future (as labeled on virtually every financial product these days).

Past performance should not be ignored. As the mutual fund giant, T. Rowe Price explains, "While the future isn't predictable, past returns can offer some insights."[2] Major asset classes are equities (stocks), fixed income (bonds), alternative investments, and cash. Each of these asset classes includes different types of securities. "The asset allocation decision is the choice among these broad asset classes, while the security selection decision is the choice of which particular securities to hold within each asset class."[3] For example, fixed income might include municipal bonds, corporate bonds, and high-yield bonds. Equities might include large cap growth, small cap value, and foreign large cap securities. Cash might include money markets, CDs, or US Treasuries. Alternative investments might include hedge funds, venture capital, and real estate. Within each of these alternative investments, there are components or subsectors providing additional means for diversification. For instance, there are different types of REITs that fall under the two central areas for REITs. "There are two principal kinds of REITs. *Equity trusts* invest in real estate directly, whereas *mortgage trusts* invest primarily in mortgages and construction loans. REITs generally are established by banks, insurance companies, or mortgage companies, which then serve as investment managers to earn a fee."[4]

UNDERSTANDING THE REIT MARKET

The REIT market has grown quite large and is not just domestic. Figure 10.2 shows a comparison among the FTSE NAREIT, S&P 500, and Russell 2000. With the REIT market evolving, it has become more specialized. "REITs today are less diversified than they used to be. By and large, REIT management are eschewing property diversification in favor of focusing on one property type. Put another way, REIT executives are moving their companies toward specialization rather than generalization."[5] REITs are accessible most places around the globe, providing even more diversification possibilities. One can select different REITs from Europe, Asia, or the United States, as well as a specific type of REIT such as office or hotel. REIT subsectors can have a wide range of performance. For example, in the first

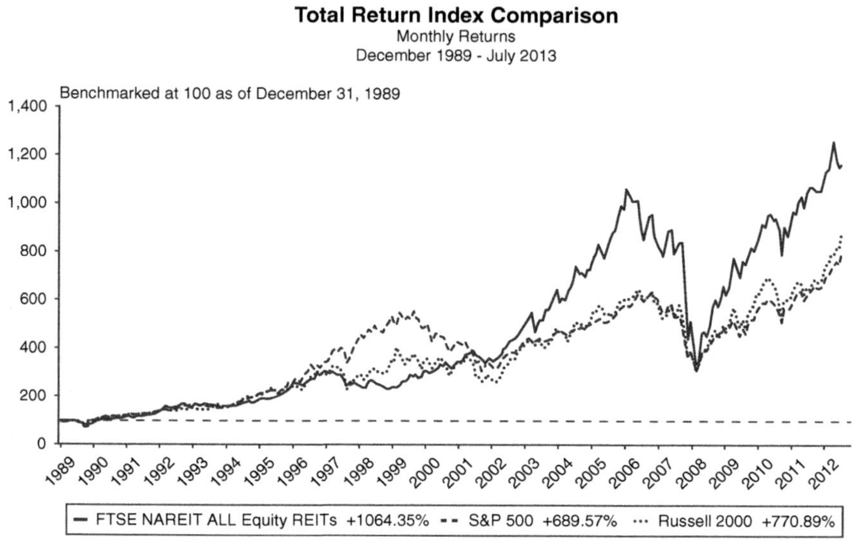

Figure 10.2 Total Return Index Comparison.

Source: Author; NAREIT® (National Association of Real Estate Investment Trusts), FactSet.

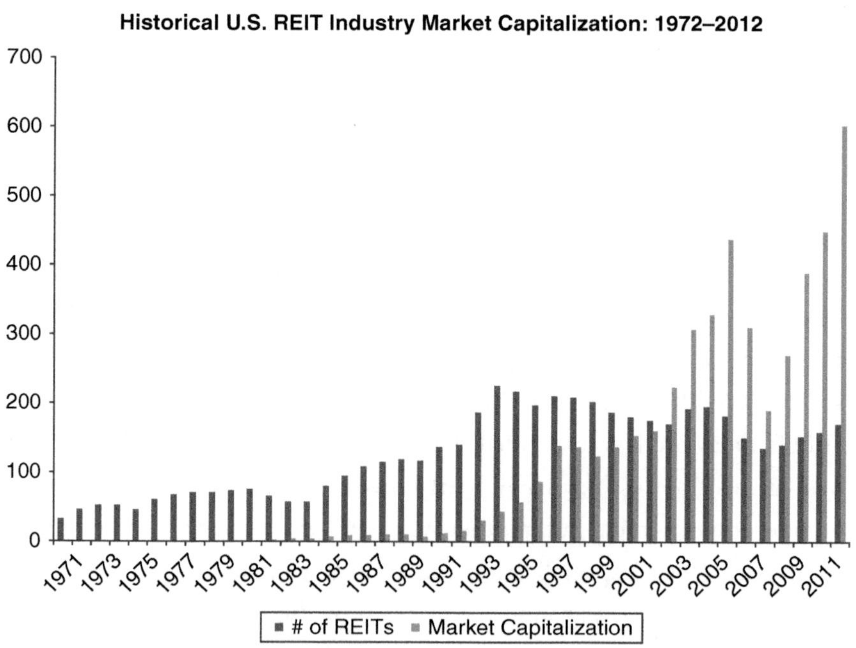

Figure 10.3 Number of REITs and Market Capitalization from 1972 to 2012.

Source: "US REIT Industry Equity Market Cap," REIT.com, March 29, 2013.

quarter of 2013, commercial mortgage performances were up 22.6 percent and manufactured homes were up 17.2 percent while regional malls were only up 2.6 percent and apartments were down 0.03 percent.[6] Figure 10.3 is a chart showing how large the REIT market has grown till the end of 2011.

REITs are investments in publicly traded companies. "Today there are 129 equity REITs representing a combined market cap of more than $500 billion."[7] There are also private closed-end real estate funds. "The money in closed-end private real estate funds pursuing debt strategies is surging. And with $2 trillion in commercial property loans maturing over the next five years, the funds have plenty of takers in the property world."[8]

MANAGER SELECTION

Manager selection can be sometimes confused with security selection. SMAs or separately managed accounts enable an individual or institution to select a money manager with a unique style such as large cap growth stocks or small cap value. Selecting money managers or fund managers is not easy for an individual or institution. Alternative investments, like stocks and bonds, have varying rates of return and levels of price volatility over time. By diversifying with different types of alternatives and adding them to a stock and bond portfolio, it might lower risk and increase returns. Just by adding more securities, whether they are alternative investments or not, does not necessarily mean one is lowering risk. "Ultimately, however, even if we include a large number of risky securities in our portfolio, we cannot avoid risk altogether. To the extent that virtually all securities are affected by the common macroeconomic factors, we cannot eliminate our exposure to these risk sources."[9] Careful selection of the type of investment might help lower risk. Manager selection is not immaterial:"U.S. state pension plans with higher allocations to alternative investments generally experienced better 10-year returns than those with less exposure, a new analysis from consultant Cliffwater LLC shows. Contrary to common market wisdom, researchers at Cliffwater, based in Marina Del Rey, Calif., also found that those decade-long returns owed more to manager and fund selection than to the size of the alternatives allocation."[10] Figure 10.4 is the US State Pension asset allocation for 2011.

If an investor adds alternative investments to a portfolio, it might be prudent to look into different types, research them thoroughly, examine

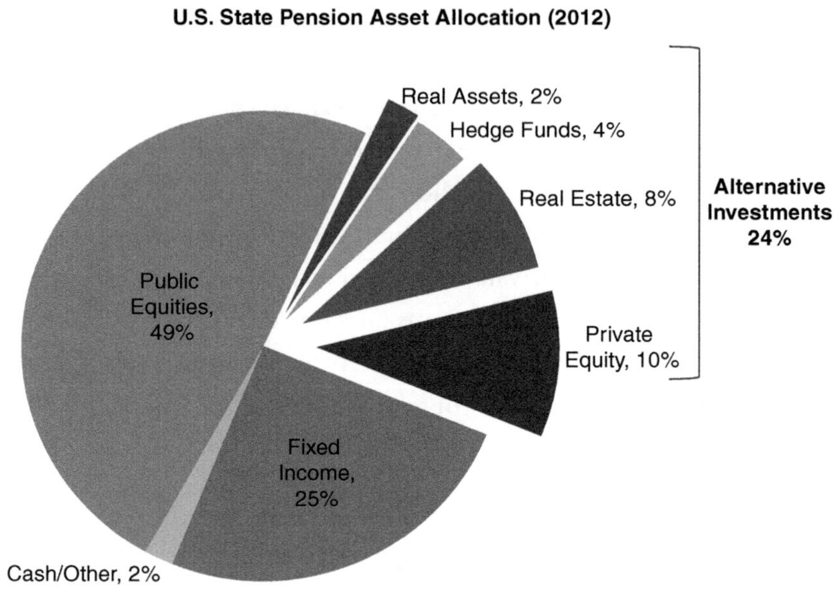

Figure 10.4 US State Pension Asset Allocation in 2012.

Source: Author; "Cliffwater 2013 Report on State Pension Performance and Trends," Cliffwater LLC, July 2013.

asset allocation, review risk, decide what is best for your needs, and consider when and how much to add. Certain alternative investments might be suitable while others might not be, depending on the investor. Alternative investments are misunderstood by the general population and take time to really understand so it might also be wise to gradually add them over time. Dollar cost averaging has been used for decades for those that want to gradually enter the market with equities or not be bothered with highs and lows of the market. Hypothetically, one could use dollar cost averaging with alternative investments. In short, there is no excuse to not look into alternative investments but one needs to do some homework first. Unless one is an investment professional, investing in alternative investments is not easy. Investing in alternative investments takes years to master. Similar to getting exercise and eating right, alternative investments can be beneficial for an investment portfolio's health.

Regarding investing, there are "three legs to a stool": fixed income, equities, *and* alternative investments. "Locking in a static mix of stocks and bonds may not provide a sufficient buffer against volatility. Creating a lower-risk portfolio using alternative investments may provide more stability than the traditional tactic of moving money from stocks into bonds, as new risks emerge among troubled global credit markets."[11] For decades, the focus has primarily revolved around two areas: stocks and bonds. On occasion, cash is thrown into the equation. For the past century, numerous studies have been conducted regarding stocks and bonds. For example, the mutual fund giant, T. Rowe Price, along with Ibbotson, has compiled data geared towards pessimists that shows there are actually more years with good returns than bad years. Morningstar Advisor showed that the S&P500 had more than ten declines of -13 percent or more from January 1926 to November 2008 (Figure 10.5).

However, it depends when an investor enters the market. As a new client joked with me, "Whenever I invest, the market always seems to go down." Investors tend to believe their market timing is always wrong, which might not be the case. Poor timing can be devastating. Hypothetically, if an investor put $1 million into the market in 1999 when the market seemed ideal, they would have lost substantial amounts of money the next three years from 2000 to 2002 when the S&P500 was off around 51 percent. If this investor had $500k left, it would take many more years to recover. Essentially, the investor would now need to earn 100 percent return on his/her money just to break even. Let us assume that the investor has nerves of steel after losing half their money and they have not sworn, yelled at, thrown things, or fired their financial advisor. The advisor and client ultimately decide to stay the course or "Stocks for the Long Run!" as Jeremy Siegel would say. 2003 was a very good year, with +28.36 percent followed by 10.74 percent

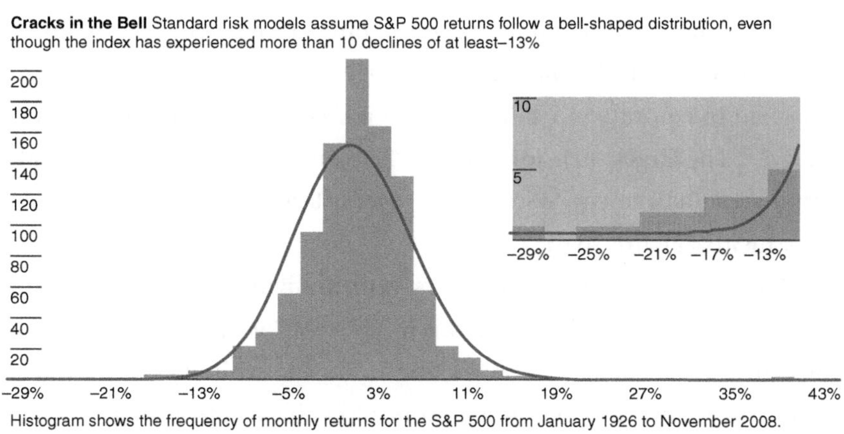

Figure 10.5 Frequency of Monthly Returns for the S&P 500.

Source: Paul D. Kaplan, "Déjà Vu All Over Again," *Morningstar Advisor*, February–March 2009, 30.

in 2004, 4.83 percent in 2005, 15.61 percent in 2006, and 5.48 percent in 2007. The recovery looked good. Then 2008 transpired, with a massive loss of -36.58 percent. Timing is important and so is proper allocation, which includes alternative investments.

Alternative investments might be considered for virtually any portfolio. The weighting of each alternative investment that an investor ultimately selects, and when they select them, all depends on market conditions, the wave, risk tolerance, age, income needs, retirement goals, and other variables. The goal should be to build a better, more diversified portfolio to protect against downside risk. Arguably, the "smart money" large institutions have a fair amount devoted to alternatives that sometimes is classified as "other," as seen in Table 10.2 with the top 20 largest retirement funds.

Institutional investors, including the largest ones with significant holdings in alternative investments, are adding more of them after the recent financial downturn. "The largest institutions are increasing allocations to alternatives, whilst those at the other end of the scale are, at most, just maintaining the small presence that they took when they first invested in alternatives a few years ago."[12] One of the largest and better performing pension funds, Texas Teachers, appears to use Wave Theory. Texas Teachers appears to add alternative investments at precisely the right time. The Austin-based pension fund is $109.1 billion and has over 115 manager relationships. However, it is in the process of reducing this large number to a smaller number. Around $20.2 billion is presently in alternative investments, primarily private equity and real assets. "In all, the system has $14.3 billion targeted but not yet invested—$7.1 billion in private equity and $7.2 billion in real assets. This year alone, system officials plan to commit $3.2 billion in real assets and $1.5 billion in private equity."[13] The largest pension fund in the United States, California Public Employees' Retirement Systems also uses a large amount of alternative investments (Figure 10.6).

An argument by many investors, both individual and small institutions, is that we do not have "billions in asset" or "we do not have access to alternative investments." However, the landscape with alternative investments is changing and becoming more accessible to the average investor. For example, private equity is attracting more interest: "Private Equity

Table 10.2 Top 20 Largest Retirement Funds/Sponsors Ranked by Total Assets, in US Millions, As of September 30

Rank	2009 rank	Sponsor	Assets	Change	Total DB	Total DC	DB stocks	DB bonds	DB cash	DB other
1	1	**Federal Retirement Thrift**	**$264,013**	12.6%		$264,013				
2	2	**California Public Employees**	**$214,387**	7.9%	$213,066	$1,321	52.1%	23.8%	1.5%	22.6%
3	3	**California State Teachers**	**$138,888**	6.5%	$138,630	$258	53.0%	23.0%		24.0%
4	4	**New York State Common**	**$133,023**	5.8%	$133,023		55.1%	25.9%	1.3%	17.7%
5	5	**Florida State Board**	**$123,373**	7.6%	$117,802	$5,571	61.0%	25.0%	1.0%	13.0%
6	6	**New York City Retirement**	**$115,204**	3.2%	$96,801	$18,403	58.7%	33.7%	0.1%	7.5%
7	7	**General Motors**	**$101,541**	2.4%	$87,807	$13,734	27.4%	45.8%		26.8%
8	8	**Texas Teachers**	**$100,280**	9.8%	$100,280		56.0%	21.6%	1.1%	21.4%
9	11	**IBM**	**$83,095**	7.5%	$49,692	$33,403	35.3%	47.3%	30.0%	17.1%
10	10	**New York State Teachers**	**$80,324**	3.5%	$80,324		60.8%	23.0%	1.4%	14.8%
11	13	**Boeing**	**$79,411**	11.6%	$48,670	$30,741	34.0%	51.0%		15.0%
12	12	**Wisconsin Investment Board**	**$77,812**	6.5%	$75,355	$2,457	59.0%	27.0%		14.0%
13	9	**AT&T**	**$76,183**	−5.0%	$46,090	$30,093	41.0%	33.3%	0.7%	25.0%
14	14	**North Carolina**	**$75,314**	6.4%	$69,746	$5,568	50.3%	38.1%		11.6%
15	18	**Ohio Public Employees**	**$72,157**	6.7%	$71,727	$430	61.9%	26.5%	0.3%	11.3%
16	15	**New Jersey**	**$70,803**	3.1%	$70,230	$573	43.7%	37.1%	3.3%	15.9%
17	19	**Washington State Board**	**$61,637**	8.7%	$52,035	$9,602	37.0%	21.0%	1.2%	40.8%
18	18	**Ohio State Teachers**	**$61,007**	4.8%	$60,587	$420	64.7%	18.0%	3.2%	14.1%
19	17	**General Electric**	**$60,843**	4.4%	$42,728	$18,115	49.0%	20.0%	4.0%	27.0%
20	20	**Oregon Public Employees**	**$55,216**	7.2%	$54,152	$1,064	44.0%	26.0%		30.0%

Source: Pensions & Investments, February 7, 2011.

California Public Employees' Retirement System
Alternative Investment & Other Asset Classes
March 31, 2011

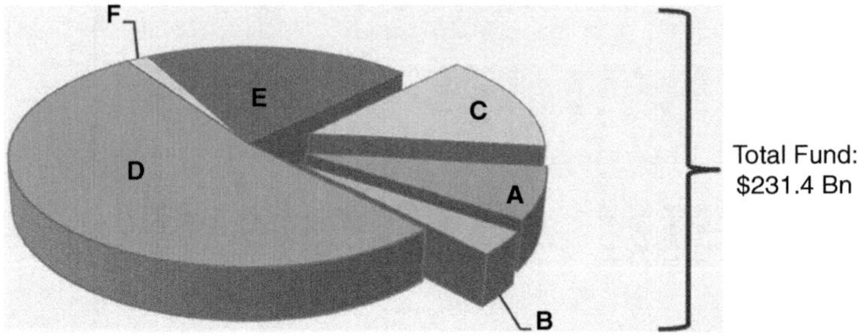

Alternatives		Non-Alternatives	
A. Real Estate (8%)	$17.7 bn	D. Global Equity (53%)	$122.9 bn
B. Inflation Leaked (3%)	$8.0 bn	Global Fixed Income (20%)	$47.8 bn
C. Alternative Investment Management (14%)	$33.2 bn	Cash Equivalents (2%)	$3.9 bn

Figure 10.6 CALPERS: Alternative Investments.
Source: Author and Calpers.ca.gov

funds provide investments opportunities that otherwise would be unavailable to most institutions and most high net worth individuals to achieve higher returns than traditional investments by investing in non-public companies with particular prospects for increasing their productivity and value through operational improvements, usually including new capital spending. As a result, private buyout related investments grew from 12 transactions valued at $13 million in 1970 to 2,474 transactions involving total equity investment of $70 billion in 2007."[14] Today, the number has not only grown, but there are several ways to gain exposure to private equity such as mutual funds or ETFs. Minimums can be as low as $1,000.

Too often investors are heavily weighted in just one security or sector, dramatically increasing their risk. It is a simple notion: the higher the concentration, the higher the risk. One of my high net worth clients once asked me how he should visualize asset allocation with alternative investments, which I thought was a very astute question. Typically, if one wants to arrive at a certain destination, one might use a road map. Asset allocation helps steer the road map otherwise known as the investment policy statement. While some institutions utilize investment policy statements, very few financial advisors make the effort or spend the time to write them for their clients.

Asset allocation is important but it is not a panacea. Over the past four decades, asset allocation was thought to be the holy grail to investing. Anyone working on Wall Street or involved with finance claimed that "93.6 percent" of performance was because of asset allocation. Few advisors or investment professionals questioned how this conclusion was derived. Oddly, very few advisors challenged this number. Investors naively followed along. Multiple definitions of asset allocation sprang up along the way but failed to address alternative investments. The focus was on stocks, bonds, and cash. Investors still misconstrue the definition of asset allocation in 2013. I once had a high net worth client tell me he was "very well diversified" and yet he was 100 percent in stocks (and nothing else). The stocks were all large growth, which he refused to sell. While this strategy worked well in the 1990s, large growth eventually went out of favor. Nothing works forever in finance. The investor ultimately got clobbered. He told me that he wished he had listened more and finally learned what diversification means.

ASSET ALLOCATION VERSUS SECURITY SELECTION OR MARKET TIMING

In "Determinants of Portfolio Performance," Brinson, Hood, and Beebower examined 91 large pension plans over 1974–1983 and found that asset allocation is far more important than security selection or market timing (Figure 10.7). Brinson and his colleagues state, "Our goal is to determine, from historical investment data on U.S. corporate pension plans, which investment decisions had the greatest impacts on the magnitude of total return and on the variability of that return."[15] They found that investment policy dominates 93.6 percent of the variation in total plan return. Later, they examined 82 large pension plans from 1977 to 1987 and found that "asset allocation policy, however determined, is overwhelmingly dominant contributor in total return."[16] For decades after these Brinson studies were released, banks, investment firms, insurance companies, mutual funds, pension consultants, financial planners, and others preached this gospel and viewed

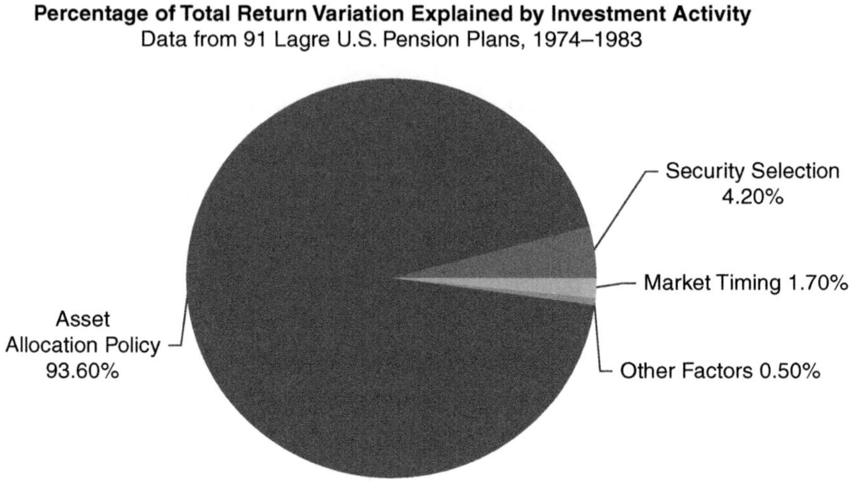

Figure 10.7 Brinson, Hood, and Beebower: US Pension Plan Total Return Variation Explained by Investment Activity (1974–1983).

Source: Gary P. Brinson, L. Randolph Hood, and Gilbert L. Beebower, "Determinants of Portfolio Performance," *Financial Analysts Journal*, July–August 1986, pp. 39–44. Copyright 1986, CFA Institute. Reproduced and republished from the *Financial Analysts Journal* with permission of CFA Institute. All rights reserved.

asset allocation as the holy grail to investing. As Roger Ibbotson states, "The idea that asset allocation policy explains more than 90 percent of performance has become accepted folklore."[17] Even Randolph Hood who was one of the original authors admitted: "It might be one of the most quoted numbers in applied finance: 93.6 percent. Ironically, it is also often misquoted or taken out of context."[18] However, very few finance "experts" even bothered to read Brinson, Beebower, and Hood's papers let alone understand why they initially performed this research. The reason behind the studies is most intriguing. At the time, Brinson, Beebower, and Hood were concerned that asset allocation had too little importance. In fact, asset allocation was somewhat ignored at the time. One of Brinson's colleagues, Randolph Hood, explains: "In the early 1980s, Gary Brinson and I were wondering why our institutional pension clients spent so much time and effort in manager searches and so little time in reviewing their asset allocation policies. It was not as if all our clients had identical risk tolerances, liability streams, and funding policies."[19] Consultants, probably afraid of being fired, focused on manager selection and not enough on asset allocation.

During the 1970s, manager selection appeared to be the primary focus, which was convenient for the pension consultants. If a manager did not perform well, they had someone to blame. Blame shifted to the managers and how well they performed, not the asset allocation that the consultant devised. If the consultant focused mainly on asset allocation and was wrong, he or she probably would get fired. "Poor outcomes resulting from asset allocation policies are difficult to blame on investment managers."[20] It was not the first nor the last time, someone in finance attempted to shift the blame. While nothing is set in stone, the best route might be somewhere in the middle of the road as opposed to the extremes. In other words, active management or security/manager selection might be similar in importance as to asset allocation and not be heavily slanted one way or the other. Both appear to be useful, especially with alternative investments. "For the U.S. equity funds, asset allocation policy excess market returns accounts for 48 percent of the excess market return variations for the average equity funds; active portfolio management accounts for 41 percent. The residual 11 percent is a result of the interaction effect."[21] Post Great Recession, active management appears to be increasing in importance. "After being trounced by the stock market for years, so-called active managers are on a hot streak."[22]

While asset allocation is important, it is not a panacea, especially when adding alternative investments to a portfolio. In other words, it is not prudent to buy a bunch of alternative investments, throw them into a portfolio, and walk away. When an investor adds alternative investments or reduces them, it is crucial to be aware of the market and how the alternative investments fit into the mix. Alternative investments typically have a low and sometimes negative correlation with stocks and bonds. They are an entirely different asset class and for the most part, act differently. Security selection and tactical asset allocation (formerly called "market timing" by Brinson and others) are both more important than one would think with alternative investments. Are you buying gold at its all-time high? Are you adding venture capital at the height of the tech bubble? Some even argue that it is more or less rebalancing of a portfolio than just market timing.

Regardless of what an investor wants to call it, changes to a portfolio are needed from time to time. As Dan Moisand stated in *The Retirement Advisor*, "Buying at the bottom or selling at the top certainly beats missing them both... rebalancing is not market timing."[23] The phrase "market timer" used to be as derogatory as calling someone a style drifter. Over time, advice changed and timing strategies became more accepted—for example, the adage "sell in May and go away." While Wall Street folklore exists, this strategy appears to have some merit for equities. Historically, advisors would literally draw a style box (large cap growth, large cap blend, large cap value, mid cap growth, mid cap blend, mid cap value, small cap growth, small cap blend, and small cap value) and advisors would then put various money managers with different "styles" into each box so that a pension plan or individual would be properly allocated.

However, times changed after the tech bubble. There is a desire today to have managers that are nimble and try to protect capital. The decisions these managers make tend to be shorter-term decisions. Investment policy statements typically include a set asset allocation that must be rebalanced according to a mandate. Rebalancing in this respect will occur from time to time. What used to be called "style drift" and was frowned upon is much more acceptable today than in the past. The frequency one makes changing a portfolio and shifting assets, will, of course, vary amongst the type of investor. Investors, whether they are an individual or institutional, should have their own set of goals and objectives.

"OTHER ASSETS" CATEGORY

Apparently, overlooked by the financial world for decades, the old Brinson, Hood, and Beebower study involved equity, bonds, and cash equivalents as well as a category called "other." It is most interesting to note why there was a category called "other". According to the authors of the research, the "other" category was an enigma. "Because the composition of the 'other assets' category was unknown, its weight was allocated to the equity, bond and cash components in proportion to their respective weights."[24] Why does this matter? It is relevant because "a few plans had extraordinarily large allocations to the 'other' category over the period; these 'outliers' were omitted from the analysis."[25] Alternative investments were not widely understood at the time Brinson and his colleagues ran their numbers. As of the beginning of 2013, alternative investments are still unknown to many investors. But decades ago, they were even less understood. Interestingly enough, the miscellaneous "other" category included "convertible securities, international holdings, real estate, venture capital, insurance contracts, mortgage-backed bonds and private placements."[26] Sound familiar? Today, most if not all of this "other" category would be considered to be alternative investments. One can clearly see that if parts of the study pertaining to alternative investments were eradicated and their "weight" allocated to stocks, bonds, and cash, the conclusion of the study might have shown security selection and market timing to be much more important. Even a few short years later (after the original study), as the market changed, the same study revealed that asset allocation was 91.5 percent versus 93.6 percent. Decades later, most still think asset allocation (is most if not all) the key to investing (Figure 10.8).

A skeptic might believe that the plans with extraordinarily higher allocations to the "other asset" category were high risk and high return. Yet this belief is unjustified. "The two plans with extraordinarily low risk had higher allocations to the 'other asset' class—perhaps real estate, given the low volatility."[27] Brinson and his partners identified alternative investments but did not know how to include them at the time; they were somewhat of a mystery at the time and there was not enough data to use. The gathering of data with alternatives is not easy nor was it simple to show that waves exist with alternative investments, similar to securities such as bonds or stocks. Information regarding alternative investments is often hard to

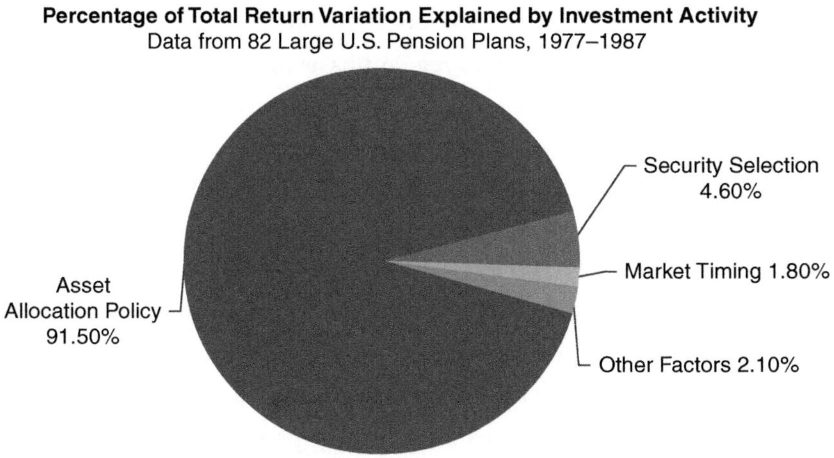

Figure 10.8 Brinson, Hood, and Beebower: US Pension Plan Total Return Variation Explained by Investment Activity (1977–1987).

Source: Gary P. Brinson, Brian D. Singer, and Gilbert L. Beebower, "Determinants of Portfolio Performance II: An Update," *Financial Analysts Journal*, May–June 1991, pp. 40–48. Copyright 1991, CFA Institute. Reproduced and republished from the *Financial Analysts Journal* with permission of CFA Institute. All rights reserved.

find and was never assembled in any book before *Wave Theory for Alternative Investments* was written. They did realize that alternative investments have a low correlation to stocks and bonds. "The historically low correlation between the returns of alternative assets and equities, bonds, and cash leads us to believe that it is unreasonable to assume that a mix of equities, bonds, and cash can serve as a proxy for alternative asset classes."[28]

The last study Brinson, Hood, and Beebower did ended more than a quarter of a century ago, from 1977 to 1987. Interestingly enough, they never did a follow-up or current study. If a new study showed very different results, it would not necessarily mean Brinson, Beebower, and Hood were wrong or did a bad job. However, it would be valuable for investors to have updated information. As stated in *Financial Advisor* magazine:

> For more than a decade, asset allocation has been accepted as the principal tool for helping individual investors protect from risk and accumulate wealth. A landmark study by Brinson, Hood, and Beebower, 'Determinants of Portfolio Performance,' Financial Analysts Journal, July–August 1986, found that more than 90% of portfolio performance results from allocation across asset classes. Their findings have driven financial planners to focus their energies on optimizing client portfolios. Recent years of market volatility and underperformance have raised questions about whether portfolio optimization 'science' merits such emphasis in the decisions of individual investors.[29]

What if asset allocation did not determine 93.6 percent of portfolio performance? Times have changed. Back then, alternative investments were in their infancy and not well understood. Optimal portfolio decisions depend on the details of the environment: the financial assets that are available, their expected returns and risks, and the preferences and circumstances of investors.[30] Today, we have a paradigm shift led by alternative investments. Obviously, the world of alternative investments has increased over time and the results might be very different in 2013 as opposed to 1987, showing more importance with both security selection and tactical asset allocation in the current environment. Randolph Hood never felt active asset management was unimportant. "Nothing in the original paper suggests that active asset management is not an important activity. It was not the point of our paper, and our goal was not to demonstrate otherwise."[31]

THE TRUTH ABOUT ASSET ALLOCATION

Subsequent research in fact revealed that strategic asset allocation accounted for less portfolio performance than the Brinson, Hood, and Beebower studies revealed. "Strategic asset allocation, on average, accounts for 77.5% of the variability of portfolio returns. The investment process should not be limited to strategic asset allocation, as managers can potentially add value through tactical asset allocation and security selection."[32] Some even believe that asset allocation is far less important than one would think. "Another interpretation of the BHB study is that, for the ten-year period covered in their study, asset allocation policy returns explain only 14.6 percent of the range of actual portfolio returns!"[33] There are quite a few studies showing why the 93.6 percent number is off base and present issues with the way the returns were calculated. "While the BHB study observes that asset allocation policy explains 93.6 percent of the variance of quarterly portfolio returns, when using the more appropriate standard deviation asset allocation policy explains only 79 percent of the variation of quarterly returns. Though still a big number, it does not appear to be as conclusive as the reported 93.6 percent."[34] Asset allocation plays a role and is important for investors, but it is not everything. As Roger Ibbotson explains, "Asset allocation is very important, but nowhere near 90 percent of the variation in returns is caused by the specific asset allocation mix."[35]

Alternative investments are a different breed from equities and bonds. Security selection and manager selection is extremely important when selecting alternative investments. For instance, since 1986, private equity has done well and become an attractive asset class for many investors. If one selects a good manager, returns can even be higher as shown below where there is a substantial difference between upper and lower quartile managers (Table 10.3).

Hedge fund selection is another area where careful selection is crucial. Not all hedge funds are created equal. While some hedge funds struggled during 2012, others did quite well. Hedge funds move in waves and timing is important. As we previously examined, alternative investments as a

Table 10.3 US Private Equity since Inception IRR and Multiples by Fund Vintage Year, Net to Limited Partners As of December 31, 2010

Vintage year	Upper quartile (%)	Median (%)	Lower quartile (%)	Difference between upper and lower (%)	Number of funds
1986	17.72	11.13	7.32	10.4	11
1987	15.16	10.82	8.52	6.64	12
1988	15.48	12.3	9.99	5.49	17
1989	29.18	20.51	12.57	16.61	18
1990	19.24	15.06	10.64	8.6	8
1991	44.23	38.85	16.57	27.66	11
1992	30.33	19.75	13.38	16.95	14
1993	33.54	21.73	8.74	24.8	25
1994	15.97	9.67	−0.45	16.42	21
1995	30.9	11.28	0.64	30.26	33
1996	12.8	8.27	0.74	12.06	38
1997	13.13	7.29	−1.23	14.36	51
1998	14.57	9.65	1.6	12.97	52
1999	17.87	11.45	6.31	11.56	55
2000	20.93	12.35	7.56	13.37	72
2001	39.61	22.28	10.47	29.14	22
2002	27.58	21.36	11.23	16.35	32
2003	19.88	14.43	7.07	12.81	34
2004	13.19	8.74	4.49	8.7	62
2005	12	6.99	2.31	9.69	78
2006	11.6	4.04	0	11.6	72
2007	13.19	5.92	−3.86	17.05	70
2008	16.89	0.09	−19.77	36.66	54
2009	25.94	11.66	−0.73	26.67	14
2010	N/A	N/A	N/A	N/A	7

Source: "U.S. Private Equity Index," Cambridge Associates LLC, December 31, 2010.

Table 10.4 The Top Ten Hedge Funds to Watch in 2013

Fund	2012 return*	AUM
Greenlight Capital	10.90%	$7.7 billion
Maverick Capital	21%	$9 billion
Third Point	11%	$8.8 billion
Omega Advisors	22%	$7 billion
Appaloosa Management	22%	$14 billion
Saba Capital Management	9%	$5.8 billion
Metacapital Management	34%	$1.4 billion
Bridgewater Associates	23%	$130 billion
Winton Capital Management	33.40%	$29 billion
Jana Partners	11.20%	$2.5 billion

Source: "The Elite List," Worth Magazine, December–January 2013, p. 72.
* As of December 31, 2012.

whole move in waves and so do the individual style of hedge funds. Hedge funds can lower risk and increase returns if used correctly (Table 10.4).

Concerning alternative investments, both security selection and tactical moves are more important than was concluded in the two Brinson studies conducted decades ago. Securities change over time and so should research. It is analogous to comparing students that used to visit the college library years ago to modern-day students going online with an iPad for research. Years ago, there was no Internet and one had to use a card catalogue to find a book in a library (hopefully, the majority of my readers will have a clue as to what I am talking about here). I made a reference, while lecturing students at Wharton, to a card catalogue, and one of the students asked me after my lecture what I was talking about. They never heard of a card catalogue! There is now evidence that both security selection and tactical asset allocation might play an even more important role with alternative investments than stocks and bonds. In "Strategic Asset Allocation and Other Determinants of Portfolio Returns," Hoernemann, Junkans, and Zarate came up with a different or more updated study than Brinson and his colleagues. In their "alternative study," the Wells Fargo team "concluded that strategic asset allocation, on average, accounts for 77.5% of the variability of portfolio returns. We end by asserting that the investment process should not be limited to strategic asset allocation, as managers can potentially add value through tactical asset allocation and security selection."[36] The group adopted what most finance professionals call tactical asset allocation instead of "market timing," which Brinson and his partners had used. Brinson defined active asset allocation as "Temporarily deviating from the policy asset mix in order to benefit from a state of capital market disequilibrium with respect to the investment fundamentals underlying the policy mix."[37]

As the Wells Fargo team explained, "Tactical asset allocation involves slightly deviating from the investor's strategic asset allocation for a short period of time in order to take advantage of temporary inefficiencies in pricing between asset classes."[38] Their study was conducted differently from the Brinson study using "synthetic portfolios." It also had a longer time horizon over 35 years (1970–2004). Finally, the Wells Fargo study included alternative assets (Figure 10.9).

While the Wells Fargo team used different means to gather data, as opposed to Brinson and his partners who gathered data from 91 US Pension Plans (and later 82 large US Pension Plans) over a shorter time period, the results clearly showed that managers can add value with security selection and tactical asset allocation. There was a big difference in time periods

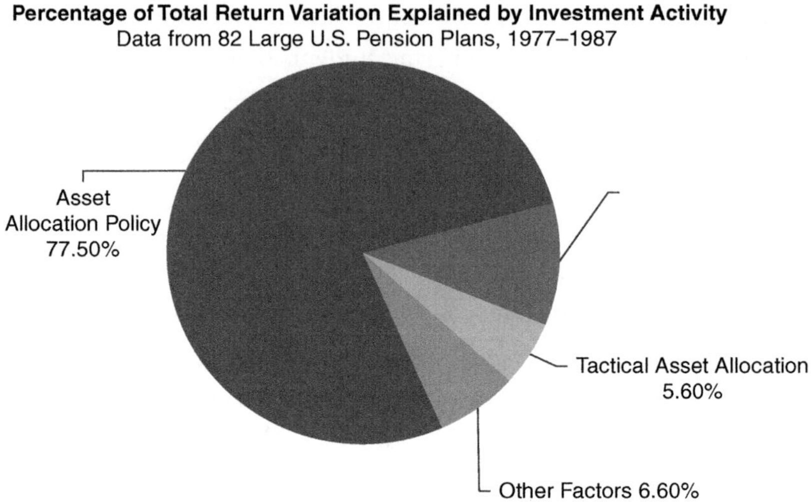

Figure 10.9 Hoememann, Junkans, and Zarate: US Pension Plan Total Return Variation Explained by Investment Activity (1977–1987).

Sources: Author; Jeffrey T. Hoernemann, Dean A. Junkans, and Carmen M. Zarate, "Strategic Asset Allocation and Other Determinants of Portfolio Returns," *The Journal of Wealth Management*, Winter 2005, pp. 26–38.

between the two studies (Brinson et al.'s studies were between 1974–1983 and 1977–1987) while the Wells Fargo team focused on 35 years or 1970–2004. The addition of alternative investments appears to be the main factor that changed the percentage of total return variation explained by investment activity. That is, the major difference between the studies was the use of alternative investments. By adding alternative investments, asset allocation policy was less important, achieving returns (93.6–77.5 percent). Security selection was also more important over this longer time period (4.2–10.3 percent). Market timing, otherwise known as tactical asset allocation, was also found to be more important (1.7–5.6 percent). Thus, investors might be able to potentially increase value by tactical asset allocation as well as with security selection.

SECURITY SELECTION AND TACTICAL ASSET ALLOCATION

Security selection and tactical asset allocation might not have not have been as important 50 years ago. However, the market has changed and investments do not just revolve around stocks, bonds, and cash any more, like they did back in the 1960s and 1970s. That was then, this is now, as they say. An investor might be remiss today just focusing on stocks and bonds and excluding alternative investments. A number of studies have shown that if an investor misses a few days in the stock market, returns will diminish, which makes stocks unattractive. From 1991 through 2010, the S&P500 averaged a yearly gain of 9.1 percent but that return was nearly slashed in half, to 5.4 percent, if you were out of the market on merely the 10 best days over those two decades and if you missed the 20 best days, your average annual return slumped to 3 percent.[39] While this "go with the flow" mentality does not address active versus passive managers or mutual funds/money managers actively managing money versus passive indexes, it relies heavily on the assumption that you will have your money invested during all of those 20 years. However, people invest at different times and might add or take funds out. They might start investing 12 years ago. How many of the best days did they miss? What if they had a wedding, needed to buy a house, had to live off their income, had to take care of expensive hospital bills, got divorced, were laid off, or had some other expense? Twenty years does not sound like a lot but that amounts to about 5,000 trading days (using 250 a year days on average that the stock market is open, excluding holidays and weekends). Therefore, if one misses just 10 days out of 5,000, returns dwindle. One might ask, is this the best way to invest?

Some investors today merely throw their money into an index fund and a bond fund, figuring that is the best way to invest. They then select an inexpensive index, betting that passive (indexes) will outperform active (money managers/mutual funds). Yet this thinking might be flawed. As of September 1, 2011, America's 8,000 equity funds had an average 10-year annual gain of just 4.7 percent, a bit better than the S&P's 500's measly 2.7 percent rise.[40] A 200 basis point difference is not minor. Depending on the market, active frequently beats passive investing but not always. Purveyors of index funds frequently like to select certain time periods or add unreasonable fees to mutual funds, trying to somehow demonstrate that passive is better than active. Yet there is no definitive study to prove this sentiment is valid.

Generally, preconceived notions and strong opinions based without facts invariably can lead to poor decision making with investing. For instance, I have had some risk adverse clients over the years who demanded all bonds. They refused to listen to any other ideas for diversifying and had little to no knowledge concerning asset allocation. Other clients, especially those that were relatively young, wanted millions put into equities. Institutional investors also can make poor investment decisions. I recall meeting an institutional client (a college endowment) that had $100 million in just government bonds. The board was completely remiss and had no idea what they were doing. Worse yet, they imposed strict government like rules to submitting a RFP (request for proposal) or request for proposal. Another client felt that owning a gold-mining stock gave her suitable exposure to alternative investments. While extremes are seldom beneficial, I noticed a particular set of investors that seemed to do the best over time. That is, having a combination of stocks, bonds, and alternative investments appeared to be the best combination. Performance could be tweaked by when alternative investments were added or removed and the types of investment vehicles selected.

When CEOs select which companies to acquire, it behooves retail or institutional investors to act the same way. "Our perspective is that diversification is intrinsically neither good nor bad; it depends on whether the parent company adds more value to the businesses it owns than any other potential owner could, making it the best owner of those businesses in the circumstances."[41] An individual investor should carefully consider risk as well as return for any security they are considering adding to their portfolio. In other words, careful consideration should be administered when adding alternative investments and not done haphazardly or blindly.

11

MODERN PORTFOLIO ALLOCATION

A number of institutional and individual clients that I helped over the years had heavy weightings to alternative investments. These clients either had alternative investments to begin with or wanted more of them to add to existing portfolios. Clients with alternative investments tended to outperform the portfolios of clients demanding all equities, fixed income, cash, or a combination of the three. A number of the largest endowments have heavy weightings to alternative investments. A larger allocation to alternative investments most likely explains why endowments had better performance compared to public pensions over the past ten years. According to the National Association of College and University Business Officers, "Endowments with assets over $1 billion generated the highest average return for all periods."[1] "Big government-employee pensions reported median returns of 13.43 percent for the year. Funds with less than $1 billion in assets, which don't invest as much in so-called alternatives like private equity, hedge funds and real estate, had median returns of 12.47 percent, according to Wilshire."[2]

In the introduction of *Wave Theory for Alternative Investments,* I explained the purpose of diversification using alternative investments: Diversification is a means to lower risk or standard deviation. It is a common risk management tool. The objective is to have minimal covariance with the securities in a portfolio. Covariance is simply a measure of how much or how little two variables change together. By diversifying and owning different types of securities that do not move in lockstep together, risk will most likely be reduced. Alternative investments can possibly lower risk and can help diversify away beta. Beta is a measure of the volatility, or systematic risk, of a security or a portfolio in comparison to the market as a whole.[3]

I believe it is prudent to utilize what I call Modern Portfolio Allocation (MPA), which might be useful as an updated or more current method of investing. MPA should not be confused with MPT (Modern Portfolio Theory). As investors, we typically frame securities. Cognitive abilities of investors are somewhat narrow and confined. As a result, investors tend to box securities. In "Behavioral Portfolio Theory," authors Hersh Shefrin and Meir Statman explain:

> Labels, such as 'stock' or 'bond' provide help in processing information as they frame complex information into simple boxes. Behavioral investors begin the process of security screening by eliminating from consideration securities whose labels indicate that they are not likely to be suitable for a given layer. For example, investors might eliminate securities that carry the 'stock' label from consideration for the downside protection layer because they know that, in general, stocks lack the desired properties for downside protection securities."[4]

As if labels were not bad enough, Wall Street has the bad habit of using acronyms for everything: ETF, CD, FOF, LBO, VC, MPT, and hundreds more. MPT is no longer modern and might not be as helpful today as it was in the past. "Modern Portfolio Theory did not fail during the credit crisis—portfolio construction did. Many investors did not have exposure to enough different asset classes."[5] MPA involves alternative investments. Alternative investments have a negative correlation. *Correlation* is a numerical measure of the similarity (or difference) in the performance of two investments.[6] MPA revolves around using both tactical (short-term investing) as well as strategic (long-term investing). I have worked with a lot of high net worth individuals and institutions. Wealthy individuals want to be treated like institutions. MPA might be considered by either institutions or individuals.

WAVES WITH ALTERNATIVE INVESTMENTS

While I gathered information for many years regarding alternative investments, it was an arduous task to prove or show the possibility of waves existing. In order to show patterns, trends, and cycles with a security or investment, a fair amount of data needed to be gathered. In *Valuation Measuring and Managing the Value of Companies*, Tim Koller, Marc Goedhart, and David Wessels, from McKinsey & Company, acknowledge the possibility of taking advantage of market declines. When the market undergoes a period of irrational behavior, smart managers can detect and perhaps exploit the resulting market deviations.[7] Wave Theory might not just involve alternative investments but traditional securities as well. A financial historian at New York University's Stern School of Business, Professor Sylla, has studied the market back more than two centuries and discovered certain patterns with equities. "Using 10-year averages of annual market returns, including dividends and adjusted for inflation, Prof. Sylla and his colleagues found that U.S. stocks have risen and fallen in surprisingly consistent waves for more than 200 years. The pattern has become even steadier since World War II."[8] MPT utilizes a quantitative tool called Mean Variance Optimization (MVO). MVO revolves around the efficient frontier curve. The more the risk incurred, the higher the rate of return, while the antithesis is true; the less risk one takes the lower the return. "The efficient-frontier curve consists of portfolios with the maximum return for a given level of risk or the minimum risk for a given level of return. The algorithm used to generate the curve is known as mean variance optimization (MVO), since what is being optimized is return versus standard deviation, or *variance* from the *mean* return."[9]

An investor makes his or her portfolio allocation with the goal to maximize expected returns while selecting a certain level of risk. Yet MVO can be problematic with alternative investments; MVO does not take into account the "tail risks" that investors abhor like rogue waves where they can lose a lot of money. "The financial crises served as a reminder that short-term realties stubbornly co-exist within long-term theory. The portfolios that are arrayed along the frontier represent different estimations of return and risk, given enough time for the performance of asset classes to reach equilibrium. In the short term, however, the market can be scarily irrational and inefficient, and apparently with greater frequency and severity than the normal distribution of returns envisioned by MPT."[10] MVO revolves around the mean and variance parameters of a normal distribution: "The Markowitz mean-variance optimization, or MVO, fails to account for the 'tail risks' that investors seek to avoid. The Markowitz mean-variance optimization framework relies only on the mean and variance parameters of a normal distribution, even though asset class returns are not normally distributed."[11] If something is positively skewed it means that the tail of the distribution is on the right since the outcomes were positive, while negatively skewed means there are rogue waves or some other large losses so it would be negatively skewed.

MOVING BEYOND MODERN PORTFOLIO THEORY

MPT is not modern. Harry Markowitz introduced MPT in 1952. For centuries, mathematicians have been studying what is normal. "Understanding of the normal curve was advanced in the early 19th century by two mathematicians, Carl Friedrich Gauss and Pierre Simon de Laplace. Gauss, a maths genius, was using the curvature of the Earth to improve the accuracy of geographic measurements in the Bavarian hills. He observed that the distribution of estimates varied widely, but tended to cluster around a mean with symmetry either side... [Laplace] showed mathematically that the sum of a large number of mutually independent, identically distributed random variables is approximately normally distributed."[12] Asset classes, as we know, are not normally distributed:

> Empirically, almost all asset classes and portfolios have returns that are not normally distributed. Many asset return distributions are asymmetrical. In other words, the distribution is skewed to the left (or occasionally to the right) of the mean (expected) value. In addition, most asset return distributions are more leptokurtic, or fatter tailed, than are normal distributions. The normal distribution assigns what most people would characterize as meaninglessly small probabilities to extreme events that empirically seem to occur approximately 10 times more often than the normal distribution predicts.[13]

In essence, MPT is beyond its time. It is not useless but it is also not very helpful today. As Peter Swisher and Gregory Kasten explain, "The problem is that while we have an elegant mathematical model for describing the perfect investment—called modern portfolio theory (MPT)—that model is wrong. Not wrong in the sense that the overall theory is no good, just wrong in the specific sense that it produces inefficient (and sometimes silly) portfolios. And we've known it for decades."[14]

MODERN PORTFOLIO ALLOCATION

How might one construct a better portfolio? While there are no guarantees and past performance might not be indicative of the future, Modern Portfolio Allocation might be a method one could utilize. MPA is current. At the time of MPT, there were few alternative investments and the focus was primarily around stocks and bonds. Similarly, there was a buy and hold mentality. MPT has never really been tested during extreme periods of risk. Rogue waves and extreme market volatility have been more commonplace. Expecting the unexpected appeared to be the motto through the tech bubble bursting and the real estate market imploding. "Though mathematicians and many investors have long known market behavior isn't a pretty picture, standard portfolio construction assumes returns fall along a tidy, bell-curve-shaped distribution. With that approach, a 2008-type decline would fall near the skinny left tail, indicating its rarity."[15] Unlike MPT (which is no longer modern since it was conceived almost 60 years ago), MPA includes investments that are not necessarily liquid or easily valued nor traded on an exchange. In other words, it includes the use of alternative investments to possibly increase returns while lowering risk at the same time.

There are five aspects to MPA. First, a diversified portfolio is needed with assets that are not highly correlated. Second, alternative investments are carefully selected and added to stock and bond portfolios in order to create a more diversified portfolio. Third, the goal of MPA is to lower risk and increase returns. Fourth, tactical and strategic asset allocation are used. In other words, both short- and long-term strategies are used with the asset allocation model. Fifth, new risk measurements are used to achieve better expectations with investors (Figure 11.1).

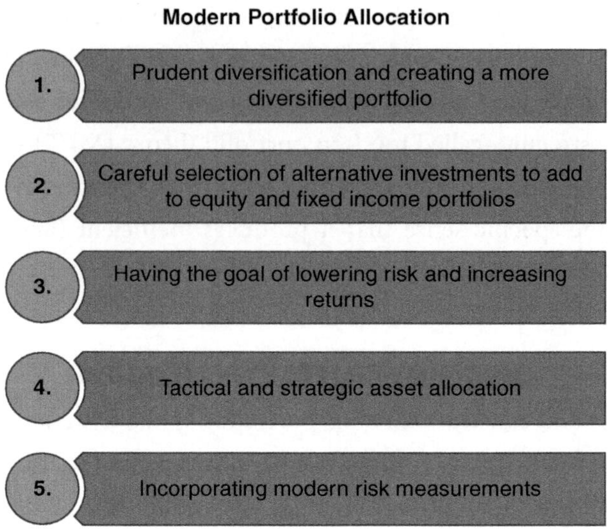

Figure 11.1 Modern Portfolio Allocation.
Source: Author.

MPA can be used by either institutions or individuals. Used correctly, returns can possibly be increased while risk is lowered. Used incorrectly, the antithesis can occur. If one incorporated an equal investment amongst various alternatives along with stock, bonds, and cash, the average return would satisfy most investors. Returns might be normal while risk is lowered. The idea of MPA revolves around using alternative investments to further diversify. MPA examines how one is allocated and when one invests as well as the type(s) of asset classes being added such as alternative investments (hedge funds, real estate, managed futures, commodities, private equity, or venture capital). "It is worth noting that the three main strategies available to investors for improving a portfolio's risk-adjusted return are *strategic asset allocation, market timing, and security selection.* Security selection seeks to add value within an asset class by picking securities (or funds) with positive expected alpha."[16] If one limits or narrows investment selection because of bias, lack of information, or trepidation, they might be doing themselves more harm than good. Figure 11.2 shows REITs and gold outperforming equities and fixed income for the past decade. I have found it is always best to examine adding a new asset class or security to a portfolio before dismissing it.

Alternative investments are still relatively new and evolving because of the growth and the rapidly changing investment climate. Today's financial

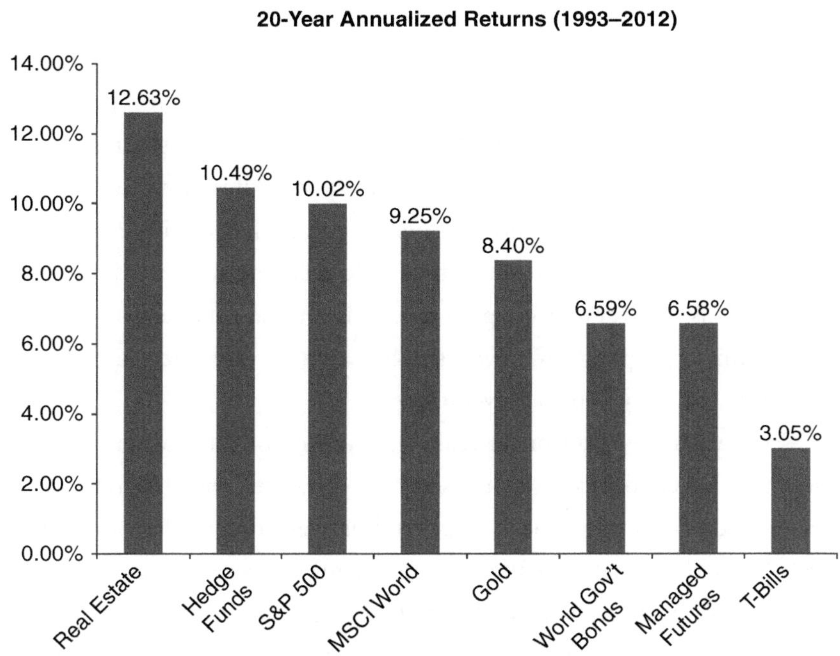

Figure 11.2 Twenty-year Annualized Returns from 1993 to 2012.

Source: "2011 Alternative Survey of US Institutions and Financial Advisors," *Morningstar & Barron's*, p. 4, May 2012.

markets have reduced if not eliminated a buy and hold strategy for stocks. When something is new, it is not necessarily proven nor completely understood. There are no road maps or guidelines. Therefore, one needs to be careful in how these rules are used regardless if they are an individual or institution. Even some of the best and brightest institutions have lost money. JP Morgan, for example, was unsuccessful using one of the new risk measurements called value-at-risk (Var) for a highly complex new derivative product they built: Some lawmakers are eyeing a new risk model used by J.P. Morgan's Chief Investment Officer that failed to reflect the giant position traders had taken on a derivative index. Risk models are mathematical formulas that track various metrics of trades, including how much a position swings from day to day compared to an average. The model in question, known as value-at-risk, measures how much a firm can lose in a normal trading day.[17]

While the JP Morgan employees were using a current risk measurement with a new complex product for institutions, it serves as a lesson to not get carried away. Jumping to the conclusion that something is bulletproof is also not wise. Learning about various alternative investments and examining risk measurements to decide which ones to add or remove from a portfolio, is prudent. Blindly throwing money into an esoteric product and not examining the downside is negligent. Alternative investments carry risk that will vary. There is different risk affiliated with each vehicle an investor might select to gain exposure to an alternative investment. For instance, risk will vary with a gold bar, ETF, mutual fund, jewelry, futures, gold mining company, etc., even though each vehicle offers exposure to gold. Risk will vary with each vehicle.

Even with the addition of real estate as one of the alternatives (after the Great Recession that was caused by real estate), the risk, return, and beta looked favorable. The two portfolios were designed from 2000 to 2009 (after the Great Recession). The net result was returns were higher with a lower beta and less volatility. It is no coincidence why the top 200 pension funds in the United States increased their exposure to alternative investments including real estate. Adding alternative investments to a stock and bond portfolio can possibly reduce risk while simultaneously increase returns. Yet it is important to note that market risk can never be entirely eliminated. "The stock market is risky because there is a spread of possible outcomes. The usual measure of this spread is the standard deviation or variance…Investors can eliminate unique risk by holding a well-diversified portfolio, but they cannot eliminate market risk. All the risk of a fully diversified portfolio depends on its sensitivity to market changes."[18]

UNDERSTANDING RISK

Risk can never be totally eliminated but it can be reduced. Risk can be lowered by examining when and how an investment is made. Further, risk can be reduced depending on when securities are bought or sold as well as the types of securities that are ultimately selected. Understanding risk can help investors build better, stronger portfolios and manage expectations better. What is risk compared with standard deviation? While investors have different risk tolerances, risk is simply the possibility of losing an investment. Investors do not know when they will lose money. What is the downside of an investment? What return will the investment provide and

Table 11.1 Adding Long/Short Hedge Funds, 2001–2010

HFRI equity hedge allocation	0%	20%
Equity allocation	60% SP500	40% SP500
Fixed income allocation	40% Barclays Agg.	40% Barclays Agg.
Average annual return (%)	**3.53**	**4.32**
Average standard deviation (%)	**9.82**	**8.04**

Source: Author.

how reliable is it? "Risk in investment means that future returns are unpredictable. This spread of possible outcomes is usually measured by standard deviation."[19] The Markowitz Mean-Variation Optimization involves standard deviation.

Standard deviation involves dispersion of returns. Standard deviation can be defined as the square root of the variance, which is a measure of the dispersion of a random variable; equals the expected value of the squared deviation from the mean.[20] A variance is simply a measure of variability or the mean squared deviation from the expected value. The variability can measure variability of individual securities as well as that of a portfolio. "The variability of a well-diversified portfolio reflects mainly the covariances."[21] A covariance is the measure of the co-movement between two variables. The importance here is that diversification can reduce variability of a portfolio. By diversifying more, it lowers variability. Adding an equity hedge can possibly lower risk while increase returns, as Table 11.1 shows.

Hypothetically, if an investor just had 20 percent allocated to hedge funds, 40 percent to the SP500 (equity index), and 40 percent to Barclays Aggregate (fixed income index), the investor would achieve lower risk and higher return than an investor with roughly 60 percent SP500 and 40 percent Barclays Aggregate.

The MVO process entails selecting a group of asset classes in order to find the best place on the efficient frontier for lowering risk and increasing returns. Yet a primary fault with MVO is that it assumes normal distributions:

> In an MVO, we use the normal distribution when forming asset-class assumptions. What is nice about the normal distribution is that it is very intuitive: Roughly two thirds of the time, returns are within one standard deviation away from the mean (average) return;

more than 95% of the time, returns are within two standard deviations; and returns are within three standard deviations of the mean about 99.7% of the time. This means, according to normal distribution mathematics, there is approximately a 0.13% probability of an extremely large gain or loss (100% less 99.74% divided by 2).[22]

Asset classes, however, are not normally distributed. "The normal distribution is flawed, however, in that it is a bell-shaped curve that assumes symmetry (a loss is just as probable as a gain) and thin tails (trivial probabilities assigned to three-sigma events, those greater than three standard deviations away from the mean).[23]MPT revolves around finding the ideal mix of measurable securities based on risk versus return. MPT concerns underlying analysis and evaluation of rational portfolio choices based on risk-return trade-offs and efficient diversification.[24] Figure 11.3 is a graph showing standard deviation and return over the past 20 years with and without alternative investments.

In my experience working with investors (institutional or individual), I have found that they are more interested in how much they could potentially lose as opposed to the dispersion of returns. A number of newer risk measures have evolved, which help show the downside. These measures

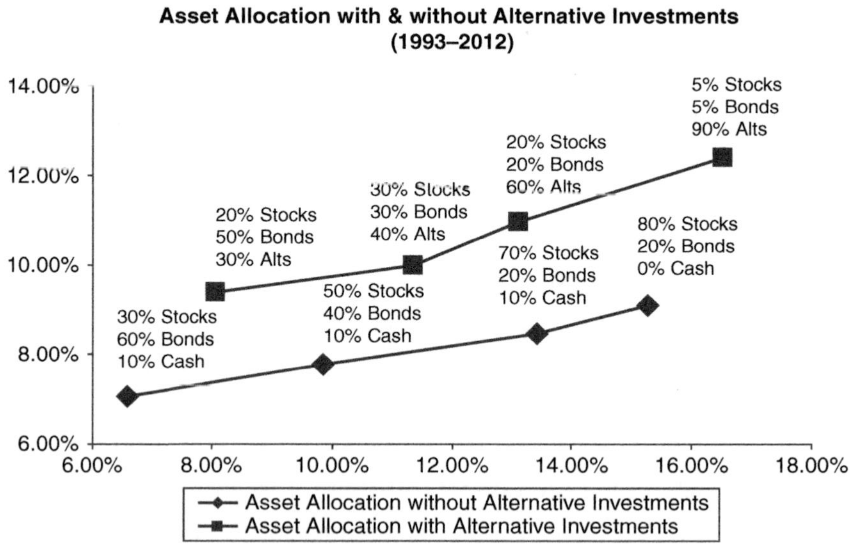

Figure 11.3 Asset Allocation with and without Alternative Investments, 1993–2012.
Source: Author.

appear to work better especially when alternative investments are included in the asset mix.

Alternative investments are often illiquid, have no developed market, or are difficult to track: "Pricing data on equities, investment-grade bonds, and cash instruments in developed markets are readily available and not subject to significant pricing problems or survivorship bias. Passive investment in these asset classes is readily accomplished through separate accounts, mutual funds, or ETFs. This is not the case with alternative investment classes, which require a new approach to evaluating the risk return profile."[25] When something is illiquid or difficult to assign a value, risk and reward charts can become somewhat meaningless for investors. There is no linear relationship between portfolios and portfolio values in terms of illiquidity. As Acerbi and Scandolo explain in Liquidity Risk Theory and Coherent Measures of Risk: "The first important thing we want to stress is the conceptual difference between *assets* and *portfolios*...Indeed the very concept of 'value of an asset' will turn out to be meaningless and so we will not try (nor need) to define it. An asset does not have any value *per se*. Its value will depend on the portfolio in which we put it and its only objective reality is the list of prices at which we can buy or sell it."[26] While one could view or prefer one risk measure over another, the following is a brief guide defining various terms used to describe risk (that may or may not be applicable to a specific alternative investment:

RISK AND RETURN RATIOS

1. Treynor Ratio

The Treynor ratio is simply the ratio of excess return to beta. The formula is as follows:

$$\text{Treynor ratio} = \frac{E(R_A) - R_f}{\beta_A}$$

-$E(R_A)$ = *Asset A's return*

-R_f = *Risk-free rate*

-β_A = *Asset A's Beta*

The Treynor Ratio tells us the reward-to-risk ratio of Asset A. In other words, it gives the risk premium per "unit" of systematic risk of Asset A.[27]

2. Sharpe Ratio

A ratio developed by Nobel laureate William F. Sharpe to measure risk-adjusted performance. The Sharpe ratio is calculated by subtracting the risk-free rate—such as that of the 10-year US Treasury bond—from the rate of return for a portfolio and dividing the result by the standard deviation of the portfolio returns.[28]

$$\text{Sharpe ratio} = \frac{\overline{r}_p - r_f}{\sigma_p}$$

Where:

$\overline{r}_p$ = Expected porfolio return

r_f = Risk-free rate

σ_p =Portfolio standard deviation

The Sharpe ratio is used to show how well the return of an asset compensates the investor for the risk that they are willing to take. Ideally, the investor wants a higher Sharpe ratio, not lower. While well known in finance, the Sharpe ratio is far from perfect. "The reward-to-variability ratio (as it was originally labeled) remains a hardy perennial for evaluating money managers and investment strategies...But fame doesn't change the fact that the Sharpe ratio falls well short of capturing the full spectrum of risks in the money game."[29] The main problem is that market returns do not always exhibit a normal statistical distribution. "The non-random aspect of returns is commonly measured instead by skewness, a measure of probability asymmetry, and kurtosis, which measures how "peaked" the random variables are."[30] Returns are not normally distributed. "Standard deviation can be used to analyze data for any distribution curve, but it's not particularly well suited for profiling the non-normality of investment returns...Those who assume that returns are normally distributed, then, run the risk of underestimating the potential for big losses, particularly over short periods of time."[31] These "fat tails" occur when the market experiences huge losses found in recessions or other market downturns. "Tailness and peakness are both components of kurtosis."[32] Kurtosis is from the Greek word kurtosis, which means bulging.

3. Sortino Ratio

This is a ratio developed by Frank A. Sortino, which helps show the difference between good and bad volatility in the Sharpe ratio. It is a variation of the Sharpe ratio.

$$\text{Sortino ratio} = \frac{<R> - R_f}{\sigma_d}$$

Where:

$<R>$ = Expected return
R_f = Risk-free rate of return
σ_d = Standard deviation of negative asset returns

The ratio takes excess return and divides it by lower partial standard deviation (LPSD). LPSD is computed like the usual standard deviation but uses only "bad" returns.[33]

RISK MEASUREMENTS

Value at Risk (VaR) is a measure of risk and commonly used. It is a popular measure of risk and commonly used in the finance industry. VaR is a technique used to estimate the probability of portfolio losses based on the statistical analysis of historical price trends and volatilities.[34] There are different types of VaR. The basic VaR estimates a portfolio's potential for maximum loss at a given confidence level (typically set at 95 percent).[35] While VaR is not that complex, it is still misunderstood and in some cases misused. Perhaps the most well-known case of a problem using VaR rests with JP Morgan and the $8 billion blow-up:

> To justify increasing their risk, JP Morgan admitted that it started to use a different measure by which they gauge how risky an investment is, something called, Value-At-Risk. This new calculation, which no one outside of JP Morgan apparently knew about up until last week, allowed the bank to increase its risk without setting off alarm bells. Obviously the risk it took was far more dangerous than anyone thought. A simple hedging exercise designed to protect something as benign as a corporate bond blew up in their faces.[36]

Some experts have doubt about using VaR. "VaR is not a coherent risk measure because it simply doesn't fulfill one of the axioms of coherence."[37] Understanding risk is crucial whether it is a retail investor with a small account or a big bank.

Modified Value at Risk (MVaR)

Because VaR is based on normally distributed returns, which is somewhat unrealistic, newer variations of VaR have evolved such as MVaR (or Cornish Fisher Value-at-Risk). "MVaR is an attempt at finding a compromise between realism and computational simplicity. MVaR provides an estimate of the risk that accompanies the non-normal aspect of return distributions, but only up to a given confidence level. If we're using a 95% level, the worst losses at the 5th percentile and beyond are undefined with MVaR (or VaR)."[38] MVaR is basically a generalization of VaR that allows for the returns distribution to be both skewed and have excess kurtosis. Returns are non-normal and MVaR takes this into consideration by allowing the distribution to be skewed and have excess kurtosis (which is referred to as the third and fourth moments of the distribution). MVaR, in other words, is a more realistic risk measurement. MVaR can be helpful with alternative investments. "It has become a popular risk measure for (among others) alternative investments which typically exhibit non-Gaussian returns."[39] Gaussian returns or distributions are basically the "normal distribution" and often described as a "bell-shaped curve." The Gaussian function was named after Carl Friedrich Gauss, a German mathematician born in 1777. "Many asset return distributions are more leptokurtic than normal or Gaussian distributions—a condition characterized by a higher peak in the center, "thinner waist" or fewer values between the center and the tails, and most importantly, "fatter tails."[40] Yet MVaR might not be the holy grail given that some of the worst financial storms (such as Rogue Waves) happen in this 5 percent or fat tail. "Confidence levels below 95.84% should never be used for the Modified Value-at-Risk to be consistent with investors' preferences for kurtosis. In addition, the use of higher confidence levels is restricted by the value of the skewness. Failure to respect these restrictions on confidence levels results in mistakenly assessing risk and potentially overweighting assets which exhibit undesirable properties in terms of higher moments."[41] The Tech Bubble and the Great Recession are two good examples of extreme market movements. Examples of severe financial storms go back for centuries. They typically lead to recessions or depressions.

Conditional Value at Risk (CVaR)

Another VaR measurement called CVaR provides an estimate of risk taking into consideration extreme losses in the tail. CVaR can be viewed as the tail VaR or expected tail loss. "Conditional Value-at-Risk (CVaR), defined as the mean of the tail distribution exceeding VaR, has attracted much attention in recent years."[42] CVaR is designed to constrain tail loss risk. It is a risk assessment technique often used to reduce the probability a portfolio will incur large losses and performed by assessing the likelihood (at a specific confidence level) that a specific loss will exceed the value at risk.[43] CVaR focuses on the left tail. CVaR is similar to VaR but is somewhat more comprehensive and does not just look at one point of distribution: "VaR estimates the loss that is expected to be exceeded with a given level of probability over a specified time period while CVaR is calculated by taking a probability weighted average of the possible losses conditional on the loss being equal to or exceeding the specified VaR; CVaR is a comprehensive measure of the entire part of the tail that is being observed, and for many, the preferred measurement of downside risk."[44] Table 11.2 shows sound allocations using conservative risk, moderate risk, and aggressive risk:

CVaR takes a probability-weighted average of the possible losses conditional on the loss being equal to or exceeding the specified VaR.[45] "CVaR is approximately proportional to the kurtosis, i.e., the higher the kurtosis, the fatter the tail, so the higher the CvaR."[46] High kurtosis has a distinct peak near the mean, declines, and has fat tails. Low kurtosis has a flat top near the mean. Higher kurtosis means that more of the variance is due to rare, big deviations. MVO uses standard deviation for measuring risk. CVaR takes into consideration the non-normal nature of returns, unlike VaR. Regardless of whether one prefers basic VaR or conditional VaR, there will always be risk. "There's no perfect measure of risk and there are many types of risk. Perspective, then, is the only game in town. Risk is multi-dimensional, which implies that our tool kit for measuring risk should be no less... Ultimately,

Table 11.2 Allocation to Alternative Strategies Based on 20-Year Monthly Returns Ending December 2011

	Conservative risk		Moderate risk		Aggressive risk	
	20/80/0	2/80/15	60/40/0	45/40/15	80/20/0	65/20/15
Monthly mean return	0.56	0.55	0.58	0.57	0.59	0.58
Standard deviation	1.76	1.43	2.96	2.47	3.71	3.21
Excess kurtosis	1.80	1.41	2.16	2.44	1.97	2.17
Skewness	−0.51	−0.44	−0.75	−0.84	−0.75	−0.83
Range of returns	13.26	10.46	21.30	18.13	26.46	22.81
Geometric average monthly return	0.54	0.54	0.54	0.54	0.52	0.53
Sharpe ratio	0.57	0.69	0.33	0.40	0.25	0.30
5% VAR	−2.40	−2.13	−4.89	−3.84	−6.58	−5.48
CVAR	−3.85	−3.01	−7.06	−5.82	−9.01	−7.76
ER-to-CVAR	0.075	0.095	0.040	0.050	0.030	0.036

Equities represented by the MSCI All Country World Index. Bonds represented by a blend of 95 percent Barclay's Global Aggregate Bond Index and 5 percent Barclay's Global High Yield Index. Alternative strategies represented by the HFRI Fund of Funds Index. Past performance is no guarantee of future performance. Index performance is provided for illustration purposes only and does not reflect the performance of any principal product. Investors cannot invest directly in an index.

Source: Dave Reichart, Senior Vice President, Principal Funds.

estimating risk is about getting comfortable with what could go wrong under different scenarios. That includes thinking about the weak link in your choice of risk metrics."[47] Any good investor, financial advisor, or consultant will know the amount of risk they are willing to incur. No investor should be clueless. Problems occur when investors fail to understand the risk. When losses occur, the investor then looks for someone to blame. Like any investment, alternative investments are not risk-free. They carry unique risks that are not easily measured.

The alternative investments chart shows annualized returns and risk for six alternative investments (NAREIT, S&P GSCI, CAMB US Venture Cap, CAMB US Private Equity, BARC CTA, and HFRI Fund Weighted Comp) as well as the S&P500 Composite and Barclay Cap Agg Bond. Three ratios are examined: Sharpe, Sortino, and Treynor. In an ideal world, daily or monthly data would be splendid. However, both LBO and venture capital data is hard to collect and track. Fortunately, The Private Capital Research Institute is gathering research from 15 private equity firms for a research database. "The main problem is academics cannot re-create private equity research to test their results because there isn't a comprehensive database."[48] Alternative investments typically have a low or negative correlation with stocks and bonds.

Modified-Conditional Value-at-Risk (M-CVaR)

Ibbotson, a Morningstar company, examined the M-CVaR optimizations that take into account fat tails and skewness for identifying the best asset allocation. "We find that both skewness and kurtosis (fat tails) impact the M-CVaR optimization and lead to substantially different allocations than the traditional mean-variance optimizations. In particular, the combination of negative skewness coupled with a fat tail has the greatest impact on the optimal asset allocation weights."[49] Skewness is a measure of symmetry if the right side looks like the left side. The majority of asset classes have returns that are not normally distributed. Return distribution is skewed to the left or right of the mean or expected value. MVaR is different from CVaR. "M-CVaR maximizes return for a given level of CVaR, or equivalently, minimizes CVaR for a given level of return. CVaR measures the expected loss in the left tail given (i.e., conditional on) that a particular threshold has been met, such as the worst first or fifth percentile of outcomes in the distribution of possible future outcomes."[50] Ideally, the dream investment is leptokurtic with positive skewness and has low semi-variance. "M-CVaR optimization tends to pick positively skewed and thin-tailed assets."[51]

Let us look at equities, fixed income, and alternative investments over a 20-year time period and examine a number of Calculations (VaR, CVaR, and MvaR) as well as standard deviation and average returns (Table 11.3).

The percentile used for this example using data from the past 20 years (1991–2011) is 5%. The probability level for the VaR and CVaR is set at 5 percent with a confidence level of 95 percent. Essentially, around 5 percent of the time, the S&P500 shows that the S&P500 index (using VaR) will produce returns at least -6.36 percent on a monthly basis and -11.10 percent on a quarterly basis. As illustrated in *Wave Theory for Alternative Investments*, multiple months of negative returns can occur. During 2008, the S&P500 had a total of eight negative months of returns throughout the year. There were two times, the index produced back-to-back negative returns three months in a row. Based on how an advisor or investor constructs a particular portfolio (in these examples alternative investments are included), what are the chances of having negative returns for a given portfolio. In other words, how bad can things really get with a particular portfolio and what

Table 11.3 Venture Capital and Private Equity Only Have Quarterly Not Monthly Data

Percentile 5%	Monthly						Quarterly					
	Weights	Returns		VaR Calculations			Weights	Returns		VaR Calculations		
		Average	Std Dev	VaR	CVaR	MVaR		Average	Std Dev	VaR	CVaR	MVaR
S&P 500*	**20%**	0.76%	4.36%	−6.42%	−9.00%	−6.23%	**20%**	2.34%	8.40%	−11.47%	−17.32%	−11.17%
S&P GSCI*	**20%**	0.73%	6.20%	−9.47%	−12.78%	−9.12%	**20%**	2.30%	11.51%	−16.63%	−23.75%	−15.54%
Barclays Capital Aggregate Bond*	**20%**	0.52%	1.05%	−1.21%	−2.17%	−1.19%	**20%**	1.57%	1.89%	−1.54%	−3.90%	−1.56%
Barclay CTA Index*	**10%**	0.47%	2.16%	−3.09%	−4.46%	−3.06%	**10%**	1.38%	3.27%	−3.99%	−6.74%	−3.94%
NAREIT All Equity REITS*	**10%**	1.06%	5.81%	−8.49%	−11.97%	−7.35%	**10%**	3.26%	10.48%	−13.98%	−21.62%	−12.63%
Cambridge US Venture Capital**	**0%**	N/A	N/A	N/A	N/A	N/A	**0%**	4.36%	12.92%	−16.90%	−26.66%	−8.66%
Cambridge US Private Equity**	**0%**	N/A	N/A	N/A	N/A	N/A	**0%**	3.66%	5.35%	−5.15%	−11.04%	−4.85%
HRFI Fund Wghtd Comp	**20%**	0.80%	2.03%	−2.55%	−4.20%	−2.41%	**20%**	2.33%	4.32%	−4.77%	−8.90%	−4.60%
Portfolio	**100%**	0.71%	2.36%	−3.17%	−4.87%	−2.83%	**100%**	2.17%	4.33%	−4.95%	−8.93%	−4.33%

Source: Author.

is the likelihood that such a negative occurrence will take place? Anyone investing (especially with alternative investments) should strive to understand the risk they might incur either adding or taking away a particular security. It is important to understand what one could lose and what the gain or return might be before executing a particular strategy.

The standard deviation in both the monthly and quarterly columns shows how much variability is in distribution. Just like with bonds and stocks, alternative investments vary. One example is venture capital. The return distribution skews to the right of the mean (or expected value) because there are blockbuster quarters that in turn pull up the average. Regarding using VaR, at 5 percent when things are bad, what is the threshold if one examines the past 20 years? If one looks at the VaR for REITs, it was -13.72 percent. Using CVaR, it was -21.51 percent. The real estate REIT index that was used was the NAREIT index, an unmanaged total return index that is designed to measure the growth and performance of the REIT industry. The index includes all REITs traded on the New York Stock Exchange and the Nasdaq. If a 5 percent extreme event occurs, what would you expect to lose if one had all REITs. In 1987, for example, the market was decimated. It was a Six Sigma event. When that happens, what is the average negative return? What might an investor expect? CVaR assumes returns are normal hence the word, "conditional." However, almost everyone does not think returns are normal all the time. Therefore, MVaR was created, which assumes returns are not normal and that the tails are fatter. There is a higher degree or number of losses with a "fat tail" return distribution. Using REITs again as an example, MVaR would be around -12.39 percent. "MVaR makes a valiant effort at balancing parsimony with reality. Ideally, risk estimates should be easy to calculate, they should use a minimal number of variables, and they should accurately model the true distribution of asset returns."[52] The standard deviation for REITs over this time period is 10.43 percent, with average returns of 3.44 percent. One can compare these numbers to equities, fixed income, and other alternative investments to achieve a better asset allocation model.

MPA uses both tactical (short-term investing) and strategic (long-term investing). Tactical asset allocation is considered a dynamic investment strategy that changes a portfolio's assets over shorter time period in order to lower risk and increase returns. "By understanding risk premiums change with market conditions, it may be possible to employ tactical asset allocation strategies to improve investment returns."[53] Some do not view short-term investing as tactical but rather as trading. "Confusion abounds about the distinction between trading and investing. Trading is focused on short-term price changes that occur for any variety of reasons. Investing is a process focused on future economic cash flows from business activities that ultimately determine the value of an investment."[54] Alternative investments, just like stocks or bonds, can be added to a portfolio with a short-term or longer-term view, or even a combination of the two. In other words, one can have a long-term portfolio with assets they intend to hold for the long haul while adding or selling other alternative investments on a short-term basis. An investor might have a short-term allocation to alternative investments (IPOs, private equity, ETFs, real estate REITs, etc.) and a longer-term asset allocation (venture capital, real estate, timber, hedge funds, LBO, etc.) that they add to a stock and bond portfolio (Figure 11.4).

Van Vliet and David Blitz "propose a dynamic strategic asset allocation." One could hold any security for the long haul but could sell it if certain red

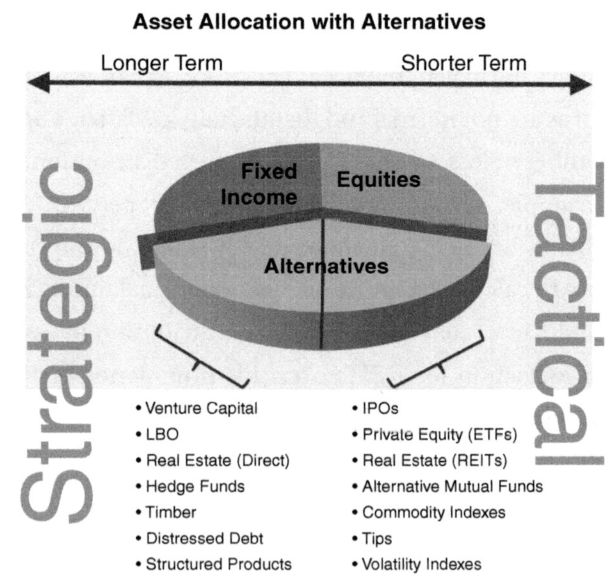

Figure 11.4 Strategic and Tactical Asset Allocation with Alternatives.
Source: Author.

flags developed. Therefore, you would have something you intend to keep for a long time but could sell shares or buy shares in the short term. Dahlquist and Harvey described a tactical overlay on a portfolio, "Our approach is based on linking the time-varying risk and return characteristics of the investment opportunity set over the economic cycle to the asset allocation decision."[55] There is nothing wrong with shorting or making moves to protect a portfolio. If a trend develops, it might be prudent to adjust a portfolio. "Following the onset of a market crisis, a Managed Futures strategy will be one of the select (few) strategies which are able to adapt to take advantage of the persistent trends across the wide range of asset classes they trade in delivering crisis alpha to their investors."[56] Some investors do not believe in long term investing. "With computerized traders that 'hold' stocks for only a few seconds at a time and markets that can swing wildly in a matter of moments, long-term investing seems to be on the verge of extinction."[57] Others do not believe in short-term trading. Individuals as well as institutions can lose money with short-term trades. No strategy or investment should ever be summarily dismissed. There might be merit to having both a long-term and short-term or opportunistic strategy to invest. The less confined and more nimble, the better.

12

DEVISING PORTFOLIOS WITH ALTERNATIVE INVESTMENTS (ACTIVE VS. PASSIVE)

ACTIVE MANAGEMENT

There are now two main styles of management for portfolios with alternative investments (active and passive). Given that investors can select alternative mutual funds, diversification has become easier to achieve. Mutual funds are quite common and owned by many investors, whether as part of a retirement plan or in a non-retirement account such as a wrap account or fee-based account. Mutual funds have plenty of attractive features. However, performance tends to vary, sometimes outperforming the indexes while other times failing to outperform them. Alternative mutual funds are no different. Persistence also is an issue. While one might have an initial aversion to investing in a leveraged buyout fund (private equity funds as they are frequently called), private equity or a leveraged buyout funds can be defined as: To briefly review the concept, in an LBO a small group of equity investors, usually including current management, acquires a firm in a transaction financed largely by borrowing. The debt is serviced with funds generated by the acquired company's operations and, often, by the sale of some of its assets. Generally, the acquiring group plans to run the acquired company for a number of years, boosts its sales and profits, and then take it public again as a stronger company.[1]

LBO mutual funds are new and might be incorporated into a diversified portfolio of funds. To further show the importance of alternative investments, a comparison was run with six different portfolios both with and without alternative investments over a decade ending December 31, 2010. Diversification with alternative investments and asset allocation is important. Likewise, active management with alternative investments has its merits as compared to passive management. That is, manager selection appears to play an important role with alternative investments. While there are numerous funds and investment options that one can select, certain funds were selected merely for illustrative purposes. The funds selected are all liquid, have low minimums, and available to most investors.

Portfolio 1: The first asset allocation (#1) has all equities, no bonds, and no alternative investments. This portfolio did well in the final year but poorly over the other times periods and averaged 2.71 percent return over the decade. A passive equity index fund was used called Vanguard 500 Index Admiral. Risk was somewhat high and the Sharpe ratio one of the lowest over the times period.

Portfolio 2: The second allocation (#2), on the other hand, was comprised of all fixed income and did not include equities or alternative investments. The Vanguard Long-Term Bond Index was used. Over a decade, the index averaged 7.13 percent return with lower risk and a Sharpe ratio of .55.

Portfolio 3: The third asset allocation (#3) included 50 percent fixed income and 50 percent equities, using the same passive index funds of #1 and #2 allocations. The returns were in between allocations #1 and #2 with averaging a 5.36 percent return.

Portfolio 4: The fourth allocation (#4) used 25 percent fixed income, 25 percent equities, and 50 percent alternatives (25 percent REIT and 25 percent commodities). Passive indexes were selected for the alternative investments. The Vanguard REIT Index was used for REITs and the Powershares DB Commodity Index was used for commodities. The returns for allocation (#4) surpassed the previous combinations of all stock, all bonds, or a 50 percent stock/50 percent bond combination, with the new stock, bond, and alternative portfolio averaging 7.88 percent over the decade. While the three-year number underperformed, all other time periods did well including the one-year return of 25.18 percent. Further, risk was 12.77 as opposed to equities 15.84 and a little higher than bonds, which had a risk of 9.81. The Sharpe ratio was also high, with 0.50 compared to only 0.12 for equities and comparable to bonds with 0.55.

Portfolio 5: The fifth allocation (#5) used 25 percent equities, 25 percent fixed income, and 50 percent REITs. Despite the collapse of the real estate market in the later part of the decade, the diversified portfolio with the addition of an alternative investment, produced a 24.99 percent return over one year, 7.52 percent return over three years, 5.19 percent over five years, and 8.54 percent return over ten years. While returns and the Sharpe ratio were higher, risk also increased.

Portfolio 6: The final or sixth allocation had 25 percent fixed income, 25 percent equities, and 50 percent alternative investments that were actively managed, as opposed to indexes. Using Morningstar, a total of 27 alternative mutual funds were identified using criteria such as the requirement of having a one, three, five, and ten-year track record. These mutual funds offer real estate to commodity exposure such as global gold. Some of the funds offer hedge fund strategies such as market neutral or risk arbitrage. Having 50 percent of the portfolio (with actively managed alternative investment funds) produced the highest return over the past decade, with 10.18 percent return, beating every other combination. By way of comparison, the Vanguard 500 Index returned only 2.71 percent and the Vanguard Long-Term Bond Index only returned 7.13 percent. The much touted 50 percent stock/50 percent bond portfolio returned only 5.36 percent as compared to 10.18 percent return of the actively managed alternative investments portfolio with stock and bonds. The alternative mutual funds were all LW (load waived). Even if a 1 percent fee was charged to purchase these funds, that would equate to a 400 basis point difference (Table 12.1).

The alternative mutual funds selected involve different types of alternative investments. Table 12.2 shows the criteria used to narrow the list.

An investor should periodically examine all their holdings (whether it be indexes or mutual funds) to see how much or how little exposure they have to alternative investments before adding or eliminating any alternative investments.

Portfolio Asset Allocation - Diversifying with Alternatives

Portfolio	#1	#2	#3	#4	#5	#6
Mix						
Equities	**100.00%**	**0.00%**	**50.00%**	**25.00%**	**25.00%**	**25.00%**
Vanguard 500 Index Admiral	100.00%	0.00%	50.00%	25.00%	25.00%	25.00%
Fixed Income	**0.00%**	**100.00%**	**50.00%**	**25.00%**	**25.00%**	**25.00%**
Vanguard Long-Term Bond Index Inv	0.00%	100.00%	50.00%	25.00%	25.00%	25.00%
Alternatives	**0.00%**	**0.00%**	**0.00%**	**50.00%**	**50.00%**	**50.00%**
Vanguard REIT Index Inv	0.00%	0.00%	0.00%	25.00%	50.00%	0.00%
Powershares DB Commodity Index	0.00%	0.00%	0.00%	25.00%	0.00%	0.00%
Mutual Funds**	0.00%	0.00%	0.00%	0.00%	0.00%	50.00%
Return						
1 year	30.66%	2.74%	16.41%	25.18%	24.99%	24.02%
3 year	3.39%	7.98%	6.32%	2.31%	7.52%	5.23%
5 year	2.96%	7.66%	5.78%	5.66%	5.19%	6.70%
10 year	2.71%	7.13%	5.36%	7.88%	8.54%	10.18%
Risk*						
3 year	21.24	12.72	13.34	20.28	25.17	20.32
5 year	17.88	10.37	10.95	16.27	20.82	16.52
10 year	15.84	9.81	9.26	12.77	16.07	13.38
Sharpe Ratio*						
3 year	0.25	0.64	0.51	0.2	0.4	0.34
5 year	0.15	0.59	0.4	0.31	0.26	0.37
10 year	0.12	0.55	0.39	0.5	0.47	0.64

* 1-year data for Risk & Sharpe Ratio are not provided by Morningstar

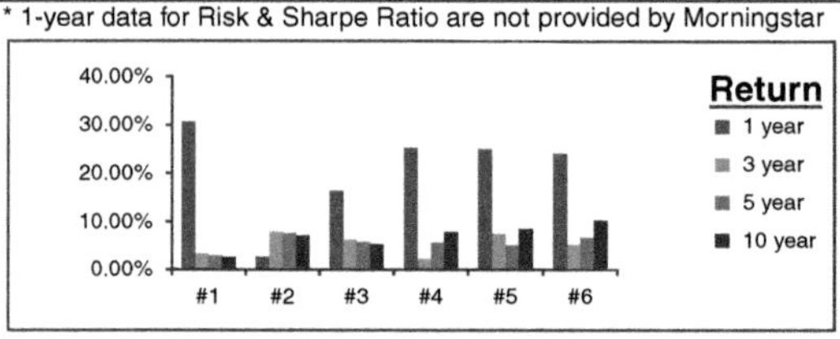

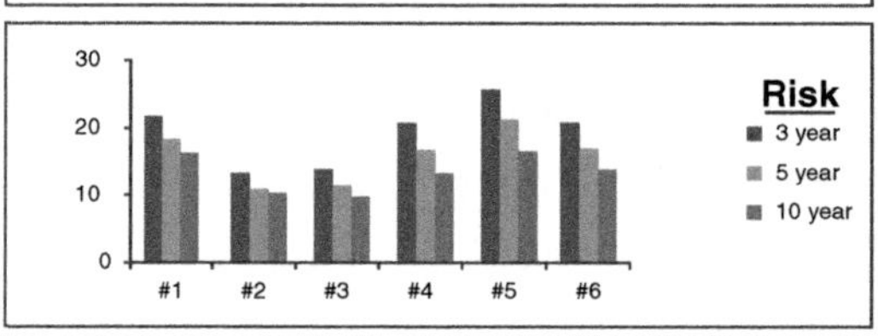

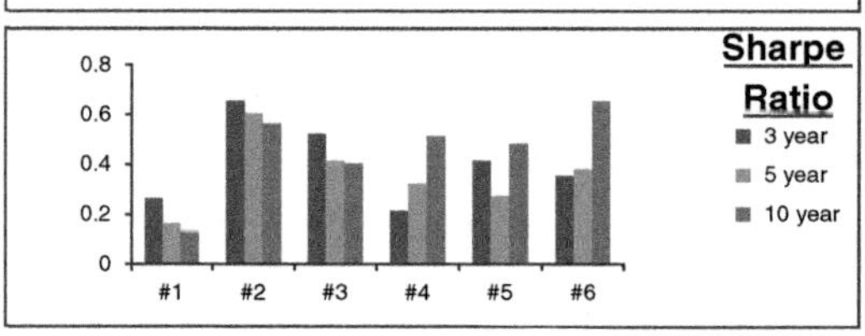

**List of 27 Funds from Morningstar

Franklin Gold and Precious Metals A LW
Blackrock Natural Resources Inv A LW
Van Eck Intl Investors Gold A LW
American Century Global Gold A LW
Prudential Global Real Estate A LW
Franklin Real Estate Securities A LW
Ivy Real Estate Securities A LW
Lord Abbett Emerging Markets Curren A LW
American Century Real Estate A LW
Calamos Market Neutral Income A LW
Rs Global Natural Resources A LW
Oppenheimer Commodity Strat Total R A LW
Spirit Of America Real Estate Inc & Gr A LW
Van Eck Global Hard Assets A LW
Cohen & Steers Realty Income A LW
Alliancebern Glbl Real Est Invmt A LW
Morgan Stanley Real Estate A LW
Ing Global Natural Resources
Franklin Natural Resources A LW
Franklin Templeton Hard Currency A LW
Putnam Global Natural Resources A LW
Oppenheimer Gold & Special Minerals A LW
Ivy Global Natural Resources A LW
Virtus Real Estate Securities A LW
Forward Real Estate Long/Short A LW
Wells Fargo Advantage Precious Meta A LW
Prudential Jennison Natural Resourc A LW

Table 12.1 Portfolio Asset Allocation—Diversifying with Alternatives.
Source: Author and *Morningstar*.

Besides instant liquidity, another benefit of the alternative mutual funds is that there are no storage costs for precious metals that an investor has to worry about. Some individuals have expensive safes to store gold bullion and jewelry. Others use private storage facilities or use banks to store their gold. If gold happens to decline in value, storage costs remain and gold pays no dividends. When buying alternative mutual funds, it is

Table 12.2 Criteria Used for Selecting Morningstar Alternative Mutual Funds

1	Each alternative mutual fund must be at least 10 years old as of Dec. 29, 2010		
2	Each alternative mutual fund must be load-waived (does not require its investors to pay fees)		
3	Each alternative mutual fund must not be an inverse fund (does not short sell)		
4	Each alternative mutual fund must belong to one of the following Morningstar categories:		
	Natural resources	Commodities	Equity precious metals
	Real estate	Currency	Bear-market
	Global real estate	Long-short	Market-neutral

Source: Author and *Morningstar*.

also prudent to pay attention to the general direction of the stock market. Is the market heading into a recession or is it in a raging bull market? Alternative investments and mutual funds are not immune from market corrections or collapses. One should also be aware of various aspects of the economy such as inflation. "Inflation tends to be cyclical and not all cycles are the same—either in terms of the prices most affected or the resulting impact on stock and bond markets."[2]

Alternative mutual funds are mutual funds that invest publicly traded securities that are in the same industry or area found in actual alternative investments. For instance, an alternative mutual fund might invest in publicly traded stocks such as gold and silver equities (otherwise known as mining stocks) whereas an ounce of gold or silver is the actual alternative investment. Mutual funds permit style drift and are not exact replacements for the actual alternative investment. For example, one might notice a few names in the alternative investment fund portfolio that would not ordinarily be expected to be seen. A commodity-oriented mutual fund might invest in storage companies or fertilizer companies. Holdings can be changed any time. Technically, buying precious metals as an alternative investment entails investing directly in the metal such as buying gold bullion or gold futures. Investing in a gold miner as a proxy for investing in gold is different. Gold stocks can have wild fluctuations and might not necessarily correlate with the price of gold. In fact, when gold went from 250 to above 1,800 (August 2011) over the course of a decade, a number of miners did not fare so well because of acquisitions. For instance, Barrick Gold (ABX) lost value after buying the copper company Equinox. Barrick is considered one the largest and well-known gold stocks. However, it did not fare well despite the rising price of gold after this acquisition. As can be seen with any commodity, miners carry a different set of risk and reward as compared to the actual underlying commodity (Figure 12.1).

Gold miners have hedging risk. "There are also risks that investors positively want companies to take. For example, investors in gold-mining companies and oil production companies buy those stocks to gain exposure to often-volatile gold or oil prices. If gold and oil companies attempt to hedge their revenues, that effort merely complicates life for their investors, who then have to guess how much price risk is being hedged and how and whether management will change its policy in the future."[3] The vast majority of the precious metal mutual funds own equities not the actual gold bullion. However, First Eagle, a mutual fund family, owns both. One must decide which type of fund is best suited for them and carefully evaluate any nuances. Real estate is another example where a mutual fund might own a number of hotel stocks as compared to an investor that buys a hotel. The hotel's value might be very different from that which is owned by the mutual fund. Obviously, there are pros and cons to each. One could

GDX - Gold Miners ETF Market Vectors - Monthly OHLC Chart

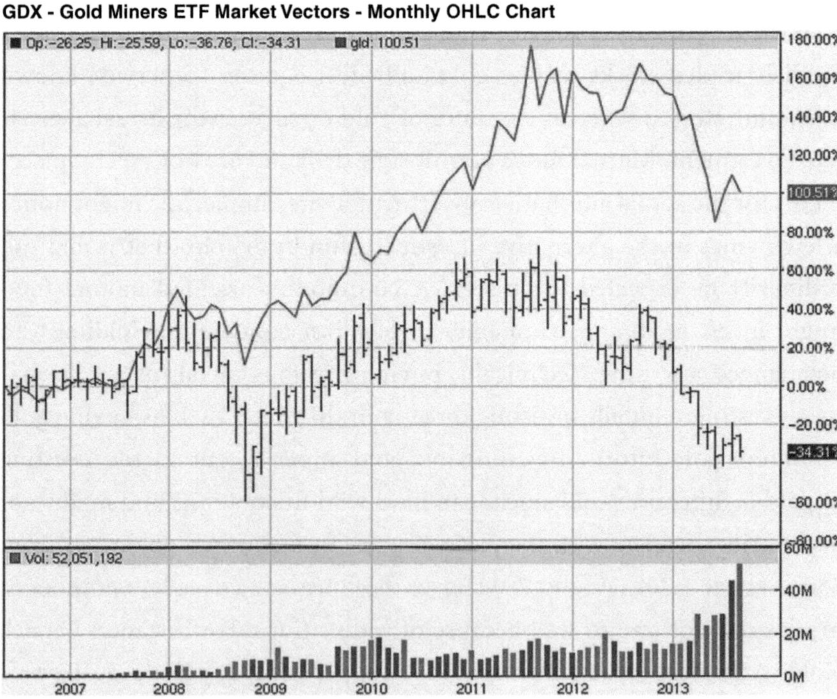

Figure 12.1 Risk and Rewards of Gold Miners.

Source: Author.

hypothetically invest $10,000 in a real estate mutual fund versus buying a hotel for $50 million; there are diversification benefits and different acquisition costs. Therefore, one could argue that buying a mutual fund focusing on alternative investments is not the same as buying the underlying asset.

ALTERNATIVE INVESTMENTS (PASSIVE MANAGEMENT)

Hypothetically, if an investor were to have a balanced portfolio over the past 20 years (1990–2010) that is passively run using a strategic or long-term asset allocation of 50 percent equities (S&P 500 Composite) and 50 percent fixed income (Barclay Aggregate), the average return would have been 8.04 percent. As seen in the following chart, bonds returned an average of 6.28 percent while equities returned 9.80 percent. During this time period, there were several recessions with bull and bear markets affecting both asset classes. For example, if one had 100 percent in stocks, they would have had higher returns over this time period provided they did not sell or buy in the interim. Substantial losses in stocks occurred in 2000, 2001, 2002, and 2008. The best year was 1995 with a return of 37.20 percent and the worst year was 2008 with a loss of -36.58 percent. Fixed income or bonds did not fluctuate as much with a small loss in 1994 of -2.92 percent and a return of 18.47 percent in 1995. Yet over the two decades, bonds averaged 6.28 percent versus equities which despite the volatility, produced an average of almost +300 basis points more than bonds (Table 12.3).

While those enamored with stocks or bonds might cringe, what would be the result during the same time period if an investor added alternative investments to the mix? If one kept 20 percent in equities and 20 percent in fixed income but added 60 percent in alternative investments over the same time period, how would that affect returns for an investor? For argument's sake, one could equally weight six of the main alternative investments by allocating 10 percent to each of the six primary alternative investments to comprise the 60 percent allocation to alternative investments. The six alternative investments used in this example are as follows: NAREIT, S&P GSCI, Cambridge US Venture Capital, Cambridge US Private Equity, Barclay CTA Index, and the HFRI Fund Weighted Composite (Table 12.4).

Table 12.3 20 Years—50% Fixed Income and 50% Equities

Date	BarCap Aggregate Bnd	S&P 500 Composite	NAREIT Composite	S&P GSCI	CAMB US Venture Cap	CAMB US Private Equity	BARC CTA Index	HFRI Fund Wghtd Comp	Total Return
Weight	**50.00%**	**50.00%**	**0%**	**0%**	**0%**	**0%**	**0%**	**0%**	
1993	9.75	9.97	18.55	−12.33	19.22	21.89	10.37	30.88	**9.86**
1994	−2.92	1.33	0.81	5.29	17.12	16.37	−0.65	4.1	**-0.80**
1995	18.47	37.2	18.31	20.33	46.22	27.48	−13.64	21.5	**27.84**
1996	3.63	23.82	35.75	33.92	41.89	23.2	9.12	21.1	**13.73**
1997	9.65	31.83	18.86	−14.07	34.18	39.63	10.89	16.79	**20.74**
1998	8.69	28.34	−18.82	−35.75	30.84	11.7	7.01	2.62	**18.52**
1999	−0.82	20.89	−6.48	40.92	288.25	50.51	−1.19	31.29	**10.04**
2000	11.63	−9.03	25.89	49.74	26.22	−14.24	7.86	4.98	**1.30**
2001	8.44	−11.85	15.5	−31.93	−39.74	−6.74	0.84	4.62	**−1.71**
2002	10.26	−21.97	5.22	32.07	−33.72	−7.59	12.36	−1.45	**−5.86**
2003	4.1	28.36	38.47	20.72	−3.94	26.96	8.69	19.55	**16.23**
2004	4.34	10.74	30.41	17.28	15.38	24.2	3.3	9.03	**7.54**
2005	2.43	4.83	8.29	25.55	6.9	30.94	1.71	9.3	**3.63**
2006	4.33	15.61	34.02	−15.09	17.55	29.73	3.54	12.89	**9.97**
2007	6.97	5.48	−17.83	32.67	15.31	10.83	7.64	9.96	**6.23**
2008	5.24	−36.58	−37.84	−46.49	−16.61	−23.63	14.09	−19.02	**−15.67**
2009	5.93	25.92	27.8	13.48	3.25	21.74	−0.1	19.98	**15.93**
2010	6.54	15.06	27.56	9.02	13.83	21.45	7.05	10.49	**10.80**
2011	4.62	0	7.28	2.07	13.14	10.9	−3.09	−5.56	**2.31**
2012	4.23	15.99	19.7	0.26	7.17	13.8	−1.7	4.79	**10.11**
Average	**6.28**	**9.80**	**12.57**	**7.38**	**25.12**	**16.46**	**4.21**	**10.39**	**8.04**

Source: Author.

Table 12.4 20 Years—Diversifying with Alternatives

Date	BarCap Aggregate Bnd	S&P 500 Composite	NAREIT Composite	S&P GSCI	CAMB US Venture Cap	CAMB US Private Equity	BARC CTA Index	HFRI Fund Wghtd Comp	Total Return
Weight	**20.00%**	**20.00%**	**10.00%**	**10.00%**	**10.00%**	**10.00%**	**10.00%**	**10.00%**	
1993	9.75	9.97	18.55	−12.33	19.22	21.89	10.37	30.88	**12.80**
1994	−2.92	1.33	0.81	5.29	17.12	16.37	−0.65	4.1	**3.99**
1995	18.47	37.2	18.31	20.33	46.22	27.48	−13.64	21.5	**23.15**
1996	3.63	23.82	35.75	33.92	41.89	23.2	9.12	21.1	**21.99**
1997	9.65	31.83	18.86	−14.07	34.18	39.63	10.89	16.79	**18.92**
1998	8.69	28.34	−18.82	−35.75	30.84	11.7	7.01	2.62	**7.17**
1999	−0.82	20.89	−6.48	40.92	288.25	50.51	−1.19	31.29	**44.34**
2000	11.63	−9.03	25.89	49.74	26.22	−14.24	7.86	4.98	**10.57**
2001	8.44	−11.85	15.5	−31.93	−39.74	−6.74	0.84	4.62	**−6.43**
2002	10.26	−21.97	5.22	32.07	−33.72	−7.59	12.36	−1.45	**−1.65**
2003	4.1	28.36	38.47	20.72	−3.94	26.96	8.69	19.55	**17.54**
2004	4.34	10.74	30.41	17.28	15.38	24.2	3.3	9.03	**12.98**
2005	2.43	4.83	8.29	25.55	6.9	30.94	1.71	9.3	**9.72**
2006	4.33	15.61	34.02	−15.09	17.55	29.73	3.54	12.89	**12.25**
2007	6.97	5.48	−17.83	32.67	15.31	10.83	7.64	9.96	**8.35**
2008	5.24	−36.58	−37.84	−46.49	−16.61	−23.63	14.09	−19.02	**−19.22**
2009	5.93	25.92	27.8	13.48	3.25	21.74	−0.1	19.98	**14.99**
2010	6.54	15.06	27.56	9.02	13.83	21.45	7.05	10.49	**13.26**
2011	4.62	0	7.28	2.07	13.14	10.9	−3.09	−5.56	**3.40**
2012	4.23	15.99	19.7	0.26	7.17	13.8	−1.7	4.79	**8.45**
Average	**6.28**	**9.80**	**12.57**	**7.38**	**25.12**	**16.46**	**4.21**	**10.39**	**10.83**

Source: Author.

By adding a mix of six different alternative investments, the average return went from 8.04 percent to +10.83 percent. The lowest return was Barclays CTA or managed futures with 4.21 percent. While this number is the lowest, it is most interesting to note the importance of this alternative investment. During 2000, 2001, and 2002, the S&P 500 index lost -9.03 percent, -11.85 percent, and -21.97 percent respectively. Managed futures, on the other hand, produced 7.86 percent, 0.84 percent, and 12.36 percent during these extremely negative years for the stock market, which demonstrates the low correlation that alternative investments typically have with both equities and fixed income. Likewise, the S&P 500 was down -36.58 percent in 2008 and managed futures (Barclay CTA Index) returned 14.09 percent! And what is behind managed futures that drives such admirable performance when the stock market craters? Managed futures involve trend-following. "The primary driver of most managed futures is trend-following or momentum investing; that is, buying assets that are rising and selling assets that are declining. These strategies are typically applied to liquid exchange-traded futures contracts on various commodities, equity indices, currencies and/or government bonds."[4]

MANAGED FUTURES

When something is unfamiliar, by nature it is scary. Alternative investments scare many investors and they shut them out before even listening. Excluding any investment is ill-advised and will narrow options for an investor. For example, if an investor is unfamiliar with managed futures, they frequently cringe just hearing the name. Yet managed futures can help an investor build a better portfolio if used correctly. Managed futures offer a number of compelling features (Table 12.5).

Managed futures did well during the past two downturns in the market. "Equity and energy prices had been declining, government bond prices had been rising, and currencies with high interest rates had been depreciating. This led to managed futures funds being positioned short equities, short energies, long government bonds and gold, and short "carry" currencies."[5] By adding managed futures and other alternative investments, an investor can possibly generate better returns while lowering risk.

Table 12.5 Ten Reasons to Consider Adding Managed Futures to Your Portfolio

1. Diversify beyond the traditional asset classes
2. Reduce overall portfolio volatility
3. Increase returns and reduce volatility
4. Returns evident in any kind of economic environment
5. Strong performance during stock market declines
6. Successful pension plan sponsors use them
7. Commodity Trade Advisors (CTAs) and Pool Operators (CPOs) have access to a wide variety of global futures products that are liquid and transparent
8. CTA/CPO community is regulated and trades on regulated futures exchanges
9. Risk management and clearing
10. Overall industry growth has been exceptional

Source: "10 Reasons to Consider Adding Managed Futures to your Portfolio," *CME Group*, 2010, pp. 1–2.

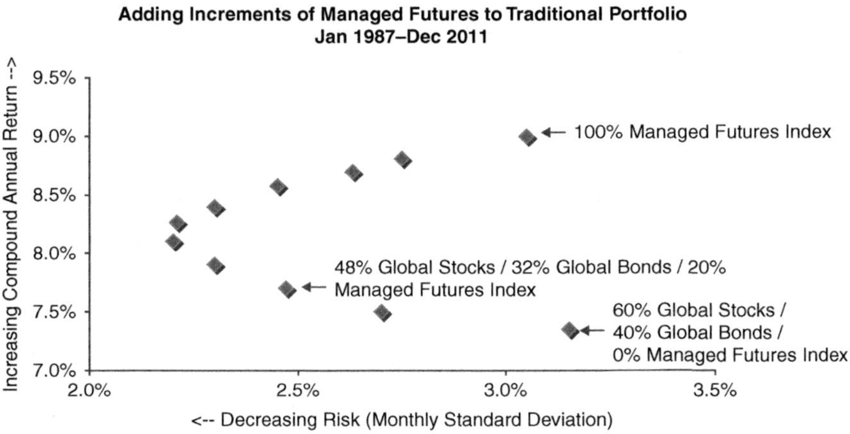

Figure 12.2 Traditional Portfolios with Additions of Managed Futures.
Source: Millburn Ridgefield Corporation.

Figure 12.2 is a chart showing the benefits of adding managed futures to a diversified portfolio.

Managed futures are gaining popularity not just amongst institutions but advisors: "For the second year in a row, advisors again cited managed futures as the asset to which they were most likely to increase their exposure, while currency funds didn't make their top five...Institutions flagged managed futures as the third most popular strategy for increased allocation, while long/short equity (or debt) and private equity/venture capital were the top two strategies for increased allocation."[6] Adding alternative investments to a portfolio of stocks, bonds, and cash will help an investor further diversify, manage risk, possibly achieve better returns, make an investor more aware of asset allocation, and make one more open to alternative investments. There are many benefits to alternative investments. Managed futures tend to do well in very bad stock markets and have a low correlation with equities. In the 20-year wave chart, managed futures and other alternative investments such as hedge funds, LBO, venture capital, real estate, currencies, and commodities were compared to stocks, bonds, and cash (Figure 12.3 and Table 12.6).

Venture Capital

The best-performing alternative investment asset class was venture capital, with an average return of +27.06 percent. Strangely, many investors would not even look at or consider venture capital after the Great Recession. However, this sentiment eventually changed and there is an ever growing interest in venture capital. A lot of the smart money has also attracted attention by the media for investments in the venture capital space. While one could literally write a book about it, Table 12.7 shows a handful of venture capital deals that billionaires invested in to further diversify their portfolios.

LBO Funds

LBO funds are very different from equity mutual funds and involve long term-investments into private companies. "There are about 260 private-equity firms in the market trying to raise $214 billion from investors, according to Preqin, a research firm."[7] Qualified investors invest in private equity. A qualified investor is an individual whose net worth, or joint net worth with a spouse, exceeds $1,000,000; or whose individual income exceeded $200,000 or whose joint income with a spouse exceeded $300,000 in each of the two most recent years that can be expected to meet that income in the current year.[8] The duration for private equity can be ten years with no liquidity. Equity mutual funds, on the other hand, invest in public companies. The funds are liquid, transparent, and have low minimums. Private equity (LBO funds) tend to be persistent and have a number of other positive attributes. Steven Kaplan from the University of Chicago Booth School of Business and Antoinette Schoar from the Sloan School of Management at MIT have written extensively on private equity performance. "Kaplan and Schoar find that GPs whose funds outperform the industry in one fund are likely to outperform the industry in

The Wave Chart: 20-Year Ranking of Asset Class Returns for Equities, Fixed Income, and Alternative Investments

	1991	1992	1993	1994	1995	1996	1997	1998	1999	2000
Best Return	NAREIT Composite 35.68%	HFRI Fund Wghtd Composite 21.22%	Int'l Stk 32.94%	CAMB US Venture Cap 20.07%	CAMB US Venture Cap 47.81%	NAREIT Composite 35.75%	CAMB US Venture Cap 54.40%	CAMB US Venture Cap 35.89%	CAMB US Venture Cap 319.77%	S&P GSCI 49.74%
	HFRI Fund Wghtd Composite 32.19%	CAMB US Private Eqty 16.38%	HFRI Fund Wghtd Composite 30.88%	CAMB US Private Eqty 16.37%	S&P 500 Composite 37.20%	S&P GSCI 33.92%	CAMB US Private Eqty 39.63%	S&P 500 Composite 28.34%	CAMB US Private Eqty 50.51%	NAREIT Composite 25.89%
	S&P 500 Composite 30.23%	NAREIT Composite 12.18%	CAMB US Private Eqty 21.89%	Int'l Stk 8.06%	CAMB US Private Eqty 27.48%	CAMB US Venture Cap 30.18%	S&P 500 Composite 31.83%	Int'l Stk 20.33%	Average 44.55%	BarCap Aggregate Bnd 11.63%
	CAMB US Venture Cap 20.58%	CAMB US Venture Cap 10.61%	CAMB US Venture Cap 21.87%	S&P GSCI 5.29%	HFRI Fund Wghtd Composite 21.50%	S&P 500 Composite 23.82%	NAREIT Composite 18.86%	CAMB US Private Eqty 11.70%	S&P GSCI 40.92%	BARC CTA Index 7.86%
	BarCap Aggregate Bnd 16.00%	Currency 10.27%	NAREIT Composite 18.55%	Average 4.61%	S&P GSCI 20.33%	CAMB US Private Eqty 23.20%	Average 16.97%	BarCap Aggregate Bnd 8.69%	HFRI Fund Wghtd Composite 31.29%	Cash 5.96%
	Average 15.55%	S&P 500 Composite 7.49%	Average 13.06%	Cash 4.24%	Average 18.75%	HFRI Fund Wghtd Composite 21.10%	HFRI Fund Wghtd Composite 16.79%	BARC CTA Index 7.01%	Int'l Stk 27.30%	Average 5.49%
	Int'l Stk 12.50%	BarCap AggregateBnd 7.40%	BARC CTA Index 10.37%	HFRI Fund Wghtd Composite 4.10%	BarCap Aggregate Bnd 18.47%	Average 18.09%	Currency 11.35%	Average 6.43%	S&P 500 Composite 20.89%	HFRI Fund Wghtd Composite 4.98%
	Currency 10.94%	Average 7.35%	S&P 500 Composite 9.97%	S&P 500 Composite 1.33%	NAREIT Composite 18.31%	BARC CTA Index 9.12%	BARC CTA Index 10.89%	Currency 5.71%	Cash 4.74%	Currency 4.45%
	CAMB US Private Eqty 9.57%	S&P GSCI 4.42%	BarCap Aggregate Bnd 9.75%	NAREIT Composite 0.81%	Int'l Stk 11.55%	Currency 6.69%	BarCap Aggregate Bnd 9.65%	Cash 5.06%	Currency 3.12%	S&P 500 Composite -9.03%
	Cash 5.75%	Cash 3.62%	Cash 3.09%	BARCCTA Index −0.65%	Currency 11.49%	Int'l Stk 6.36%	Cash 5.25%	HFRI Fund Wghtd Composite 2.62%	BarCap AggregateBnd −0.82%	Int'l Stk −13.96%
	BARC CTA Index 3.73%	BARC CTA Index −0.91%	Currency −3.33%	BarCap Aggregate Bnd −2.92%	Cash 5.75%	Cash 5.25%	Int'l Stk 2.06%	NAREIT Composite −18.82%	BARC CTA Index −1.19%	CAMB US Private Eqty −14.24%
Worst Return	S&P GSCI −6.13%	Int'l Stk −11.85%	S&P GSCI −12.33%	Currency −5.96%	BARC CTA Index −13.64%	BarCap Aggregate Bnd 3.63%	S&P GSCI −14.07%	S&P GSCI −35.75%	NAREIT Composite −6.48%	CAMB US Venture Cap −17.75%

	2001	2002	2003	2004	2005	2006	2007	2008	2009	2010
Best Return	NAREIT Composite 15.50%	S&P GSCI 32.07%	Int'l Stk 39.17%	NAREIT Composite 30.41%	CAMB US Private Eqty 30.94%	NAREIT Composite 34.02%	S&P GSCI 32.67%	BARC CTA Index 14.09%	Int'l Stk 32.46%	NAREIT Composite 27.56%
	BarCap Aggregate Bnd 8.44%	BARC CTA Index 12.36%	NAREIT Composite 38.47%	CAMB US Private Eqty 24.20%	S&P GSCI 25.55%	CAMB US Private Eqty 29.73%	Int'l Stk 11.63%	BarCap Aggregate Bnd 5.24%	NAREIT Composite 27.80%	CAMB US Private Eqty 21.45%
	HFRI Fund Wghtd Composite 4.62%	BarCap Aggregate Bnd 10.26%	S&P 500 Composite 28.36%	Int'l Stk 20.70%	CAMB US Venture Cap 14.71%	Int'l Stk 26.86%	CAMB US Venture Cap 11.09%	Currency 3.50%	S&P 500 Composite 25.92%	CAMB US Venture Cap 18.51%
	Cash 4.09%	Currency 6.29%	CAMB US Private Eqty 26.96%	S&P GSCI 17.28%	Int'l Stk 14.02%	S&P 500 Composite 15.61%	CAMB US Private Eqty 10.83%	Cash 1.80%	CAMB US Private Eqty 21.74%	S&P 500 Composite 15.06%
	Currency 2.71%	NAREIT Composite 5.22%	S&P GSCI 20.72%	Average 12.24%	Average 10.32%	CAMB US Venture Cap 14.99%	HFRI Fund Wghtd Composite 9.96%	CAMB US Venture Cap −17.36%	HFRI Fund Wghtd Composite 19.98%	Average 11.55%
	BARC CTA Index 0.84%	Cash 1.70%	HFRI Fund Wghtd Composite 19.55%	CAMB US Venture Cap 11.06%	HFRI Fund Wghtd Composite 9.30%	HFRI Fund Wghtd Composite 12.89%	Average 7.80%	Average −18.12%	Average 14.05%	HFRI Fund Wghtd Composite 10.49%
	Average −6.33%	Average −0.76%	Average 18.21%	S&P 500 Composite 10.74%	NAREIT Composite 8.29%	Average 11.96%	BARC CTA Index 7.64%	HFRI Fund Wghtd Composite −19.02%	S&PGSCI 13.48%	S&PGSCI 9.02%
	CAMB US Private Eqty −6.74%	HFRI Fund Wghtd Composite −1.45%	Currency 11.08%	HFRI Fund Wghtd Composite 9.03%	S& P500 Composite 4.83%	Cash 4.76%	BarCap Aggregate Bnd 6.97%	CAMB US Private Eqty −23.63%	CAMB US Venture Cap 6.28%	Int'l Stk 8.21%
	S&P 500 Composite −11.85%	CAMB US Private Eqty −7.59%	BARC CTA Index 8.69%	BarCap Aggregate Bnd 4.34%	Cash 3.00%	BarCap Aggregate Bnd 4.33%	S&P 500 Composite 5.48%	S&P 500 Composite −36.58%	BarCap Aggregate Bnd 5.93%	BARC CTA Index 7.05%
	Int'l Stk −21.21%	Int'l Stk −15.66%	BarCap Aggregate Bnd 4.10%	BARC CTA Index 3.30%	BarCap Aggregate Bnd 2.43%	BARC CTA Index 3.54%	Cash 4.74%	NAREIT Composite −37.84%	Currency 0.91%	BarCap Aggregate Bnd 6.54%
	S&P GSCI −31.93%	S&P 500 Composite −21.97%	CAMB US Venture Cap 2.18%	Currency 2.36%	BARC CTA Index 1.71%	Currency −0.12%	Currency 2.59%	Int'l Stk −43.06%	Cash 0.16%	Currency 3.05%
Worst Return	CAMB US Venture Cap −34.05%	CAMB US Venture Cap −29.63%	Cash 1.07%	Cash 1.24%	Currency −1.21%	S&P GSCI −15.09%	NAREIT Composite −17.83%	S&P GSCI −46.49%	BARC CTA Index −0.10%	Cash 0.13%

Figure 12.3 The Wave Chart.

Table 12.6 Managed Futures

Managed futures provided portfolio protection during the worst 15 quarters for the S&P 500 Index since 1987

Period	Event	S&P 500 Index	Managed Futures Index	Difference
Fourth quarter 1987	Black Monday—global stock markets crash	−22.50%	16.90%	39.40%
Fourth quarter 2008	Bear market in US equities led by financials	−21.90%	8.70%	30.70%
Third quarter 2002	WorldCom scandal	−17.30%	9.40%	26.70%
Third quarter 2001	Terrorist attacks on World Trade Center & Pentagon	−14.70%	4.10%	18.80%
Third quarter 2011	Turmoil surrounding the Greek Bailout	−13.90%	1.80%	15.70%
Third quarter 1990	Iraq invades Kuwait	−13.70%	11.20%	25.00%
Second quarter 2002	Continuing aftermath of technology bubble bursting	−13.40%	8.50%	21.90%
First quarter 2001	Bear market in US equities led by technology	−11.90%	6.00%	17.80%
Second quarter 2010	Sovereign debt crisis	−11.40%	−1.90%	9.50%
First quarter 2009	Continuing bear market in US equities led by financials	−11.00%	−1.80%	9.30%
Third quarter 1998	Russia defaults on debt, LTCM crisis	−9.90%	10.50%	20.50%
First quarter 2008	Credit crisis, commodity prices rally	−9.40%	5.90%	15.40%
Third quarter 2008	Credit crisis, government-sponsored bailout of banks	−8.40%	−3.70%	4.70%
Fourth quarter 2000	DotCom bubble bursts	−7.80%	19.80%	27.60%
Third quarter 1999	Anxiety during run-up to Y2k	−6.20%	−0.70%	5.60%

Source: Millburn Ridgefield Corporation.

Table 12.7 Smart Money Going Into Venture Capital—Recent Billionaire Investments

Billionaire	Company	Industry
Randal Kirk	New River Pharma	Pharmaceuticals
Jeff Bezos	General Fusion	Energy
Eric Schmidt	Backplane	Social media
Ron Burkle	Airbnb	Travel
Mark Cuban	Toygaroo	Toys
Eduardo Saverin	Qwiki	Search engine
Steve Case	Vinfolio	Wine
Sean Parker	Spotify	Online music
Ted Turner	Ted's Montana Grill	Restaurants
Jay Walker	Priceline	Travel

Source: Author

the next and vice versa. These findings are very different from those for mutual funds. In mutual funds, persistence has been difficult to detect and, when detected, tends to be driven by persistent under-performance rather than over-performance."[9] Historically, private equity has had very good returns. Private equity covers a number of subcategories. "Among the most common investment strategies in private equity are venture capital, buyout capital (leveraged buyout, expansion, and acquisition financing) mezzanine capital and recapitalization capital (distressed investments)."[10] LBO funds have grown into a major asset class. Nihat Bulent Gultejin, associate professor of finance at the Wharton School of the University of Pennsylvania and the former governor of the Central Bank of the Republic of Turkey, describes the phenomenal growth of private equity funds: "Private equity funds currently have exceeded $2 trillion in capital committed globally, from a figure of around $8 billion in the U.S. in 1991."[11] "In 1986 and again in 1987, about $40 billion worth of LBOs took place, and 1988 brought about LBO deals worth over $50 billion."[12] LBO funds move in waves just like all the other alternative investments. "Private equity activity appears to experience recurring boom and bust cycles that are related to past returns and to the level of interest rates relative to earnings."[13] The LBO market in 2006–2008 had a number of big deals: TXU ($43.2 billion), Equity Office Properties ($34.1 billion), and HCA ($33.0 billion). Figure 12.4 shows 30 years of global LBO versus US IPO activity.

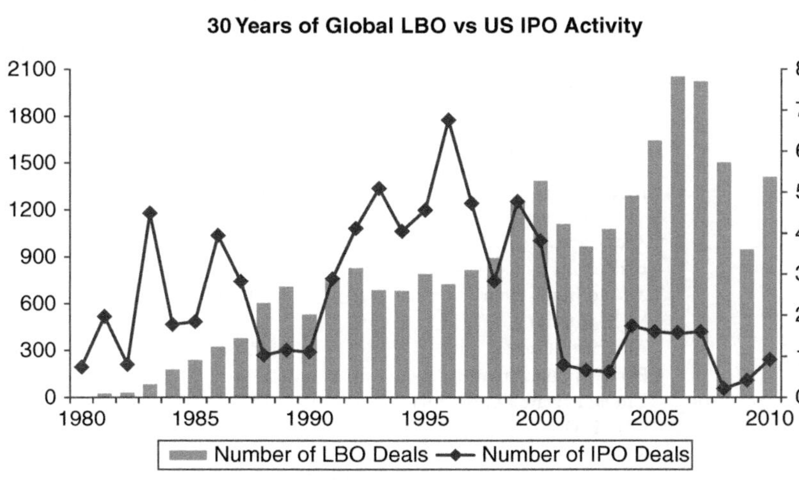

Figure 12.4 Global LBO vs. US IPO activity.

Source: Author.

While it is not apples to apples, an investor could gain exposure (or at least more knowledge about private equity and LBO funds) by investing in publicly traded companies of private equity firms. However, buying the publicly traded company of a private equity firm is not the same as investing in the particular funds that the company has set up. Each private equity company has different funds, with different styles and/or geographic locations or areas of focus. One fund might invest in LBO deals in Asia while another one will focus on mid-cap domestic LBO deals. Table 12.8 lists the publicly traded private equity companies.

Carlyle Group was the most recent high-profile private equity firm to go public. Carlyle Group went public, selling 30.5 million shares at $22.00 per share, which valued the company at around $7 billion on May 3, 2012. Compared with mutual fund companies, private equity firms tend to have lower price to earnings ratios. Compared with mutual fund companies, private equity firms tend to have lower price to earnings ratios. Private equity firms are still growing and becoming more global. They are attracting a lot of assets and beginning to rival mutual fund companies. Private equity funds are not too dissimilar from mutual fund families; mutual fund companies offer different styles of investing. As private equity firms grow, they are expanding beyond just LBOs. For example, Blackstone has 76 percent of its $190 billion in assets in areas outside private equity, like hedge funds and credit. Carlyle Group has diversified even more. The trend of buy-out firms ditching buy-outs will accelerate in 2013.[14] Since private equity companies are still relatively new public offerings, there is some concern: "Investors and analysts have a range of concerns about these companies: among them

Table 12.8 Publicly Traded Private Equity Firms

Investment	Ticket
Ares Capital	ARCC
Blackstone	BX
Apollo Investment	AINV
MCG Capital	MCGC
American Capital	ACAS
Fortress Investment	FIG
Global Private Equity Port.	PSP
Carlyle Group	CG
KKR	KKR

Source: Author

are their ability to reap substantial investment gains, their complex corporate structure—shares are called units and have special tax treatment, for example—and the volatility of the firms' short-term results."[15] The special tax treatment that many firms received in the past might not continue in the future, which might pose new risk to investors: "American private-equity bosses owe their tremendous fortunes in part to favourable tax treatment. For years they dodged any change to the treatment of "carried interest", but this will also end in 2013, as America closes tax loopholes."[16]

PRIVATE EQUITY ETFS

A number of new ETFs and funds focusing on private equity have also emerged. For instance, Powershares Global Listed Private Equity Portfolio is an exchange-traded fund in the United States. The fund seeks "investment results that correspond generally to the price and yield of the Red Rocks Listed Private Equity Index, which includes more than 30 U.S. publicly listed companies with direct investments in more than 1,000 private businesses."[17] Owning private companies through such a vehicle is not the same as investing in a leveraged buyout fund and carries its own set of risks. However, for an investor seeking some type of exposure to private companies, something might be better than having nothing. The fund is also liquid and been around since 2010 so it is not brand new; it is developing a track record (not that past performance is necessarily any guarantee of future returns). Similar to private equity ETFs, there are ETFs with hedge fund like strategies such as Global X and AlphaClone that buy the stocks that hedge funds are buying. "Alternative or hedge-fund-like investments are fast emerging as a distinct asset class…Dozens of mutual funds have launched in recent years which try to perform like hedge funds by using derivatives and exotic strategies."[18]

REAL ESTATE

Real estate investing is very broad. One area that did quite well after the Great Recession was farmland. Farmland appreciated in value and farmers became very wealthy in the United States. "High corn and soybean prices and low interest rates have made Iowa land an attractive investment."[19] Nationwide, the per-acre value of farm real estate in 2012 averaged $2,650, up 10.9 percent from 2011.[20] While one might not have the means and wherewithal to buy a farm for diversification purposes, certain mutual funds and hedge funds invest directly or indirectly in farmland. Farmland moves in waves just like the rest of the real estate market and other alternative investments.

Despite the real estate collapse, the NAREIT composite averaged 12.57 percent, handsomely beating both equities and fixed income. Despite Bernie Madoff and the mass exit of hedge funds after 2008, hedge funds averaged 10.39 percent, beating both equities and fixed income as well. Private equity also beat fixed income and equities with an average return of 16.46 percent. There were even hedge funds that did quite well during the real estate collapse, such as John Paulson. "Hedge funds are known for taking outsize bets that can lead to big winnings—or huge losses. A hedge fund run by John Paulson of Paulson & Co. had gains of as much as 590% in 2007 thanks to a wager against the subprime mortgage market. But another Paulson & Co. fund, Advantage Plus, lost more than half its value in 2011 after ill-fated bets on financials and gold."[21] After reviewing the performance of alternative investments, one might ask why anyone would even bother with either equities or fixed income. What if an investor constructed a portfolio of 100 percent alternative investments and totally did away with any allocation devoted to equities and bonds? For most investors, this notion would be simply unconscionable. Table 12.9 shows the results of eradicating fixed income and equities, using just alternative investments.

A portfolio of 100 percent alternative investments (NAREIT composite, S&P GSCI, Cambridge US Venture Capital, Cambridge US private equity, Barclays CTA Index, and the HFRI Fund Weighted Composite) produced an average return of 12.69 percent from 1993 to 2012. Equities produced 9.80 percent while fixed income averaged 6.28 percent. Hypothetically, one could have all alternative investments as a core and use equities and fixed income as satellite investments. Years ago, I had the good fortune of meeting and investing with one of the wealthiest families in the United States. They completely abandoned stocks and bonds and focused solely on alternative investments. As a result, the family outperformed the S&P 500.

Table 12.9 20 Years—All Alternatives

Date	BarCap Aggregate Bnd	S&P 500 Composite	NAREIT Composite	S&P GSCI	CAMB US Venture Cap	CAMB US Private Equity	BARC CTA Index	HFRI Fund Wghtd Comp	Total Return
Weight	**0.00%**	**0.00%**	**16.67%**	**16.67%**	**16.67%**	**16.67%**	**16.67%**	**16.67%**	
1993	9.75	9.97	18.55	−12.33	19.22	21.89	10.37	30.88	**14.76**
1994	−2.92	1.33	0.81	5.29	17.12	16.37	−0.65	4.1	**7.17**
1995	18.47	37.2	18.31	20.33	46.22	27.48	−13.64	21.5	**20.03**
1996	3.63	23.82	35.75	33.92	41.89	23.2	9.12	21.1	**27.50**
1997	9.65	31.83	18.86	−14.07	34.18	39.63	10.89	16.79	**17.71**
1998	8.69	28.34	−18.82	−35.75	30.84	11.7	7.01	2.62	**−0.40**
1999	−0.82	20.89	−6.48	40.92	288.25	50.51	−1.19	31.29	**67.22**
2000	11.63	−9.03	25.89	49.74	26.22	−14.24	7.86	4.98	**16.74**
2001	8.44	−11.85	15.5	−31.93	−39.74	−6.74	0.84	4.62	**−9.58**
2002	10.26	−21.97	5.22	32.07	−33.72	−7.59	12.36	−1.45	**1.15**
2003	4.1	28.36	38.47	20.72	−3.94	26.96	8.69	19.55	**18.41**
2004	4.34	10.74	30.41	17.28	15.38	24.2	3.3	9.03	**16.60**
2005	2.43	4.83	8.29	25.55	6.9	30.94	1.71	9.3	**13.78**
2006	4.33	15.61	34.02	−15.09	17.55	29.73	3.54	12.89	**13.77**
2007	6.97	5.48	−17.83	32.67	15.31	10.83	7.64	9.96	**9.76**
2008	5.24	−36.58	−37.84	−46.49	−16.61	−23.63	14.09	−19.02	**−21.58**
2009	5.93	25.92	27.8	13.48	3.25	21.74	−0.1	19.98	**14.36**
2010	6.54	15.06	27.56	9.02	13.83	21.45	7.05	10.49	**14.90**
2011	4.62	0	7.28	2.07	13.14	10.9	−3.09	−5.56	**4.12**
2012	4.23	15.99	19.7	0.26	7.17	13.8	−1.7	4.79	**7.34**
Average	**6.28**	**9.80**	**12.57**	**7.38**	**25.12**	**16.46**	**4.21**	**10.39**	**12.69**

Source: Author.

13

THE ASSET ALLOCATION PROCESS AND SAMPLE PORTFOLIOS

Asset Allocation Process

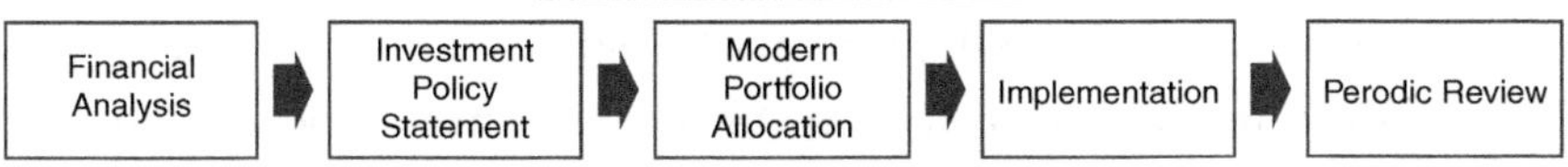

Financial analysis: Analysis entails information gathering. It is similar to getting a checkup at a doctor's office where a number of tests and measurements are run such as a blood test, weight and height measurements, urine analysis, blood pressure, temperature, stress test, cholesterol, and other important diagnostics. Financial analysis starts with what an investor owns at a given point in time. How are your assets allocated? Investors frequently candy-coat this financial information just like when they tell white lies to a doctor who asks any of the following question, "Are you watching your weight? Are you exercising? Are keeping a control of your smoking? How is the drinking? When is the last time you had any alcohol? Are you eating proper?" The number of patients that answer these questions honestly are a very small minority. Investors need to be completely honest not only to themselves but also with the financial advisor seeking information about their financial health. If an advisor does not have all the facts (similar to a patient lying to his or her doctor), the results will invariably be poor. Distorting the truth will only harm an investor in the long run. Facts are important. What is your age, annual income, needs, objectives, investing experience, time horizon to invest, liquidity needs, tax status, net worth, existing assets, risk tolerance, and any other pertinent information? These questions need candid answers.

If an advisor is dealing with an individual, numbers are important but so is really knowing the client. Learning about the investor's experiences and listening to their stories is equally if not more important. As my friend Charles W. Collier states in his "Wealth in Families," "There is more to family wealth than the financial dimension. Human capital refers to who individual family members are, and what they are called to do; intellectual capital refers to how family members learn and govern themselves; social capital denotes how family members engage with society at large; and financial capital stands for the property of the family."[1] If a financial advisor is a good one, they will attempt to really know a client. Otherwise, recommending alternative investments for the sake of recommending them is not helpful and will most likely run into problems down the road.

Once it is clear what is important to the family or individual, it is necessary to focus on the asset allocation at hand. How many stocks, bonds, and alternative investments does one own? Are there any real alternative investments? How are they allocated? What percentage of a portfolio is taxable versus tax deferred or tax free? What vehicles are being used such as money managers, indexes, ETFs, mutual funds, or hedge funds? Financial analysis also includes an investors risk tolerance. How much of a drop in their portfolios can they take? Ninety percent of the investors that I met in the late 1990s wanted "low risk" portfolios with "a minimum of 20–30% returns." An investor's liquidity needs are important. If you cannot feed Spot, as I have said in the past, then do not invest. A number of alternative investments are illiquid. Not everyone can handle illiquidity. Individuals as well as institutions routinely make this mistake. Even some of the largest endowments in the country run into liquidity issues. Taxes are another concern. If you are an individual, what tax bracket are you in? Are you in the maniac bracket? How much do you pay in tax each year? Do you mind paying them late? A number of alternative investments issue K1s and one will need to go on extension. If you are used to paying taxes on time, this might come as a shock to the system. I once managed the money of a CEO who wanted income and not to lose money in the stock market. As a result, he was primarily in bonds and sailed through the market collapse. When I met with him and showed him he earned an additional $1 million in income (a fair amount of which was taxable), he was upset. Taxes are a consideration with alternative investments. Age is also important. Many financial planners allocate more bonds for older people as opposed to younger ones where they suggest using more equities. The thinking is that younger people have a longer time horizon and can accept more risk. Mature investors need income and to live off their portfolio. They cannot experience huge losses so they will need safer, more liquid securities such as bonds. At first blush, many advisors write off alternative investments for older clientele. Yet this might be a mistake. No asset classes should ever be summarily dismissed whether or not the client is an individual or institution. It does not matter. Narrowing the investment spectrum is never wise. Each investor's needs must be carefully assessed. Understanding which alternative investment to add and when to add one is no easy task. Neither is selling or eliminating an alternative investment. Alternative investments can play a role in many different types of portfolios regardless of age since they act differently from bonds (fixed income) and stocks (equities). In other words, they have similar characteristics but do not necessarily correlate with the traditional asset classes. Alternative investments have a low correlation with equities and fixed income.

Investment Policy Statement (IPS): Whether one's investment history is abysmal or stellar, an investment policy statement or "IPS" helps one develop a map of where they would like to go. An IPS states the steps needed to reach one's goals and objectives. An IPS typically has a horizon or time period attached to it. In addition, an IPS will have restrictions and certain assumptions. Families and boards of institutions have one thing in common—personalities. Boards of institutional clients can be as difficult as a dysfunctional family (if not worse). Therefore, I find the IPS to be invaluable. Institutions such as pension plans or foundations require investment policy standards that detail how the investments should be managed, acceptable risk, asset allocation, restrictions, and other mandates they feel are important. It is a godsend for financial advisors. Whereas financial analysis shows where an investor is at the moment, an IPS shows the direction in which one is headed or the goals that an investor would like to achieve. It is written in black and white. "Once you've created one, you can use your investment policy statement as a compass, a check to keep your investment portfolio on course to meet its goals even when the market and your emotions are telling you to run for the hills."[2] Having something multiply in writing is helpful to show to an investor.

One mistake I have seen over the years is when an IPS is too restrictive that it eliminates good ideas which could help the investor achieve proper diversification and help reach the end goal. An IPS will include performance benchmarks. What is the desired performance or satisfactory return? These goals need to be reasonable. Further, an IPS needs to be flexible so that change can occur. If a manager or parts of the portfolio underperform, how long should you give the manager or asset to improve? Instant gratification is not always a brilliant idea on how to invest. What types of vehicles should be used to achieve the goals and objectives that were laid out? Does the investor need money managers, mutual funds, indexes, or hedge funds? Can there be a combination of these vehicles?

Modern Portfolio Allocation (MPA): What type of asset allocation should one be using? Strategic, tactical, or both? Buying securities and throwing them in a pile does not translate into a well thought out asset allocation model. I have found that if one visualizes three different portfolios (conservative, moderate, or aggressive), it can help develop a cohesive plan for asset allocation. Figure 13.1 is an example.

Throughout my career, I custom tailor every single portfolio for each client whether they are an institution or ultra high net worth investor. While these three different models for asset allocation show the nuances between them, one could theoretically have countless asset allocation models. Some banks even throw out nine or ten recommended models, which is confusing to most investors. Investors can get overwhelmed. For instance, studies have been conducted with 401 (k) plans. Plans with 30–40 options tend to produce results more than plans with fewer options such as 8–15 options.

Because college endowments have a long-term view, they tend to focus on strategic asset allocation. Moreover, they can have a lot more assets that are illiquid. The smart money has discovered that alternative investments help reduce risk and simultaneously increase return. Adding alternative investments to the mix, Notre Dame improved performance of the school's endowment fund. "The endowment fund, which has more than 50% of its

Sample Tactical Asset Allocation Using Alternatives

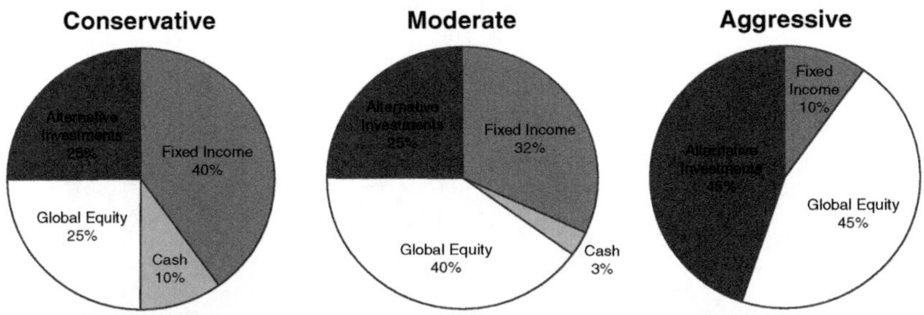

Conservative	
Cash	
Global Cash	10%
Fixed Income	
Municipal Bonds	20%
Government Bonds	5%
Corporate	15%
Global Equity	
US Equity Large	14%
US Equity Small/Mid	3%
Developed ex US	5%
Emerging Markets	3%
Alternative Investments	
Commodities/Managed Futures	4%
Hedge Funds	6%
TIPs	5%
REITs	5%
Private Equity	5%

Moderate	
Cash	
Global Cash	3%
Fixed Income	
Municipal Bonds	20%
Government Bonds	3%
Corporate	9%
Global Equity	
US Equity Large	20%
US Equity Small/Mid	10%
Developed ex US	7%
Emerging Markets	3%
Alternative Investments	
Commodities/Managed Futures	5%
Hedge Funds	5%
TIPs	5%
REITs	5%
Private Equity	5%

Aggressive	
Cash	
Global Cash	0%
Fixed Income	
Municipal Bonds	5%
Government Bonds	0%
Corporate	5%
Global Equity	
US Equity Large	20%
US Equity Small/Mid	10%
Developed ex US	10%
Emerging Markets	5%
Alternative Investments	
Commodities/Managed Futures	10%
Hedge Funds	15%
TIPs	5%
REITs	10%
Private Equity	5%

Key
- Cash
- Fixed Income
- Global Equity
- Alternative Investments

Figure 13.1 Asset Allocation Using Alternatives.
Source: Author.

assets invested in alternatives, returned 21.5% for its fiscal year ended June 30 and has consistently outperformed a traditional 60% equity, 40% fixed-income portfolio. The endowment has a 12.1% 15-year annualized return against 6.8% for the typical 60/40 plan."[3] Likewise, Smith College has a fair amount invested in alternative investments (Figure 13.2).

Yet endowments need income and funds for expenses with their schools. Some schools such as Yale and Harvard put quite a bit of money into alternative investments. When the market dropped, the value of equities plummeted as did bonds. Since Harvard could not sell its private

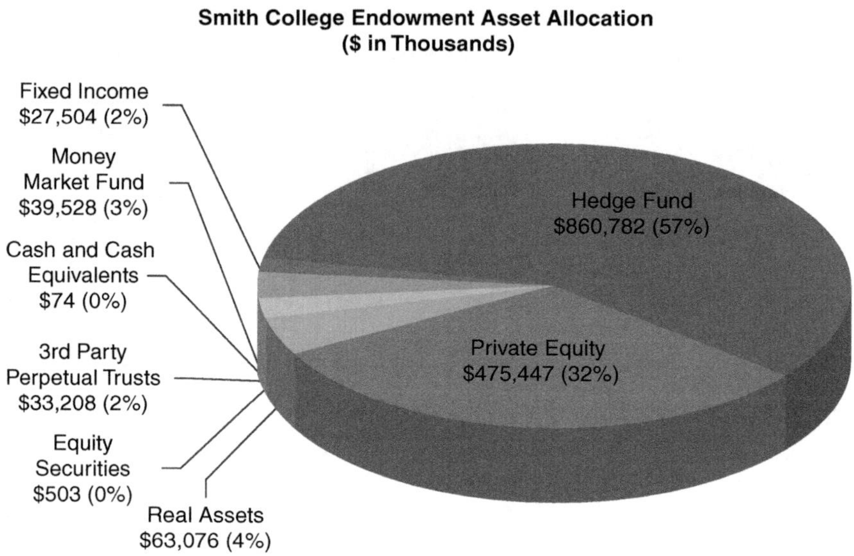

Figure 13.2 Smith College Endowment Asset Allocation ($ in Thousands).
Source: Smith College 2009–2010 Annual Report.

equity (which it attempted to do at the bottom of the market), funds were needed and Harvard resorted to borrowing money to use for its expenses. Fortunately, Harvard's alternative investments were not unloaded at fire sale prices and they rebounded. Too much of anything is generally not a good thing, including alternative investments.

There are some items that will always remain unavoidable for both institutions and individuals such as expenses. "No economic unit—firm or household or government—enjoys perfect synchronization between the seasonal patterns of its flow of receipts and its flow of expenditures."[4] Institutions and individuals need to balance their budgets. The more assets an endowment has, the more likely they will have a greater allocation to alternative investments. For instance, funds over $1 billion in assets have 60 percent in alternative investments. In some cases, they own quite a bit of alternative investments.

How would a portfolio look for an individual invested in alternative investments? The answer is that there are countless ways to invest in alternative investments and it depends on a number of variables such as age, risk tolerance, net worth, investment objectives, income, etc. that the individual has, which will affect the allocation to alternative investments. I came across an article about a successful athlete who also happens to be

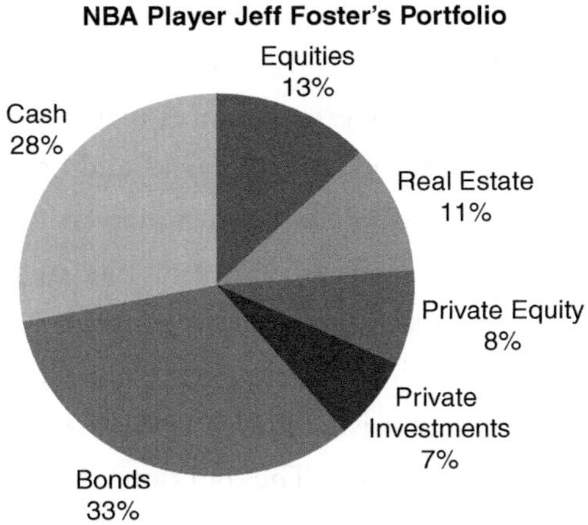

Figure 13.3 Portfolio of Jeff Foster, NBA player.
Source: "The Seven-Foot Buffett," Paul Watcher, *Bloomberg BusinessWeek*, November 2011, p. 89.

a good investor. Over two decades, I have unfortunately not come across one athlete who has been a successful investor so this article got my attention. Reading through the article to find his allocation, I became aware that Jeff Foster likes alternative investments and incorporates them into a well-thought out overall asset allocation model he uses. While each portfolio should be designed individually according to a person's risk tolerance, income needs, age, and other variables, Jeff's portfolio has approximately 26 percent devoted to alternative investments (Figure 13.3).

A number of hedge funds and money managers are buying or selling various alternative investments. For instance, Permanent Portfolio. Initially, the fund did poorly during the tech bubble and had assets of around \$52 million at the end of 2001. After changing its investment philosophy, things improved. Ten years later the fund reached \$15.6 billion in assets. According to Bloomberg, the fund had various alternative investments: 5 percent Silver, 10 percent Swiss francs and bonds, 20 percent gold, 30 percent US Stocks: half natural resources/real estate, half aggressive growth, and 35 percent high-grade corporate and Treasury bonds, with annual returns averaging 12 percent in the decade ended August 31, 2011, compared with 2.7 percent for the S&P 500.[5] Permanent Portfolio shifts its asset allocation even into asset classes that are not in favor. Frequently, what appears to be the worst time to invest when market is decimated is actually the best time to invest. "Portfolio strategies that attempt to exploit return reversals may still earn positive expected profits."[6] The particular weightings to various alternative investments such as silver, gold, real estate, currencies, and other alternatives using both tactical and strategic asset allocation illustrates MPA. Certain percentages of alternative investments are used in an overall coherent asset allocation model with stocks and bonds. Investors who merely invest in one or two asset classes are not diversified. Similarly, those that turn their noses up at alternative investments are remiss. Holding a handful of stocks and bonds without ever making any changes might not be the best method of investing: "The application of trend following offers a substantial improvement in risk-adjusted performance compared to traditional buy-and-hold portfolios…The traditional method of asset allocation of 60% in domestic equities and 40% in domestic bonds and, apart from a little rebalancing, holding these positions indefinitely increasingly appears archaic."[7] For years, many advisors used a 60 percent equity/40 percent allocation, erroneously thinking that the assets were not highly correlated and this was the best way to invest. However, the correlation is much higher than many would think. "Over the last 15 years, the correlation of returns between a 60/40 portfolio and a 100% equity portfolio was 0.99, meaning that they were almost perfectly correlated. Even a portfolio that is exceptionally overweight bonds shows a similar trend. A 30% stock/70% bond portfolio had a 0.82 correlation to a 100% stock portfolio."[8]

There is a group of millionaires that meets on a regular basis in New York City. Amongst many topics, they discuss the ideal asset allocation. The group is called "Tiger 21." Collectively, they have around 180 members and $15 billion if you add up their net worth. They frequently invite experts to speak and review other member's asset allocation especially new members. According to Tiger 21's new Member Favorites Survey, alternative investments play a major role in their asset allocation (Figure 13.4).

Members use hedge funds, private equity, real estate, commodities, currencies, and other for their investments. Provided an investor has the knowledge base or an advisor that is well versed in fixed income, equities, and alternative investments, they can decide what weighting to assign to each, followed by the types of assets in each category, and the weightings each of these should have. But before one searches for managers or specific assets to add, a suitable asset allocation model should be devised. Institutions devise asset allocation models and update them on a regular

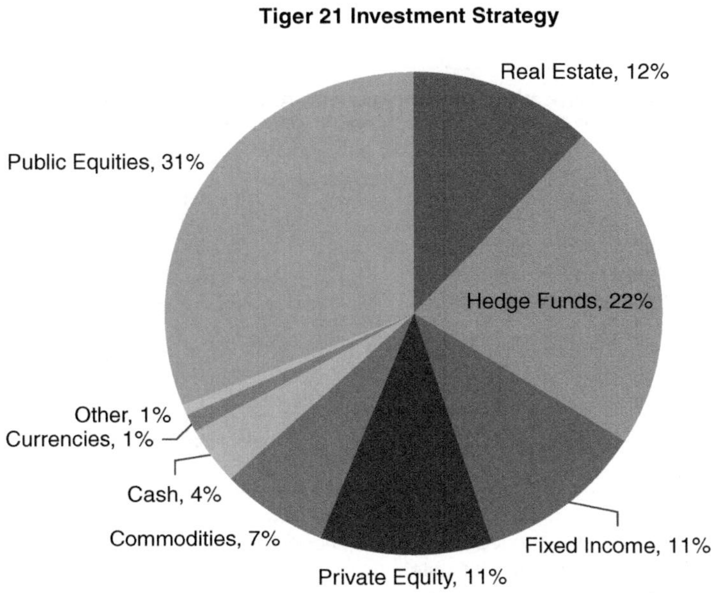

Figure 13.4 Tiger 21 Investment Strategy.
Source: Members Favorites Survey, Tiger 21, www.tiger21.com

basis. For example, the state of New Jersey changed its asset allocation model to include more alternative investments. "New Jersey Division of Investment, which manages investments for the $72.4 billion state public pension fund, has increased its target for alternative investments to 29.7% of total assets, from 26% effective July 1."[9] Likewise, the Indiana Public Retirement System, Indianapolis devised a new mix that included a fair amount devoted to alternative investments. South Carolina has approximately half of its $26 billion invested in alternative investments. "Like most public pension funds, South Carolina faces pressure to hit annual-return targets in order to satisfy pension obligations to thousands of teachers, clerks and other state employees without having to increase contributions from the state. South Carolina's fund has a $13 billion deficit. Consultants and Wall Street advisers to pension funds say hedge funds, private equity and other nontraditional investments offer the best hope to make the target."[10]

Once an investor or advisor has a suitable asset allocation with alternative investments, they can fill in the pieces by selecting managers or securities that help with this allocation. In other words, the selection process

Asset Allocation: Diversifying with Alternative Investments

Sample $5 Million Investment Portfolio with Alternative Investments

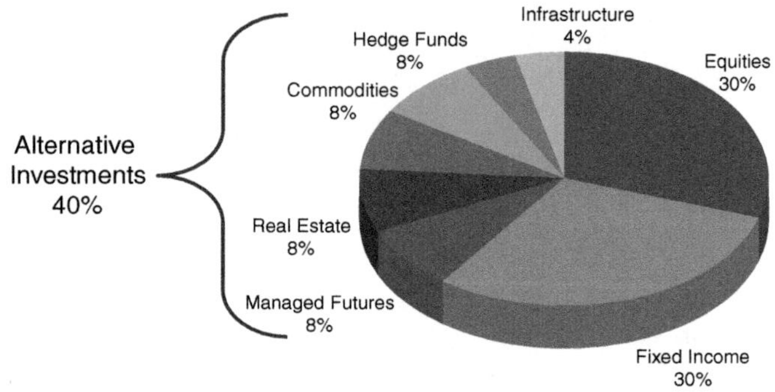

Equities	***$1,500,000***	***30%***
Fidelity Adviser Strategic Dividend & Income Fund	$300,000	6%
Fidelity Advisers New Insights	$300,000	6%
BlackRock Global Allocation	$300,000	6%
Janus Triton Fund	$300,000	6%
Schafer Cullen Capital Management	$300,000	6%
Fixed Income	***$1,500,000***	***30%***
Pimco Total Return	$300,000	6%
Templeton Global Bond	$300,000	6%
Loomis Sayles Bond Fund	$300,000	6%
JP Morgan Strategic Income	$300,000	6%
Guggenheim Enhanced Short Duration Bond ETF	$300,000	6%
Alternative Investments	***$2,000,000***	***40%***
Managed Futures		
Altegrls Winton Futures Fund	$200,000	4%
AQR Managed Futures	$200,000	4%
Real Estate		
Vanguard Global ex-U.S. Real Estate Index	$200,000	4%
ING Real Estate	$200,000	4%
Commodities		
WisdomTree Commodity Currency Fund	$200,000	4%
BlackRock Commodity	$200,000	4%
Hedge Funds		
IQ Alpha Hedge Strategy	$200,000	4%
Putnam Absolute Return 700 Fund	$200,000	4%
Private Equity		
Red Rocks Listed Private Equity	$200,000	4%
Infrastructure		
Cohen and Steers Infrastructure Fund	$200,000	4%

Figure 13.5 Diversifying with Alternative Investments.

Source: Author.

begins. Figure 13.5 shows an example of an asset allocation using regular mutual funds or ETFs.

Implementation: Security selection is another area that I find crucial with alternatives. With Brinson, security selection primarily meant picking out stocks. "In security selection the portfolio manager (or stock selector) will seek to add value by selecting individual securities within the asset category."[11] Flash forward many decades and one could view security selection with alternative investments. Timing on how and when the securities are selected is the final step. Putting together a coherent asset allocation model requires skill, experience, and patience. One needs to understand not just returns but the risk entailed and how certain combinations will work together. Sometimes (depending on the assets involved) it is necessary or prudent to write an IPS regardless of whether you are an institution or individual. Net worth also plays a role with alternative investments. For clients with assets of $25 million or more, a leading global bank's suggested allocation for wealthy individuals is shown in Figure 13.6.

Each investor will have different goals based on age, risk tolerance, income, retirement needs, time horizon, children, marital status, expenses, tax bracket, and other factors. If one does not have a written investment

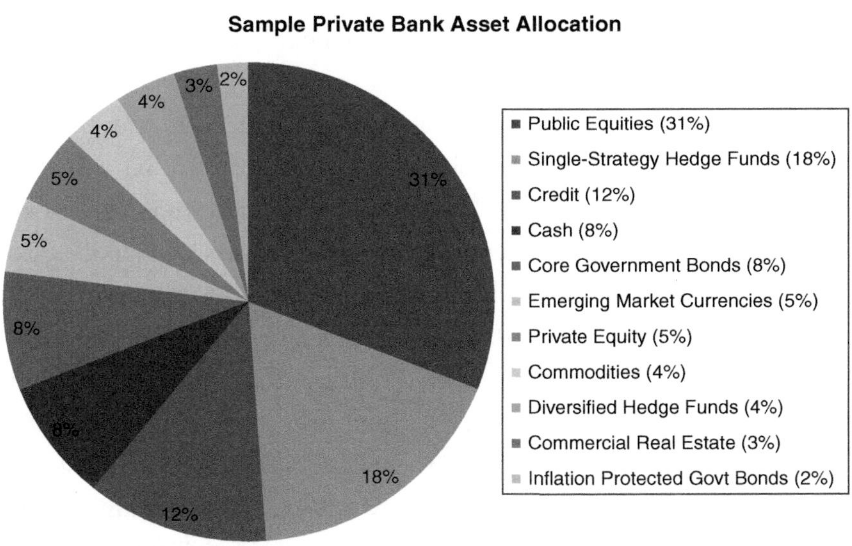

Figure 13.6 Sample Private Bank Asset Allocation.

Note: Model serves as a discussion opener. Client's goals vary.

Source: Author.

policy, a board, or a decent investment advisor, it is crucial to be aware of any behavioral science. Investing is very much psychological and it can be easy for an investor to be swept into a sea of negativity or excessive optimism or irrational exuberance. Investing is about making money. Nothing else matters. If one lets themselves be influenced by others or carried away by their own emotions, results will invariably be lackluster.

Periodic review: Haphazardly adding alternative investments to a portfolio is not prudent and can lead to loss of principal. An astute investor or advisor will study the market, understand the alternative investments they are considering adding along with any advantages or disadvantages, and see how the additions might look whether they are short or long in duration. Asset allocations with alternative investments appear to outperform those without alternative investments. Over the past 20 years, a conservative portfolio (using the old way of investing with stocks, bonds, and cash), with 60 percent devoted to bonds, 30 percent to equities, and 10 percent to cash, resulted in an average return of 7.06 percent with a standard deviation of 6.60 percent. A moderate or middle of the road approach with 50 percent stocks and 50 percent bonds and cash, resulted in an average return of 7.77 percent, with a standard deviation of 9.86 percent. If one has aggressively invested with 80 percent stocks, 20 percent bonds, and 0 percent cash, the average return was 9.12 percent with a standard deviation of 15.26 percent (Figure 13.7).

If an investor decided to add alternative investments over the past 20 years from 1993 to 2012, the risk and return changed. When I started my finance career in the early 1990s, I recall sitting on a beach with some friends. I visualized numbers and sequences with each wave but was unfamiliar with Fibonacci at the time. My premise was that perhaps one could apply mathematics with the natural world to finance. The early 1990s was not too terribly kind to equities. Because of my exposure to alternative investments (before almost anyone knew what alternative investments were at the time), I noticed that adding alternative investments helped me lower risk and increase rates of returns for my clients, which were both institutional and high net worth clients. No data existed to prove my Wave Theory. Over the years, data became more accurate and accessible but was far from perfect. I collected a lot of data on various alternative investments, which proved Wave

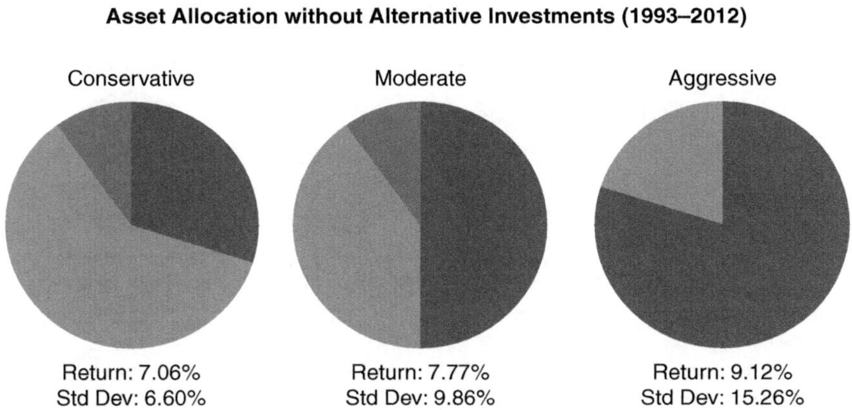

	Conservative	Moderate	Aggressive
S & P Composite	30%	50%	80%
Bar Cap Agg Bnd	60%	40%	20%
1 Year T-Bill	10%	10%	0%

Figure 13.7 Asset Allocation without Alternative Investments.
Source: Author.

Theory worked. While one can argue over active versus passive investing, the 20-year history of alternative investments is interesting for anyone building an investment portfolio or considering adding alternative investments.

Hypothetically, if one constructed a diversified portfolio using alternative investments, they could possibly have lowered risk and increased returns over that period of time. While it might not have been considered "conservative" 20 years ago, a conservative alternative investment portfolio would have a lesser weighting than stocks and bonds. Only recently have investors started adding alternative investments. The top Barron's advisors did not have much in alternative investments five years ago but had around 30 percent devoted to alternative investments in 2012. Twenty years ago (1993–2012), an investor might have invested 40 percent into stocks, 40 percent into bonds, and 20 percent into alternative investments, which would have resulted in an average return of 8.94 percent, with a standard deviation of 10.05 percent. A conservative allocation with alternative investments using 20 percent alternative investments outperformed an aggressive allocation of 80 percent stocks and 20 percent bonds with far less risk! If one elected a middle of the road approach, with 40 percent

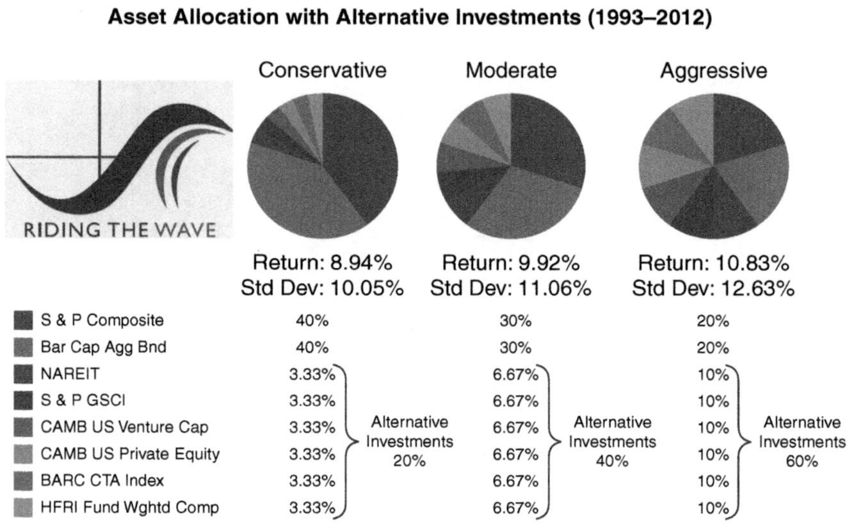

Figure 13.8 Asset Allocation with Alternative Investments (1993–2012).
Source: Author.

alternative investments, 30 percent stocks, and 30 percent bonds, standard deviation would have nominally increased but returns would have averaged 9.92 percent with a standard deviation of 11.06 percent over these two decades. If an aggressive investor allocated 60 percent to alternative investments, 20 percent to equities, and 20 percent to bonds 20 years ago, the result would be a standard deviation of 12.63 percent and a return of 10.83 percent. The aggressive portfolio with 60 percent alternative investments readily beat the aggressive portfolio using the old method of investing in just stocks, bonds, and cash. The aggressive portfolio with alternative investments produced an average annual return of 10.83 percent versus a return of just 8.94 percent for a portfolio with 80 percents stocks and bonds. Standard deviation for the aggressive portfolio with alternative investments was 12.63 percent versus 15.26 percent for the aggressive portfolio with no alternative investments (Figure 13.8).

It is now feasible to place certain alternative investments on the efficient frontier using historical returns. That is, one can create a strategic asset allocation model for the efficient frontier if the goal is more long-term investing (Figure 13.9).

Using alternative investments, whether strategic or tactical, can possibly lower risk and increase returns. Investing in alternative investments can

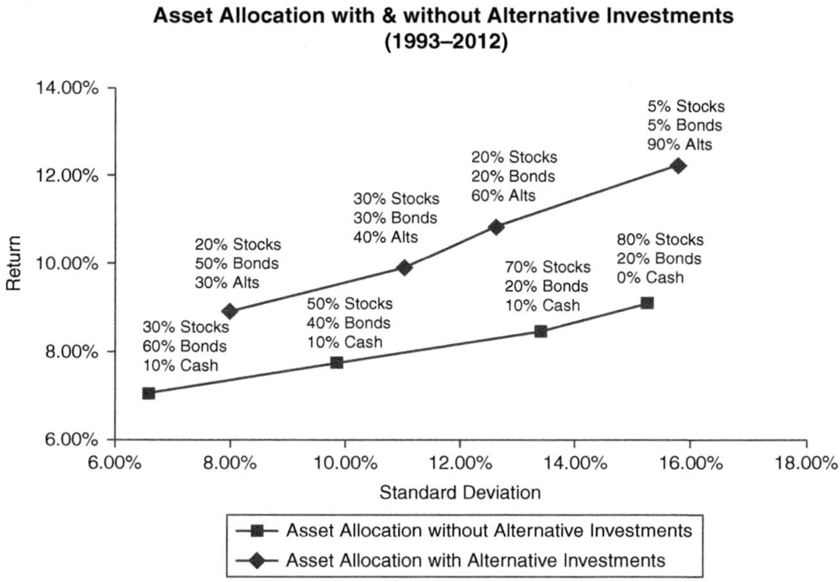

Figure 13.9 Asset Allocation with and without Alternative Investments (1993–2012).
Source: Author.

be rewarding but it takes time and experience to master. Nothing is easy in life but rewards do not come to those that are idle or complacent. One can choose to sit on the beach and watch others ride the wave or one can be proactive. The market for alternative investments is growing and will play an even more important role than it has in the past.

NOTES

INTRODUCTION: THAT WAS THEN, THIS IS NOW

1. Zvi Bodie, Alex Kane, and Alan Marcus, *Investments*, 9th ed., New York, NY: McGraw-Hill, 2011, 8.
2. Corrie Driebusch, "Firms Boost Alternative Investments on Client Demand," *Dow Jones Newswires*, November 21, 2012.
3. Anthony Cowell Partner and Andrew Stepaniuk, "Transformation: The Future of Alternative Investments," *KPMG s Investment Management Practice*, June 2010, 2.
4. Kevin Olsen, "NJ Commits $1.745 Billion to Alts," *Pensions and Investments*, August 6, 2012, 22.
5. Diana Britton, "Alternatives Going Mainstream," *Wealth Management*, June 2012, 22.
6. Juliet Chung, "Fidelity Offers Hedge-Fund Access Via Arden Tie," *Wall Street Journal*, December 7, 2012.
7. Lewis Braham, "Serving Up Disappointment," *Bloomberg Markets*, July 2012, 102.
8. Wayne Lin, "Risk {Re}considered," Legg Mason Perspectives, 2010.
9. Douglas Cumming, Lars Helge Haβ, and Denis Schweizer, "Strategic Asset Allocation and the Role of Alternative Investments," *European Financial Management*, March 19, 2012.
10. Michel Ochi, *Ocean Waves: The Stochastic Approach*, New York, NY: Cambridge University Press, July 2005, 252.
11. David Benoit, "S&P Cuts Ratings for Global Banks," *Wall Street Journal*, November 30, 2011, C3.
12. Eugene Brigham, *Fundamentals of Financial Management,* Chicago, IL: Dryden Press, 1989, 104.
13. Lloyd Hanford, "Is the Real Estate Market Recovering?" February 6, 2011, http://www.lloydhanford.com/?p=75 (accessed May 2011).
14. Stephen Todd Walker, *Wave Theory for Alternative Investments,* New York, NY: McGraw-Hill, 2011, 3.
15. Frank Margan and Ben Finney, *A Pictorial History of Surfing*, Sydney: Paul Hamlyn Press, 1961, 39–250.
16. Shourun Guo, et al., "Do Buyouts (Still) Create Value?" *The Journal of Finance*, August 2009, 1.
17. Robert S. Harris, Tim Jenkinson, andSteven N. Kaplan, "Private Equity Performance: What Do We Know?" Fama-Miller Working Paper; *Chicago Booth Research Paper No. 11–44; Darden Business School Working Paper No. 1932316.* April 2, 2013. http://dx.doi.org/10.2139/ssrn.1932316
18. Rudiger Stucke, "Updating History," *University of Oxford*, December 1, 2011, 1–22.

19. David Robinson and Berk Sensoy, "Cyclicality, Performance Measurement, and Cash Flow Liquidity in Private Equity," *National Bureau of Economic Research*, September 20, 2011, 1.
20. Lloyd Hanford, "The Real Estate Bubble," November 27, 2009, http://www.lloydhanford.com/?p=40 (accessed May 2011).
21. Lawrence Yun, "Government Support and the Good Boom," *Realtor Magazine*, March–April 2012.
22. Nick Timiraos, "Housing Market Posts Gains," *Wall Street Journal*, November 20, 2012, B1.
23. Lisa Gibbs, "Housing Play the Rebound," CNN Money, January–February 2013.
24. Adrian Pagan and Kirill Sossounov, "A Simple Framework for Analyzing Bull and Bear Markets," *Journal of Applied Economics*, October 8, 2002, 1.
25. Nicholas Barberis, et al., "A Model of Investor Sentiment," *Journal of Financial Economics*, February 1998, 314.
26. Andrew Lo and A. MacKinlay, "When Are Contrarian Profits Due to Stock Market Overreaction?" *Review of Financial Studies*, May 1989, 1.
27. Brian Hurst, Yao Hua Ooi, and Lasse H. Pedersen, "Understanding Managed Futures," *AQR Capital Management*, Winter 2010, 3.
28. The Editors, "Biggest Distressed Debt Investor Marks Europe With 19% Returns," *Bloomberg Markets*, August 2011, 55.
29. Richard Teitelbaum, "Most Influential 50 Money Managers: Ray Dalio," *Bloomberg Markets*, October 2011, 44.
30. Pascal Tremblay, "Welcome to Canada!" *Private Capital Prive*, Summer 2012.
31. Inyoung Hwang, "Strategists' Recommended Allocations for Stocks, Bonds, Cash," *Bloomberg*, April 29, 2013, http://www.bloomberg.com/news/2013–04–29/strategists-recommended-allocations-for-stocks-bonds-cash.html (accessed October 2013).
32. Stephen L. Nesbitt, "Trends in State Pension Asset Allocation and Performance," *Cliffwater*, June 26, 2012, 6.
33. Jeremy Siegel, "Valuing Growth Stocks: Revisiting the Nifty Fifty," *AAII Journal*, October 1998, 20.
34. Gaia Serraino and Stan Uryasev, "Protecting Equity Investments: Options, Inverse ETFs, Hedge Funds, and AORDA Portfolios," *Aorda*, October 2011, 2.
35. Hersh Shefrin and Meir Statman, "The Disposition to Sell Winners Too Early and Ride Losers Too Long: Theory and Evidence," *The Journal of Finance*, Vol. 40, No. 3, Papers and Proceedings of the Forty-Third Annual Meeting American Finance Association, Dallas, Texas, July 1985, 778.
36. Gaia Serraino and Stan Uryasev, "Protecting Equity Investments: Options, Inverse ETFs, Hedge Funds, and AORDA Portfolios," October 2011, 2.
37. "*Trends in State Pension Asset Allocation and Performance*," Cliffwater, June 26, 2012, 1.
38. Hersh Shefrin and Meir Statman, "Behavioral Portfolio Theory," November 1997, 16.
39. Werner De Bondt and Richard Thaler, "Does the Stock Market Overreact?" *The Journal of Finance*, Vol. 40, No.3, Papers and Proceedings of the Forty-Third Annual Meeting American Finance Association, Dallas, Texas, December 28–30, 1984, 794.
40. J. B. De Long, et al., "Positive Feedback Investment Strategies and Destabilizing Rational Speculation," *The Journal of Finance*, June 1990, 381.
41. Roy Batchelor and Richard Ramyar, "Magic Numbers in the Dow," *Cass Business School*, September 2006, 10.

42. Gjergji Cici, "WRDS Guide to IPO Databases and Research," *Wharton Research Data Services*, May 30, 2005, http://wrds-web.wharton.upenn.edu/wrds/research/applications/guides/ipo/index.cfm (accessed February 2014).
43. Liam Pleven, "All Commodities Aren't Equal," *Wall Street Journal*, June 3, 2011, C6.
44. John Campbell and Luis Viceira, "Strategic Asset Allocation," *Harvard University*, April 2001, 7.

1 DOES THE UNIVERSE MOVE IN WAVES?

1. Robert Dinwiddie, *Oceans: The World's Last Wilderness Revealed*, DK Adult, New York, NY, 2008.
2. The Editors, "Protests: Not Quite Together," *The Economist*, October 22, 2011, 73.
3. "RIA Merger & Acquisitions Activity For First Quarter of 2013 Records Highest Number of Deals Since Q1 2012," Charles Schwab, May 2, 2013.
4. E.S. Browning and David Benoit, "Big-Bank Pioneer Now Seeks Breakup," *Wall Street Journal*, July 26, 2012, A1.
5. Wikipedia, "Wave," http://en.wikipedia.org/wiki/Wave (accessed July 2011).
6. Paul Steinhardt and Neil Turok, *Endless Universe: Beyond the Big Bang*, New York, NY: Doubleday, May 2007, xiv.
7. Lauris Baum, Dr. Paul Frampton, and Louis J. Rubin Jr., "Endless Universe Made Possible by New Model," *University of North Carolina at Chapel Hill*, January 2007, http://www.unc.edu/news/archives/jan07/newmodel012907.html (accessed July 2011).
8. Carl Sagan, *Broca's Brain: Reflections on the Romance of Science*, 1st ed., New York and Toronto: Ballantine Books, 1986.
9. "The CGWA Mission," *Center for Gravitational Wave Astronomy*, 2011, http://phys.utb.edu/department/CGWApage/index.shtml (accessed July 2011).
10. Robert Dinwiddie, *Oceans: The World's Last Wilderness Revealed*, New York, NY: DK Adult, 2008.
11. Jared Kaltwasser, "Tech Firm Launches its Smart-Buoy Trial," *NJ Business Journal*, August 29, 2011, 3.
12. Michel Ochi, *Ocean Waves: The Stochastic Approach*, New York: Cambridge University Press, July 2005, 112.
13. Ibid., 166.
14. Ibid., 252.
15. Stephen Miller, "Surf Swami Knew When to Hang Ten," *Wall Street Journal*, December 30, 2011, A6.
16. Ibid.
17. Katy Burne and Tom Lauricella, "Secret Panel Holds Fate of Greek Credit-Default Swaps," *Wall Street Journal*, February 29, 2012.
18. "Are CDOs Sneaking Added Risk into Your Client's Portfolio?" *Financial Advisor Magazine*, July 2007, 26.
19. Richard Tomlinson and David Evans, "CDO Boom Masks Subprime Losses, Abetted by S&P, Moody's, Fitch," *Bloomberg*, May 31, 2007, http://www.bloomberg.com/news/print/2007–05–31/cdo-boom-masks-subprime-losses-abetted-by-s-p-moody-s-fitch.html (accessed January 2014).
20. The Editors, "Citigroup's Deal with SEC Got the Treatment It Deserved: View," *Bloomberg*, November 29, 2011, http://www.bloomberg.com/news/2011–11–29/citigroup-s-deal-with-sec-got-the-treatment-it-deserved-view.html (accessed May 2011).

21. Jean Eaglesham and Jeanette Neuman, "US Beats Clock," *Wall Street Journal*, July 19, 2012, C3.
22. "Are CDOs Sneaking Added Risk into Your Client's Portfolio?" *Financial Advisor Magazine*, July 2007, 26.
23. Seth Lubove and Daniel Taub, "The Subprime Sinkhole," *Bloomberg Markets*, July 2007, 36.
24. "Are CDOs Sneaking Added Risk into Your Client's Portfolio?" *Financial Advisor Magazine*, July 2007, 26.
25. David Henry, "A Chain Reaction in Shaky Debt?" *BusinessWeek*, November 25, 2007, 32.
26. Tim Koller, Marc Goedhart, and David Wessels, *Valuation: Measuring and Managing the Value of Companies*, Hoboken, New Jersey: John Wiley and Sons, Inc., 2010, 325.
27. David Henry and Mathew Goldstein, "This Investment Could Turn Ugly," *BusinessWeek*, June 18, 2007, 25.
28. The Editors, "The Bloomberg 20," *Bloomberg Markets*, April 2008, 26.
29. Amir Efrati, "US Probes Morgan Stanley," *Wall Street Journal*, May 11, 2010, A1.
30. D. Wade Hands, "Back to the Ordinalist Revolution," *Metroeconomica*, 2011, 386.
31. Mitch Anthony, "I Saw the Movie," *Financial Advisor Magazine*, January 2012, 42.
32. Gerhard Bry and Charlotte Boschan, *Cyclical Analysis of Time Series*, National Bureau of Economic Research, 1971, 12.
33. Ben Levisohn, "Is It Value's Turn to Shine?" *Wall Street Journal*, November 25, 2012, B9.
34. Robert J. Shapiro, "The Role of the Private Equity Sector Promoting Economic Recovery," *Private Equity Growth Capital Council*, March 2009, 2.
35. Ibid.
36. "The Big Long", *The Economist*, December 1, 2012, 77.
37. A.G. Barnett, Jolieke C. van der Pols, and Annette J. Dobson, "Regression to the Mean: What It Is and How to Deal with It," University of Queensland, August 2004, 1.
38. Carolyn Cui and Patrick McGee, "Key Bond Index Gets Bitten," *Wall Street Journal*, April 13, 2013, C1.
39. "Mean Reversion (finance)." *Wikipedia*. Wikimedia Foundation. December 10, 2013. Web October 24, 2013.
40. Associated Press, "Morgan Stanley Posts $1.26 Billion Loss," *MSNBC*, July 22, 2009, http://www.msnbc.msn.com/id/32081818/ns/business-us_business/t/morgan-stanley-posts-billion-loss/#.UAetC7Q1-So (accessed September 2011).
41. Joe Gose, "Private Equity Jumps Big Into Commercial Real Estate Loans", *Investor's Business Daily*, November 30, 2012, A10.
42. Alan Lavine, "Improving Fundamentals", *Financial Advisor Magazine*, December 2012, 109.
43. Zvi Bodie, Alex Kane, and Alan Marcus, *Investments*, 9th ed., New York, NY: McGraw-Hill, 1989, 184.

2 NOT ALL FINANCIAL ADVISORS ARE CREATED EQUAL

1. Anne Fallon, "Advisors Turning Their Attention to Alternatives," *Reuters*, August 30, 2011, http://www.reuters.com/article/2011/08/30/idUS167331+30-Aug-2011+BW20110830 (accessed October 2011).
2. Zvi Bodie, Alex Kane, and Alan Marcus, *Investments*, 9th ed., New York, NY: McGraw-Hill, 2011, 168.

3. "Your Assets: Allocate and Diversify," *Wells Fargo*, 2012, https://www.wellsfargo.com/investing/basics/allocate_diversify (accessed January 2012).
4. "Asset Allocation," *PNC Bank*, 2012, https://www.pnc.com/webapp/unsec/Asset+Management/ Investment+Strategy/Asset+Allocation (accessed January 2012).
5. Sarah Riopelle, "Insights: RBC Select Portfolios," *Royal Bank of Canada*, June 30, 2011, 1.
6. "Asset Allocation," *Merrill Lynch*, 2012, http://www.ml.com/CarverBank/prod_asset.html (accessed January 2012).
7. "Asset Allocation," *Goldman Sachs*, 2012, http://www.goldmansachs.com/gsam/individuals/ education/asset-allocation/index.print.html (accessed January 2012).
8. Shane Romig, "Argentina to Charge Firms Involved in Falklands Drilling," *Wall Street Journal*, March 15, 2012, http://online.wsj.com/article/ SB10001424052702304459804577283853 395410044.html (accessed March 2012).
9. Jeff Cox, "Bank Layoffs Far from Over: 150,000 Likely in 2012," *CNBC*, December 16, 2011, http://www.cnbc.com/id/45696542/Bank_Layoffs_Far_From_Over_150_000_Likely_in_2012_Bove (accessed March 2012).
10. Max Abelson and Ambereen Choudhury, "After Massive Job Cuts, Wall Street's a Different Place," *BusinessWeek*, December 11, 2011, 55.
11. Thomas Coyle, "New Firm Forms for Breakaway Brokers," *Dow Jones Newswires*, April 17, 2012, http://financialadviserblog.dowjones.com/blog/stay-ahead-of-your-clients/new-firm-forms-for-breakaway-brokers (accessed April 2012).
12. Dan Fitzpatrick, "Big Banks Prepare Another Round of Cuts," *Wall Street Journal*, July 19, 2012, C1.
13. Lionel Barber, "The Fall of the Universal Bank," *The World in 2013*, 142.
14. William Wright, "Investment Banks Face an Arid Landscape," *Financial News Column*, August 14, 2012, http://www.efinancialnews.com/story/2012–08–14/investment-banks-face-an-arid-landscape (accessed August 2012).
15. Bernie Clark, "The Changing RIA," *Financial Advisor Magazine*, April 2012, 56.
16. Brian Hamburger, "Success Breeds Envy," *Financial Advisor Magazine*, April 2012, 46.
17. J. Alex Tarquinio, "Tweet, Text, Trade," *SmartMoney Magazine*, June 2012, 56.
18. "The New Diversification: Open Your Eyes to Alternative, A Conversation with Professor Christopher C. Geczy, Ph.D.", BlackRock, April 30, 2003.
19. Ed Royce, "Sarbanes-Oxley Has Devastated US IPO Market," *Investor's Business Daily*, July 30, 2012, A17.
20. Peter Wallison, "Dodd-Frank's Too-Big-to-Fail Dystopia," *Wall Street Journal*, May 24, 2012, A15.
21. Helen Kearney, "Morgan Stanley Loses 6 Advisers with $1bln of Assets," *Thomson Reuters*, May 2, 2011, http://www.reuters.com/article/2011/05/02/ubswealth-idUSN0221737720110502 (accessed July 2013).
22. Corrie Driebusch, "DJ Broker's World: Brokers Pressured to Keep Promoting High-Margin Products," *Wall Street Journal*, February 25, 2013.
23. Jack Willoughby, "How to Break up the Banks," *Barron's*, February 6, 2012, 45.
24. Colin Barr, "Costly Position Was Wager on Corporate Debt Gone Wrong," *Wall Street Journal*, May 11, 2012, A5.
25. The Editors, "Over-regulated America," *The Economist*, February 18, 2012, 9.
26. The Editors, "The Dodd-Frank Act: Too Big Not To Fail," *The Economist*, February 18, 2012, 22.
27. Michael Porter and Jan Rivkin, "What Washington Must Do Now," *The World in 2013*, 50.
28. Andrew Stepaniuk and Anthony Cowell, "Transformation: The Future of Alternative Investments," *KPMG*, June 2010, 5.

3 ACCESS TO ALTERNATIVE INVESTMENTS AND COMPETITIVE ADVANTAGES

1. Diana Britton, "Withering Wirehouses? Not Quite," *Registered Rep*, December 2012, 30.
2. Harvey Rosenblum, "Choosing the Road to Prosperity: Why We Must End Too Big to Fail—Now," 2011 Annual Report, *Federal Reserve Bank of Dallas*, May 1, 2012, 21.
3. Ning Du and John E. McEnroe, "Are Multiple Analyst Earnings Forecasts Better Than the Single Forecast?" *Journal of Behavioral Finance,* January 2011, 12 (1), 1.
4. Corrie Driebusch, "Advisers Fanning Out from Big Firm World," *Dow Jones Newswire,* July 20, 2012.
5. Anne Stausboll, "A Message from CalPERS CEO," CalPERS, April 4, 2011, http://www.calpersresponds.com/issues.php/a-message-from-calpers-ceo (accessed March 2012).
6. Zvi Bodie, Alex Kane, and Alan Marcus, *Investments*, 9th ed., New York, NY: McGraw-Hill, 2011, 481.
7. Philip S. Khinda, Donald E. Wellington, and Ellen S. Zimiles, "CalPERS Special Review: Selected Recommendation," *CalPERS*, December 2010, 3.
8. Ibid., 7.
9. Robin Sidel, Victoria McGrane, and Dan Fitzpatrick, "Bank Breakups: Not So Fast," *Wall Street Journal*, July 29, 2012, C1.
10. Dakin Campbell, "Thomas Weisel Banks On His Reputation To Bring Deals To Stifel," *Bloomberg Markets*, September 21, 2010, 36.
11. Caitlin Nish, "DJ Wachovia Loses in Stifel Adviser-Raiding Case," *Dow Jones Newswires*, April 3, 2012, http://www.nasdaq.com/article/wachovia-loses-in-stifel-adviser-raiding-case-20120403–01094 (accessed May 2012).
12. Dan Case, interview with author.
13. Rich Karlgaard, "Steve Case: An Entrepreneur's Life," *Forbes*, August 8, 2011, 26.
14. The Editors, "Dan Case: A Class Act in the Valley," *BusinessWeek*, July 15, 2002, 46.
15. The Editors, "The State of the IPO Market in the Wake of Facebook's IPO Fiasco," *PrivCo*, May 25, 2012, http://www.privco.com/facebooks-effect-on-the-ipo-and-venture-capital-markets (accessed May 2012).
16. Linda Sandler and Laura Marcinek, "Mass. Regulator Subpoenaed Citi, Goldman Over Facebook," Bloomberg, October 27, 2012, http://www.bloomberg.com/news/2012–10–26/mass-regulator-subpoenaed-citi-goldman-over-facebook.html (accessed October 2012).
17. Diana Britton, "Withering Wirehouses? Not Quite," *Wealth Management*, December 2012, 27.
18. Eric Rasmussen, "Advisors in a Darwinian World," *Financial Advisor Magazine*, January 2012, 55.
19. The Editors, "Independent Advisors on the Rise," *Financial Advisor Magazine*, October 2011, 24.
20. Francesco Guerrera, "Time to Embrace Market Risk, or to Run from It?" *Wall Street Journal*, June 12, 2012, C1.
21. E.S. Browning and David Benoit, "Big-Bank Pioneer Now Seeks Breakup," *Wall Street Journal*, July 26, 2012, A1.
22. Jason Ma, "U.S. Banks Too Big?" *Investor's Business Daily*, July 12, 2012, A1.
23. Roy Diliberto, "Demonstrating That You Care," *Financial Advisor Magazine*, December 2012, 42.
24. Damian Paletta, Dana Cimilluca, and Jon Hilseurath, "Libor Talks Go Back to Early '08," *Wall Street Journal*, July 15, 2012, B2.

25. Cass Sunstein, "Two Policies to Keep from the Fiscal Cliff," *Bloomberg BusinessWeek*, December 24, 2012, 16.
26. Brett Philbin, "Merrill Lynch Boosts Recruiting Deal for Top Brokers," *Wall Street Journal*, February 21, 2012, http://blogs.wsj.com/deals/2012/02/21/merrill-lynch-boosts-recruiting-deal-for-top-brokers/ (accessed March 2012).
27. Aaron Lucchetti, "Morgan Stanley, Citigroup to Give Brokers Big Retention Fees," *Wall Street Journal*, February 14, 2009, B1.
28. Suzanne Kapner, "Rocky Start for Marriage of Brokers," *Wall Street Journal*, April 3, 2012, C1.
29. Stratos Wealth Partners, "Financial Advisory Team Leaves Morgan Stanley Smith Barney to Join National Network," *Dow Jones Newswires*, June 12, 2012, http://www.marketwatch.com/story/ financial-advisory-team-leaves-morgan-stanley-smith-barney-to-join-national-network-stratos-wealth-partners-2012–06–12 (accessed June 2012).
30. Mindy Diamond, "The Regional Alternative," *Wealth Management*, November 2011, 98.

4 THE CHANGING FINANCIAL LANDSCAPE

1. "Aaron Dorr joins Sandler O'Neill's Investment Banking Group," Sandler O'Neill, March 16,2011, http://www.sandleroneill.com/a53acab4–99de-4f6e-96bf-dd420925812c/resource-center-press-releases-2011-detail.htm (accessed January 2012).
2. The Editors, "The Trophy Has Begun to Lose Its Shine," *Wall Street Journal*, September 15, 2004, C11.
3. Tom Frost, "The Big Danger with Big Banks," *Wall Street Journal*, May 16, 2012, A15.
4. The Editors, "Wirehouses Lose Market Share but Remain Big Dogs," *Dow Jones Newswires*, January 25, 2012, http://solutions.dowjones.com/tnt/newsletters/TNT_012512.pdf (accessed February 2012).
5. Harvey Rosenblum, "Choosing the Road to Prosperity: Why We Must End Too Big to Fail—Now," 2011 Annual Report, *Federal Reserve Bank of Dallas*, May 1, 2012, 15.
6. Sallie Krawcheck and Cyrus Sanati, "Your Big Question: Can Investors Trust Wall Street Again?" *CNN Money*, July 2013, 76.
7. Bank For International Settlements, Statistical release, BIS over-the-counter derivatives statistics: Data at end-June 2012.: Monetary and Economic Department, November 2012, 1.
8. Gregory Zuckerman and Liz Rappaport, "Rivals Go to Lunch on JP Morgan's Losses," *Wall Street Journal*, May 22, 2012, C1.
9. Carrick Mollenkamp and Serena Ng, "A Fear Gauge Comes Up Short," *Wall Street Journal*, September 28, 2011, C1.
10. Ibid.
11. Francesco Guerrera, "J.P. Morgan's Big Loss: Lessons from a Fiasco," *Wall Street Journal*, May 15, 2012, C1.
12. David Reilly, "Peering over J.P. Morgan's Hedges," *Wall Street Journal*, May 18, 2012, C10.
13. Tom Frost, "The Big Danger with Big Banks," *Wall Street Journal*, May 16, 2012, A15.
14. Francesco Guerrera, "J.P. Morgan's Big Loss: Lessons from a Fiasco," *Wall Street Journal*, May 15, 2012, C1.

15. "Global Alternatives Survey 2013: Including the Top Alternative Asset Manager Rankings," *Towers Watson*, July 2013, 12.
16. Harvey Rosenblum, "Choosing the Road to Prosperity: Why We Must End Too Big to Fail—Now," 2011 Annual Report, *Federal Reserve Bank of Dallas*, May 1, 2012, 3.
17. David Benoit, "Comp Ratios at I-Banks," *Wall Street Journal*, March 27, 2012, http://blogs.wsj.com/deals/2012/03/27/comp-ratios-at-i-banks-how-goldman-stacks-up-to-boutiques/ (accessed April 2012).
18. Anupreeta Das and Gina Chon, "Bankers Pinched As Street Gets Lean," *Wall Street Journal*, April 24, 2012, C1.
19. Michael Fischer, "Alternatives for the Masses," *Financial Advisor Magazine*, March 2011, http://www.fa-mag.com/component/content/article/38-features/7086-alternatives-for-the-masses.html?tmpl=component&print=1&page= (accessed March 2011).
20. Karen Hube, "More Stocks, Fewer Bonds," *Barron's*, March 4, 2013, 34.
21. Susanne Craig, "The Stock-Research Pact: One Small Firm Battles Internal, External Discord," *Wall Street Journal*, April 28, 2003, C1.
22. Mike Mayo, "Shouting Down Wall Street's Wall," *Wall Street Journal*, November 5, 2011, C6.
23. Francesco Guerrera, "Facebook Offering Highlights Unfair Game," *Wall Street Journal*, May 28, 2012, C1.
24. Ibid.
25. Linda Sandler and Laura Marcinek, "Mass. Regulator Subpoenaed Citi, Goldman Over Facebook," *Bloomberg*, October 27, 2012, http://www.bloomberg.com/news/2012–10–26/mass-regulator-subpoenaed-citi-goldman-over-facebook.html (accessed October 2012).
26. Suzanne Kapner and Randall Smith, "Citigroup Unit Is Fined for Disclosure Lapses," *Wall Street Journal*, January 19, 2012, C1.
27. Ben Levisohn, "How to Play Political Risk," *Wall Street Journal*, November 5, 2011, B8.
28. Art Steinmetz and Jerry Webman, "2012 Outlook: Our Long-term Investment Themes," *Oppenheimer Funds*, Q1 2012, 2.
29. Kenneth Silber, "Political Stand-Offs", *Research Magazine*, February 2013, 70–71.
30. Audrei Shleifer, Nicholas Barberis, and Robert Vishny, "A Model of Investor Sentiment," *Journal of Financial Economics*, March 1998, 49, 307.
31. Ibid.

5 I HATE TO SAY IT, BUT I TOLD YOU SO

1. "2009 Alternative Investment Survey of Institutions and Financial Advisors," *Morningstar and Barron's*, November 9, 2009, 30.
2. Reshma Kapadia and Matthew Heimer, "Investing Reinvented: A SmartMoney Master Plan," *Wall Street Journal*, June 15, 2011 http://online.wsj.com/article/SB70001424052748703916004576271511557699694.html (accessed August 1, 2013)
3. Leslie Scism, "Florida Bolsters Hurricane Coffers," *Wall Street Journal*, July 22, 2011, C1.
4. "Evaluating Investment Risk," Standard & Poor's, 2011, https://fc.standardandpoors.com/sites/client/wfs2/wfs/article.vm?topic=6066&siteContent=8358 (accessed January 2014).
5. Stocks are represented by the total returns of the S&P 500. Bonds are represented by a composite of the total returns of long-term US government bonds,

derived from yields published by the Federal Reserve, and the Barclays Long-Term Government Bond Index. T-bills are represented by a composite of the yields of three-month Treasury bills, published by the Federal Reserve, and the Barclays three-month Treasury bills, published by the Federal Reserve, and the Barclays three-month Treasury Bills index.
6. Reshma Kapadia and Matthew Heimer, "Own More 'Alternatives,'" *Smart Money*, July 2011, 54.
7. "Patience Is a Virtue," *Altegris Advisors*, August 2011, 2.
8. Thao Hua, "Worldwide AUM Hits Post-crisis Milestone," *Pensions and Investments*, June 27, 2011, 1.
9. William Gross, "Investment Outlook—Wall Street Food Chain," *PIMCO*, June 2012, 1.
10. Meir Statman, *What Investors Really Want*, New York, NY: McGraw-Hill, 2011, 4.
11. Karen Hube, "Retirement Ready," *Worth Magazine*, April–May 2011, 32.
12. "2009 Alternative Investment Survey of Institutions and Financial Advisors," *Morningstar and Barron's*, November 9, 2009.
13. Jean Lassignardie and John W. Thiel, "World Wealth Report: 2011," *Capgemini* and *Merrill Lynch Wealth Management.*, 2011, 4.
14. "Z.1 Financial Accounts of the United States," *Board of Governors of the Federal Reserve System*, Third Quarter 2013.
15. Trillion,"
16. Ron DeLegge, "Searching for Optimal ETF Portfolios," *Research Magazine Guide to ETF Investing 2013*, April 2013, 9.
17. Tim Koller, Marc Goedhart, and David Wessels, *Valuation: Measuring and Managing the Value of Companies*, Hoboken, NJ, and Canada: John Wiley & Sons, Inc.
18. Penelope Wang, "The Great Ideas about Stocks Are Wrong," *Fortune*, January 2012, 68.
19. Thao Hua, "Worldwide AUM Hits Post-crisis Milestone," *Pensions and Investments*, June 27, 2011, 1.
20. "Managed Futures: Fear Not Volatility," *Altegris Advisors*, February 2012, 7.
21. Marshall Eckblad, "A New Alternative," *Wall Street Journal*, October 5, 2011, D1.
22. Katherine Kaminski, "In Search of Crisis Alpha: A Short Guide to Investing in Managed Futures," *CME Group*, April 5, 2009, 3.
23. Brian Hurst, Lasse H. Pedersen, and Yao Hua Ooi, "Understanding Managed Futures," *AQR Capital Management*, Winter 2010, 3.
24. Karen Damato, "A Periodic Look at Performance and Investor Behavior," *Wall Street Journal*, October 5, 2011, C19.
25. Francesco Guerrera, "Hidden Danger Lurking in Money-Market Funds," *Wall Street Journal*, October 18, 2011, B10.
26. Barry Burr, "3 Ways to Enhancing Returns," *Pensions & Investments*, October 17, 2011, 15.
27. Everett Ehrlich, "The Changing Role of Hedge Funds in the Global Economy," *ESC Company*, September 2011, 11.
28. Stuart Taylor (Ed.), "2013 Preqin Investor Network Global Alternatives Report," *Preqin*, 2013, 13.

6 THE "SMART MONEY" IS GLOBAL

1. Steven Eder, "Pensions Leap Back to Hedge Funds," *Wall Street Journal*, May 27, 2011, C1.

2. Elroy Dimson, Paul Marsh, and Mike Staunton, *Triumph of the Optimists: 101 Years of Global Investment Returns*, New Jersey: Princeton University Press, 2002, 24.
3. The Editors, "This Time It's Serious," *The Economist*, February 18, 2012, 71.
4. Elroy Dimson, Paul Marsh, and Mike Staunton, *Triumph of the Optimists: 101 Years of Global Investment Returns*, New Jersey: Princeton University Press, 2011, 23.
5. Ibid.
6. The Editors, "The Celestial Economy," *The Economist*, September 10, 2011, 86.
7. Andrea Burgess, Andrew Gilbert, Conrad Co Heine, and Ian Emery, *Pocket World in Figures 2012 Edition, The Economist*, 2012, 68.
8. Shyh-Wen Tzeng, "China Leads IPO Rankings in 2012 YTD," *Dealogic*, March 20, 2012, 1.
9. Ben Levisohn, "Why China Looks Like a Buy," *Wall Street Journal*, July 16, 2011, B7.
10. Michael Milken, "Where's Sputnik?" *Michael Milken Institute*, 2Q 2011, 3.
11. "China," *U.S. Energy Information Administration*, September 4, 2012 (revised April 22, 2013), 1–2.
12. Charles Kenny, "The Case for Second Place," *BusinessWeek*, October 23, 2011, 14.
13. "China's Economy Achieved a Stabilized and Accelerated Development in the Year of 2012," *National Bureau of Statistics of China*, January 18, 2013, http://www.stats.gov.cn/english/pressrelease/t20130118_402867147.htm
14. N. Garleanu and L.H. Pedersen, "Liquidity and Risk Management," *American Economic Association*, May 2007, 193.
15. Martin Steward, "Alternatives – with Pensions DNA," *Investment and Pensions Europe*, February 2012, http://www.ipe.com/alternatives-with-pensions-dna/43893.fullarticle (accessed April 2014).
16. Zvi Bodie, Alex Kane, and Alan Marcus, *Investments*, 9th ed., New York, NY: McGraw-Hill, 1989, 3.
17. Ibid., 104.
18. Jerry Kern, "No Alternative but to Diversity," *Morningstar Advisor*, December/January 2010, 7.
19. Richard Brealey, Stewart Myers, and Franklin Allen, *Principles of Corporate Finance*, 8th ed., New York, NY: McGraw-Hill, 2006, 161.
20. Victoria Barbary and Edward Chin, "Testing Time Sovereign Wealth Funds in the Middle East & North Africa and the Global Financial Crises," *Monitor*, May 2009, 31.
21. Wharton Leadership Center, "The Brave New World of Sovereign Wealth Funds," *Knowledge@Wharton*, 2010, 40.
22. Zvi Bodie, Alex Kane, and Alan Marcus, *Investments*, 9th ed., New York, NY: McGraw-Hill, 2011, 138.
23. SEI, "Exotic to Mainstream: Growth of Alternative Mutual Funds in the U.S. and Europe," *SEI Knowledge and Strategic Insight*, May 24, 2010, 1.
24. "Chartered Alternative Investment Analyst—Level 1," *CAIA*, http://www.schweser.com/caia/info/why_pursue.php (accessed January 10, 2013).
25. Diane Henry, "iShares Diversified Alternatives Trust to Cease Trading on May 29, 2013," *Business Wire*, May 15, 2013, http://www.businesswire.com/news/home/20130515006773/en/iShares-Diversified-Alternatives-Trust-NYSEArca-ALT-Cease (accessed August 15, 2013).
26. Matt Hougan, "ALT To Shut; 1st iShares Closure Since '02," *Index Universe*, April 25, 2013, http://www.indexuniverse.com/sections/features/16611-alt-to-shut-1st-ishares-closure-since-02.html (accessed August 15, 2013).
27. "Nuveen Long/Short Commodity Total Return Fund (CTF)," *Nuveen*, http://www.nuveen.com/CommodityInvestments/Product/Performance.aspx?fundcode=CTF (accessed August 15, 2013).

28. Beverly Goodman, "An Alternative to Hedge-Fund Alternatives," *Barron's*, May 28, 2012, 35.
29. SEI, "Exotic to Mainstream: Growth of Alternative Mutual Funds in the U.S. and Europe," *SEI Knowledge and Strategic Insight*, May 24, 2010, 2.
30. J.R. Branstrader, "Safety First in New Fleet of Funds," *Barron's*, April 9, 2011, L21.
31. Jack Bogle, *Don't Count on It!*, Hoboken, NJ, and Canada: Wiley, November 2010, 441.
32. Beverly Goodman, "An Alternative to Hedge-Fund Alternatives," *Barron's*, May 28, 2012, 35.
33. Nadia Papagiannis, Josh Charney, Alexa Auerbach, and Beverly Goodman (Eds.), "2011 Alternative Survey of US Institutions and Financial Advisors," *Morningstar & Barron's*, May 2012, 4.
34. Jon Sundt and Allen Cheng, "The Case for Liquid Alternative Investments," *Altegris Advisors*, June 2012, 22.
35. Beverly Goodman, "An Alternative to Hedge-Fund Alternatives," *Barron's*, May 28, 2012, 35.
36. Yu Yuan, "Behavioral Finance—Syllabus," *Wharton School of the University of Pennsylvania*, Spring 2011, 1.
37. The Editors, "Business Education: Trouble in the Middle," *The Economist*, October 15, 2011, 71.
38. Gur Huberman, "Familiarity Breeds Investment," *Review of Financial Studies*, Fall 2001, 659.
39. Jason Kelly and Oliver Staley, "Kravis Pledges $100 Million for Columbia Business School Campus," *Bloomberg*, October 5, 2010, http://www.bloomberg.com/news/2010–10–05/henry-kravis-pledges-100-million-to-columbia-for-business-school-campus.html (accessed February 2014).
40. The Editors, "Education vs. Bureaucracy," *Investor's Business Daily*, October 31, 2011, A5.
41. "Higher Education: Not What It Used To Be," *The Economist*, December 1, 2012, 29.
42. Gillian Wee, "Giving and Getting," *Bloomberg Markets*, February 2013, 88.

7 HEDGE FUNDS: EVIL OR ANGELS IN DISGUISE?

1. Steven Eder, "Pensions Leap Back to Hedge Funds," *Wall Street Journal*, May 27, 2011, C1.
2. Andrew Stepaniuk and Anthony Cowell, "Transformation: The Future of Alternative Investments," *KPMG*, June 2010, 37.
3. Everett Ehrlich, "The Changing Role of Hedge Funds in the Global Economy," *ESC Company*, September 2011, 11.
4. Christine Williamson, "Large Endowments Grab Healthy Portfolio Gains," *Pensions and Investments*, December 12, 2011, 1.
5. William Jahnke, "The Asset Allocation Hoax," *Journal of Financial Planning*, 1 (2), February 1997, 111.
6. Christine Williamson, "Investors Changing Lanes in Drive for Hedge Funds," *Pensions and Investments*, September 17, 2011, 5.
7. Michael McDonald, "Massachusetts Pension Cuts Middlemen in Hedge-Fund Investments," *Bloomberg*, April 5, 2011, http://www.bloomberg.com/news/2011–04–05/massachusetts-state-pension-plan-cuts-middleman-in-hedge-fund-investments.html (accessed May 2012).

8. "Ohio PERS Investment Plan: 2011," *Ohio Public Employees Retirement System*, 2, https://www.opers.org/pubs-archive/investments/inv-plan/2011_Investment_Plan.pdf
9. Steven Eder, "Pensions Leap Back to Hedge Funds," *Wall Street Journal*, May 27, 2011, C1.
10. Ibid.
11. Michael Corkery and Steven Eder, "Bridgewater Goes Large," *Wall Street Journal*, June 22, 2011, C1.
12. Kenneth Heinz, "Hedge Funds End 2010 With Record Quarterly Asset Increase," *Hedge Fund Research*, p. 1, January 19, 2011.
13. Thao Hua, "Worldwide AUM Hits Post-crisis Milestone," *Pensions and Investments*, June 27, 2011, 1.
14. Ibid.
15. Christine Williamson, "Institutional Investors Pour into Hedge Funds," *Pension and Investments*, November 14, 2011, 1.
16. Julie Creswell, "Shrinking 'Quant' Funds Struggle to Revive Boom," *The New York Times*, August 19, 2010, http://www.nytimes.com/2010/08/20/business/20quant.html (accessed May 2012).
17. Anuj Gangahar, "Does Not Compute: How Misfiring Quant Funds Are Distorting the Markets," *Financial Times*, December 9, 2007, http://www.ft.com/cms/s/0/553fea68-a68e-11dc-b1f5–0000779fd2ac.html#axzz21E5Xhlkp (accessed May 2012).
18. AT Staff, "2011 Quant Gold Book," *Advanced Trading*, November 2011, 17.
19. Tom Lauricella, "Tough Era for 'Macro' Funds," *Wall Street Journal*, July 11, 2011, C1.
20. Ibid.
21. Adam Tashman and Robert Frey, "Modeling Risk Arbitrage Strategies Using Finite Mixtures," *Quantitative Finance*, 9 (5), August 2009, 495.
22. Gregory Zuckerman and Steven Eder, "As Stocks Slide, Investors Scramble," *Wall Street Journal*, August 11, 2011, C1.
23. Yu Yuan, "Behavioral Finance—Syllabus," *Wharton School of the University of Pennsylvania*, Spring 2011, 1.
24. Jianfeng Yu, Robert Stambaugh, and Yu Yuan, "The Short of It: Investor Sentiment and Anomalies," *National Bureau of Economic Research*, November 1, 2010, 5.
25. "Summary of the Dodd-Frank Wall Street Reform," *Cadwalader, Wickersham & Taft LLP*, August 10, 2010, 3.
26. Andrew Stepaniuk and Anthony Cowell, "Transformation: The Future of Alternative Investments," *KPMG*, June 2010, 20.
27. Ibid., 6.
28. Jeremy Kahn, "Treasure Island," *Bloomberg Markets*, February 2012, 59.
29. The Editors, "Economics Focus: Cause and Defect," *The Economist*, October 29, 2011, 88.
30. Tom Lauricella, "New Twist on Hedge Funds," *Wall Street Journal*, November 7, 2011, R4.
31. Juliette Fairley, "Staying Afloat," *Financial Advisor*, October 3, 2011, http://www.fa-mag.com/news/staying-afloat-8441.html?print (accessed August 15, 2013).
32. G. Cici, A. Kempf, and A. Puetz, "The Valuation of Hedge Funds' Equity Positions," *American Finance Association*, December 2011, 31.
33. Tom Lauricella, "New Twist on Hedge Funds," *Wall Street Journal*, November 7, 2011, R4.
34. Ibid.
35. Jane Kim, "Stock-Research Reform to Die?" *Wall Street Journal*, June 9, 2009, C1.

36. Roger Parloff, "The Gray Art of Not Quite Insider Trading," *Fortune Magazine*, September 2, 2013, 64.
37. Mike Spector and Greg Bensinger, "LightSquared Pulls the Plug," *Wall Street Journal*, May 15, 2012, C1.
38. Bill Alpert, "How Hedge Funds Got Hooked in a Ponzi Scheme," *Barron's*, February 27, 2012, 20.
39. Kambiz Foroohar, "A VC Who Runs a Hedge Fund," *Bloomberg*, November 2011, 100.
40. Michael Santoli, "Bubble Trouble," *Barron's*, July 25, 2011, 19.
41. Andrew Bary, "Excitement Heats for Facebook IPO Even as LinkedIn and Groupon Cool," *Barron's*, December 5, 2011, 18.
42. Ari Levy, "Tiger Global Said to Pay $20 million for LinkedIn Stake," *Bloomberg*, July 28, 2011, http://www.bloomberg.com/news/2010–07–27/linkedin-valued-at-more-than-2-billion-after-investment-by-tiger-global.html (accessed May 2012).
43. Spencer Ante, "Hedge-Fund Investors Scout Out Web Firms," *Wall Street Journal*, July 12, 2011, B1.
44. Rolfe Winkler, "LivingSocial Is Avoiding Prying Eyes," *Wall Street Journal*, December 9, 2011, C12.
45. Daniel Fisher, "How the Government is Helping Hedge Funds Make Billions Off of IPOs," *Forbes*, March 21, 2012, http://www.forbes.com/sites/danielfisher/2012/03/21/how-the-government-is-helping-hedge-funds-make-billions-off-ipos/ (accessed June 2012).
46. Alistair Barr, "Brazil's Groupon Rival Backed by Tiger Global," *Wall Street Journal*, May 6, 2011, http://articles.marketwatch.com/2011–05–06/industries/30743908_1_hedge-fund-venture-capital-benchmark-capital (accessed May 2012).
47. Ari Levy, "Tiger Global Said to Pay $20 million for LinkedIn Stake," Bloomberg, July 28, 2011, http://www.bloomberg.com/news/2010–07–27/linkedin-valued-at-more-than-2-billion-after-investment-by-tiger-global.html (accessed May 2012).
48. Daniel Fisher, "How the Government is Helping Hedge Funds Make Billions Off of IPOs," *Forbes*, March 21, 2012, http://www.forbes.com/sites/danielfisher/2012/03/21/how-the-government-is-helping-hedge-funds-make-billions-off-ipos/ (accessed June 2012).
49. Leena Rao, "Tiger Global Bought Massive Amounts of LinkedIn Stock Pre and Post IPO," *Tech Crunch*, June 4, 2011, http://techcrunch.com/2011/06/04/sec-watch-tiger-global-bought-massive-amounts-of-linkedin-stock-pre-and-post-ipo/ (accessed June 2011).
50. Pui-Wing Tam and Shayndi Raice, "Facebook's Investors Poised for Jackpot," *Wall Street Journal*, January 28, 2012, B4.
51. Rolfe Winkler, "The $100 Billion Question that Looms for Facebook," *Wall Street Journal*, November 30, 2011, C13.
52. David Benoit, "Morgan Stanley Made a Bundle on Facebook Deal," *Wall Street Journal*, June 18, 2012, http://blogs.wsj.com/deals/2012/06/18/morgan-stanley-a-bundle-on-facebook-deal/ (accessed June 2012).
53. Mike Armstrong, "Facebook Keeps on Sagging," *Philadelphia Inquirer*, May 30, 2012, A14.
54. Brian Deagon, "Facebook Worth $104 Bil after IPO Shares Sell at 38," *Investor's Business Daily*, May 18, 2012, A1.
55. Lizette Chapman, "Q&A with Facebook Investor David Sze about IPO," *Wall Street Journal*, May 21, 2012, http://blogs.wsj.com/digits/2012/05/21/qa-with-facebook-investor-david-sze-about-ipo/ (accessed June 2012).

56. Poornima Gupta and Gerry Shih, "Factbox: Facebook's IPO: Who Gets Rich?" *Reuters*, May 17, 2012, http://www.reuters.com/article/2012/05/16/us-facebook-riches-idUSBRE84F1EK20120516 (accessed May 2012).
57. Nathan Vardi, "The Richest Trade is Selling the Facebook IPO," *Forbes*, May 16, 2012, http://www.forbes.com/sites/nathanvardi/2012/05/16/the-richest-trade-is-not-betting-against-the-jpmorgan-whale-its-selling-the-facebook-ipo/ (accessed June 2012).
58. Scott Austin, "Facebook Investors' Worth on IPO Day," *Wall Street Journal*, May 17, 2012, http://blogs.wsj.com/digits/2012/05/17/facebook-investors-worth-on-ipo-day/ (accessed May 2012).
59. The Associated Press, "Facebook IPO: Who is Selling Stock?" *USA Today*, May 17, 2012, http://www.usatoday.com/tech/news/story/2012–05–15/facebook-ipo-stock-sell/54970236/1 (accessed May 2012).
60. Rolfe Winkler, "Facebook Status: Tech's Poorer Relative," *Wall Street Journal*, May 18, 2012, C10.
61. "Tiger Global," *Hedge Fund Letters*, May 18, 2012, http://www.hedgefundletters.com/category/tiger-global/ (accessed May 2012).
62. Mark Boslet, "Most Aggressive IPO Insiders Selling Facebook Were Tiger, Thiel, Goldman Sachs, and Accel," *Thomson Reuters*, May 23, 2012, http://privatemarkets.thomsonreuters.com/most-aggressive-ipo-insiders-selling-facebook-were-tiger-thiel-goldman-sachs-and-accel/21019609.article (accessed May 2012).
63. Jennifer Dauble, "CNBC Exclusive: CNBC Transcript: CNBC's Maria Bartiromo Speaks with James Gorman, Morgan Stanley Chairman & CEO, on CNBC's 'Closing Bell with Maria Bartiromo' Today," *CNBC.com*, May 31, 2012.
64. Andrew Barry, "Facebook Flops: Look Out Below," *Barron's*, May 20, 2012, 21.
65. Brett Philbin, "Facebook Mess May Renew Broker-Independence Push," *Wall Street Journal*, May 22, 2012, http://blogs.wsj.com/marketbeat/2012/05/22/facebook-mess-may-renew-broker-independence-push/ (accessed May 2012).
66. "Facebook IPO Fiasco Worsens," *PrivCo*, May 22, 2012, http://oldprod.privco.com/ breaking-news-facebook-ipo-fiasco-worsens-morgan-stanley-under-investigation-subpoena-on-selective-disclosures-of-facebook-2nd-quarter-earnings-miss-mid-ipo-earnings-warnings-unprecedented-selling-insiders-may-have-had-access-to-material-non-public-inform (accessed May 2012).
67. Andrew Osterland, "Facebook Flop Doesn't Look Good for Morgan Stanley," *Investment News*, May 29, 2012, http://www.investmentnews.com/article/20120529/FREE/120529928 (accessed June 2012).
68. Mark Boslet, "Most Aggressive IPO Insiders Selling Facebook Were Tiger, Thiel, Goldman Sachs, and Accel," *Thomson Reuters*, May 23, 2012, http://privatemarkets.thomsonreuters.com/most-aggressive-ipo-insiders-selling-facebook-were-tiger-thiel-goldman-sachs-and-accel/21019609.article (accessed May 2012).
69. Lauran LaCapra and Jennifer Saba, "Facebook Investors Look for Exits," *Reuters*, April 27, 2011, http://www.reuters.com/article/2011/04/27/us-facebook-shares-idUSTRE73Q8L720110427 (accessed May 2012).
70. James O'Toole, "Regulators Eye Morgan Stanley's Pre-Facebook IPO Actions," *CNN Money*, May 22, 2012, http://money.cnn.com/2012/05/22/markets/facebook-ipo-morgan-stanley/index.htm (accessed June 2012).
71. "Facebook IPO Fiasco Worsens," *PrivCo*, May 22, 2012, http://oldprod.privco.com/ breaking-news-facebook-ipo-fiasco-worsens-morgan-stanley-under-investigation-subpoena-on-selective-disclosures-of-facebook-2nd-quarter-earnings-miss-mid-ipo-earnings-warnings-unprecedented-selling-insiders-may-have-had-access-to-material-non-public-inform (accessed May 2012).

72. Randall Smith, "For Funds, a Groupon Deal Could Disappoint," *Wall Street Journal*, October 12, 2011, C1.
73. Joe Light, "Facebook Funds Plunge," *Wall Street Journal*, June 10, 2012, B9.
74. Aaron Lucchetti, Anupreeta Das, and Monica Langley, "Morgan Stanley Was Driver on Facebook's Wild IPO Ride," *Wall Street Journal*, June 17, 2012, A1.
75. Stephen Gandel, "Morgan Stanley Made Money on Facebook Share Drop," *CNN Money*, May 24, 2012, http://finance.fortune.cnn.com/2012/05/24/morgan-stanley-facebook-ipo-drop/ (accessed June 2012).
76. Andrew Osterland, "Facebook Flop Doesn't Look Good for Morgan Stanley," *Investment News*, May 29, 2012, http://www.investmentnews.com/article/20120529/FREE/120529928 (accessed June 2012).
77. Phil Purcell, "Shareholders Can Cure Too Big To Fail," *Wall Street Journal*, June 26, 2012, A15.
78. Andrew Bary, "In Facebook's Fiasco, Hope for Reform," *Barron's*, May 28, 2012, 39.
79. Ana Semedo, "Lowest June for US Listed IPOs since 2003," *Dealogic*, June 21, 2012, 1.
80. Rep. Darrell Issa, "Letter to The Honorable Mary L. Schapiro, Chairman of the United States Securities and Exchange Commission," Committee on Oversight and Government Reform, House of Representatives, Congress of the United States, June 19, 2012, 1.
81. Aaron Lucchetti and Jean Eaglesham, "Morgan Stanley Gets Facebook Fine," *Wall Street Journal*, December 18, 2012, A1.
82. Linda Sandler, "Has the Madoff Trustee Gone Too Far?" *BusinessWeek*, July 14, 2011, 41.
83. Malcolm Baker, Jeffrey Wurgler, and Yu Yuan, "Global, Local, and Contagious Investor Sentiment," *National Bureau of Economic Research*, October 17, 2011, 30.
84. Beverly Goodman, "Hedge Funds for Hoi Polloi," *Barron's*, July 30, 2012, 25.
85. David Cutler, James M. Poterba, and Lawrence H. Summers, "What Moves Stock Prices?" *Journal of Portfolio Management*, Spring 1989, 10.

8 THE FOOLS' GOLD OR THE REAL DEAL?

1. Tatyana Shumsky, "New Rule Could Tarnish Gold," *Barron's*, August 15, 2011, M11.
2. The Editors, "If Greece Goes," *The Economist*, "June 25, 2011, 13.
3. Liam Denning, "Gold Relies on Central-Bank Support for Momentum," *Wall Street Journal*, September 12, 2011, C8.
4. Tim Koller, Marc Goedhart, and David Wessels, *Valuation: Measuring and Managing the Value of Companies*, McKinsey & Co., 2010, 391.
5. May Day and Tatyana Shumsky, "Gold Exceeds $1,600," *Wall Street Journal*, July 19, 2011, C6.
6. Jason Zweig, "When Treasurys Aren't Safe, Then What Is?" *Wall Street Journal*, July 18, 2011, C1.
7. Jason Zweig, Liam Pleven, and Mary Pilon, "Gold Even Reigns on Stock Market," *Wall Street Journal*, August 23, 2011, C2.
8. Liam Denning, "Gold Relies on Central-Bank Support for Momentum," *Wall Street Journal*, September 12, 2011, C8.
9. The Editors, "Glittering Gold Need Not Set Off a Panic Over Inflation," *Bloomberg Markets*, June 8, 2011, 12.

10. "Global demand for gold jewellery up 12% in Q1 2013 driven by significant increases in India and China," Press Releases: May, 2013. *World Gold Council*. May 16, 2013. http://www.gold.org/media/press_releases/archive/2013/05/gdt_q1_2013_pr/
11. Rhiannon Hoyle and Yue Li, "Chinese See New Year as Golden," *Wall Street Journal*, January 18, 2012, C4.
12. Liam Pleven, "Investors in Gold Rush for the Exits," *Wall Street Journal*, May 30, 2012, B4.
13. Ronald Delegge, "Is Gold in Trouble?" *Research Magazine*, July 2012, 23.
14. Brad Zigler, "Gold Diversifier," *Financial Advisor Magazine*, November 2011, 81.
15. William Mellor, "Glencore's Soldier of Fortune," *Bloomberg Markets*, October 2011, 46.
16. William Wright, "The Ups and Downs of IPOs," *Wall Street Journal*, October 10, 2011, R7.
17. David Darst, *The Art of Asset Allocation: Principles and Investment Strategies*, New York, NY: McGraw-Hill, 2008, 181.
18. Richard Brealey and Stewart Myers, *Principles of Corporate Finance*, 4th ed., New York: McGraw-Hill, 1991, 322.
19. Michael Rothfeld, "Red Flags at Failed Broker," *Wall Street Journal*, July 13, 2012, C1.
20. Deborah Solomon, "Commodity Cop Getting Grief from All Sides," *Wall Street Journal*, July 19, 2011, B6.
21. Christopher Condon, "ETFs Passive No More in Challenge to $7.8 Trillion Market," *Bloomberg*, June 26, 2012, http://www.bloomberg.com/news/2012–06–26/etfs-passive-no-more-in-challenge-to-7–8-trillion-market.html (accessed June 2012).
22. Aaron Lucchetti, Scott Patterson, and Victoria McGrane, "Lost and Found—Maybe," *Wall Street Journal*, November 5, 2011, B1.
23. Zvi Bodie, Alex Kane, and Alan Marcus, *Investments*, 9th ed., New York, NY: McGraw-Hill, 2011, 201.

9 VENTURE CAPITAL

1. The Associated Press, "The Goal of Google+ Is Insight Into Lives," *Investor's Business Daily*, July 14, 2011, A4.
2. Thomas Black, "Call for Companies to Hand Out More Cash," *Bloomberg Markets*, October 17–23, 2011, 60.
3. Ben Casselman, "U.S. at Risk if Europe Goes Bad," *Wall Street Journal*, November 15, 2011, A4.
4. Christopher Armstrong, George Foster, John R.M. Hand, and Tony Davila, "Market-to-Revenue Multiples in Public and Private Capital Markets," *Australian Journal of Management*, 2005, 51.
5. Karen Weise, "Nike: New Funding for Startups," *Bloomberg Markets*, October 2011, 44.
6. Rossana Weitekamp and Barbara Pruitt, "Jobless Entrepreneurship Tarnishes Steady Rate of U.S. Startup Activity," Kauffman Foundation, March 7, 2011, http://www.kauffman.org/newsroom/ jobless-entrepreneurship-tarnishes-steady-rate-of-us-startup-activity.aspx (accessed March 2011).
7. "Frequently Asked Questions," Small Business Administration (SBA) Office of Advocacy, January 2011, http://www.sba.gov/sites/default/files/sbfaq.pdf (accessed February 2014).
8. Spencer E. Ante, Laura Kreutzer, and Sabrina Willmer, "Union Square Ventures Raising New Tech Fund," *Wall Street Journal*, September 15, 2011, B3.

9. Pui-Wing Tam, "After Dry Year, Start-ups Are Poised to Get Cash," *Wall Street Journal*, December 23, 2009, B1.
10. Kyle Alspach, "Sharp Rise for Mass. VC Deals," *Boston Business Journal*, July 15, 2011, 3.
11. Andrei Shleifer, J. Bradford De Long, Lawrence H. Summers, and Robert J. Waldmann, "The Survival of Noise Traders in Financial Markets," *National Bureau of Economic Research*, Working Paper #2715, September 1988, 5.
12. Shayndi Raice and Randall Smith, "Groupon's Deal Is Big Test for IPO Market, Offering Pegs Value at Nearly $13 Billion," *Wall Street Journal*, November 4, 2011.
13. Scott Thurm and Pui-Wing Tam, "Prominent Investors Miss Web IPO Payoff," *Wall Street Journal*, June 19, 2012, A1.
14. Victoria Barret, "Dropbox," *Forbes*, November 7, 2011, 82.
15. The Editors, "The Emerging Online Giants," *The Economist*, July 8, 2010, 1.
16. Adrien Henni, "Russia's Technology Boom Attracts Foreign Investors," *The Telegraph*, April 3, 2012, http://www.telegraph.co.uk/sponsored/russianow/technology/9183881/Russia-technology-foreign-investors.html (accessed April 2012).
17. Adrien Henni, "Russia's Technology Boom Attracts Foreign Investors," *The Telegraph*, April 3, 2012, http://www.telegraph.co.uk/sponsored/russianow/technology/9183881/Russia-technology-foreign-investors.html (accessed April 2012).
18. Editors, "Cryptocurrencies, The Great Hiccup," *The Economist*, February 22, 2014, 65.
19. (Yoshifumi Takemoto and Sophie Knight, "Bitcoin exchange firm files for bankruptcy," *The Philadelphia Inquirer*, March 1, 2014, A4.)
20. Editors, "Eric Holder's Hazy Vision on Pot," *Bloomberg BusinessWeek*, February 6, 2014, p. 10.
21. Department of the Treasury Financial Crimes Enforcement, "BSA Expectations Regarding Marijuana-Related Businesses," February 14, 2014, Web: February 21, 2014.
22. Andrew McAfee, "What Every CEO Needs to Know About the Cloud," *Harvard Business Review*, November 2011, 126.
23. Doug Henschen, "IBM Beats Oracle, Microsoft With Big Data Leap," *Information Week*, October 25, 2011, http://www.informationweek.com/software/information-management/ibm-beats-oracle-microsoft-with-big-data (accessed August 12, 2013)
24. Kurt Marko, "Cloud Storage Evolved," *Information Week*, April 23, 2012, 30.
25. Katharine Grayson, "El Dorado Cash Backs enStratus," *Minneapolis/St. Paul Biz Journal*, November 11, 2011, 6.
26. Charles Babcock, "Global Data Center Chains Promise Easier Backup," *Information Week*, October 17, 2011, 18.
27. J. Hoover, "The CIA Rethinks Data Centers for Big Data," *Information Week*, November 14, 2011, 13.
28. Anna Kovner, Josh Lerner, and Paul Gomper, "Specialization and Success: Evidence from Venture Capital," *Journal of Economics and Management Strategy*, 18 (3), Fall 2009, 821.
29. Pu-Wing Tam, "Venture Firm Raises $2.08 Billion for Fund," *Wall Street Journal*, May 10, 2012, C1.
30. Spencer E. Ante, Laura Kreutzer, and Sabrina Willmer, "Union Square Ventures Raising New Tech Fund," *Wall Street Journal*, September 15, 2011, B3.
31. Kyle Alspach, "Summit Partners Closes on Bigger VC Fund, Raising $520M," *Boston Business Journal*, January 13, 2012, 13.

32. Arleen Jacobius, "It's the Belle of the Ball Again, after 10-Year Funk," *Pensions and Investments*, May 14, 2012, 1.
33. "Preqin Special Report: Venture Capital Deals by Industry, Stage, and Size," *Preqin*, May 10, 2012, 19.
34. Aaron Ricadela, "Who Will Be the Green VC Giant?" *BusinessWeek*, October 22, 2009, http://www.businessweek.com/magazine/content/09_44/b4153054900653.htm (accessed November 2009).
35. Mark Johnson and Josh Suskewicz, "How to Jump-Start the Clean-Tech Economy," *Harvard Business Review*, 2011, 49.
36. Neil King, "Venture Capitol: New VC Force," *Wall Street Journal*, December 14, 2009, A1.
37. John Vomhof, "$100k Hybrid Not in Sock, but Fisker Is Selling Anyway," *Minneapolis/St. Paul Business Journal*, July 15, 2011, 3.
38. Ron Leuty, "Tom Perkins to Uncle Sam: Quit VC," *San Francisco Business Times*, December 1, 2011, 39.
39. Ryan Underwood, "Crowd Control: Crowdfunding," *Inc. Magazine*, November 2012, 21.
40. Source: "Still Not Working," *The Economist*, March 30, 2013, 74–75.
41. Ibid.
42. Jon Asmundsson, "Crowdfunding Wins in Washington," *Bloomberg Markets*, November 2012, 20.
43. John Wasik, "The Brilliance (and Madness) of Crowdfunding," *Forbes*, June 25, 2012, 144.
44. Jud Askins, Direct quote.
45. Karen Blumenthal, "On Crowdfunding and Other Threats," *Wall Street Journal*, September 23, 2012, B8.
46. John Wasik, "The Brilliance (and Madness) of Crowdfunding," *Forbes*, June 25, 2012, 144.
47. Angus Loten, "Stalled Crowdfunding Rules Leave Business Plans on Ice," *Wall Street Journal*, December 13, 2012, B1.
48. Ryan Tracy, "For Solar, No Guarantees," *Wall Street Journal*, August 31, 2011, B3.
49. The Editors, "Solargate Opens Wide," *Investor's Business Daily*, October 3, 2011, A17.
50. Lindsay Riddell, "Cleantech VC Funding Bounces Back," *San Francisco Business Times*, April 8, 2011, 8.
51. Lindsay Riddell, "Cleantech Jobs Outpace Economy," *San Francisco Business Times*, July 15, 2011, 7.
52. Yuliya Chernova, "Loan was Solyndra's Undoing," Wall Street Journal, September 15, 2011.
53. John Steele Gordon, "Government as Bad Venture Capitalist," *Barron's*, January 9, 2012, 14.
54. David Reilly, "Sandy Weill Regrets Breaking Glass," *Wall Street Journal*, July 26, 2012, C12.
55. Donna Howell, "Sun Has Not Set of U.S. Solar," *Investor's Business Daily*, September 30, 2011, B2.
56. John Tozzi, "China's Next Export: Venture Capital," *BusinessWeek*, May 27, 2012, 53.
57. Galen Moore, "VC Group Head Says Balance Coming to Industry," *Boston Business Journal*, April 15, 2011, 6.
58. Charles Passy, "What Steakhouses Won't Tell You," *Smart Money*, December 2011, 72.

59. Stephen Todd Walker, *Wave Theory for Alternative Investments,* New York, NY: McGraw-Hill, 2011, 232.
60. Anna Kovner, Josh Lerner, and Paul Gomper, "Specialization and Success: Evidence from Venture Capital," *Journal of Economics and Management Strategy*, 18 (3), Fall 2009, 820.
61. Jonathan Rockoff, "Gender Gap: The Risks of Heart Disease for Women," *Wall Street Journal*, November 1, 2011, D1.
62. Ibid.
63. Ron Winslow, ""If Only Heart Attacks Were Predictable," *Wall Street Journal*, April 16, 2012, R6.
64. Katharine Grayson, "Heart-Monitor Maker Expands Presence," *Minneapolis /St. Paul Business Journal*, March 16, 2012, 6.
65. "Welcome to CardioVax: Home," *CardioVax*, 2009, http://www.cardiovax.com /index.html (accessed July 2013).
66. Katharine Grayson, "Sunshine Heart Finishes Study," *Minneapolis/St. Paul Business Journal*, June 17, 2011, 5.
67. Katharine Grayson, "Intervalve Gets $4.7 Million for Tests of Device," *Minneapolis/St. Paul Business Journal*, September 2, 2011, 5.
68. The Editors, "A Unique Approach to Repair Heart Muscle after Attack," *New Jersey Business Journal*, August 1, 2011, 5.
69. PR Newswires, "CardioMEMS, Inc. Tops Georgia's 2010 Venture Financing List," *The Business Journals*, April 4, 2011, http://www.bizjournals.com/prnewswire /press_releases/2011/04/04/CL76535 (accessed April 2011).
70. "Technology Overview," *Circulite*, April 2012, http://www.circulite.net/products-technology/technology-overview.php (accessed May 2012).
71. Katharine Grayson, "Osprey Closes $20M Offering," *Minneapolis/St. Paul Business Journal*, April 20, 2012, 5.
72. "MyCell Products," *Cellular Dynamics International*. http://www.cellulardynamics.com/products/mycell.html
73. Aaron Tilley, "Mobile Heart Monitor Doesn't Skip a Beat," *SF Business Times*, July 25, 2012, 16.
74. "Technology," Vascular Magnetics, Inc., August 2010. http://www.vascularmagnetics.com/2010/08/technology.html
75. "Custom Films and Sensors for Flexible and Formable Touch Devices," www .canatu.com, 2013.
76. Brian Deagon, "The IPO Market Finally Sprang Back To Life In May," *Investor's Business Daily*, June 1, 2011, A4.
77. "PwC US Mid-Year M&A Outlook 2011" *PricewaterhouseCoopers*. June 8, 2011, 1. http://emarketing.pwc.com/reaction/images/Cox/PwCmid-yearM&Aoutlook-06.08.11.pdf
78. Venture-Backed Acquisitions Break All-Time Annual Record; Driven By Chinese Companies, Number of IPOs At Highest Quarterly Level Since 2000, NVCA & Thomson Reuters, January 3, 2011, 1.
79. "About Us," *SharesPost*, https://welcome.sharespost.com/about-us
80. Tiernan Ray, "Time to Friend Facebook? How to Buy in Now," *Barron's*, March 28, 2011, 12.
81. Jeff Bunder and Philip Bass, "A Study of North American Exits," *Ernst & Young: PE Insights*, 2 (2), December 2010, 3.
82. "Venture Capital Industry Raises $7.1 Billion in Q1," *Thomson Reuters* and *NVCA*, April 11, 2011, 1.

83. Clare Chachere, Lisa Peterson, and Emily Mendell, "Venture Capital Investments Rise 19% in Q2 2011," *NVCA–PWC*, July 20, 2011, 1.
84. Ibid.
85. Alan Kotok, "2011 Q2 VC Funding Up for Life Sciences, CleanTech Stalls," *Science Business*, July 21, 2011, 23.
86. Ibid.
87. Rodney Brown, "New England Venture Deals in Third Quarter up over 2010," *Boston Business Journal*, October 21, 2011, 13.
88. Ibid.
89. Clare Chachere, Lisa Peterson, and Emily Mendell, "Venture Capital Investments Rise 19% in Q2 2011," *NVCA–PWC*, July 20, 2011, 1.
90. Spencer Ante, "Tumblr Valued at $800 Million," *Wall Street Journal*, September 27, 2011, A1.
91. Ibid.
92. The Editors, "Disrupting the Disrupters," *The Economist*, September 3, 2011, 27.
93. Amir Efrati, "Funding Values Twitter at $8.4 Billion," *Wall Street Journal*, August 2, 2011, B3.
94. Michael Days, "In 2011, Twitter Exploded," *Philadelphia Inquirer*, December 25, 2011, A1.
95. Ken North, "From Medlars to Twitter," *Information Week*, April 23, 2012, 34.
96. Patrick Seitz, "The Race toward Facebook," *Investor's Business Daily*, April 30, 2012, A8.
97. Nick Wingfield, "Zynga Secures $1 Billion Cushion," *Wall Street Journal*, August 12, 2011, B4.
98. Amir Efrati, "Facebook Share Clamor Heats Up," *Wall Street Journal*, March 17, 2011, B5.
99. "Facebook and WhatsApp Getting the Message," *The Economist*, February 22, 2014, 54.
100. Robert Dinwiddie, *Oceans: The World's Last Wilderness Revealed*, DK Adult, 2008.
101. Ibid.
102. Source: Matt Craze, "Tapping the Oceans," *Bloomberg Markets,* March 2013, 92–94.
103. "The State of Desalination 2011," IDA World Congress on Desalination and Water Reuse, September 4–9, 2011.
104. Scott DeCarlo, "Earning Away From Home," *Forbes*, May 9, 2011, 138.
105. The Staff, "Preqin Special Report: Venture Capital," *Preqin*, May 2012, 19.
106. Alan Lavine, "Tiger Versus Dragon," *Financial Advisor Magazine*, July 2011, 109.
107. The Editors, "Adventures in Capitalism—Business in India," *The Economist*, October 22, 2011.
108. David Weild and Edward Kim, "Market Structure is causing the IPO crisis—and more," Capital Market Series, *Capital Markets Advisory Partners* and *Grant Thornton*, June 2010, 1.
109. Aaron Lucchetti, "U.S. Falls Behind in Stock Listings," *Wall Street Journal*, May 26, 2011, A14.
110. "Venture Capital Fundraising Q4 2011." *NVCA* and *Thomas Reuters*. January 9, 2012, 1.
111. Adam Thierer, "Tech Titans and Creative Destruction," *Forbes*, November 7, 2011, 42.
112. Michael Milken, "Where's Sputnik?" *Michael Milken Institute*, 2Q 2011, 3.
113. The Editors, "Disrupting the Disrupters," *The Economist*, September 3, 2011, 27.

114. Vipal Monga, "Companies' $2 Trillion Conundrum," *Wall Street Journal*, October 5, 2011, B5.
115. Kenton Powell, "The New Venture Capital," *Bloomberg Markets*, October 24, 2011, 40.
116. Joann Muller, "Glued, Screwed, and Rented," *Forbes*, November 21, 2011, 48.
116. Katharine Grayson, "U of M Funds Will Invest in Startups," *Minneapolis/St. Paul Business Journal*, December 7, 2012, 6.

10 ASSET ALLOCATION AND ALTERNATIVE INVESTMENTS

1. Magnus Dahlquist and Campbell R. Harvey, "Global Tactical Asset Allocation," *Duke University*, January 2011, 1.
2. Stuart Ritter, "Average Returns Aren't All That Common," *T. Rowe Price Insights*, October 2011, 13.
3. Zvi Bodie, Alex Kane, and Alan Marcus, *Investments*, 9th ed., New York, NY: McGraw-Hill, 2011, 8.
4. Ibid., 104.
5. Jennifer Popovec, "Is the Diversified REIT Dying?", *Wealth Management*, January 2013, 44 and 45.
6. A.D. Pruitt, "REIT Returns Up but Trail Broader Market," *Wall Street Journal*, April 2, 2013, C6.
7. Brad Thomas, "The Great REIT Boom," *Investment Guide Real Estate*, Forbes, December 10, 2012, 170.
8. "Private Equity Jumps Big Into Commercial Real Estate Loans," Joe Gose, *Investor's Business Daily*, November 30, 2012, A10.
9. Zvi Bodie, Alex Kane, and Alan Marcus, *Investments*, 9th ed., New York, NY: McGraw-Hill, 2011, 184.
10. Christine Williamson, "Manager Selection Trumps Allocation Size, Study Says," *Pensions and Investments*, July 9, 2012, 6.
11. John Wasik, "A World of Alternatives That Goes Beyond Stocks and Bonds," *New York Times*, October 19, 2011, F11.
12. Andrew Stepaniuk and Anthony Cowell, "Transformation: The Future of Alternative Investments," *KPMG*, June 2010, 36.
13. Arleen Jacobius, "New look for Texas Teachers' Private Equity, Real Assets," *Pensions and Investments*, June 27, 2011, 1.
14. Robert J. Shapiro, "The Role of the Private Equity Sector Promoting Economic Recovery," *Private Equity Growth Capital Council*, March 2009, 3.
15. Gary Brinson, L. Randolph Hood, and Gilbert Beebower, "Determinants of Portfolio Performance," *Financial Analysis Journal*, January–February 1995, 133.
16. Ibid., 136.
17. Roger Ibbotson, "The Importance of Asset Allocation," *Financial Analysts Journal*, March/April 2010, 18.
18. L. Randolph Hood, "Determinants of Portfolio Performance—20 Years Later," *Financial Analysts Journal*, September–October 2005, 6.
19. Ibid.
20. Ibid.
21. James Xiong, Peng Chen, Roger G. Ibbotson, and Thomas M. Idzorek, "The Equal Importance of Asset Allocation and Active Management," *Financial Analysts Journal*, March/April 2010, 4.
22. Sarah Morgan, "Being More Active Is Thus Far Good Financial Advice," *Wall Street Journal*, February 14, 2012, C8.

23. Dan Moisand, "Timing is Nothing," *Financial Advisor Magazine*, November 2011, 47.
24. Gary P. Brinson, Brian D. Singer, and Gilbert L. Beebower, "Determinants of Portfolio Performance II: An Update," *Financial Analysts Journal*, May–June 1991, 42.
25. Ibid.
26. Gary P. Brinson, L. Randolph Hood, and Gilbert L. Beebower, "Determinants of Portfolio Performance," *Financial Analysis Journal*, January–February 1995, 134.
27. Gary P. Brinson, Brian D. Singer, and Gilbert L. Beebower, "Determinants of Portfolio Performance II: An Update," *Financial Analysts Journal*, May–June 1991, 45.
28. Jeffrey Hoernemann, Dean Junkans, and Carmen Zarate, "Strategic Asset Allocation and Other Determinants of Portfolio Returns," *Journal of Wealth Management*, Winter 2005, 28.
29. Larry Fowler and Jeffrey Rattiner, "Averting Disaster," *Financial Advisor Magazine*, August 2005, 24.
30. John Campbell and Luis Viceira, "Strategic Asset Allocation," *Harvard University*, April 2001, 7.
31. L. Randolph Hood, "Determinants of Portfolio Performance—20 Years Later," *Financial Analysts Journal*, September–October 2005, 7.
32. Jeffrey Hoernemann, Dean Junkans, and Carmen Zarate, "Strategic Asset Allocation and Other Determinants of Portfolio Returns," *Journal of Wealth Management*, Winter 2005, 26.
33. William W. Jahnke, "The Asset Allocation Hoax," *Journal of Financial Planning*, August 2004, 65.
34. Ibid.
35. Roger Ibbotson, "The Importance of Asset Allocation," *Financial Analysts Journal*, March–April 2010, 20.
36. Jeffrey Hoernemann, Dean Junkans, and Carmen Zarate, "Strategic Asset Allocation and Other Determinants of Portfolio Returns," *Journal of Wealth Management*, Winter 2005, 26.
37. Gary Brinson, Brian Singer, and Gilbert Beebower, "Determinants of Portfolio Performance II: An Update," *Financial Analysts Journal*, May–June 1991, 41.
38. Jeffrey Hoernemann, Dean Junkans, and Carmen Zarate, "Strategic Asset Allocation and Other Determinants of Portfolio Returns," *Journal of Wealth Management*, Winter 2005, 29.
39. The Editors, "Funds Keep Buy-And-Hold Flame," *Investor's Business Daily*, August 19, 2011, A9.
40. Jack Willoughby, "SEC Tackles Fund Derivatives," *Barron's*, September 5, 2011, 35.
41. Tim Koller, Marc Goedhart, and David Wessels, *Valuation: Measuring and Managing the Value of Companies*, Hoboken, NJ: Wiley, 2010, 413.

11 MODERN PORTFOLIO ALLOCATION

1. Stephen Todd Walker, *Wave Theory for Alternative Investments*, New York, NY: McGraw-Hill, 2011, XXVIII.
2. Martin Z. Braun, "'Mega' Public Pensions Beat Small Funds in 2012: Wilshire," *Bloomberg Businessweek*, February 3, 2013.
3. Wayne Lin, "Risk {Re}considered", Legg Mason Perspectives, 2010.
4. Hersh Shefrin and Meir Statman, "Behavioral Portfolio Theory," *Journal of Financial and Quantitative Analysis*, November 1997, 35 (2), 16.

5. "The New Diversification: Open Your Eyes to Alternatives, A Conversation with Professor Christopher C. Geczy, Ph.D.", *BlackRock*, 2.
6. Richard Bornhoft, "Speaking of Correlation," Investor Insight Issue 2, *Equinox Fund Management*, 2013, 1.
7. Tim Koller, Marc Goedhart, and David Wessels, *Valuation: Measuring and Managing the Value of Companies*, Hoboken, New Jersey, and Canada: John Wiley & Sons, Inc., 2010, 326.
8. E.S. Browning, "A Long-Term Case for Stocks," *Wall Street Journal*, September 12, 2011, C1.
9. Pete Swisher and Gregory Kasten, "Post-Modern Portfolio Theory," *FPA Journal*, September 30, 2005.
10. Wayne Lin, "Risk {Re}considered", Legg Mason Perspectives, 2010.
11. James Xiong and Thomas M. Idzorek, "Quant Corner: The Impact of Skewness and Fat Tails on the Asset-Allocation Decision: Exploring M-CVaR Optimization, A Promising Alternative to Traditional MVO," *Morningstar Alternative Investments Observer*, Second Quarter 2011, 6.
12. Andrew G. Haldane, "Tails of the Unexpected," The Credit Crisis Five Years On: Unpacking the Crisis, *Bank of England*, June 8, 2012.
13. James Xiong and Thomas M. Idzorek, "Quant Corner: The Impact of Skewness and Fat Tails on the Asset-Allocation Decision: Exploring M-CVaR Optimization, A Promising Alternative to Traditional MVO," *Morningstar Alternative Investments Observer*, Second Quarter 2011, 6.
14. Peter Swisher and Gregory Kasten, "Post-Modern Portfolio Theory", *Journal of Financial Planning*, September 2005, 74–85.
15. Eleanor Laise, "Some Funds Stop Grading on the Curve," *Wall Street Journal*, September 8, 2009.
16. Ajay Dravid, "Managed Futures: Diversification within the Asset Class," Equinox Capital Markets Volume 2, *Equinox Fund Management*, June 2010, 1.
17. Scott Patterson, "Oversight of JP Morgan Probed," *Wall Street Journal*, June 4, 2012, C1.
18. Richard Brealey, Stewart Myers, and Franklin Allen, *Principles of Corporate Finance*, 8th ed., New York, NY: McGraw-Hill, 2006, 181.
19. Ibid., 172.
20. ZviBodie, Alex Kane, and Alan Marcus, *Investments*, 9th ed., New York, NY: McGraw-Hill, 2011, 13.
21. Richard Brealey, Stewart Myers, Franklin Allen, *Principles of Corporate Finance*, 8th ed., New York, NY: McGraw-Hill, 2006, 166.
22. Cindy Sin-Yi Tsai, "The Real World Is Not Normal," *Morningstar Alternative Investments Observer*, Third Quarter 2011.
23. Ibid.
24. ZviBodie, Alex Kane, and Alan Marcus, *Investments*, 9th ed., New York, NY: McGraw-Hill, 2011, 96.
25. Ibid., 361.
26. Carlo Acerbi and Giacomo Scandolo, "Liquidity Risk Theory and Coherent Measures of Risk," *Quantitative Finance*, October 21, 2008, 683.
27. Stephen Ross, Randolph Westerfield, and Bradford Jordan, *Fundamentals of Corporate Finance*, 8th ed., New York, NY: McGraw-Hill, 2008, 422.
28. The Editors, "Sharpe Ratio," *Investopedia*, January 16, 2012, http://www.investopedia.com/terms/s/sharperatio.asp (accessed January 2012).
29. James Picerno, "Building a Better Sharpe Ratio," *Financial Advisor Magazine*, April 2012, 129.

30. Ibid.
31. Ibid.
32. Lawrence T. DeCarlo, "On the Meaning and Use of Kurtosis," Fordham University, *Psychological Methods*, 1997, 2 (3), 292–307.
33. ZviBodie, Alex Kane, and Alan Marcus, *Investments*, 9th ed., New York, NY: McGraw-Hill, 2011, 139.
34. The Editors, "Value at Risk," *Investopedia*, January 16, 2012, http://www.investopedia.com/terms/v/var.asp (accessed January 2012).
35. James Picerno, "Building a Better Sharpe Ratio," *Financial Advisor Magazine*, April 2012, 130.
36. Cyrus Sanati, "Tossing Blame for JPMorgan Trade?" *CNN Money*, May 14, 2012, http://finance.fortune.cnn.com/2012/05/14/jpmorgan-loss-federal-reserve/ (accessed May 2012).
37. Carlo Acerbi and Dirk Tasche, "Expected Shortfall: A Natural Coherent Alternative to Value at Risk," *Economic Notes*, July 2002, 279.
38. James Picerno, "Building a Better Sharpe Ratio," *Financial Advisor Magazine*, April 2012, 130.
39. Lauren Cavenaile and Thomas Lejeune, "A Note on the Use of Modified Value-at -Risk," *The Journal of Alternative Investments*, Spring 2012, 14 (4), 79.
40. James Xiong and Thomas Idzorek, "Mean-Variance versus Mean-Conditional Value-at-Risk Optimization," *Morningstar*, February 16, 2012, 3.
41. Lauren Cavenaile and Thomas Lejeune, "A Note on the Use of Modified Value-at-Risk," *The Journal of Alternative Investments*, Spring 2012, 14 (4), 79.
42. S. Zhu and M. Fukushima, "Worst Case Conditional Value-at-Risk with Application to Robust Portfolio Management," *Operations Research*, October 2009, 1155.
43. The Editors, "Conditional Value at Risk," *Investopedia*, January 16, 2012, http://www.investopedia.com/terms/c/conditional_value_at_risk.asp (accessed January 2012).
44. James Xiong and Thomas M. Idzorek, "Quant Corner: The Impact of Skewness and Fat Tails on the Asset-Allocation Decision," *Morningstar Alternative Investments Observer*, 24, Second Quarter 2011.
45. Mallory Horejs, "Interpreting Morningstar's Alternatives Categories," *Morningstar Alternative Investments Observer*, Second Quarter 2011, 3 (2), 2–5.
46. James Xiong and Thomas Idzorek, "Mean-Variance versus Mean-Conditional Value-at-Risk Optimization," *Morningstar*, February 16, 2010, 10.
47. James Picerno, "Building a Better Sharpe Ratio," *Financial Advisor Magazine*, April 2012, 130.
48. Arleen Jacobius, "Private Equity Group Takes First Steps in Building Database," *Pensions and Investments*, April 16, 2011, 8.
49. Ibid., 3.
50. Ibid., 18.
51. James Picerno, "Building a Better Sharpe Ratio," *Financial Advisor Magazine*, April 2012, 130.
52. Ibid., 129.
53. The Staff, "Active Investment Management and Time-Varying Investor Risk Premium," *Good Harbor Financial*, 2010, 2.
54. Gary Brinson, "The Future of Investment Management," *Financial Analysts Journal*, July/August 2005, 25.
55. David Blitz and Pim Van Vliet, 'Dynamic Strategic Asset Allocation: Risk and Return Across Economic Regimes," Robeco Asset Management, July 2009, 3.

56. Katherine Kaminski, "In Search of Crisis Alpha: A Short Guide to Investing in Managed Futures," *CME Group*, April 5, 2009, 3.
57. Jason Zweig, "Why We Are Driven to Trade," *Wall Street Journal*, July 21, 2012, B1.

12 DEVISING PORTFOLIOS WITH ALTERNATIVE INVESTMENTS (ACTIVE VS. PASSIVE)

1. Eugene Brigham and Louis Gapenski, *Intermediate Financial Management*, 3rd ed., Chicago: Dryden Press, 1990, 874.
2. The Staff, "Diversifying to Fight Different Forms of Inflation," *T. Rowe Price Report*, Summer 2011, 14.
3. Tim Koller, Marc Goedhart, and David Wessels, *Valuation: Measuring and Managing the Value of Companies*, Hoboken, New Jersey, and Canada: John Wiley & Sons, Inc., 2010, 36.
4. Brian Hurst, Lasse H. Pedersen, and Yao Hua Ooi, "Understanding Managed Futures," *AQR Capital Management*, Winter 2010, 2.
5. Ibid., 3.
6. Nadia Papagiannis, Josh Charney, Alexa Auerbach, and Beverly Goodman (Eds.), "2011 Alternative Survey of US Institutions and Financial Advisors," *Morningstar & Barron's*, May 2012, 4.
7. Alexandra Suich, "Barbarians in a state", *The World in 2013*, The Economist, 146.
8. "Accredited Investors," U.S. Securities and Exchange Commission, http://www.sec.gov/answers/accred.htm.
9. Viral V. Acharya, Olivier Gottschlag, Moritz Hahn, and Conor Kehoe, "Corporate Governance and Value Creation: Evidence from Private Equity," *New York University*, November 18, 2008, 10.
10. Davis Vaitkunas, "Mezzanine Finance", *Private Capital Privé*, Fall 2012, 5 (3), 11.
11. Nihat Bulent Gultekin, "Advanced Seminar on Private Equity—Syllabus," *Wharton School of the University of Pennsylvania*, Spring 2011, 1.
12. Eugene Brigham and Louis Gapenski, *Intermediate Financial Management*, 3rd ed., South-Western College, Chicago: Dryden Press, 1990, 874.
13. Steven Kaplan and Per Stromberg, "Leveraged Buyouts and Private Equity," *University of Chicago*, June 2008, 3.
14. Alexandra Suich, "Barbarians in a state", *The World in 2013*, 146.
15. Gregory Zuckerman, "Carlyle Pitches Skeptics on IPO," *Wall Street Journal*, April 17, 2012, A1.
16. Alexandra Suich, "Barbarians in a state", *The World in 2013*, 146.
17. The Editors, "Powershares Global Listed Private Equity Portfolio," *Bloomberg Terminal* (accessed March 2011).
18. Shefali Anand, "Alternative Funds: How Do You Pick?" *Wall Street Journal*, June 4, 2012, C11.
19. Alan Bjerga, "The Iowa Land Grab," *Bloomberg Businessweek*, December 24, 2012, 99.
20. Mary Ahearn, "Beginning Farmers And Ranchers At A Glance: 2013 Edition," *Economic Brief Number 22*, United States Department of Agriculture Economic Research Service, January 2013, 4.
21. Joe Light, "Build Your Own Hedge Fund," *Wall Street Journal*, December 15, 2012, p. B7.

13 THE ASSET ALLOCATION PROCESS AND SAMPLE PORTFOLIOS

1. Charles W. Collier, *Wealth in Families*, Harvard University, 2001, 8.
2. Christine Benz, "Making Your Investment Policy Statement," *Morningstar*, October 1, 2009, http://news.morningstar.com/articlenet/article.aspx?id=309575 (accessed May 2012).
3. Kevin Olsen, "Notre Dame Endowment CIO Malpass Honored," *Pensions and Investments*, May 28, 2012, 8.
4. J. Tobin, "Liquidity Preference as Behavior Towards Risk," *Review of Economic Studies*, February 1958, 25 (2), 65.
5. Charles Stein, "Sticking With a Mix That Excels in Tough Times," *BusinessWeek*, September 26, 2012, 56.
6. Andrew Lo and A. MacKinlay, "When Are Contrarian Profits Due to Stock Market Overreaction?" *Review of Financial Studies*, May 1989, 3 (2), 1.
7. Andrew Clare, James Seaton, Peter N. Smith, and Stephen Thomas, "The Trend is Our Friend: Global Asset Allocation Using Trend Following", Cass Business School, London and University of York, UK, May 31, 2012, 1.
8. "The New Diversification: Open Your Eyes to Alternative, A Conversation with Professor Christopher C. Geczy, Ph.D.", *BlackRock*.
9. Robert Steyer, "New Jersey Hikes Alts," *Pensions and Investments*, May 28, 2012.
10. Michael Corkery, "Weaning Off 'Alternative' Investments," *Wall Street Journal*, January 30, 2012, C1.
11. Carl Bacon, "Practical Portfolio Performance Measurement and Attribution," Great Britain: John Wiley & Sons, Ltd., September 2004, 88.

INDEX

GPSR Compliance

The European Union's (EU) General Product Safety Regulation (GPSR) is a set of rules that requires consumer products to be safe and our obligations to ensure this.

If you have any concerns about our products, you can contact us on ProductSafety@springernature.com

In case Publisher is established outside the EU, the EU authorized representative is:

Springer Nature Customer Service Center GmbH
Europaplatz 3
69115 Heidelberg, Germany

Batch number: 10705162

Printed by Printforce, the Netherlands